P9-CDZ-521

"A Few Acres of Snow"

Documents in Canadian History,
1577–1867

"A Few Acres of Snow"

Documents in Canadian History, 1577–1867

edited by Thomas Thorner

broadview press

Canadian Cataloguing in Publication Data

Main entry under title:
    "A few acres of snow": documents in Canadian history 1577–1867

Includes bibliography references.

ISBN 1-55111-150-0

1. Canada -- History -- Sources.   I. Thorner, Thomas.

FC18.F49 1997   971   C97-931535-2
F1026.F49 1997

Copyright © 1997, Broadview Press Ltd.

broadview press
P.O. Box 1243
Peterborough, Ontario
K9J 7H5   Canada

broadview press
3576 California Road
Orchard Park, NY
14127   USA

B.R.A.D. Book Representation
& Distribution Ltd.
244a, London Road
Hadleigh, Essex
SS7 2DE United Kingdon

Bruce Watson,
St. Clair Press
P.O. Box 287
Rozelle, NSW
2039 Australia

printed in Canada

Contents

Acknowledgements

A project of this size was not without its problems. Support arrived from several sources. Kwantlen University College provided me with the services of a work study student, Bettie Ann Moroz, who for one semester scanned several early chapter prototypes. My colleagues Frank Abbott and Thor Frohn-Nielsen never wavered in their support for this project and adopted the early drafts without reservation as required readings for their courses. Thor, in particular, assisted by revising all and writing some of the chapter introductions. My debt to him is rather significant. Frank Leonard of Douglas College proved to be my best sounding board and source for alternative ideas. On various occasions when total termination of this project loomed large, Frank always managed to persuade me that the book had merit. Comments and suggestions from students at Kwantlen University College who read the various drafts of these readings also made this a better text.

Introduction

"You realize that these two countries have been fighting over a few acres of snow near Canada, and they are spending on this splendid struggle more than Canada itself is worth."
Voltaire, *Candide*, 1759

Voltaire's remark, although unflattering, remains one of the best-known descriptions of early Canada. The modern reader must find it ironic that one of the leading thinkers of the Enlightenment could utterly dismiss an area, which he never visited, that would come to be one of the world's wealthiest and most highly developed societies. Published in 1759, when French dreams of a religious utopia or commercial success in North America lay in shambles, the remark could be attributed to bitterness or Eurocentrism. Yet many high-ranking French government officials shared his assessment of Canada. With this short incisive remark, Voltaire also satirized his fellow philosophers such as Montaigne and Rousseau who romanticized about the garden paradise and natural goodness found in the New World. But four years after *Candide* Voltaire published another novel, *L'Ingenu*, that contradicted his earlier views. Its protagonist, a French Canadian raised by Huron native people, employs his morality and ingenuity to rise above the corrupt Parisian environment he is forced to confront.[1]

Nonetheless, Voltaire's image has served as and still remains a powerful characterization of this country. Whether they wrote exploration diaries, natural histories, guide books, immigration tracts, or essays, early Canadian writers often concentrated upon the physical environment. As the ink froze in her pen, Anna Brownell Jameson recorded that human character and behaviour "depend more on the influence of climate than the pride of civilized humanity would be willing to allow" and went on to pity the poor immigrants who were as "yet unprepared against the rigour of the season."[2] While some such as Catherine Parr Trail experienced "infinite delight ... contemplating these pretty frolics of Father Frost,"[3] many other Canadians perceived their relationship with winter in hostile terms. One is reminded of Thomas Keefer's lament that "from Canada there is no escape: blockaded and imprisoned by Ice and Apathy."[4] A partial explanation for these various opinions may be that Canadian winter meant different things to different people. According to

Judith Fingard, "To the successful merchant and his family winter represented a time of entertainment, sport, cultural activity or, at worst, boredom," while to the labourer winter was "synonymous with hardship, cold, hunger, and gloomy unemployment or underemployment."[5] What meaning indigenous people placed upon winter is not as well documented, but they too experienced vast differences. The winter village ceremonies of the West Coast would, for example, contrast sharply with those of the Cree hunting bands of the prairies.

The bleakness inherent in the image of "a few acres of snow" is also in harmony with the disappointment and subsequent transiency of the colonial population. Some like Susannah Moodie described Upper Canada as a "prison house." Whether it was groups such as Black Loyalists who chose Sierra Leone over Nova Scotia or individuals such as Samuel Cunard or Thomas Chandler Haliburton, many sought to escape the limitations of Canada and moved elsewhere. For the Irish arriving at Grosse Isle or the navvies working on the Beauharnois canal, as the following accounts reveal, the promise of a better life was often illusionary.

What follows is a volume that attempts to bring together compelling excerpts of divergent eyewitness perspectives on specific topics in Canadian history. The fascination of primary sources like the Voltaire quote lies in their personal perspective and the immediacy of experience they convey. However lacking in objective insight they may be, they were written by people at or close to the source of the events they describe.

Many collections of Canadian readings on the market today reprint articles from academic journals as models of scholarship. Although such articles may certainly be of great value, they naturally tend to be written with a scholarly audience in mind. Coupled with standard survey texts, the near-total reliance upon secondary sources has had wide-ranging consequences. A student registering for a course on the Victorian novel would, no doubt, expect to read Victorian novels, not simply digest what secondary sources had to say about them. Even if the raw materials were as dense, drab and dull as the popular perception of Canadian history makes them out to be, bypassing them would be disturbing. But primary sources are far from dull. What historians usually find most enjoyable about the craft is research — the labyrinthine quest in primary sources for answers about the past. In the same way, readers of this book are encouraged to analyze the arguments and information in the sources for themselves.

This is still very much a book aimed at those largely unfamiliar with the subject. In order to make available the greatest possible amount of original material that is interesting and important, some less pertinent passages have been deleted. Exercising even a minimal shaping hand will sacrifice some dimensions of the past, but even if the occasional reader feels uncomfortable that the integrity of some documents has been violated, one hopes that in the interests of engaging a wider readership and lifting the veil of boredom from Canadian history, the end will have justified the means.

Some may also wish to hear less in a volume such as this one from the voices of white men. Despite efforts to the contrary, the unfortunate fact is that for many topics one has to rely upon the opinions of the white, male elite. Even those women who did provide detailed records of their experiences in early Canada often reflected their origin and class more closely than their gender. On the rare occasions when one comes upon a substantial native commentary, it has invariably been transcribed by Europeans, rendering its contents highly suspect.

Editors of document collections such as this must also be sensitive to Emma Larocque's criticism that reproducing historical documents such as these perpetuates negative images, particularly about native people, and as such constitutes hate literature.[6] Without a doubt many documents written by ethnocentric Europeans, with their emphasis on native violence, are elements of a literature of hate written to justify white domination. But it hardly follows that reprinting these inaccuracies constitutes disseminating hate literature. Instead these documents may provide a means of exposing these lies, of demonstrating the basis of intolerance, and of understanding that prejudice is commonplace. In some respects these documents may be used to confront the current complacency or smugness of Canadians who assume that especially compared to the United States, ours has been a kinder, gentler history and therefore lacks the foundation for bigotry and racism.

Notes

1. Greg Gatenby, *The Wild is Always There* (Toronto: Alfred A. Knopf, 1993), pp. 177, 458–459. For some the qualifier "near Canada" in the famous *Candide* quote has also been taken to invalidate its wider application. On this debate, Gatenby cites "L'Opinion de Voltaire sur le Canada," *Séances et Travaux de L'Académie*

des Sciences Morales et Politiques: Compte Rendu (Paris, 1900). Even if the *Candide* remark did not refer exclusively to Canada, the association between Canada and snow is unequivocal in Voltaire's remark of October 13, 1759, "We French had the bright idea of establishing ourselves in Canada, on top of the snow between the bears and the beavers."

2. Anna Brownell Jameson, *Winter Studies and Summer Rambles in Canada* (London: Saunders and Otley, 1838), vol. 1, pp. 27–28.

3. Catherine Parr Trail, *The Backwoods of Canada* (London: Charles Knight, 1836), p. 245.

4. Thomas Keefer, *Philosophy of Railroads* (Montreal: Armour and Ramsay, 1850), p. 1.

5. J. Fingard, "The Winter's Tale: The Seasonal Contours of Pre-Industrial Poverty in British North America, 1815–1860," *Canadian Historical Association Papers*, 1974, p. 65.

6. Emma Larocque, "On the Ethics of Publishing Historical Documents" in J. Brown and R. Brightman (eds.), *"The Orders of the Dreamed": George Nelson on Cree and Northern Ojibwa Religion and Myth, 1823* (Winnipeg: University of Manitoba Press, 1988).

1

"Make More Haste Homeward"

Early European Exploration

DOCUMENTS

A) Account of the Second Voyage of the Frobisher Expedition, 1577
George Beste

B) Northern Voyages, 1624
Jens Munck

What did these early explorers want? Was it land in the name of king and country? Perhaps fabulous wealth from unexplored resources? Some sought new souls for the church, or the rush of fame and glory. There were as many reasons for exploration as there were explorers, and most expedition leaders likely combined several motivations.

A number of captains and expedition leaders from several European nations confidently and boldly chose to explore Canada's high Arctic during the sixteenth and seventeenth centuries. They, unlike most of their crews, enjoyed the benefit of some knowledge, financial support, potential rewards, and often egos large enough to crush niggling feelings of trepidation. Of those adventurers who survived to tell their tales, many later retired to their home-lands as minor heroes, living on government pensions and royalties from their published memoirs. Their harrowing stories indeed captivated the imagina-tion of kings and bourgeoisie alike, and made them much in demand on the social circuit. Why? Partly because they expanded Europe's horizon the way our astronauts enlarge ours. Europeans coveted the potential of the new worlds: there were fortunes to be made, national prestige to enhance, strate-gic one-upmanship, and the titillation of the unknown: dangerous and exotic. These explorers formed the vanguard of what became the largest imperialis-tic enterprise in human history.

The following selections are but two examples of such memoirs, one representing a quintessentially English view, the other offering a more stoical Danish perspective. We know little of George Beste's early life, though evidence suggests he was an English professional soldier. He signed on, in 1577, as Second-in-Command under Martin Frobisher, a man seasoned to the Arctic through a previous voyage seeking the elusive Northwest Passage. They did not find it, but Frobisher's effort generated excitement anyway. He returned from the high Arctic with rock samples that he insisted contained gold, and the ensuing interest raised enough capital from optimistic investors for a second mission, this one entirely focused on mineral wealth.

Frobisher and his 200 men set sail early in 1577, and arrived in what he called *Meta Incognita* (the "Unknown Land") on July 17. His crew then began chipping and carting 200 tons of ore from the barren landscape, to the ship, by hand, with picks, shovels, and baskets. He originally planned to spend the winter, but Frobisher changed his mind by the end of the short summer, headed home to Britain, and returned the following year with a much larger fleet of 15 ships. This time he optimistically hoped to establish a permanent English mining settlement in Canada's far north and, ever on the lookout for new conquests, claimed Greenland for Britain *en route*. Refining the ore proved impossible despite his best intentions, boundless enthusiasm, back-breaking work, and enormous expense. Frobisher finally admitted defeat in 1583 after financial losses ruined his patron, Michael Lok. Beste, who published his account in 1578, offers modern historians significant information about Canada's north, particularly the intriguing observation that the Inuit already knew about European trade goods by the time of Frobisher's arrival.

Jens Munck (1579–1628) spent virtually his entire life at sea, cutting his teeth as a cabin boy and quickly rising through the ranks to command his own merchant ship. Luckily for him, he lived during the reign of one of the most able and aggressive nation builders in Denmark's history. King Christian IV wanted to strengthen Denmark's commercial economy by exploiting the world's known northern resources: minerals, furs, and whales. To that end, he hired capable adventurers to assert his claim over Greenland and Canada's eastern Arctic. Munck thus obtained a naval commission in 1611 and set sail on his first Arctic expedition in 1619. He and his crew entered Hudson's Bay that summer, claimed it for Denmark, and prepared to winter on the Churchill River estuary. Little did they know what was to come! That long, dark winter tested them beyond endurance. Scurvy, for which they had no cure, took a bitter toll, slowly and painfully killing over half Munck's men by the following March. That June, 61 men rested in shallow graves on the beach or slowly decomposed in the fetid, rat-infested hulk of the ship. Only Munck and two others survived.

Undaunted by the tragic results, Munck planned a second expedition to establish a permanent settlement based upon the fur trade. This, however, did not come to pass and he never returned to Canada. He did publish his memoirs, entitled *Northern Voyages*, in 1624 and the king made him an admiral in the Danish navy the following year.

A) Account of the Second Voyage of the Frobisher Expedition, 1577
George Beste

Being furnished with one tall ship of Her Majesty's, named the *Ayde,* of two hundred ton, and two other small barques, the one named the *Gabriel* the other the *Michael,* and being fitly appointed with all things necessary for the voyage, the said Captain Frobisher, with the rest of his company, came aboard his ships the five and twentieth day of May in the year of our Lord God, 1577.

The eighth of June we set sail from the Orkney Islands having a merry wind by night, and lost sight of all the land, keeping our course west-north-west for the space of twenty-eight days without sight of any land, and saw many monstrous fish, and strange fowl which seemed to live only by the sea.

The fourth of July the *Michael* (being foremost ahead) shot off a piece of ordnance and struck all her higher sails, indicating to the rest that they descried land, and about ten of the clock at night we made the land, and knew it to be Freeseland.

It is a marvellous thing to behold, of what great bigness and depth some islands of ice be here, some seventy, some eighty fathoms under water, besides that which is above, seeming to be islands more than half a mile in circuit. All these ice islands are fresh in taste, and seem to be bred in the sounds thereabouts, or in some land near the pole, and with the wind and tides are driven along the coasts.

Having spent four days and nights sailing along this land and finding the coast subject to bitter cold and continual mists, our General determined to spend no more time therein but to bear out his course towards the straits called Frobisher Straits, after the General's name.

Our General on the morning of the 17th day of July descried land from our main top. And about noon, we made the North Foreland perfect, which otherwise is called Hall's lesser island, whence the ore was taken up which was brought into England by Captain Frobisher this last year. At our arrival here all the seas about the coast were so covered over with huge quantities of great ice that we thought these places might only deserve the name of Mare Glaciale, and be called the Icie Sea.

God having blessed us with so happy a landfall we bore into the straits and came as near the shore as we might for the ice, and upon the 18th day of July our General, taking the goldfinders with him, attempted to go on shore with a small rowing pinnace upon the small island where the ore was, to prove whether there were any store thereof to be found. But he could not get, in all that island, another piece so big as a walnut.

However, our men which sought the other islands thereabouts, found them all to have good store of the ore, whereupon our General with these good tidings returned aboard.

On Friday the 19th of July, in the morning early, with his best company of gentlemen and soldiers (to the number of forty persons) the General went on shore to discover the habitation of the country people, as also to find out some fit harbour for our ships.

Passing towards the shore with no small difficulty, by reason of the abundance of ice which lay along the coast so thick, we arrived at length upon Hall's greater island.

Leaving our boats here with sufficient guard, we passed up into the country about two English miles and reached the top of a high hill on the top whereof our men made a cross of stones heaped up of a good height, and solemnly sounded a trumpet, and said certain prayers, honouring the place with the name Mount Warwick. This done, we retired our companies, not seeing anything here worth further discovery, the country seeming barren and full of ragged mountains, in most parts covered with snow. And thus marching back towards our boats, we espied certain of the country people, waving us back again, and making great noise, with cries like the bellowing of bulls, seeming greatly desirous of conference with us. Whereupon the General being therewith better acquainted, answered them again with the like cries, whereat, and with the noise of our trumpets, they seemed greatly to rejoice, skipping, laughing and dancing for joy. And hereupon we made signs unto them, holding up two fingers, commanding two of our men to go apart from our companies, whereby they might do the like. So that forth-with two of our men and two of theirs met together a good space from the company, neither party having their weapons about them.

Our men gave them pins and such trifles as they had. And they likewise bestowed on our men two bow cases, and such things as they had. They earnestly desired our men to go up into their country, and our men offered them like kindness aboard our ships, but neither party (as it seemed) admit-ted or trusted the other's courtesy.

The day being thus well near spent, we retired in haste into our boats again, minding forthwith to search along the coast for some harbour fit for our ships; considering that all this while they must lay off-and-on between the two headlands, being continually subject to great danger from fleeting ice.

When the people perceived our departure, they earnestly called us back again, following us almost to our boats; whereupon our General, taking his master with him, went apart unto two of them, meaning if they could to lay sure hold upon them and forcibly to bring them aboard, with intent to bestow certain toys and apparel upon the one, and so to dismiss him with all arguments of courtesy, and to retain the other for an interpreter.

The General and his master being met with the two savages, they sud-denly laid hold upon them. But the ground underfeet being slippery, their handfast failed, and their prey escaping, ran away and lightly recovered their bows and arrows which they had hid not far from them behind the rocks.

Though being the only two savages in sight, they now so fiercely, des-perately, and with such fury assaulted and pursued our General and his master, (who were altogether unarmed) that they chased them to their boats, and hurt the General in the buttocks with an arrow.

Our soldiers (which were before commanded to keep to their boats) per-ceiving the danger, and hearing our men calling for shot, came speedily to the rescue. When the savages heard the shot of one of our culivers, they ran away. But a servant of my Lord of Warwick, called Nicholas Conyer, overtook one of them and, being a Cornishman and a good wrestler, showed his victim such a Cornish trick that he made his sides ache for a month after. And so being stayed, one savage was taken alive and brought away, but the other escaped.

Thus with their strange and new prey, our men repaired to their boats and passed to a small island where they resolved to tarry all night, for even now a sudden storm was grown so great at sea, that by no means could they return to their ships.

Here every man refreshed himself with a small portion of victuals, having neither eaten nor drunk all the day before. But because they knew not how long the storm might last, nor how far off the ships might put to sea, nor whether they should ever return to them again or not, they made great spare of their victuals. For they knew full well that the best cheer the country could yield them was golden rocks and stones (a hard food to live upon withal) and that the country people were more likely to eat them, than to give them something to eat. And thus keeping very good watch and ward, they lay there all night upon hard cliffs of snow and ice, both wet, cold and comfortless ...

This day were divers storms, and by nine of the clock at night the storm was grown so great and continued such until the morning, that it put our ships in no small peril, for having mountains of fleeting ice on every side, some scraped us, and some happily escaped us; but the least of all of them were as dangerous to strike as any rock, and able to have split asunder the strongest ship of the world. Indeed every man on board, both better and worse, had enough to do, with his hands to haul ropes, and with his eyes to look out for danger.

The next morning, being the 20th of July, as God would, the storm ceased, and the General espying the ships, came happily aboard and then from this northern shore we struck over towards the southerland.

The 21st of July, we discovered a bay which ran into the land, that seemed a likely harbour for our ships, wherefore our General rowed thither with his boats to make proof thereof, and with his goldfinders to search for ore. Here all the sands and cliffs did so glitter that it seemed to be all gold, but upon trial being made it proved no better than black lead and verified the proverb — All is not gold that shineth.

Upon the 22nd of July we bare farther into Frobisher's Strait and came to anchor thinking ourselves in good security. But we were soon greatly endangered with a piece of drift ice which struck on our stern such a blow that we feared lest it had struck away our rudder. Being forced now to cut our cable to escape, we were fain to set our foresail to run further up within a very narrow channel.

Upon a small island called Smith's Island (because our smith set up his forge there) was found a mine of silver, but the ore was not won out of the rocks without great labour. Here our gold finders made assay of such ore as they had found upon the Northerland, and found four sorts thereof to hold gold in good quantities.

Upon another small island here was also found a great dead fish which, so it seemed, had been embalmed with ice. It was round like to a porpoise, being about twelve foot long, and having a horn of two yards length growing out of the snout or nostrils. This horn is wreathed and straight, like in fashion to a taper made of wax and may truly be thought to be the sea Unicorn. This horn is to be reserved as a jewel by the Queen Majesty's commandment, in her wardrobe of robes.

Tuesday the 23rd of July divers of the gentlemen desired our General to suffer them, to the number of twenty or thirty persons, to march up thirty or forty leagues in the country, to the end they might explore the inland and do some acceptable service for their country. But the General, well considering the short time he had in hand, and the greedy desire our country hath for gain, bent his whole endeavour only to find a mine to freight his ships, and to leave the exploration (by God's help) hereafter to be accomplished.

Therefore the twenty-sixth of July he departed over to the Northland with the two barques, leaving the *Ayde* riding in Jackman's Sound.

The barques came the same night to anchor in a sound upon the Northland, where the tides did run so swift, and the place was so subject to indrafts of ice, that by reason thereof they were greatly endangered. They found a very rich mine, and had got almost twenty ton of ore together when, upon the 28th of July, the ice came driving into the Sound where the barques rode, in such sort that they were therewith greatly distressed. The *Gabriel,* riding astern the *Michael,* had her cable torn asunder by a piece of driving ice, and lost another anchor. Having but one cable and anchor left (for she had lost two before) and the ice still driving upon her, she was (by God's help) well fenced from the danger by one great island of ice which came aground hard ahead of her which, if it had not so chanced, I think surely she had been cast upon the rocks with the ice ...

Toward the morning we weighed anchor and went further up the straits, leaving our ore which we had digged, behind us.

In one of the small islands here we found a tomb wherein the bones of a dead man lay and, our savage being with us, we demanded by signs whether his countrymen had slain this man and eaten his flesh. He made signs to the contrary, and indicated that he was eaten by wolves and wild beasts.

Here also was found hid under stones good store of fish, and sundry other things of the inhabitants: as sleds, bridles, kettles of fish skins, knives of bone, and such other like. Taking in his hand one of those country bridles, our savage caught one of our dogs and hampered him handsomely therein as we do our horses, and with a whip in his hand he taught the dog to draw a sled, as we do horses in a coach. They thus use dogs for that purpose as we do our horses. And we found since that the lesser sort of dogs they feed fat, and keep them as domesticated cattle in their tents for their eating.

The 29th of July, about five leagues from Beare's Sound, we discovered a bay which was a fit harbour for our ships, and this is the furthest place that this year we have entered up within the straits. It is reckoned from the cape of the Queen's Foreland, which is the entrance of the straits, not above ninety miles.

Upon this island was found good store of the ore, which in the washing held gold plainly to be seen; whereupon it was thought best to load here, than to seek further for better ore, and spend time with jeopardy. Therefore our General, setting the miners to work, and showing first a good precedent of a painful labour, and a good captain in himself, gave good examples for others to follow him; whereupon every man, both better and worse, with their best endeavours, willingly laid to their helping hands.

The next day, being the 30th of July, the *Michael* went over to Jackman's Sound for the *Ayde* and the whole company to come thither.

Upon the main land over against the Countess of Warwick's Island, we discovered and beheld to our great marvel the poor caves and houses of those country people, which same serve them for their winter dwellings. They are made two fathom underground, in compass round like to an oven, having holes like to a fox to enter by.

From the ground upward they build with whale bones (for lack of timber) which, bending one over another, are handsomely compacted in the top, and are covered over with seal skins which, instead of tiles, fenceth them from the rain. In each house they have only one room, having the one half of the floor raised with broad stones a foot higher than the other, whereon after strewing moss, they make their nests to sleep in. They defile these dens most filthily with their beastly feeding, and dwell only in one place until they are forced to seek a sweeter air, and a new home. They are (no doubt) a dispersed and wandering nation, as the Tartars, and live in hordes and troups without any certain abode, as may appear by sundry circumstances of our experience.

Here our captive (being ashore with us to declare the use of such things as we saw) stayed alone behind the company, and did set up five small sticks round in a circle, one by another, with one small bone placed just in the midst of all: which thing, when one of our men perceived it, he called us back to behold the matter, thinking that he had meant some charm or witchcraft therein. But the best conjecture we could make thereof was that he would thereby signify to his countrymen the memory of our five men which they betrayed the last year, and also that he himself was taken and kept prisoner.

Thereupon, we calling the matter to his remembrance, he gave us plainly to understand by signs that he had knowledge of the taking of our five men the last year. And when we made him signs that they were slain and eaten, he earnestly denied it, and made signs to the contrary.

The first of August, Captain Yorke, with the *Michael*, came into Jackman's Sound and declared unto us that the last night past he came to anchor in a certain bay where he discovered tents of the country people. Going with his company ashore, he entered into them, but found the people departed, as it should seem, for fear of their coming. But amongst sundry strange things which they found in these tents there was raw and new killed flesh of unknown sort, with dead carcasses and bones of dogs, and I know not what. They also beheld (to their greatest marvel) a doublet of canvas made after the English fashion, a shirt, a girdle, three shoes for contrary feet and of unequal bigness, which they well conjectured to be the apparel of our five poor countrymen which were intercepted the last year by these country people.

Which informations, when he had delivered them to the company, we determined forthwith to investigate the matter. Hereupon Captain Yorke, accompanied by thirty or forty persons in two small rowing pinnaces, made towards the place where they had discovered the tents of those people and here he set some of the company ashore under the mate, to encompass the savages on the one side, whilst the Captain and his boats might entrap them on the other side. Landing at last at the place where the people had been, they found the tents removed. Notwithstanding this, our men marched up into the country, passing over two or three tedious mountains, and by chance espied certain tents in a valley and, besetting them about, determined to take the people if they could. But the savages, having descried our company, launched one great and another small boat, being about sixteen or eighteen persons, and very narrowly escaping, put themselves to sea.

Whereupon our soldiers on the shore discharged their pieces and followed them, thinking the noise, being heard by our boats at sea, would bring our boatmen to that place. And thereupon, indeed, our men which were in the boats did come and forced the country people to put themselves ashore again upon a point of land. Our men so speedily followed that they had little leisure left them to make any escape. So soon as the savages landed each of them broke his oar, thinking by that means to prevent us carrying away their boats, for want of oars. Then, desperately turning upon our men, resisted them manfully in their landing, so long as their arrows and darts lasted, and after that, by gathering up those arrows which our men shot at them, yes, and even plucking our arrows out of their bodies, so they encountered us afresh and maintained their cause until both weapons and life utterly failed them. When they found they were mortally wounded (being ignorant what mercy meaneth) with deadly fury they cast themselves headlong from the rocks into the sea, lest perhaps their enemies should prey off their dead carcasses (for they supposed us to be eaters of man's flesh).

In this conflict one of our men was dangerously hurt in the belly with one of their arrows, but of the savages five or six were slain. The rest escaped among the rocks, saving two women, whereof the one being old and ugly, our men thought she had been a devil or some witch, and therefore let her go. The other, being young and encumbered with a sucking child at her back, hiding herself behind the rocks, was espied by one of our men who, supposing she had been a man, shot through the hair of her head and pierced through the child's arm, whereupon she cried out and was taken. Our surgeon, meaning to heal her child's arm, applied salves thereto. But she was not acquainted with such kind of surgery and plucked those salves away, and by continual licking with her own tongue (not much unlike our dogs) healed up the child's arm.

And now considering their sudden flying from our men, and their desperate manner of fighting, we began to suspect that we had heard the last news of our men, which last year were betrayed of these people. And considering also their ravenous and bloody disposition in eating any kind of raw flesh or carrion, however stinking, it is to be thought that they had slain and devoured our men. For the doublet which was found in their tents had many holes therein, being made with their arrows and darts.

Having now got a woman captive, for the comfort of our savage man, we brought them both together, and every man desired to behold the manner of their meeting, the which was more worth the beholding than can be well expressed by writing. At their first encounter they beheld each the other for a good time without speech or word uttered, with great change of colour and countenance, as though it seemed the grief and disdain of their captivity had taken away the use of their tongues and utterance. The woman at the first turned away and began to sing, as though she thought upon another matter; but being again brought together, the man broke up the silence first, and with stern countenance began to tell a long solemn tale to the woman, whereunto she gave good hearing. Afterwards, they being grown into more familiar acquaintance I think the one would hardly have lived without the comfort of the other. Yet, insofar as we could perceive (albeit they lived continually together) yet did they never use each other as man and wife. The woman did all necessary things that appertained to a good housewife, as in making clean their cabin, and every other thing that appertained to his ease. When he was seasick, she would make him clean, she would kill and flay the dogs for their eating, and dress his meat. Only I think it worth the noting that the man would never shift himself, except he had first caused the woman to depart out of his cabin; and they both were most shameful lest any of their private parts should be discovered either of themselves or any other person.

On Monday, the 6th of August, the Lieutenant, with all the soldiers, for the better guard of the miners, pitched their tents in the Countess' Island, and fortified the place for their better defence as well as they could; when, being all at labour, they perceived upon the top of a hill a number of the country people waving with a flag and making great outcries unto them. These were of the same company which had lately encountered our men, being come to complain of their late losses and to entreat (as it seemed) for restitution of the woman and child. Whereupon the General taking the savage captive with him, and setting the woman where they might best perceive her, in the highest place of the island, went over to talk with them.

This captive, at the first encounter with his friends, fell so into tears that he could not speak a word for a great space; but after a while, overcoming his weakness, he talked with his companions and bestowed upon them such toys and trifles as we had given him. Whereby we noted that they are very kind one to the other, and greatly sorrowful for the loss of their friends.

Our General, by signs, required his five men back which they took captive the last year, and promised them not only to release those which we had taken, but also to reward them with great gifts and friendship. Our savage made signs in answer from them, that our men should be delivered us, and were yet living, and made signs likewise unto us that we should write letters unto them.

The next morning early, being the 7th of August, they called again for the letter which, being delivered unto them, they speedily departed, making signs with three fingers, while pointing, to the sun, that they meant to return within three days ...

Saturday, the 11th of August, the people showed themselves again, and called unto us from the side of a hill over against us. The General (with good hope to hear of his men) went over unto them. There were only three in sight, but greater numbers were hid behind the rocks and our men, justly suspecting them, kept aloof. In the meanwhile, others of our men who stood on the Countess' Island saw divers of the savages creeping behind the rocks towards our men; whereupon the General presently returned without tidings of his missing men, nor did we ever after hear aught of them.

Now our work was growing towards an end. Though having only five poor miners, and the help of a few gentlemen and soldiers, we had brought aboard almost two hundred tons of gold ore in the space of twenty days. And upon Wednesday, being the 21st of August, we fully finished the whole work. And it was now good time to leave; for, as the men were well wearied, so their shoes and clothes were well worn, their basket bottoms torn out, their tools broken, and the ships reasonably well filled.

Some, with over-straining themselves, received hurts not a little dangerous, some having their bellies broken, and others their legs made lame. And about this time the ice began to congeal and freeze about our ship's sides at night, which gave us a good argument of the sun's declining southward, and put us in mind to make more haste homeward.

B) Northern Voyages, 1624
Jens Munck

Anno Domini 1619: His Royal Majesty's ship *Unicorn*, and the sloop *Lamprey*, having been properly made ready, provisioned, and prepared with other necessaries for the voyage to search for the North West Passage, I, Jens Munk, in the name of God, sailed with the said two ships from Copenhagen on the 9th of May with forty-eight men aboard the *Unicorn* and sixteen aboard the *Lamprey*.

On the 18th of May it happened, early in the morning, while we were sailing along, that one of my men who was walking on the deck suddenly jumped overboard and plunged his head under water without, however, so it appeared, sinking as quickly as he desired. But, as it was blowing hard, no one could save him; which I should much have wished. He therefore went down and was lost.

On the 25th of May, while off southern Norway, the *Lamprey* sprang a leak so that I was obliged to run into Karmsund. On examination I found that three bolt-holes had been left open by the carpenters and afterwards filled with pitch. While I stayed at Karmsund one of my two coopers died, wherefore I caused three young men to be engaged so as to maintain my full complement of men.

On the 30th of May I sailed from Karmsund and shaped our course for Shetland. On the 4th of June we sailed round the east end of the Faeroe Islands and shaped our course west and west-by-north ...

Thus we sailed on in a westerly direction until the 20th of June when we encountered much ice, so that we were obliged to turn eastward again toward the open sea. We kept sailing back and forth, with gales and bad weather, until June 30th, when we sighted the southern cape of Greenland which the English call Cape Farewell. Doubtless whoever named that place did not intend to return thither. We had then arrived at Davis Strait and when I had got free of this ice I shaped my course west by north on which track we encountered much more ice.

On the 8th of July we sighted the land on the American side but could not reach the shore for the quantity of ice, so we sailed to and fro outside the ice and could effect nothing.

On July 9th there was such a fog in the night, and so great a cold, that icicles were hanging from the rigging six inches long, and none of the men could stand the cold. But before three o'clock on the same day the sun was shining so hotly that the men threw off their overcoats, and some of them their jackets as well.

Then I stood in among the ice into a great bay which, according to my English pilots, ought to have been the proper entrance to Hudson's Strait, but which after long investigation we found not to be the right entrance.

Leaving this bay we shaped our course southerly along the coast which we found to consist everywhere of broken land and high rocks, until we came to Resolution Island on the north side of the entrance into Hudson's Strait.

On the 12th I sent my Lieutenant with some of the crew on shore at this island in order to fetch water and to ascertain what was to be found there, because it seemed a likely place for finding harbours and for obtaining water. In the evening they returned with water, but reported that there was no anchorage. On the same day I shot two or three birds with a gun; but at the last discharge the same gun burst into pieces and took the brim clean off the front of my hat.

On the 13th of July, towards evening, we were in the greatest distress and danger in the Strait of Hudson, and did not know what counsel to follow, because we could not advance any farther by tacking, the ice pressing us hard on all sides. Being in such a perilous situation we took in all the sails and fastened the *Lamprey* to the *Unicorn*. We then commended all into the hand of God and drifted along and into the ice again ...

On the 17th of July I ordered the *Lamprey* to sail ahead of us to find where we could anchor, and followed after with the *Unicorn*. We then found a good harbour where we cast anchor in the name of God.

The following day I sent men out with orders to search whether any people were to be found on the land, and toward midday they returned without having noticed any people. They had, however, found many places where people had been.

On the 18th of July we observed that there were people on the southern side of the harbour, wherefore I at once had my boat manned and went myself thither in it.

When the natives saw that I was coming on shore they remained standing, having laid down their arms and implements behind some stones. When I approached them they returned whatever salutations I offered them; but were careful to keep between me and the place where their arms were laid.

I took up some of their arms and implements and examined them, upon which they at once made me understand that they would rather lose all their garments and go naked, than lose their arms and implements; and they pointed to their mouths thereby signifying that it was by means of their arms and implements that they obtained their food. When I again laid down their things they clapped their hands, looked up to heaven, and showed themselves very merry and joyful. Thereupon I presented them with knives and all sorts of iron goods. One of my men, who had a very swarthy complexion and black hair, they embraced, no doubt thinking that he was one of their own nation and countrymen.

On the 19th of July I had hoped to have had further intercourse with the natives, but it was altogether in vain for, though I remained lying here until July 22nd, none of the natives came to me, from which it is to be concluded that they are doubtless subject to some authority which must have forbidden them to come to us again.

On the 23rd of July we found ourselves so entirely surrounded by ice on all sides that we could not get away from it. We therefore made the *Lamprey* fast to the *Unicorn*, brought down the topmasts (as a violent gale was commencing) and then drifted whither the wind or the ice might carry us. In the next night the ice pressed on us so hard and we were so firmly fixed in it that we could not give way, and the ice crushed four anchors to pieces on the bow of the *Lamprey*. At the same time the ice forced itself under the *Lamprey*'s keel so that one might pass one's hand along the keel from stem to stern.

On the 25th I nearly lost two men who were ordered to fetch back a grapnel which had been thrown onto a large mass of ice in order to turn the ship. On the same day the rudder head of the *Unicorn* was broken to pieces. The following day the ships remained in the same place, drifting neither outward nor inward, so that we were now in the greatest distress and danger. We did not know of any measures we could take, but commended the whole matter into the hand of God.

On July 31st we were carried inward by the flood tide over some rocks, and thus came into a small bay where we were somewhat more secure against the ice. The men were now so entirely worn out that they could not any longer have sustained the hard work entailed in pushing great quantities of ice from the ship, and by the incessant veering and hauling.

During August 5th the ice commenced to thin somewhat and drift away; wherefore I had the hold trimmed and ordered the beer to be put into fresh casks, water fetched, and everything made ready to proceed. But on August 8th so much snow fell that all the mountains were covered with it and, on the deck, the snow was more than six inches deep. On this same day we buried one of our seamen named Anders Staffuanger in this place, which we have called Haresund because we caught many hares here.

Thus did our journey proceed for many days until in time we came out of Hudson's Strait and set our course south-west-by-south for three days and three nights sailing, to reach the land again at Jens Munk's Wintering-place, as I have called the river mouth which we discovered on the western shore of the great bay.

September 7th. Now that I had come into the harbour aforesaid, though with great difficulty on account of wind and storm, snow, hail and fog, I ordered a watch on the land, and maintained a fire in order that the *Lam-*

prey, which had strayed from us during a great gale, might find us again. She joined us on the 9th of September.

The crews having suffered much from the aforesaid gale, and other hardships and trouble, and a part of them in consequence being down sick, I caused the sick people to be brought on shore and we gathered cloud-berries, gooseberries and other berries for them. I also had a good fire made on the shore every day for the sick, whereby they were comforted and in time nicely regained their health.

On the 10th and 11th of September there was such a terrible gale and snowstorm that nothing could be done.

Early the next morning a large white bear came down to the water near the ship and began eating the flesh of a white-whale which I had caught the day before. I shot the bear, and the men all desired its flesh for food, which I allowed. I ordered the cook just to boil it slightly and then to keep it in vinegar for a night, and I myself had two or three pieces of this bear's flesh roasted, for the cabin. It was of good taste and did not disagree with us ...

While we now thought that the ship was well protected against drift ice and bad weather, such a tremendous drift of ice came upon us on the 27th, with the low ebb tide, that if the ship had not been resting so firmly on the ground, we should have been carried away. We were obliged to let go all four hawsers by which the ship was moored, and part of them went to pieces. The ship also became so leaky that at flood tide we pumped out 2,000 strokes of water. I ordered the carpenters, and others who could ply an axe, to make five bridge-piles while the other men hauled timber and stones for these piles which I caused to be placed before the bow of the ship in order to turn off the ice so it would not hurt us.

Everything being now well finished and the ship and sloop protected against the ice and tempest, I ordered the cannon to be placed in the hold and a part of our goods to be brought on shore, in order that the deck might be clear and that the ship should not suffer so much from the great weight resting on her deck. I also distributed to the crew clothes, shirts, shoes and boots and what ever else could be of use as a protection against the cold ...

The weather being fine on [October] 7th I journeyed up the river to see how far I could get with a boat but there were so many stones in it that I could not advance beyond a mile and a half. On my return I came to a promontory and found there a picture on a stone, drawn with charcoal, and fashioned like the half of a devil: wherefore I called the place Devil's Cape.

In many places where we came we could quite well see where people had been and had had their summer abodes. In the forest there are in many places great heaps of chips where they have cut wood or timber, and the chips look as if they have been cut off with curved iron tools. I am of the opinion that the said people have some kind of idolatry connected with fire and, if that is so, it is to be wished that these poor, blinded pagans might come to the profession of the true Christian Faith. As regards their food and mode of living, it would seem they use much in a half-cooked state because, wherever we found that they had had their meals, the bones did not seem to have been very well roasted.

On the 10th of October I began to give the men rations of wine; but beer they were allowed to drink according to their want, as much as every man himself liked. At the same time I made regulations for keeping a watch, the fetching of wood, and burning of charcoal, so that everyone knew what he was to do and how to conduct himself.

On October 22nd the ice became very firm and there was a terribly hard frost, and on the same night we caught a black fox. The crew now commenced to go ashore in the daytime in pursuit of game. A part went into the forest to set traps to catch animals, and some of these built a hut wherein to lie in ambush for animals. Another part of the men betook themselves to open country for shooting, because there was plenty of ptarmigan and hares as long as the snow was not too deep. At this time, and until Christmas, the men liked to go ashore when the weather was fine, because they never went without they carried home something good to eat which was a sufficient inducement to them to move about.

On November 10th, which was St. Martin's Eve, the men shot some ptarmigan, with which we had to content ourselves instead of the traditional St. Martin's goose. I ordered a pint of Spanish wine be given to each of the men beside their daily allowance, wherewith the whole crew were satisfied, even merry and joyful. And of the ship's beer there was given them as much as they liked. But afterwards, when the frost got the upper hand, the beer froze to the bottom so that I was afraid to let the men drink of it before they had well melted and boiled it again. However in this matter I let the men follow their own inclination because the common people, after all, are so disposed that, whatever is most strongly forbidden them, they are most apt to do on the sly without considering whether it be beneficial or hurtful to them.

In the middle of the month two of the men commenced to use the ambush hut and in the first night they caught two black foxes and a cross fox, which were very beautiful. This same night a large black dog came to the ship on the ice; but the man on watch, not knowing but that it was a black fox, shot him and with much exultation dragged him into the cabin thinking that he had got a great prize. But when we examined it, we found it to be a large dog which no doubt had been trained to catch game because it had been tied round the nose with small cords so that the hair was rubbed off. His right ear was cleft, and perhaps his owner was not very pleased to lose him. I should myself have been glad to have caught him alive, in which case I should have made a pedlar of him and have let him go home to where he had come from, carrying a pack of small goods.

On November 7th there was a very sharp frost by which all the glass bottles we had (which contained all kinds of precious waters) were broken to pieces; wherefore it is observed that whoever intends to navigate such cold seas should supply himself well with tin bottles, or other such that are able to resist the frost.

On December 12th one of my two surgeons, David Velske by name, died and his corpse had to remain on the ship unburied for two days because the frost was so very severe that nobody could get ashore to bury him; and even on the 14th the cold was so intense that many of the men got frost-bites when they met the wind with uncovered face.

On Christmas Eve I gave the men wine and strong beer, which they had to boil afresh, for it was frozen to the bottom. Nevertheless, they had quite as much as they could stand, and were very jolly, but no one offended another with as much as a word.

The Holy Christmas Day we all celebrated and observed solemnly, as a Christian's duty is. We had a sermon, and after it we gave the priest an of-fertory, according to ancient custom, each in proportion to his means. There was not much money among the men but they gave what they had. Some of them gave white fox skins, so that the priest got enough wherewith to line a coat. However, sufficiently long life to wear it was not granted to him.

During all the Holy Days the weather was rather mild; and, in order that the time might not hang on hand, the men practised all kinds of games, and whoever could imagine the most amusement was the most popular. The crew, most of whom were at that time in good health, consequently had all sorts of larks and pastimes. And thus we spent the Holy Days, with the merriment that was got up.

Anno Domini 1620.

On New Year's day there was a tremendously hard frost and I ordered a couple of pints of wine to every bowl to be given to the people, over and above their allowance, in order that they might keep themselves in good spirit. During these days we had the sharpest frost that we had yet experienced during the whole winter, and we suffered more severely from that terrible frost than from anything else.

On January 10th, the priest, Mr. Rasmus Jensen, and the surgeon, M. Casper Caspersen, took to their beds having for some time felt unwell. And after that time violent sickness commenced among the men, which day by day prevailed more and more. The illness which then raged was peculiar, and the sick were generally attacked by dysentery about three weeks before they died. On this same day my head cook died.

On the 21st of January it was fine, clear weather and sunshine, and on that date thirteen of us were down with sickness. Then, as I had often done before, I asked the surgeon, M. Caspersen (who was also lying mortally ill), whether he knew of any good remedy that might be found in his chest and which might serve for the recovery or comfort of the crew; requesting him to inform me of it. To this he answered that he had already used as many remedies as he had, to the best of his abilities, and that if God would not help, then he could not employ any further remedy at all that would be useful for recovery.

On the 23rd of January died one of my two Mates, Hans Brock by name, who had been ill and in and out of bed for nearly five months. On this day it was fine weather and beautiful sunshine and the priest sat up in his berth and gave the people a sermon, which sermon was the last he ever delivered in this world.

On the 25th, I had the body of Hans Brock buried, and ordered two falconets to be discharged, which was the last honour I could show him. But the trunnions burst off both falconets and the man who fired them very nearly lost both his legs, so brittle had the iron become on account of the sharp and severe frost.

Two days later Jens Helsing, seaman, died and on the same day my Lieutenant, the well-born Mauritz Stygge, took to his bed for good, after having been ailing for some time. Also on this day the men saw tracks of five reindeer which had been chased by a wolf, wherefore I sent a party after them.

But on account of a great fall of snow which overtook the men, they could not trace the animals and returned without catching any.

The next day the cold was so severe that a tin pot with water in it, which the boy had forgotten in the cabin, burst in the night by frost. So I do not know in what kind of vessels any precious waters may be preserved on voyages to such cold seas as these.

On February 5th a seaman named Laurids Bergen died, and I again sent to the surgeon with an urgent request that, for God's sake, he would do his utmost if he knew of any remedy or good advice. Or, inasmuch as he was himself very ill and weak, if he would let me know what medicine or remedy I could use for the benefit of the crew. To which he answered as before that, if God would not help, he could not help either.

February 10th. During these past days the weather was rather mild, but there was much sickness and weakness amongst the crew. Two of them died on this day.

On the 12th we caught two ptarmigan which were very welcome for the use of the sick; and on the following day I ordered for each person at each meal, one-third of a pint of wine and, in the morning, a whole measure of whisky, beyond the ordinary allowance.

During these days there was nothing but sickness and weakness and every day the number of the sick was continuously increased so that by the 17th, there were only seven persons in health that could fetch wood and water and do whatever work there was to be done on board. On this day also, there died a seaman who had been ill the whole voyage and of whom one may truly say that he was as dirty in his habits as an untrained beast.

On the next day Rasmus Kiobenhauffn died and, of the crew, there had then already died twenty persons. On this day we got a hare, which was very welcome.

On the 20th died the priest.

On the 29th of February the frost was so severe that nobody could get on shore to fetch water or wood, and that day the cook was obliged to take for fuel whatever he could find. I was obliged to mind the cabin myself, for this day my servant had also fallen ill and taken to his bed altogether.

On March 4th the weather was mild and we caught five ptarmigan in the open country, which was very welcome to us. I ordered broth to be made of them and had that distributed amongst the sick. But of the meat they could eat nothing because of their mouths being badly afflicted by the scurvy.

On the 8th died Oluf Boye who had been ill nearly nine weeks; and on the 9th died Anders, the cooper, who had been ill since Christmas.

March 21st. During the past days the weather had been changeable, being sometimes fine and clear, at other times sharp and severe. As regards the crew, most of them were, alas, down with illness, and it was very miserable and melancholy either to hear or see them. On this day died the surgeon, and Povel Pedersen, both of whom had been ill almost since Christmas. Now, and afterwards, the sickness raged more violently every day, so that we who were still left suffered great trouble before we could get the dead buried.

March 24th. These days were fine and mild, without frost. One of the men who got on shore and climbed a high rock, saw open water outside the inlet, which filled us with confident expectations of release. But on the following day the skipper, Jan Ollufsen, died.

I was myself now much ashore collecting herbs where the snow had melted off. They were as fresh in such places as if it had been autumn, but one had to be careful to gather them as soon as they appeared from under the snow, because otherwise they withered speedily. I also gathered a quantity of berries which I distributed among the men.

On the 27th of March I looked over the surgeon's chest and examined its contents in detail because, no longer having a surgeon, I had now to do the best I could myself. But it was a great neglect and mistake that there was not some list supplied by the physicians, indicating what the various medications were good for and how they were to be used. I am certain, and would venture my life on it, that there were many kinds of medicaments in that chest which my surgeon did not know — much less did he know for what purpose, and in what way, they were to be employed. All the names on them were written in Latin, of which he had not forgotten much in his lifetime, for want of ever knowing any. Whenever he was going to examine any bottle or box, the priest had to read the label for him.

On March 29th died Ismael Abrahamsen and Christen Gregersen, whose dead bodies were buried according to our opportunity and ability at that time.

On March 30th there was a sharp frost and on this date died Svend Arffuedsen, carpenter. And at this time commenced my greatest sorrow and misery, and I was then like a wild and lonely bird. I was now obliged myself to run about in the ship, to give drink to the sick, to boil drink for them, and get for them what I thought might be good for them, to which I was not accustomed, and of which I had but little knowledge.

The next day my second mate, Johan Pettersen died, and the following day my nephew Erich Munk; and his and Pettersen's dead bodies were placed together in one grave.

On April 3rd it was a fearfully sharp frost, so that none of us could uncover himself for cold. Nor had I anyone now to command, for they were all lying under the hand of God, so that there was great misery and sorrow. On this day died Iffuer Alsing.

On the 5th died Christoffer Opsloe, Rasmus Clemendsen and Lauritz Hansen, but the number of men in health was now so small that we were scarcely able to bury the bodies of the dead.

On the 8th died William Gordon, our English pilot, and towards evening Anders Sodens died so that these two were also buried in one grave, which we who were then alive could only manage with great difficulty, on account of the miserable weakness which was upon us, in consequence of which not one of us was well enough to go into the forest and fetch wood or fuel. Thus we were obliged to collect everything that was in the ship which would serve as fuel, and when that was consumed, we were obliged to burn our shallop for fuel ...

On the 14th there was a sharp frost. On that day only four besides myself had strength enough to sit up in the berths and listen to the homily for Good Friday. Then, on Easter Day, died Anders Aroust and Jens the cooper and, as the weather was fairly mild, I got their bodies buried. I also promoted the captain of the hold to be my skipper, even though he too was ill, in order that he might assist me as far as his strength was able, because I was myself then quite miserable and abandoned by all the world. And in the night died Hans Bendtsen.

The next day died my servant Olluff Andersen who during seven years had served me faithfully and well, and after him died Peter Amundsen.

On the 21st of April the sunshine was beautiful wherefore some of the sick crawled forth from their berths in order to warm themselves by the sun. But as they were so very weak, some of them swooned, so that it did not do them any good, and I had enough to do before I got them back again, each to his bunk.

On the 25th the wild geese began to arrive, at which we were delighted, hoping that the summer would now come soon. But in this expectation we were disappointed for the cold lasted on much longer.

May 4th. By this day many others had died, and now not a man left his berth save myself and the under-cook who still could do a little. And on this day died Anders Marstrand and Morten Marstrand who had both been long ill.

On May 7th the weather became a little milder and we three poor men who still had a little strength left could get the dead men buried but, on account of our extreme weakness, it was so difficult for us that we could not carry the dead bodies to their burial in any other way than by dragging them on a little sledge which had been used in the winter for the transport of wood.

May 10th. The foregoing days were very severe with cold and frost which greatly weakened and hindered us, but on this day the weather was fine and numbers of geese arrived. We got one of them, which sufficed for two meals. We were, at that time, eleven persons alive, counting the sick. On the following day it was very cold and we remained quietly in our bunks because, in our extreme weakness, we could not stand any cold; our limbs being paralysed and, as it were, crushed with cold.

On the next day died Jens Jorgensen the carpenter, and Svend Marstrand. And God knows what misery we suffered before we got their bodies buried. And these were the last that were buried in the ground.

On the 16th died the new skipper Jens Hendrichsen, and on the 19th died Erich Hansen Li who, throughout the voyage, had been very industrious and willing and had neither offended anyone or deserved any punishment. He had dug many graves for others, but now there was nobody who could dig his, and he had to remain unburied.

On the 22nd of May the sunshine was as fine and warm as anyone could wish from God and, by Divine Providence, a goose which three or four days before had had a leg shot off, came near the ship. We caught and cooked it, and we had food for two days off it.

Until the 28th there was nothing to write about except that we seven miserable persons who were still lying there alive, looked mournfully at each other, hoping every day that the snow would thaw and the ice drift away.

As regards the symptoms of the illness which had fallen upon us, it was a rare and extraordinary one. All the limbs and joints were so miserably drawn together, with great pains in the loins, as if a thousand knives were thrust through them. The body, at the same time, was blue and brown as when one gets a black eye; and the whole body was quite powerless. The mouth also was in a very bad and miserable condition, as all the teeth were loose and we could not eat any victuals.

During these days when we were lying in bed, so altogether bad, there died Peder Nyborg, carpenter, Knud Lauritzen Skudenes, and Jorgen, the cook's boy, all of whom remained on the steerage, for there was then nobody that could bury their bodies or throw them overboard.

On June 4th, which was Whitsunday, there remained only three alive, besides myself; all lying down unable to help one another. The stomach was ready enough, and had appetite for food, but the teeth would not allow it. The cook's boy lay dead beside my berth, and three men on the steerage. Two of the living were on shore, and would gladly have been back on ship but it was impossible for them to get there as they had not sufficient strength. We had now, for four days, had nothing for the sustenance of the body. Accordingly I did not now hope for anything but that God would put an end to this my misery; and thinking that it would have been the last I wrote in this world, I penned as follows:

> Inasmuch as I have now no more hope of life in this world, I request for the sake of God, if any Christian men should happen to come here, that they will bury in the earth my poor body, together with the others which are found here, expecting their reward from God in Heaven. And, furthermore, that this, my journal, may be forwarded to my most gracious Lord and King (for every word that is found herein is altogether truthful) in order that my poor wife and children may obtain some benefit from my great distress and miserable death. Herewith, goodnight to all the world; and my soul into the hand of God.

June 8th. As I could no longer stand the bad smell and stench from the dead bodies, I managed as best I could to get out of the berth, considering that it would not matter where, or among what surroundings I died. I spent that night on the deck using the clothes of the dead. Next day, when the two men who were on shore saw me and perceived that I was still alive (I had thought that they were dead long ago) they came out on the ice to the ship and assisted me to the land.

Then for some time we had our dwelling on shore, under a bush, and there we made a fire in the daytime. We crawled about everywhere near, wherever we saw the least green growing out of the ground, which we dug up and sucked the main root thereof. This benefited us and, as the warmth now commenced to increase nicely, we began to recover. But while we thus continued on the shore, the sailmaker who had remained aboard the ship now died.

June 18th. After the ice had drifted away from the ship we got a net for catching flounders, out of the sloop, and when the ebb had run out one-quarter, we went out dryshod and set it. When the flood returned, God gave us six large trout which I cooked myself, while the other two men went aboard the *Lamprey* to fetch wine, which we had not tasted for a long time, none of us having any appetite for it.

We now every day got fresh fish which was well cooked. It comforted us much, although we could not eat any of the meat, but only the broth, with which we drank wine, so that by degrees we recovered somewhat. At last we got a gun on shore and shot birds, from which we obtained much refreshment; so that day by day we got stronger and fairly well in health ...

When we boarded the *Unicorn* we threw overboard the dead bodies, which were then quite decomposed, as we could not move about or do anything there for bad smell and stench. Yet we required to take out of the *Unicorn*, and place aboard the *Lamprey*, victuals and necessaries for our use in crossing the sea.

It was not until the 16th of July that we were able to set sail from that place. At that time it was as warm as it might have been in Denmark, but there was such a quantity of mosquitoes that in calm weather they were unbearable. Before setting out I drilled some holes in the *Unicorn* in order that the water would rise in her, with the tide, and so keep her always firm on the ground in this harbour which I have called Jens Munk's Bay.

On the 17th we met much ice and stood off and on in front of it until later when we stuck firm in it and were so held for several days. On the 20th, while we were drifting in the ice, a large white bear came close to the ship. When he saw us he took flight across the ice and through the water, followed by a large dog which I had with me. The dog strayed from the vessel in consequence and never returned, though for a couple of days we could still hear him howl ...

Thus did we sail eastward through Hudson's Strait into the sea where we met storm and tempest. On the 4th of September we had tremendous rain, and wind amounting to a gale, and we could not at all leave off pumping. Toward evening the wind commenced to be more favourable and, as we were quite exhausted with pumping, we drifted the whole night without sails, in order to get some rest — as far as the pump would allow us to rest ...

Thus we bore on until the 20th of September when we saw Norway, and toward evening of the next day I steered into a bay, where I dropped anchor and thus remained without being moored as I had no boat wherewith to carry a hawser on shore ...

As I had now seen the ship safe, and had returned into a Christian country, we poor men could not hold our tears back, for the great joy; and we thanked God that he had graciously granted us this happiness at the end of our journey.

2

"An Inconvenient Wind"

Missionaries and Natives

DOCUMENTS
A) New Relation of Gaspesia, 1691
   Christien Le Clerq
B) Letters, 1640–1668
   Marie de l'Incarnation

The French government, ever nervous of social instability and rifts among its citizens, wished to create a purely Catholic state, both at home and in the empire. That would hopefully avoid future civil wars between Protestants and Catholics such as the one that ravaged France until Cardinal Richelieu brought it to a bloody end in 1628. The entire settlement process of New France, therefore, had an official religious dimension that logically included, as of the early 1600s, plans to assimilate North American native people. Transforming "heathen savages" into God-fearing Frenchmen certainly had a healthy dose of missionary zeal about it. There were, of course, less cynical reasons for converting native people too. Whatever the rationale, however, "Black Robes" and other Europeans infiltrated native encampments shortly after European contact, and soon left a permanent mark on the indigenous social fabric.

Men like Christien Le Clerq, born in 1641, formed the vanguard of a Catholic missionary effort that fanned out across New France. He joined the Recollect order, arrived on the Gaspé Peninsula in 1675, and began a long and generally sympathetic relationship with the local Micmac, whom he called "Gaspesians." Le Clerq was much more than an intolerant Eurocentric religious bigot harvesting souls for the Catholic church. Although the disciplines did not exist then, he was, by today's standards, an amateur anthropologist and linguist. Perhaps Le Clerq cared more for studying his audience than converting them. He spent eleven years wandering through what is now southern Quebec and northern New Brunswick, living with the local people, and absorbing as much of their culture as he could. He apparently learned languages and dialects very quickly, and even invented syllabic characters to create the first Micmac dictionary. Le Clerq's writings, based upon his lengthy stay with the Micmac and his obvious linguistic skills, stand as one of the best early ethnographic accounts historians have. They also offer one of the few accounts of native speeches from this period.

Despite his efforts, or perhaps because of them, Le Clerq concluded by 1679 that his missionary efforts failed to bear fruit. Did he spend too much time observing, too little preaching? In any case, he did not sculpt a new enclave of Frenchmen out of the Gaspesians. He considered resigning, but changed his mind and remained among the Micmac until finally retiring to France in 1686. There he took goose quill in hand and began his memoirs which he published in 1691. The following document comes from this work.

Marie Guyart, born in 1599 and better known as Marie de l'Incarnation, wanted to join a convent from the time she was a child. Her family, however, thwarted her ambitions and insisted she marry. Rebelling against family wishes, especially for a girl, was both disloyal and potentially disastrous. Marie obeyed. Fate ironically intervened, however, when her husband died after his business failed. She was, at barely twenty, a destitute mother of an infant son, but now free to join the Ursuline order which she did in 1633 when her son was twelve. Thus began her long, torturous and, arguably obsessive preparations for a life dedicated to God. She saw visions of spreading the Gospel on a fog-covered island, wore hair shirts, slept on a hair mattress, and engaged in self-flagellation, all to prove her worthiness, and to set an example of ultimate devotion to God. Missionary work among the "heathen" in the wilds of Canada could obviously appeal to someone combining religious fervour with an apparent penchant for masochism. There was, as well, a chance for the supreme sacrifice: martyrdom. This attitude, rather extreme by today's standards, was not particularly odd then. Seventeenth-century missionaries firmly believed that suffering was an essential element of a holy life.

Her religious director finally permitted her and two other nuns to set sail for New France in 1639. This was a permanent appointment. Male missionaries generally perceived a posting to New France as a temporary career assignment, but Marie and the other nuns never expected to see France again. Her mission in the new world was to evangelize native girls in the colony, a task she undertook with a vengeance. Her school opened a week after her arrival. She shrewdly learned both Iroquoian and Algonkian and, like Le Clerq, created several useful dictionaries. Discouragement also set in swiftly. Try as she might, native girls simply would not conform to her expectations for them, and she instead turned most of her attention to educating the colony's more malleable French girls. Her boarding school flourished briefly, but the mid-1600s was a difficult time for New France. The fragile economy teetered on collapse as war with the Iroquois threatened to destroy the lifeblood and social viability of the fledgling colony. Marie de l'Incarnation began to doubt whether it, let alone her school, could even survive. Louis XIV thankfully pumped fresh blood and money into New France in 1663. He made it a royal province, and his direct involvement gave her cause for cautious optimism. Still, she died at Quebec in 1672, frustrated and angry that her fervent dreams had not materialized.

Was she a self-serving zealot with serious emotional problems or a saint deserving canonization? The jury remains out. Some accuse her of the former, and there have been several attempts to secure her sainthood. Regardless of her motivation, she could certainly write about New France! Many of the 13,000 letters she penned were to her beloved son in France. He published the first collection of these in 1681, almost a decade after her death, and they form an important glimpse into the realities, aspirations, and perceptions of the day.

The native side of the early missionary story remains hidden. Historians must unfortunately interpret this critical period in Canada's early history from a decidedly one-sided, Eurocentric, and imperialistic perspective. That is both inappropriate and dangerous, but unlikely to change. The evidence for the other side simply does not exist: native people did not leave written records, and the accuracy of oral history is compromised by time and drastic cultural changes. It is, however, possible to make a few tentative observations on the native view, based largely upon reading between the lines of the missionaries' writings. Historians can ascertain, for example, that some natives converted, abandoning their traditional religious values for new and foreign life patterns. Others accepted aspects of Christianity, though often not the central tenets, either for ideological reasons, or because lip service to Catholicism might improve trade. Most indigenous people, however, generally clung to their religion as tenaciously as the missionaries tried to convert them. They repeatedly reaffirmed their own pantheon, and strenuously resisted Christianity, either by avoiding the missionaries or by refusing to accept their teachings. They remained deeply suspicious of the message of the "Black Robes," and clearly recognized the cruel irony that promised them heaven and also brought them hell as both an abstract concept and a reality, as disease often arrived in unison with the European clergy.

A) New Relation of Gaspesia, 1691
Christien Le Clerq

No matter what can be said of this reasoning, I assert, for my part, that I should consider these Indians incomparably more fortunate than ourselves, and that the life of these barbarians would even be capable of inspiring envy, if they had the instructions, the understanding, and the same means for their salvation which God has given us that we may save ourselves by preference over so many poor pagans, and as a result of His pity; for, after all, their lives are not vexed by a thousand annoyances as are ours. They have not among them those situations or offices, whether in the judiciary or in war, which are sought among us with so much ambition. Possessing nothing of their own, they are consequently free from trickery and legal proceedings in connection with inheritances from their relatives. The names of sergeant, of attorney, of clerk, of judge, or president are unknown to them. All their ambition centres in surprising and killing quantities of beavers, moose, seals, and other wild beasts in order to obtain their flesh for food and their skins for clothing. They live in very great harmony, never quarrelling and never beating one another except in drunkenness. On the contrary, they mutually aid one another in their needs with much charity and without self-seeking. There is continual joy in their wigwams. The multitude of their children does not embarrass them, for, far from being annoyed by these, they consider themselves just that much the more fortunate and richer as their family is more numerous. Since they never expect that the fortunes of the children will be larger than those of their fathers, they are also free from all those anxieties which we give ourselves in connection with the accumulation of property for the purpose of elevating children in society and in importance. Hence it comes about that nature has always preserved among them in all its integrity that conjugal love between husband and wife which ought never to suffer alteration through selfish fear of having too many children. This duty, which in Europe is considered too onerous, is viewed by our Indians as very honourable, very advantageous, and very useful, and he who has the largest number of children is the most highly esteemed of the entire nation. This is because he finds more support for his old age, and because, in their condition in life, the boys and girls contribute equally to the happiness and joy of those who have given them birth. They live, in fact, together — father and children — like the first kings of the earth, who subsisted at the beginning of the world by their hunting and fishing, and on vegetables and sagamité, or stew ...

It is certainly true that our Gaspesians had so little knowledge of bread and wine when the French arrived for the first time in their country, that these barbarians mistook the bread which was given them for a piece of birch tinder, and became convinced that the French were equally cruel and inhuman, since in their amusements, said the Indians, they drank blood without repugnance. It was thus they designated wine. Therefore they remained some time not only without tasting it, but even without wishing to become in any manner intimate, or to hold intercourse, with a nation which they believed to be accustomed to blood and carnage. Nevertheless, in the end, they became accustomed gradually to this drink, and it were to be wished that they had still to-day the same horror of wine and brandy, for they drink it even to drunkenness, to the prejudice of their salvation and of Christianity; and it makes them commit cruelties much greater than those which they had imagined in the conduct of the French.

Many persons without doubt are surprised that, and have difficulty in understanding how, a missionary can live whole years together in the Indian manner. I admit frankly that he experiences very fully the vexations of this life, especially at first, when these are always very trying. But one soon overcomes all repugnance towards it when one has such good and succulent meats as those of moose, of beaver, of seal, of porcupine, of partridge, of wild goose, of teal, of ducks, of snipe, of cod, of salmon, of bass, of trout, and of plenty of other fish and of waterfowl which serve as the usual food of the Indians.

The months of January and February are for these barbarians, as a rule, a time of involuntary penitence and very rigorous fasting, which is also often very sad as well, in view of the cruel and horrible results which it causes among them. Nevertheless they could very easily prevent its unfortunate consequences if they would but follow the example of the ants, and of the little squirrels, which, by an instinct as admirable as it is natural, accumulate with care in summer the wherewithal to subsist in plenty during the winter. But, after all, our Gaspesians are of those people who take no thought for the morrow, though this is much more because of laziness in collecting good provisions than through zeal in obeying the counsel which God has given thereon in His Holy Gospel. They are convinced that fifteen to twenty lumps of meat, or of fish dried and cured in the smoke, are more than enough to support them for the space of five to six months. Since, however, they are a people of good appetite, they consume their provisions very much sooner than they expect. This exposes them often to the danger of dying from hunger, through lack of provision which they could easily possess in abundance if they would only take the trouble to gather it. But these barbarians, being wanderers and vagabonds, do not plough the ground, nor do they harvest Indian corn, or peas, or pumpkins, as do the Iroquois, the Hurons, the Algonquins, and several other nations of Canada. In consequence they are sometimes reduced to so great need that they have neither the strength nor the spirit to leave their wigwams in order to go seek in the woods the wherewithal for living. It is then impossible to behold without compassion the innocent children, who, being nothing more than skin and bone, exhibit clearly enough in their wholly emaciated faces and in their living skeletons, the cruel hunger which they are suffering through the negligence of their fathers and mothers, who find themselves obliged, along with their unhappy children, to eat curdled blood, scrapings of skin, old moccasins, and a thousand other things incompatible with the life of man. All this would be little if they did not come sometimes to other extremes far more affecting and horrible.

It is surprising to learn that they find themselves often reduced to extremities so great and cruel that one cannot even hear of them without shuddering, and nature cannot endure them without horror. We have seen a sufficiently deplorable example thereof at the River of Sainte Croix, otherwise called Miramichis, in the month of January 1680, when our Indians consumed all their meat and their smoked fish much sooner than they had expected. Matters reached such a pass that, since the season was not yet suitable for hunting, nor the rivers in condition for fishing, they found themselves reduced to suffer all the worst that can be experienced in a famine, which resulted in their deaths to the number of forty or fifty. The French who were then at the Fort of Sainte Croix, aided them as much as they could at a juncture when the obligation to aid one's neighbour, whom the Gospel command us to love as ourselves, appeared too obvious not to be discharged with all the compassion and the charity possible. Madame Denis gave orders to her servants to distribute to the Indians, according to the needs of each wigwam, bread, flour, peas, meat, fish and even also corn ...

In a depression so great, and a desolation so general, which afflicted greatly both the French and the Indians, one of our Gaspesians was found, who, unable to endure any longer the hunger which was devouring him alive, was so barbarous and cruel as to resolve to kill and to eat his wife. She, perceiving the sinister design of her husband, and in order to save her own life, put it into his mind to break the heads and cut the throats of two of their children, one aged five to six years, and the other seven to eight. "It is true," said this cruel hard-hearted mother to her husband, her heart all pierced with grief, "that thou hast cause to complain, and that the need in which we are is extreme; but in fact if thou wilt kill some member of thy family, is it not much better that we put to death some of our children, and that we eat them together, in order that I may be able to rear and to support the smaller ones who can no longer live if once they come to lose their mother?" She pleaded her cause in her own favour so well that with common consent the man and his wife slew, by cutting their throats, these two poor innocents, paying no attention to the tears and lamentations of the little girl, who implored her father and mother not to murder her. She was not able to obtain this favour from these inhuman monsters, and both children received their death from those who had given them life. They then cut the bodies of these children into pieces, and placed them in a boiling kettle; and finally, with unheard of cruelty, the simple recollection of which makes the Gaspesian nation shudder to this very day, these monsters of nature ate them, in company with one of their brothers, who was obliged to flee with the others to the River of Saint Jean, for fear lest the leading men of our Indians, surprising them in this cruel feast, might break their heads. And in fact these leading men were as much exasperated as surprised at the news of a deed so black and so barbarous. It is true that these unhappy persons, on the return of spring, which proved very favourable for hunting, were inconsolable for the miserable nature of the death of their children, whom they had inhumanely sacrificed for the preservation of their own lives ...

Such were the words and the feelings of these poor unhappy persons. I did all in my power to console them, promising them all the protection and the aid that I could, and representing to them that while in truth their crime was monstrous, yet in fact God had more goodness and compassion for them than they had of wickedness and cruelty in thus putting to death those to whom they had given life. They believed in my words, and received my leaflets, well resolved to do and to practise exactly everything with which I could inspired them of good, in order to appease the justice of God and to invite His mercy.

Such are the grievous accidents to which, without doubt, our Indians expose themselves every year by their laziness, and by the little care that they take to accumulate in summer enough to enable them to avoid and prevent a thousand ills which very often overwhelm them in winter, as they themselves know only too well through the sad experience which they have had thereof. These Gaspesians quite agree with us, but it seems as if the abundance which they find in spring, summer, and autumn makes them forget the misfortunes which they have suffered during the winter.

After all, I declare that one cannot sufficiently admire the fortitude with which they endure the hardships of hunger, and it can be said that they fast with perhaps as much, or even with more, patience and austerity than the most rigid and the most self-mortifying of the anchorites. It is somewhat surprising to see that they make an entire occupation of singing immoderately, and of dancing sometimes like fools, when they have a consuming appetite, and when they have nothing with which to satisfy it. This they do in order to lose, say they, through this amusement, the desire which they would have for eating. It is not difficult for them to go three or four days without food, especially when they are hunting, and are chasing some wild beasts, such as the moose. They never take any meal before this exercise, however severe it may be for them. But in the evening, when they return to the wigwam, they regale themselves with all the best that there is, boiling, frying or roasting, according to the tastes of each, all that they have, without any reserve, and without any apprehension lest any one count their pieces. On the contrary, these barbarians consider that it is a very praiseworthy and glorious thing to eat a great deal. That is why, not being able to submit to the rules of temperance and of economy, which nevertheless would be very useful and invaluable to them, they make all their good to consist, and find their happiness, in eating to excess, in granting to their appetite beyond that which it desires, and in eating as they please, as well by day as by night, making a perfect pleasure and happiness of their bellies. Hence it is a proverb among us in Canada, that it needs only four or five good meals to restore them from the fatigues and the weakness of several months of illness.

They preserve inviolably among them the manner of living which was in vogue during the golden age, and those who imagine a Gaspesian Indian as a monster of nature will understand only with difficulty the charity with which they mutually comfort one another. The strong take pleasure in supporting the feeble; and those who by their hunting procure many furs, give some in charity to those who have none, either in order to pay the debts of these, or to clothe them, or to obtain for them the necessaries of life. Widows and orphans receive presents, and if there is any widow who is unable to support her children, the old men take charge of them, and distribute and give them to the best hunters, with whom they live, neither more nor less than as if they were the actual children of the wigwam. It would be a shame, and a kind of fault worthy of eternal reproach, if it was known that an Indian, when he had provisions in abundance, did not make gift thereof to those whom he knew to be in want and in need. This is why those who kill the first moose at the beginning of January or February, a time at which those people suffer greatly, since they have consumed all their provisions, make it a pleasure to carry some of it themselves very promptly to those who have none, even if these are distant fifteen to twenty leagues. And, not content with this liberality, they invite these latter also, with all possible tenderness, to join their company and to remove closer to their wigwams, in order that they may be able to aid these people more conveniently in their necessity and in their most pressing need, giving a thousand promises to share with them the half of their hunting. This is good example, without doubt, for those pitiless rich, and those hearts of stone, who have only bowels of iron for their like, and who never take any trouble whatever to relieve the extreme misery of so many poor persons who are in anguish, and who suffer hunger and nakedness, whilst these wicked rich wallow in a superabundance of property and riches, of which Providence has made them only trustees, and which he has placed in their hands only in order that they may make a holy use of them as alms and charity to the needy members of the Saviour ...

Many find it difficult to understand the manner in which the Indians boiled their meat before they were given the use of our kettles, which they now find extremely convenient. I have learned from themselves that before they obtained our kettles, they used little buckets or troughs of wood, which they filled with water; into this they threw glowing stones, which they made red hot in the fire, and they did this so often, that little by little the water grew warm, and finally boiled by virtue of the warmth and the heat of these hot rocks, until the meat was amply cooked for eating in the Indian manner, that is to say, half raw, as they eat it still to this day, and in a manner which is wholly disgusting. For it is true that these people are distinguished in their manner of living by an uncleanness which turns the stomach. I cannot believe that there is any nation in the world so disgusting in its manners of drinking and eating as the Gaspesian, excepting, perhaps, some other peoples of this new world. Hence it is true that of all the troubles which the missionaries suffer at first in order to accustom themselves to the manner of life of the Indians for the sake of instructing them in the maxims of Christianity, this is without a doubt one of the most difficult to endure, because it very often causes a rising of the stomach. Our Gaspesians never clean their kettles except the first time they use them, because, they say, they are afraid of the verdigris, which is in no danger of attaching itself to them, when they are well greased and burnt. Nor do they ever skim it off, because it seems to them that this is removing grease from the pot, and just so much good material is lost. This causes the meat to be all stuffed with a black and thick scum, like little meat balls which have nearly the appearance of curdled milk. They content themselves with removing simply the largest moose hairs, although the meat may have been dragged around the campfire for five or six days, and the dogs also may have tasted it beforehand. They have no other tables than the flat ground, nor other napkins for wiping their hands than their moccasins, or their hair, on which they sedulously rub their hands. In a word there is nothing that is not rough, gross and repellent in the extraordinary manner of life of these barbarians, who observe neither in drinking nor in eating any rules of politeness or of civility ...

The Gaspesians do not know how to read nor how to write. They have, nevertheless, enough understanding and memory to learn how to do both if only they were willing to give the necessary application. But aside from the fickleness and instability of their minds, which they are willing to apply only in so far as it pleases them, they all have the false and ridiculous belief that they would not live long if they were as learned as the French. From this it comes that they are pleased to live and to die in their natural ignorance. Some of these Indians, however, for whose instruction some trouble has been taken, have in a short time become philosophers and even pretty good theologians. But, after all, they have ever remained savages, since they have not had the sense to profit by their considerable advantages, of which they have rendered themselves wholly unworthy by leaving their studies in order to dwell with their fellow-countrymen in the woods, where they have lived like very bad philosophers, preferring, on the basis of a foolish reasoning, the savage to the French life ...

They have much ingenuity in drawing upon bark a kind of map which marks exactly all the rivers and streams of a country of which they wish to make a representation. They mark all the places thereon exactly and so well that they make use of them successfully, and an Indian who possesses one makes long voyages without going astray ...

They count the years by the winters, the months by the moons, the days by the nights, the hours of the morning in proportion as the sun advances into its meridian, and the hours of the afternoon according as it declines and approaches its setting. They give thirty days to all the moons, and regulate the year by certain natural observations which they make upon the course of the sun and the seasons ...

They are all naturally well built in body, of a fine size, tall, well-proportioned, and without any deformity, powerful, robust, dexterous, and of surprising agility, especially when they pursue the moose, whose swiftness is not less than that of fallow deer and stags. The men are taller than the women, who are nearly always short; but both are of a deportment grave, serious, and very modest.

They walk with dignity as if they had always some great affair to think upon, and to decide, in their minds. Their colour is brown, tawny, and swarthy, but their teeth are extremely white, perhaps because of the fir gum which they chew very often and which communicates to them this whiteness. Their colour, however, does not lessen at all the natural beauty of the features of their faces, and it can be said with truth that there are seen in Gaspesia as fine children, and persons as well built, as in France; whilst among them there are as a rule neither humpbacks nor crippled, one-eyed, blind, or maimed persons.

They enjoy a perfect health, not being subject to an infinity of diseases as we are. They are neither too stout nor too thin, and one does not see among the Gaspesians any of those fat bellies full of humours and of grease. Consequently the very names of gout, stone, gravel, gall, colic, rheumatism, are entirely unknown to them.

They all have naturally a sound mind, and common sense beyond that which is supposed in France. They conduct their affairs cleverly, and take wise and necessary steps to make them turn out favorably. They are very eloquent and persuasive among those of their own nation, using metaphors and very pleasing circumlocutions in their speeches, which are very eloquent, especially when these are pronounced in the councils and the public and general assemblies.

If it is a great good to be delivered from a great ill, our Gaspesians can call themselves happy, because they have neither avarice nor ambition — those two cruel executioners which give pain and torture to a multitude of persons. As they have neither police, nor taxes, nor office, nor command-ment which is absolute (for they obey, as we have said, only their head men and their chiefs in so far as it pleases them), they scarcely give themselves the trouble to amass riches, or to make a fortune more considerable than that which they possess in their woods. They are content enough provided that they have the wherewithal for living, and that they have the reputation of being good warriors and good hunters, in which they reckon all their glory and their ambition. They are naturally fond of their repose, putting away from them, as far as they can, all the subjects for annoyance which would trouble them. Hence it comes about that they never contradict any-one, and that they let everyone do as he pleases, even to the extent that the fathers and the mothers do not dare correct their children, but permit their misbehaviour for fear of vexing them by chastising them.

They never quarrel and never are angry with one another, not because of any inclination they have to practise virtue, but for their own satisfac-tion, and in the fear, as we have just said, of troubling their repose, of which they are wholly idolaters.

Indeed, if any natural antipathy exists between husband and wife, or if they cannot live together in perfect understanding, they separate from one another, in order to seek elsewhere the peace and union which they cannot find together. Consequently they cannot understand how one can submit to the indissolubility of marriage. "Does thou not see," they will say to you, "that thou hast no sense? My wife does not get on with me, and I do not get on with her. She will agree well with such a one, who does not agree with his own wife. Why dost thou wish that we four be unhappy for the rest of our days?" In a word, they hold it as a maxim that each one is free: that one can do whatever he wishes: and that it is not sensible to put constraint upon men. It is necessary, say they, to live without annoyance and disquiet, to be con-tent with that which one has, and to endure with constancy the misfortunes of nature, because the sun, or he who has made and governs all, orders it thus. If some one among them laments, grieves, or is angry, this is the only reasoning with which they console him … In a word, they rely upon liking nothing, and upon not becoming attached to the goods of the earth, in order not to be grieved or sad when they lose them. They are, as a rule, always joyous, without being uneasy as to who will pay their debts …

It is not the same, however, when they are ill-treated without cause, for then everything is to be feared from them. As they are very vindictive against strangers, they preserve resentment for the ill-treatment in their hearts until they are entirely avenged for the injury or for the affront which will have been wrongly done them. They will even make themselves drunk on purpose, or they will pretend to be full with brandy, in order to carry out their wicked plan, imagining that they will always be amply justified in the crime which they have committed if they but say to the elders and heads of the nation, that they were tipsy, and that they had no reason or judgment during their drunkenness …

They are so generous and liberal towards one another that they seem not to have any attachment to the little they possess, for they deprive themselves thereof very willingly and in very good spirit the very moment when they know that their friends have need of it. It is true that this generous disposition is undergoing some alteration since the French, through the commerce which they have with them, have gradually accustomed them to traffic and not to give anything for nothing; for, prior to the time when trade came into use among these people, it was as in the Golden Age, and everything was common property among them.

Hospitality is in such great esteem among our Gaspesians that they make almost no distinction between the home-born and the stranger. They give lodging equally to the French and to the Indians who come from a distance, and to both they distribute generously whatever they have obtained in hunting and in the fishery, giving themselves little concern if the strangers remain among them weeks, months, and even entire years. They are always good-natured to their guests, whom, for the time, they consider as belonging to the wigwam, especially if they understand even a little of the Gaspesian tongue. You will see them supporting their relatives, the children of their friends, the widows, orphans, and old people, without ever expressing any reproach for the support or the other aid which they give them. It is surely necessary to admit that this is a true indication of a good heart and a generous soul. Consequently it is truth to say that the injury most felt among them is the reproach that an Indian is Medousaoüek, that is to say, that he is stingy. This is why, when one refuses them anything, they say scornfully: "Thou art a mean one," or else, "Thou likest that; like it then as much as thou wishest, but thou wilt always be stingy and a man without heart."

They are nevertheless ungrateful towards the French, and they do not, as a rule, give anything for nothing. Their ingratitude reaches even to a point that, after having been supported and provided with the necessaries of life in their needs and their necessities, they will demand of you a compensation for the least service they will render you ...

It can be said, to the praise and the glory of our Gaspesian women, that they are very modest, chaste, and continent, beyond what could be supposed; and I can say with truth that I have specially devoted myself to the mission of Gaspesia because of the natural inclination the Gaspesians have for virtue. One never hears in their wigwams any impure words, not even any of those conversations which have a double meaning. Never do they in public take any liberty — I do not say criminal alone, but even the most trifling; no kissing, no badinage between young persons of different sexes; in a word, everything is said and is done in their wigwams with much modesty and reserve ...

I do not claim, however, to affirm that chastity has an absolute empire in all the hearts of our Gaspesian women, for one does see among them some girls and women who are libertines and who live in dishonour. But indeed it is a fact that the drinking of brandy and drunkenness causes these lapses ... For those who do not drink are so jealous of their honour that not only do they not abandon themselves to evil, but, on the contrary, they even go so far as to defeat and put to confusion, by their strong and brave resistance, those who have the insolence and temerity to solicit them to the least criminal action which can turn them from their duty.

They are naturally fickle, mockers, slanderers, and dissimulators. They are not true to their promises except in so far as they are restrained either by fear or by hope; and they believe any person would have no sense who would keep his word against his own interest.

... [I]n fact they do not know what civility is, nor decorum. Since they consider themselves all equal, and one as great, as powerful, and as rich as another, they mock openly at our bowings, at our compliments, and at our embracings. They never remove their hats when they enter our dwellings; this ceremony seems to them too troublesome. They throw their presents on the ground at the foot of the one to whom they wish to give them, and they smoke a pipe of tobacco before speaking. "Listen!" say they, "Take the present which I give thee with all my heart." That is the sole compliment which they make on this occasion; but, nevertheless, all is affability among them, for everything which gives contentment to the senses passes for virtue.

They are filthy and vile in their wigwams, of which the approaches are filled with excrements, feathers, chips, shreds of skins, and very often with entrails of the animals or the fishes which they take in hunting or fishing. In their eating they wash their meat only very superficially before putting it upon the fire, and they never clean the kettle except the first time that they use it. Their clothes are all filthy, both outside and inside, and soaked with oil and grease, of which the stink often produces sickness of the stomach. They hunt for vermin before everybody, without turning aside even a little. They make it walk for fun upon their hands, and they eat it as if it were something good. They find the use of our handkerchiefs ridiculous; they mock at us and say that it is placing excrements in our pockets. Finally, however calm it may be outside of the wigwam, there always prevails inside a very inconvenient wind, since these Indians let it go very freely, especially when they have eaten much moose ...

Their opposition to Christianity is great, from the side of their indifference, insensibility, and other faults which we have noted. But it is also no less from the point of view of drunkenness, which is the predominant vice of our Gaspesians; and I can even say with truth, that this is one of the most powerful obstacles to the conversion of these peoples.

These barbarians, who formerly mistook wine for blood, and brandy for poison, and who fled with horror from the French who would give them these liquors, are today so enamoured with these kinds of drinks that they make it a principle of honour to gorge themselves therewith like beasts; and they only drink, properly speaking, in order to get drunk. It is this which compels the missionaries to regard with grief the immoderate traffic in brandy in Canada, and to view it as the most pernicious of the obstacles which the Devil has been able to raise against the salvation of the Indians, and against the establishment of the faith among these pagan and barbarous nations. For all the vices and crimes, which are usually found separate from one another, are united in the single trade in brandy when it is made without regulations and moderation.

Avarice, self-seeking, and the immoderate desire to amass riches, all of which the Son of God has condemned by the choice which He has made of evangelical poverty, is the unhappily fertile source of the surprising disorders which are committed by those who trade and traffic in brandy with the Indians. For you will note, if you please, that the traders make them drunk quite on purpose, in order to deprive these poor barbarians of the use of reason, so that the traders can deceive them more easily, and obtain almost for nothing their furs, which they would not sell except for a just and reasonable price if they were in their right minds. This trade is fraudulent, and liable to restitution in proportion to what the thing is worth, according to the customs of trade, these barbarians not having in their drunkenness the liberty nor the judgment which is necessary for concluding a deed of sale or purchase, which requires a free and mutual consent from both parties.

Although it is not allowable to sell water for wine or for brandy, yet this is very often done by the mixing of these liquors in the sale and distribution of these kinds of drinks. This is therefore the second irregularity of which our traders in brandy are guilty; and they colour this injustice by the title of charity, alleging as their reason, that they make this mixture in order not to get the Indians drunk. It is true that the traders would be to some extent excusable if they made up the difference by other goods, but it is well known that they do nothing of the kind. On the contrary, they take the same profit as if they sold honestly, and they still make the Indians drunk by these mixed liquors, thus rendering themselves, by this miserable kind of trading, the masters not only of the furs of the Indians, but also of their blankets, guns, axes, kettles, etc., which the traders have sold them at a very dear rate. Thus these poor barbarians find themselves wholly naked, and deprived of the furs and goods which they had brought and traded for their own use, and for the support of their families.

Lewdness, adulteries, incests, and several other crimes which decency keeps me from naming, are the usual disorders which are committed through the trade in brandy, of which some traders make use in order to abuse the Indian women, who yield themselves readily during their drunkenness to all kinds of indecency, although at other times, as we have said, they would be more like to give a box on the ears than a kiss to whomsoever wished to engage them to evil, if they were in their right minds.

Injuries, quarrels, homicides, murders, parricides are to this day the sad consequences of the trade in brandy; and one sees with grief Indians dying in their drunkenness: strangling themselves: the brother cutting the throat of the sister: the husband breaking the head of his wife: a mother throwing her child into the fire or the river: and fathers cruelly choking little innocent children whom they cherish and love as much as, and more than, themselves when they are not deprived of their reason. They consider it sport to break and shatter everything in the wigwams, and to bawl for hours together, repeating always the same word. They beat themselves and tear themselves to pieces, something which happens never, or at least very rarely, when they are sober. The French themselves are not exempt from the drunken fury of these barbarians, who, through a manifestation of the anger of God justly irritated against a conduct so little Christian, sometimes rob, ravage, and burn the French houses and stores, and very often descend to the saddest extremes.

I abbreviate an infinity of other disturbances resulting from the immoderate trade which is made to our Indians in wine, brandy, and all other intoxicating drinks, in order that I may justify the zeal of Monseigneur the Bishop of Quebec, the Recollects, and other missionaries who have strongly declared themselves against these disturbances, and with so much more of justice since, through long experience, they have recognized the sad cause of the loss of the spiritual and temporal good of the French and of the Indians of New France. They have recognized, too, that among a great number of obstacles — from superstition, from insensibility, from blindness, from indifference, from impurity — which are opposed to the conversion of these pagan nations, there will always be much less likelihood of establishing solidly a true Christianity among these peoples so long as they are made drunk, and so long as no rule or moderation is observed in the distribution and sale of brandy. It was also this, perhaps, which a young libertine wished to express to me. He, not giving himself any concern about the salvation of the Indians, provided that he had their furs in order to satisfy his ambition and selfishness, boasted that he could do more evil with a bottle of brandy than the missionaries could do good with a bottle of holy water; that is to say, that he could damn more Indians by making them drunk, than the missionaries could save by instructing them in the truths of Christianity.

I do not wish to stop here to consider the arguments which the traders advance to justify the injustice of their proceedings. They say that it would be necessary to close the public-houses in France: that it is not a sin to make a Frenchman drunk, still less an Indian, even when he has been induced to drink, and although it is known that they take brandy only in order to become drunk, these barbarians not finding pleasure in this drink except so far as it makes them entirely lose their understanding and reason: that it would ruin absolutely the commerce and trade of the colony if brandy were not given to the Indians, because these barbarians would betake themselves to the English and the Hollanders of New England and New Holland: and that, finally there was needed a regulation of police, and above all, no favouritism of persons, neither of relatives nor friends, so that the trade should be free to everybody to use it with moderation ...

They are all by nature physicians, apothecaries, and doctors, by virtue of the knowledge and experience they have of certain herbs, which they use successfully to cure ills that seem to us incurable.

It is a fact that our Gaspesians generally enjoy perfect health right up to a fine old age, for they are not subject to several of the maladies which affect us in France, such as gout, gravel, scrofula, itch, etc. This is either because they are begotten by parents who are healthy and active, with a humour and blood which are well tempered, or else because they live, as we have described, in perfect harmony and concord, without lawsuits and without quarrelling for the goods of this world. Consequently they never lose their repose and their habitual tranquillity ...

There is no one, however, more to be pitied than the sick persons, who endure without complaint the hubbub, the noise, and the fuss of the juggler [somewhat analogous to a shaman] and of those in the wigwam. It seems indeed that our Gaspesians, who in other respects seem sufficiently humane and kindly, are lacking in regard to charity and consideration for their sick. It can in fact be said that they do not know how to take care of them, they give them indifferently everything which they desire, both to drink and to eat, and whenever they ask it. They take the sick persons along, and carry or embark them with themselves on their voyages when there is any appearance of recovery. But if the recovery of the sick man is wholly despaired of, so that he can no more eat, drink, nor smoke, they sometimes break his head, as much to relieve the suffering he endures as to save themselves the trouble which they have in taking him everywhere with them.

Nor have they any better idea what it means to comfort a poor invalid, and from the moment when he no longer eats or smokes any more tobacco, or when he loses speech, they abandon him entirely, and never speak to him a single word of tenderness or comfort ...

B) Letters
Marie de l'Incarnation

i) *To a Lady of Rank, Quebec, 3 September 1640*

… We have every reason then, Madame, to praise the Father of mercies for those he has so abundantly poured upon our Savages since, not content with having themselves baptized, they are beginning to become settled and to clear the land in order to establish themselves. It seems that the fervour of the primitive Church has descended to New France and that it illuminates the hearts of our good converts, so that if France will give them a little help towards building themselves small lodges in the village that has been commenced at Sillery, in a short time a much further progress will be seen.

It is a wonderful thing to see the fervour and zeal of the Reverend Fathers of the Company of Jesus. To give heart to his poor Savages, the Reverend Father Vimont, the Superior of the mission, leads them to work himself and toils on the land with them. He then hears the children pray and teaches them to read, finding nothing lowly in whatever concerns the glory of God and the welfare of these poor people. The Reverend Father Le Jeune, the principal cultivator of this vineyard, continues to perform marvels there. He preaches to the people every day and has them do everything he wishes, for he is known to all these nations and is held among them as a man of miracles. And indeed he is indefatigable beyond anything that might be said in the practice of his ministry, in which he is seconded by the other Reverend Fathers, all of whom spare neither life nor health to seek those poor souls that the blood of Jesus Christ has redeemed.

There has been a great persecution among the Hurons in which one of the Fathers was almost martyred by the blow of a hatchet. A club was broken upon him in detestation of the faith he preached. There has been a like conspiracy against the others, who were overjoyed to suffer. Despite all this, at least a thousand persons have been baptized. The devil has worked in vain. Jesus Christ will always be the Master — may he be praised forevermore …

It would take me too long to speak to you separately of them all but I shall tell you in general that these girls love us more than they love their parents, showing no desire to accompany them, which is most extraordinary in the Savages. They model themselves upon us as much as their age and their condition can permit. When we make our spiritual exercises, they keep a continual silence. They dare not even raise their eyes or look at us, thinking that this would interrupt us. But when we are finished, I could not express the caresses they give us, a thing they never do with their natural mothers ...

It is a singular consolation to us to deprive ourselves of all that is most necessary in order to win souls to Jesus Christ, and we would prefer to lack everything rather than leave our girls in the unbearable filth they bring from their cabins. When they are given to us, they are naked as worms and must be washed from head to foot because of the grease their parents rub all over their bodies; and whatever diligence we use and however often their linen and clothing is changed, we cannot rid them for a long time of the vermin caused by this abundance of grease. A Sister employs part of each day at this. It is an office that everyone eagerly covets. Whoever obtains it considers herself rich in such a happy lot and those that are deprived of it consider themselves undeserving of it and dwell in humility. Madame our foundress performed this service almost all year; today it is Mother Marie de Saint-Joseph that enjoys this good fortune ...

But after all it is a very special providence of this great God that we are able to have girls after the great number of them that died last year. This malady, which is smallpox, being universal among the Savages, it spread to our seminary, which in a very few days resembled a hospital. All our girls suffered this malady three times and four of them died from it. We all expected to fall sick, because the malady was a veritable contagion, and also because we were day and night succouring them and the small space we had forced us to be continually together. But Our Lord aided us so powerfully that none of us was indisposed.

The Savages that are not Christians hold the delusion that it is baptism, instruction, and dwelling among the French that was the cause of this mortality, which made us believe we would not be given any more girls and that those we had would be taken from us. God's providence provided so benevolently against this that the Savages themselves begged us to take their daughters, so that if we had food and clothing we would be able to admit a very great number, though we are exceedingly pressed for buildings. If God touches the hearts of some saintly souls, so that they will help us build close to the Savages as we have the design to do, we will have a great many girls. We are longing for that hour to arrive, so that we will be more perfectly able to do the things for which Our Lord sent us to this blessed country.

ii) To her son, Quebec, 4 September 1641

My very dear and well-loved son:

... For myself, my very dear son, what you say is true — I have found in Canada something quite other than I thought, but I mean this in another sense than you do. Travails here are so gentle and so easy for me to bear that I experience the words of Our Lord: My yoke is gentle and my burden is light. I have not lost my pains in the thorny study of a foreign and savage tongue; it is so easy to me now that I have no trouble teaching our holy mysteries to our converts, whom we have had this year in great number — namely, more than fifty seminarians and more than seven hundred visits from passing Savages, all of whom we have assisted spiritually and corporally. The joy my heart receives in this holy employment wipes away all the fatigues I may from time to time experience, I assure you. So have no anxiety for me on this point.

I see that you have none, but on the contrary I am very sensibly consoled by the good wish you make for me — namely, that I should be a martyr. Alas, my very dear son, my sins will deprive me of this great boon; I have done nothing until now that could have won the heart of God and obliged him to do me this honour ...

iii) To her son, Quebec, 1647

My very dear and well-loved son:

Since I inform you every year of the graces and benedictions that God pours upon this new Church, it is right that I should also acquaint you with the afflictions he permits to befall it. He consoles us sometimes like a loving father and sometimes chastises us like a severe judge — and me, in particular, who incite his anger more than all others by my continual infidelities. He has made us feel the weight of his hand this year by an affliction that is very sensible to those zealous for the salvation of souls. This is the rupture of the peace by the perfidious Iroquois, whence has followed the death of a great number of Frenchmen and Christian Savages and, above all, of the Reverend Father Jogues.

What brought these barbarians to break a peace we believed so well established was the aversion several Huron captives gave them to our Faith and prayer by telling them it was these that had attracted all sorts of misfortunes upon their nation, that had infected them with contagious maladies and made their hunting and fishing more sterile than when they lived according to their ancient customs. Almost at the same time mortality attached itself to their nation and spread throughout their villages, where it harvested many of their people in a little time, and the contagion engendered a sort of worm in their corn, which devoured it almost completely. These mishaps easily persuaded the Iroquois that what the Huron captives said was true.

When the Reverend Father Jogues went to visit them to confirm the peace on behalf of Monsieur the Governor and all the Christians, both French and Savage, he left with his host, as a pledge for his return, a casket in which were some books and church furnishings. The barbarians believed that these were demons he had left among them and that they were the cause of their misfortunes ...

Meanwhile Monsieur the Governor, who knew nothing of this reversal, readied some Frenchmen to go with some Hurons to visit them. The Reverend Father Jogues, who had already begun to sprinkle this ungrateful land with his blood, joined with them to give them advice and necessary assistance during the voyage. They departed from Trois-Rivières on the 24th of September 1646 and arrived in the country of the Agneronon Iroquois greatly fatigued on the 17th of October in the same year.

Upon their arrival they were treated in a manner they were not expecting. The barbarians did not even wait to mistreat them till they had entered the cabins but first stripped them quite naked, then greeted them with blows from fists and clubs, saying, "Do not be astonished at the treatment you are given, for you will die tomorrow. But console yourselves. You will not be burned but struck down with the hatchet and your heads placed on the palisade that encloses our village, so your brothers will see you again after we capture them."

This reception showed them very clearly that the spirits of the Iroquois were soured to such an extent that there was no hope of mercy. So they prepared themselves for death in the little time that remained to them. The next day passed quietly, however, which made them believe that the barbarians were slightly softened. But towards evening a Savage of the Bear clan took Father Jogues into his cabin to sup. Behind the door another barbarian was waiting and struck at him with a hatchet, so that he fell dead on the spot. As much was done to a young Frenchman named Jean de la Lande, a native of Dieppe, who had given himself to the Father to serve him. The barbarian at once cut off their heads and erected them as trophies on the palisade, then threw their bodies in the river.

Thus this great servant of God consummated his sacrifice. We honour him as a martyr and he is one indeed, since he was massacred in detestation of our holy Faith and of prayer, which these perfidious ones hold to be spells and enchantments. We can even say that he is thrice a martyr — as many times, that is to say, as he went to the Iroquois nations. The first time he did not die but suffered quite enough to die. The second time he did not suffer and died only in desire, his heart burning continually with the desire for martyrdom. But the third time God accorded him what he had for so long desired.

It seemed that God had promised him this great favour, for he wrote to one of his friends in a prophetic spirit, "I shall go and shall not return," and thence it appears that he was awaiting this blessed moment with a saintly impatience.

Oh, how sweet it is to die for Jesus Christ! It is for this reason that his servants so ardently desire to suffer. As the saints are always ready to do good to their enemies, we do not doubt that this one, being in heaven, asked God for the salvation of the man that had dealt him the mortal blow, for this barbarian was captured soon afterwards by the French and, after being converted to the Faith and receiving Holy Baptism, was put to death in the sentiments of a true Christian ...

Before they went farther, they burned alive a Christian who had been dangerously wounded, lest he die on the way of too easy a death. We learned that, before they left the place, these barbarians, who are more cruel than the ferocious beasts, crucified a little child aged but three years, who had been baptized. They stretched his body upon a great piece of bark and pierced his feet and hands with sticks pointed like nails. Oh, how fortunate was that child to have deserved in his state of innocence a death like unto that of Jesus Christ! Who would not envy this holy infant, who was more fortunate, in my opinion, than those whose death honoured the birth of our divine Saviour?

The afflicted group was conducted to the country of the Iroquois where they were received like prisoners of war — that is to say, they were beaten with clubs and their sides pierced by blazing firebrands. Two great scaffolds were raised, one for the men, one for the women, where they were exposed quite naked to the laughter and taunts of the barbarians. They asked for Father Jogues — the Christians so they might confess, the catechumens so they might be baptized. The only reply to their beseeching was mockery, but some captive Algonkin women quietly approached the ignominious scaffolds and told the new prisoners that he had been killed by a blow from a hatchet and that his head was on the palisade. At these words they saw that they could not expect gentler treatment and that, having no priest to confess to, they could expect help and consolation in their suffering only from God.

Indeed, after they had been the plaything of old and young, they were taken down to be led to the three villages of the Agneronon Iroquois. In one their nails were torn out, in another their fingers were cut off, in the third they were burned, and everywhere they were beaten with clubs, which added new wounds continually to the old. The lives of the women, girls, and children were spared, but the men and the youths capable of bearing arms were distributed throughout the villages to be burned, boiled, and roasted.

The Christian I spoke of that made the public prayers was roasted and tortured with a most barbarous cruelty. They began to torment him before sundown, and throughout the night he was burned from his feet to his waist. Next day he was burned from the waist to the neck. They were waiting to burn his head on the night to come but, seeing that his strength was failing, his tormentors threw his body into the fire, where it was consumed. He was never heard to utter a word of complaint or give any sign of a downcast heart. Faith gave him strength within and enabled him to perform acts of resignation without. He raised his eyes incessantly to heaven, as to the place to which his soul aspired and must soon go. You may call him a martyr or by whatever other name it pleases you, but it is certain that prayer was the cause of his sufferings and that the reason he was tortured more cruelly than the others was that he prayed aloud at the head of all the captives ...

iv) To her son, Quebec, 24 September 1654

My very dear son:

... If this peace endures, as there is occasion to hope it will, this country will be very good and very suitable for the establishment of the French, who multiply greatly and get along quite well by cultivating the land, which is becoming good now that the great forests that made it so cold are being cut down. After three or four years' tillage, the farms are as good as, and in places better than, those in France. Beasts are raised for food and for milk products. This peace increases trade, especially in beaver, which are in very great number this year because there has been freedom to go everywhere to hunt without fear. But traffic in souls is the satisfaction of those that crossed the seas to seek them so as to gain them for Jesus Christ. It is hoped that there will come a great harvest from the initiative of the Iroquois.

Some very distant Savages say there is a very spacious river beyond their country that leads into a great sea that is held to be the China Sea. If with time this is found to be true, the way will be very much shortened, and the workers for the Gospel will be able to go easily into those vast and peopled kingdoms. Time will make us certain of all things.

This, then, is a little abridgement of the general affairs of the country. As for what concerns our Community and our seminary, everything is in quite a good state, thanks to Our Lord. We have some very good seminarians, whom the Iroquois ambassadors came to see each time they were on embassy here. As the Savages love singing, they were delighted, as I have already said, to hear our girls sing so well in the French style and, as a sign of affection for them, they reciprocated with a song in their own mode, which had not so ordered a measure.

We have some Huron girls that the Reverend Fathers have judged suitable to be reared by us as French girls for, as all the Hurons are now converted and live near the French, it is believed that with time they may intermarry, which will not be possible unless the girls are French in both tongue and manners.

It was suggested in the treaty of peace that the Iroquois should bring us some of their girls, and the Reverend Father Le Moyne was to have brought us five daughters of women chiefs when he returned from their country, but the occasion was not propitious. These women chiefs are women of rank among the savages, who have a deliberative voice in the councils and reach conclusions like the men, and it was they that delegated the first ambassadors to treat for peace.

In conclusion, the harvest will be large and I believe we shall have to find labourers. It is suggested and urged upon us that we establish ourselves at Montreal but we cannot consent to this unless a foundation is assured, for one finds nothing laid out in this country and nothing can be accomplished except at great expense. So, however willing we are to follow the inclination of those that call us there, prudence does not permit us to do so.

Help us praise God's goodness for his great mercies towards us and for not only giving us peace but wishing to make our greatest enemies his children so that they may share with us the blessings of so good a Father.

v) *To her son, Quebec, September 1661*

My very dear son:

… Since that time there has been nothing but massacres. The son of Monsieur Godefroy had set out from Trois-Rivières to go to the Attikamegues with a group of Algonkins when they were attacked and put to death by the Iroquois, after defending themselves valiantly and killing a great number of Iroquois.

These barbarians have made many like thrusts, but Montreal has been the chief scene of their carnage. Madame d'Ailleboust, who made a journey here, told me some utterly terrible things. She told me that several persons were killed in a surprise attack in the woods, without anyone's knowing where they were or what had become of them. No one dared go in search of them or even leave the settlement for fear of being involved in a like misfortune. Finally the place was discovered by means of some dogs that were seen to return each night, drunken and covered with blood. This made it believed they were tearing some dead bodies, which afflicted everyone sensibly.

Each one armed himself to go out to discover the truth. When they arrived at the place, they found here and there bodies cut in half, others all mangled and stripped of their flesh, with heads, legs, and hands scattered on all sides. Each one gathered up what he could so as to render the duties of Christian burial to the deceased. Madame d'Ailleboust, who told me this story, unexpectedly encountered a man who had the trunk of a human body pressed to his stomach and his hands full of legs and arms. This sight so startled her that she almost died of fright. But it was quite otherwise when those that carried the remains of the bodies went into the town, for then one heard only the lamentable cries of the wives and children of the deceased.

We have just learned that an ecclesiastic of the Company of the Gentlemen of Montreal, having just said Mass, withdrew a little distance away to tell his hours in silence and meditation, though still quite close to seven of their domestics who were at work. When he was least thinking of the mishap that befell him, sixty ambushed Iroquois discharged a volley of musket shots upon him. Although pierced by shots, he still had the courage to run to his people to warn them to withdraw, and immediately he fell dead. The enemies pursued him and were there as soon as he was. Our seven Frenchmen defended themselves as they retreated but could not prevent one of their number from being killed and another captured.

The barbarians then gave extraordinary howls as a sign of their joy at killing a Black Robe. A renegade among them stripped the body and dressed himself in his robe and, putting a shirt over it for a surplice, paraded around the body in derision of what he had seen done in church at the obsequies of the dead. Then they cut off his head, which they carried off, retiring in haste lest they be pursued by the soldiers of the fort.

That is how these barbarians make war. They attack, then retire into the woods where the French cannot go.

We had baleful portents of all these misfortunes. After the departure of the vessels in 1660, signs appeared in the sky that terrified many people. A comet was seen, its rods pointed towards the earth. It appeared at about two or three o'clock in the morning and disappeared towards six or seven, with the day. In the air was seen a man of fire, enveloped in fire. A canoe of fire was also seen and, towards Montreal, a great crown likewise of fire. On the Island of Orleans a child was heard crying in its mother's womb. As well, confused voices of women and children were heard in the air giving lamentable cries. On another occasion a thunderous and horrible voice was heard. All these mishaps caused such fear as you may imagine.

As well, it was discovered that there are sorcerers and magicians in this country. This became apparent in the person of a miller who came from France at the same time as Monseigneur our Prelate and whom His Highness forced to abjure heresy because he was a Huguenot. This man wished to marry a girl that had travelled with her father and mother in the same vessel, saying that she had been promised to him, but, because he was a man of bad habits, no one would listen to him. After this refusal, he wished to obtain his ends by the ruses of his diabolic art. He caused demons or goblins to appear in the girl's house, and with them spectres that caused her a great deal of distress and fear. However, no-one knew the cause of this invention until, the magician himself appearing, there was reason to believe this wretch had cast an evil spell, for he appeared to her day and night, sometimes alone and sometimes accompanied by two or three others, whom the girl called by name though she had never seen them before.

Monseigneur sent Fathers and went there himself to drive away the demons by the prayers of the Church. However, nothing improved and the din became louder than ever. Phantoms appeared, drums and flutes were heard playing, stones were seen to detach from the wall and fly about, and always the magician was there with his companions to trouble the girl. Their design was to make her marry that wretch, who wished it also but wished to corrupt her first.

The place is far from Quebec and it was a great fatigue to the Fathers to go so far to work their exorcism. So, seeing that the devils were trying to exhaust them with this travail and weary them with their antics, Monseigneur ordered the miller and the girl brought to Quebec. The former was put in prison and the latter shut up in the house of the Hospitalières. Thus the matter remains. Many extraordinary things came to pass which I shall not tell, to avoid tedium and make an end of the matter. The magician and the other sorcerers have not yet been willing to confess. Nor is anything said to them, for it is not easy to convict persons in crimes of this nature.

After this pursuit of sorcerers, all these regions were afflicted with a universal malady, of which it is believed they are the authors. This was a sort of whooping cough or mortal rheum which spread like a contagion in all the families so that not a single one has been free of it. Almost all the children of the Savages, and a great part of the French children, are dead from it. We had never yet seen a like mortality, for the malady terminated in pleurisy accompanied by fever. We were all attacked by it; our boarders, our seminarians, and our domestics were all at the extremity. In a word, I do not believe twenty persons in Canada were free from this sickness, which was so universal that there is a strong foundation for the belief that those wretches had poisoned the air.

Such then are the two scourges with which it has pleased God to try this new Church — one is that of which I have just spoken, for no one has ever seen so many persons die in Canada as died this year, and the other is the persecution of the Iroquois, which keeps the entire country in continual apprehension, for it must be confessed that if they had the skill of the French and knew our weakness they would already have exterminated us. But God blinds them in his goodness towards us, and I hope he will always favour us with his protection against our enemies, whoever they may be. I beseech you to pray him to do so.

vi) To her son, Quebec, 10 August 1662

My very dear son:

I spoke in another letter of a cross, which I said was heavier to me than all the hostilities of the Iroquois. Here is what it is. There are in this country Frenchmen so wretched and lacking in fear of God that they destroy all our new Christians by giving them very violent liquors, such as wine and brandy, to extract beaver from them.

These liquors destroy all these poor people — the men, the women, the boys, and even the girls, for each is master in the cabin when it is a question of eating and drinking. They are immediately drunken and become almost mad. They run about naked with spears and other weapons and put everyone to flight, be it night or day. They run through Quebec, without anyone's being able to prevent them. Thence follow murders, violations, and monstrous and unheard-of crimes. The Reverend Fathers have done all they can to halt this evil, both on the French side and on the Savage; all their efforts have been in vain.

When our Savage day-pupils came to our classes, we pointed out the evil into which they would be precipitated if they followed the example of their kinsmen; they have not since set foot in our seminary. Such is the nature of the Savages. In the matter of behaviour, they copy everything they see the people of their nation do, unless they are well strengthened in Christian morality.

An Algonkin chief, an excellent Christian and the first baptized in Canada, came to visit us and lamented, saying, "Onontio" — that is Monsieur the Governor "is killing us by permitting people to give us liquors."

We replied, "Tell him so he will forbid it."

"I have already told him twice," he answered, "and yet he does nothing. You beg him to forbid it. Perhaps he will obey you."

It is a deplorable thing to see the fatal mishaps that spring from this traffic. Monseigneur our Prelate has done everything that can be imagined to halt its course, as a thing that tends to nothing less than the destruction of faith and religion in these regions ...

vii) To her son, Quebec, 9 August 1668

My very dear son:

... I wrote to you by all the ways, but as my letters may perish, I shall repeat here what I have said elsewhere about our employment, since you desire that I should discuss it with you ...

The Savage girls lodge and eat with French girls, but it is necessary to have a special mistress for their instruction, and sometimes more, depending upon how many we have. I have just refused seven Algonkin seminarians to my great regret because we lack food, the officers having taken it all away for the King's troops, who were short. Never since we have been in Canada have we refused a single seminarian, despite our poverty, and the necessity of refusing these has caused me a very sensible mortification; but I had to submit and humble myself in our helplessness, which has even obliged us to return a few French girls to their parents. We are limited to sixteen French girls and three Savages, of whom two are Iroquois and one a captive to whom it is desired that we should teach the French tongue. I do not speak of the poor, who are in very great number and with whom we must share what we have left. But let us return to our boarding pupils.

Great care is taken in this country with the instruction of the French girls, and I can assure you that if there were no Ursulines they would be in continual danger for their salvation. The reason is that there are a great many men, and a father and mother who would not miss Mass on a feast-day or a Sunday are quite willing to leave their children at home with several men to watch over them. If there are girls, whatever age they may be, they are in evident danger, and experience shows they must be put in a place of safety.

In a word, all I can say is that the girls in this country are for the most part more learned in several dangerous matters than those of France. Thirty girls give us more work in the boarding-school than sixty would in France. The day-girls give us a great deal also, but we do not watch over their habits as if they were confined. These girls are docile, they have good sense, and they are firm in the good when they know it, but as some of them are only boarders for a little time, the mistresses must apply themselves strenuously to their education and must sometimes teach them in a single year reading, writing, calculating, the prayers, Christian habits, and all a girl should know.

Some of them are left with us by their parents till they are of an age to be provided, either for the world or for religion. We have eight, both professed and novices, who did not wish to return to the world and do very well, having been reared in great innocence, and we have others that do not wish to return to their parents since they feel comfortable in God's house.

In the case of Savage girls, we take them at all ages. It will happen that a Savage, either Christian or pagan, wishes to carry off a girl of his nation and keep her contrary to God's law; she is given to us, and we instruct her and watch over her till the Reverend Fathers come to take her away. Others are here only as birds of passage and remain with us only until they are sad, a thing the Savage nature cannot suffer; the moment they become sad, their parents take them away lest they die. We leave them free on this point, for we are more likely to win them over in this way than by keeping them by force or entreaties. There are still others that go off by some whim or caprice; like squirrels, they climb our palisade, which is high as a wall, and go to run in the woods ...

viii) Quebec, 1 September 1668

My very dear son:

... If His Majesty desires this [that we should raise a number of little Native girls to be French], we are willing to do so, because of the obedience we owe him and, above all, because we are all prepared to do whatsoever will be for the greatest glory of God. However, it is a very difficult thing, not to say impossible, to make the little Savages French or civilized. We have more experience of this than anyone else, and we have observed that of a hundred that have passed through our hands we have scarcely civilized one. We find docility and intelligence in these girls but, when we are least expecting it, they clamber over our wall and go off to run with their kinsmen in the woods, finding more to please them there than in all the amenities of our French houses.

Such is the nature of the Savages; they cannot be restrained and, if they are, they become melancholy and their melancholy makes them sick. Moreover, the Savages are extraordinarily fond of their children and, when they know they are sad, they leave no stone unturned to get them back and we have to give them up.

We have had Hurons, Algonkins, and Iroquois; these last are the prettiest and the most docile of all. I do not know whether they will be more capable of being civilized than the others or whether they will keep the French elegance in which we are rearing them. I do not expect it of them, for they are Savages and that is sufficient reason not to hope ...

3

"Advantages and Inconveniences"

The Colonization of Canada

DOCUMENTS

A) To the King and the Lords of His Council, 1618
   Samuel de Champlain

B) True and Genuine Description of New France Commonly Called Canada, 1664
   Pierre Boucher

C) Memoir on Canada, 1673
   Jean Talon

D) To the Minister, November 10, 1679
   Jacques Duchesneau

E) Memoir Respecting Canada Prepared for the Marquis de Seignelay in January, 1690
   Jacques-Rene de Brisay de Denonville

F) Memoir to His Royal Highness the Duc d'Orleans, Regent of France, December 12, 1715, Paris
   Ruette d'Auteuil

G) Journal of a Voyage to North America; Letter X, Montreal, April 22, 1721
   P. F. X. de Charlevoix

H) Memoir of the King to Serve as Instructions for Sr. Hocquart, Commissary General of the Marine and *Ordonnateur* in New France, March 22, 1729

I) Memoir to the Minister Containing a Characterization of the French-Canadian Population, November 8, 1737
   Gilles Hocquart

So why did France want its new North American colonies? The answer depends upon a variety of factors and changed over time. Thus Champlain's aims and objectives in 1608 varied considerably from Hoquart's more than a century later. Is this surprising? Hardly. There were, however, threads throughout the following documents that cumulatively wove an overview of French aspirations, successes, and failures.

Historians know little of Samuel de Champlain's (1570?–1635) early life, and his family background remains largely conjecture. He claimed that, apart from a stint as a soldier, he spent much of his early life at sea. His own account certainly tells of heroic voyages to Spanish colonies in the new world, but some doubt exists. Perhaps Champlain fabricated part of his past to gain prestige and power. If that was the case, it worked. He certainly had influential friends and contacts, and he did achieve some success. All the same, he was an excellent draftsman and cartographer, both critical skills in the age of exploration.

Originally Champlain did not venture to Canada in any official capacity, simply travelling with Guy de Monts, who enjoyed exclusive trading privileges in North America. De Monts and his crew set sail for the new world in 1603 and eventually penetrated the Gulf of St. Lawrence. At Tadoussac Champlain observed the native fur trade for the first time. Considering Tadoussac inappropriate as a location for either a permanent trading establishment or settlement, they chose to make their first serious effort further south in Acadia. There Champlain and the crew spent the miserable winter of 1604–1605 huddled against the bitter cold and the horrors of scurvy, for which they had no cure. They barely survived and eventually emerged to search for a safer location. De Monts chose Port Royal, where they remained until the French government revoked his trading privileges in 1607. Though better than their first location, that tiny settlement, too, survived by the skin of its teeth, and disaster always loomed. Perhaps that is why Champlain, ever jovial and fond of food and drink, diverted everyone's attention by founding Canada's oldest surviving social club: the Order of Good Cheer.

He returned to Canada in 1608 without his patron, but finally in an official capacity as Guy de Monts' lieutenant. This time he and his crew settled at what is today Quebec City, and once again suffered through a terrible winter of scurvy, cold, hunger, and internal conflict. Yet Champlain never contracted scurvy, always remained fit and robust, kept his enthusiasm, eagerly wanted to see and do everything, and reputedly maintained his humour. His good health defies statistical probability and makes one wonder if he had a secret stash of apples or other fruit high in vitamin C. The following July Champlain also earned the dubious distinction of leading the first French military campaigns against the Iroquois. He worked tirelessly for the new colony throughout his long tenure, right up to his death at Quebec in 1635. A combination of private and colonial business saw him cross the Atlantic twenty-one times.

While his dispatch sets out his hopes and dreams for New France, their realization is a matter of some debate. Certainly, settlement began, but to what extent? His little post clung to life, and even disappeared entirely for several years after an attack by English privateers led by the Kirke brothers. Agriculture essentially did not exist by the end of his life, despite his best efforts, but the fur trade expanded enormously.

Pierre Boucher (1622–1717) came to Canada from Normandy in 1635. Little evidence remains of his family background, only that his father practiced carpentry. Boucher served as an assistant to the Jesuits in Huronia between 1637 and 1644. There he learned Iroquoian and acted in the vital role of interpreter for the French garrison. This helped his rapid rise through the ranks, first as an employee for the Company of One Hundred Associates, and in 1651 as captain of the garrison at Trois Rivières. Ever ambitious and capable, Boucher received the rank of Governor of Trois Rivières, and finally gained ennoblement in 1661. That year his fellow settlers, on the verge of losing their little colony to the Iroquois, chose Boucher to represent them in France. This he accomplished, simultaneously arousing interest and sympathy for New France in the home country. Louis XIV, the young "Sun King," even made New France a royal province in 1663. This was a major psychological, financial, and social boost to the fledgling settlement, for which Boucher can take much credit. The French government made him a judge that same year, and he obtained a seigneurie in 1667. A dominant figure in New France society for the rest of his life, Boucher used his influence to set the tone for future development. He, like Champlain before him, wanted French and natives to unite, which he underscored by taking a Huron wife.

The royal province of New France received the same administrative structure as existed in France. While the governor had responsibility for diplomacy and military affairs, the intendant took care of economic affairs, a particularly vital role in a new area. Jean Talon (1626–1694), who became intendant in 1665, proved very capable and helped put New France on reasonably firm footing. He initially served until 1668, but conflicts with the governor made his life miserable and he asked to be replaced. Colbert, his superior in France, convinced him to return in 1670, which he did, but only for two years. A tireless enthusiast, Talon tackled everything from the economy to population control. He began a shipyard with his own money, and started a tar works, hemp production, lumbering, potash, fishing, and beer brewing. New France, he believed, needed a triangular trade network, which he set about creating between it, the French West Indies, and France. He also established an exploration program that pushed the boundaries of New France back into the heart of modern Canada, the Ohio country of the United States, and toward the Gulf of Mexico.

Talon's allegiance was to the French king, and he regularly wrestled the Catholic church for supremacy in New France. The church's primary loyalty to Rome, after all, constituted a potential threat to his king. Talon resented priests who meddled in civil affairs, particularly in the intendant's jurisdiction over taxation and the profitable use of alcohol in the fur trade. This altered the little colony's administrative tone, and religious grounds for maintaining New France became secondary to commerce.

Although Talon retired to France with a sense of accomplishment, few of his economic programs survived him. Mercantalism reigned as the governing commercial principle in mother France, which Talon's scheme for self-sufficiency threatened. His voice, though loud, could simply not compete against the whiny cacophony of French business interests. At least he could take satisfaction from the high birth rate that his initiatives set in motion.

Jacques Duchesneau (?–1696) replaced him, and thus began a seven-year period of destructive bickering between intendant and governor. Surprising? No. The two, plus the bishop, theoretically worked as a team, but vested interests, titanic egos, differing ideologies, and personal agendas invariably pitted them against one another. The governor, after all, enjoyed a higher noble rank and had the right of veto. This, plus the desperately slow lines of communication between mother country and colony, virtually ensured that assertive governors, such as Frontenac and Denonville, ruled the day. Obviously this was not always in New France's best interests.

Jacques-Rene de Brisay de Denonville (1637–1710), a rabid perfectionist, deeply honest, and an insufferable moralizer, liked little about New France. He labeled the people debauched, undisciplined, and without respect for authority, and concluded that the colony could not defend itself let alone tackle the growing British menace to the south. Seigneuries should be closer together, more tightly defended, and French territory consolidated to the point where he could drive England from North America. He probably had a point, but set about achieving his ends in a most undiplomatic, arrogant manner. In the end, he lost the support of both the local population and the French king.

Ruette d'Auteuil (1657–1737) arrived in New France as a four-year-old with his father who became attorney general to the Sovereign Council. He returned to France in his early teens, studied law, and gained his degree in 1678, then went back to New France to follow his father's footsteps as attorney general the following year. D'Auteuil, an aggressive and proud man, soon ran afoul of Governor Frontenac, but that was not his only problem. Questions arose over his integrity and impartiality, and some described him as completely lacking practical common sense: hardly attributes appropriate to a man in a lofty post! There was an inquiry. In the end, he lost his commission and fled to France, overwhelmed with disgrace and humiliation. His side of the story appeared in a memoir published shortly after. That could have been the end, but d'Auteuil later gathered settlers and fishermen, intending to colonize Acadia in 1722. Like the rest of his projects, it too failed.

P.F.X. de Charlevoix (1682–1761) arrived in New France in 1705 as a young scholar charged with teaching grammar at the Jesuit college. He did not remain long, returning to France in 1709 where he completed theological studies to become an ordained Jesuit priest. The Prince Regent sent him back to New France in 1720 to search for the mythical western sea, and that three-year mission took him to Lake Superior, down the Mississippi, and as far as New Orleans on the Gulf of Mexico. He never enjoyed life in North America, suffered chronic ill health, and soon fled. He did, however, write a report on his exploration, plus a series of thirty-six letters describing his adventures to the Duchess de Lesdiguières. These eventually appeared, some twenty years later, published as *Histoire et Description Générale de la Nouvelle France*, the first noteworthy history of the French colony. He was also Marie de l'Incarnation's first biographer and edited the Jesuit monthly review *Journal de Travoux*.

King Louis XV's instructions to Gilles Hocquart came from Frédéric de Maurepas, Minister of Marine, the man directly responsible for the French empire. At this time France enjoyed considerable prosperity, trade soared, and the French North American empire extended from the West Indies, up through Louisiana, the Ohio valley and Mississippi rivers, and included much of present-day Canada. Did France really control this vast region? Only partially, but it did create a sense of optimism that fostered further investment around the globe. Mercantalism remained the order of the day, but in a slightly different guise: private enterprise, not the state, took more responsibility to fund and fuel trade and progress. Government still encouraged expansion, but not at the expense of the royal purse. This was, in other words, an era of cutbacks, restraint, cost-cutting, and his majesty's bureaucrats doing more with less. The emphasis became political stability and peaceful commercial rivalry with their old foe, England. Commercial victory would spring from a closely integrated empire with vibrant trade between all French Atlantic possessions, plus less emphasis on the fur trade in favour of agriculture and industry.

Gilles Hocquart's career (1694–1783) illustrates the pervasive nature of nepotism in early Canada. He, like his father, was intendant of both Toulon and Le Havre. Still, Hocquart was a good administrator: not particularly innovative or bold, but a steady, reasonably efficient and honest plodder who got the job done. All the same, friends in high places are handy, and they probably helped his promotion to intendant of New France in 1729. But the colony needed a daring visionary, someone like Talon, not Hocquart. Regardless, New France did diversify, enjoying a stable economy, and he managed to increase the volume of its trade during his nineteen years as intendant. He saw himself as a failure, particularly after his recall in 1748: merchants stuck to the lucrative fur trade instead of diversifying. The bureaucracy, which he controlled, remained understaffed, inefficient, and underpaid, and New France still lacked the overall population and material resources for truly dynamic expansion.

A) To the King and the Lords of His Council, 1618
Samuel de Champlain

Sire: The Sieur de Champlain represents to you most humbly that for sixteen years he has toiled with laborious zeal as well in the discoveries of New France as of divers peoples and nations whom he has brought to our knowledge, who had never been discovered save by him; which peoples have given him such and so faithful report of the north and south seas that one cannot doubt but that this would be the means of reaching easily to the Kingdom of China and the East Indies, whence great riches could be drawn; besides planting there the divine worship ... in addition to the abundance of merchandise from the said country of New France ... Should this said country be given up and the settlement abandoned, for want of bestowing upon it the needed attention, the English or Flemings, envious of our prosperity, would seize upon it, thereby enjoying the fruits of our labours, and preventing by this means more than a thousand vessels from going to the dry and green fisheries, and for whale-oil ...

Firstly. — His said Majesty will establish the Christian faith among an infinite number of souls, who neither hold nor possess any form of religion whatsoever, and nevertheless wish only for the knowledge of divine and human worship, according to the reports of all those who have made the voyage to the said New France.

Secondly. — The King will make himself master and lord of a country nearly eighteen hundred leagues in length, watered by the fairest rivers in the world and by the greatest and most numerous lakes, the richest and most abundant in all varieties of fish that are to be found, and full also of the greatest meadows, fields, and forests, for the most part of walnut-trees, and very pleasant hills upon which there is found a great abundance of wild vines, which yield grapes as large as or larger than ours, cultivated as these are.

Thirdly. — The Sieur de Champlain undertakes to discover the South Sea passage to China and to the East Indies by way of the river St. Lawrence, which traverses the lands of the said New France, and which river issues from a lake about three hundred leagues in length, from which lake flows a river that empties into the said South Sea, according to the account given to the said Sieur de Champlain by a number of people, his friends in the said country; whom he has visited and become acquainted with, having ascended the said river St. Lawrence for more than four hundred leagues into the said lake of three hundred leagues in length, on which voyage he found numerous fortified towns, encircled and enclosed with wooden palisades ... which towns can furnish two thousand men armed after their fashion; others less.

That His said Majesty would derive a great and notable profit from the taxes and duties he could levy on the merchandise coming from the said country, according to the memorial submitted, as likewise from the customs' duties on the merchandise that would come from China and from the Indies, which would surpass in value at least ten times all those levied in France, inasmuch as all the merchants of Christendom would pass through the passage sought by the Sieur de Champlain, if it please the King to grant them leave to do so, in order to shorten the said journey by more than a year and a half, without any risk from pirates and from the perils of the sea and of the voyage, on account of the great circuit it is necessary now to make, which brings a thousand inconveniences to merchants and travellers ...

The Sieur de Champlain humbly begs to be heard concerning certain facts which he wishes to present to you for the honour and glory of God, for the increase of this realm and for the establishment of a great and permanent trade in New France, as is specified in the following articles:

The advantage that would accrue in the first place from the cod-fishery, which would be carried on annually thanks to the permanent settlement of the people inhabiting the said country of New France, where salt could be made in considerable quantity, and two kinds of fishing could be carried on, namely dry and green, ... and through the industry of the fishermen more than a million livres would be earned annually.

Likewise the salmon fishery, which fish are in such abundance in the harbours and rivers that one could produce annually 100,000 livres.

Likewise the sea-sturgeon fishery, as also that of the sea-trout, which are so abundant in most places that they might be sold ... in regions where this fish is much in demand, annually for 100,000 livres.

Likewise eels, sardines, herrings and other fish are so plentiful that there could be obtained annually for 100,000 livres.

Likewise the whale-oils, in which the country abounds of which one can make in the said country annually to the value of 200,000 livres.

Likewise whale-bone from the said whales, and walrus-tusks, which are better than elephant's teeth ... and an abundance of seals; and of these commodities there might be taken annually to the value of 500,000 livres.

Likewise from the forests, which are of marvellous height, a number of good vessels might be built, which could be laden with the above-mentioned merchandise and other commodities, as will be stated below. From the said forests could be made ships' masts of several sizes, beams, joists, planks of many varieties, such as oak, elm, beech, walnut, plane, maple, birch, cedar, cypress, chestnut, hemlock, pine, fir and other woods; there could be made stave-wood, sawed oak for window frames amd wainscoting and for other interior decoration, for which the most part of the said woods are suitable; and there would be obtained from them annually to the value of 400,000 livres.

Likewise there could be obtained a quantity of gum, the smell of which resembles incense.

Likewise of the useless woods one could make ashes, from which there could be obtained annually to the value of 400,000 livres.

From the pines and firs could be obtained pitch, tar and resin to the value annually of 100,000 livres.

As for the nature of the soil, it is certain that it yields to the native tillers corn, maize, beans, peas, roots the dye of which makes a colour similar to cochineal; and if the said root were cultivated one could obtain from it annually to the value of 400,000 livres.

Likewise a notable profit could be gained from the hemp, which the same soil yields without cultivation and which in quality and texture is in wise inferior to ours; and there could be obtained from it annually to the value of 300,000 livres.

In addition is to be considered the profits to be derived from several kinds of mines, such as those of silver, steel, iron which yields 45 per cent., lead which yields 30 per cent., copper 18 per cent., and whatever other minerals, or things not yet come to our knowledge which a permanent settlement in the country may discover; and there could be derived from the said mines annually more than 1,000,000 livres.

Likewise cloths, such as sail-cloths, could be made from the hemp of the said country; as well as cables, ropes, and rigging for all sorts of vessels, to the value of more than 400,000 livres.

Likewise the traffic and trade in furs is not to be scorned, not only marten, beaver, fox, lynx and other skins, but also deer, moose and buffalo robes, which are commodities from which one can derive at present more than 400,000 livres.

Likewise from the said country can be obtained marble, jasper, alabaster, porphyry and other kinds of valuable stones; and a notable profit may be made therefrom.

Vines are in abundance in the said country, which the soil yields of itself; and if they were cultivated they would yield great profits; as likewise corn and other things, which the permanent settlements will be able to supply through the industry of the inhabitants of the said country.

Besides all these things one may expect in the future the same abundance of cattle that is seen in Peru since the Spaniards introduced them there … and from the Spaniards' account more than a million in gold is obtained annually from the hides. For New France is so well watered everywhere that the fertility of the meadows ensures the feeding and multiplying of the said cattle, whenever they are introduced here …

B) True and Genuine Description of New France Commonly Called Canada, 1664, Paris
Pierre Boucher

… But how can we make money there? What can we get out of it all? This is a question that has often been put to me, and that gave me an inclination to laugh every time it was put to me; I seemed to see people who wanted to reap a harvest before they had sowed any thing. After having said that the country is a good one, capable of producing all sorts of things, like France, that it is healthy, that population only is wanting, that the country is very extensive, and that without doubt there are great riches in it which we have not been able to bring to light, because we have an enemy who keeps us pent up in a little corner and prevents us from going about and making discoveries; and so he will have to be destroyed, and many people will have to come into this country, and then we shall know the riches of it; but some one will have to defray the cost of all this; and who shall do it if not our good King? He has shown an inclination to do it, and may God be pleased to keep him still of the same mind.

Our neighbours, the English, laid out a great deal of money at the out-set on the settlements they made; they threw great numbers of people into them; so that now there are computed to be in them fifty thousand men capable of bearing arms; it is a wonder to see their country now; one finds all sorts of things there, the same as in Europe, and for half the price. They build numbers of ships, of all sorts and sizes; they work iron mines; they have beautiful cities; they have stage-coaches and mails from one to the other; they have carriages like those in France; those who laid out money there, are now getting good returns from it; that country is not different from this; what has been done there could be done here …

It seems to me that I hear some one say: "you have told us much about the advantages of New France but you have not shown us its disadvantages, nor its inconveniences, yet we know well that there is not a country in the world however good it may be, in which something that is disagreeable is not met with." I answer that you are right. It has been my study all along to make these things known to you; but in order to enable you to understand them more clearly, I shall here specify in detail what I consider the most troublesome and disagreeable things …

The first is that our enemies, the Iroquois keep us so closely pent up that they hinder us from enjoying the advantages of the country. We cannot go to hunt or fish without danger of being killed or taken prisoners by those rascals; and we cannot even plough out fields, much less make hay, without continual risk: They lie in ambush on all sides, and any little thicket suffices for six or seven of those barbarians to put themselves under cover in, or more correctly speaking in an ambush, from which they throw themselves upon you suddenly when you are at your work, or going to it or coming from it. They never attack but when they are the strongest; if they are the weakest they do not say a word; if by accident they are discovered they fly, leaving every thing behind them; and as they are fleet of foot it is difficult to catch them; so you see we are always in dread, and a poor fellow does not work in safety if he has to go ever so little a way off to his work. Wives are always uneasy lest their husbands, who have gone away to their work in the morning, should be killed or taken prisoners and they should never see them again; and these Indians are the cause of the greater number of our settlers being poor, not only through our not being able to enjoy the advantages of the country as I have just said, but because they often kill cattle, sometimes hinder the gathering in of the harvest, and at other times burn and plunder houses when they can take people by surprise. This is a great evil, but it is not beyond remedy, and we expect one from the benevolence of our good King, who has told me that he wishes to deliver us from it. It would not be very difficult to do so, for there are not among them more than eight hundred or nine hundred men capable of bearing arms. It is true they are warlike men, and very dexterous at fighting in the woods; they have given proof of this to our Commanders from France who despised them; some of these were killed and others were forced to admit that one must not neglect to take precautions when one goes to war with them, that they understand the business, and that on this score they are not barbarians; but after all a thousand or twelve hundred men well led would give occasion for its being said, "they were but they are not;" and to have exterminated a tribe that has caused so many others to perish and is the terror of all these countries, would raise the reputation of the French very high throughout New France ...

Here is another set of questions that have been put to me, namely: how we live in this country whether justice is administered, if there is not great debauchery, seeing that numbers of worthless fellows and bad girls come here, it is said.

I will answer all these questions one after the other, beginning with the last. It is not true that those sort of girls come hither, and those who say so have made a great mistake, and have taken the Islands of Saint Christophe and Martinique for New France; if any of them come here, they are not known for such; for before any can be taken on board ship to come here some of their relations or friends must certify that they have always been well-behaved; if by chance there are found among those who have, some who are in disrepute, or who are said to have misconducted themselves on the voyage out, they are sent back to France.

As for the scapegraces, if any come over it is only because they are not known for what they are, and when they are in the country they have to live like decent people, otherwise they would have a bad time of it; we know how to hang people in this country as well as they do elsewhere, and we have proved it to some who have not been well behaved.

Justice is administered here, and there are Judges; and those who are not satisfied with their decisions can appeal to the Governor and the Sovereign Council, appointed by the King, and sitting at Quebec.

Hitherto we have lived pleasantly enough, for it has pleased God to give us Governors who have all been good men, and besides we have had the Jesuit Fathers who take great pains to teach the people what is right so that all goes on peaceably; we live much in the fear of God, and nothing scandalous takes place without its being put to rights immediately; there is great religious devotion throughout the country.

Several persons after having heard me speak of New France, whether they felt inclined to come to it or not, have put these questions to me: "Do you think I would be fit for that country? What would have to be done in order to get there? If I took four or five thousand francs with me, could I with such a sum make myself tolerably comfortable?" And after these several other questions which I shall mention after having answered these.

You ask me in the first place whether you are fit for this country. The answer I make you is that this country is not yet fit for people of rank who are extremely rich, because such people would not find in it all the luxuries they enjoy in France; such persons must wait until this country has more inhabitants, unless they are persons who wish to retire from the world in order to lead a pleasant and quiet life free from fuss, or who are inclined to immortalize themselves by building cities or by other great works in this new world.

The people best fitted for this country are those who can work with their own hands in making clearings, putting up buildings and otherwise;

for as men's wages are very high here, a man who does not take care and practice economy will be ruined; but the best way is always to begin by clearing land and making a good farm, and to attend to other things only after that has been done, and not to do like some whom I have seen, who paid out all their money for the erection of fine buildings which they had to sell afterwards for less than the cost.

I am supposing myself to be speaking to persons who would come to settle in this country with a view to making a living out of it, and not to trade.

It would be well for a man coming to settle, to bring provisions with him for at least a year or two years if possible, especially flour which he could get for much less in France and could not even be sure of being always able to get for any money here; for if many people should come from France in any year without bringing any flour with them and the grain crops should be bad here that year, which God forbid, they would find themselves much straitened.

It would be well also to bring a supply of clothes, for they cost twice as much here as they do in France.

Money is also much dearer; its value increases one third, so that a coin of fifteen sous is worth twenty, and so on in proportion.

I would advise a man having money enough to bring two labouring men with him, or even more if he has the means, to clear his land; this is in answer to the question whether a person having three thousand or four thousand francs to employ here could do so with advantage; such a person could get himself into very easy circumstances in three or four years if he choose to practice economy, as I have already said.

Most of our settlers are persons who came over in the capacity of servants, and who, after serving their masters for three years, set up for themselves. They had not worked for more than a year before they had cleared land on which they got in more than enough grain for their food. They have but little, generally when they set up for themselves, and marry wives who are no better off than they are; yet if they are fairly hard working people you see them in four or five years in easy circumstances and well fitted out for persons of their condition in life.

Poor people would be much better off here than they are in France, provided they are not lazy; they could not fail to get employment and could not say, as they do in France, that they are obliged to beg for their living because they cannot find any one to give them work; in one word, no people are wanted, either men or women, who cannot turn their hands to some work, unless they are very rich.

Women's work consists of household work and of feeding and caring for the cattle; for there are few female servants; so that wives are obliged to do their own house work; nevertheless those who have the means employ valets who do the work of maidservants ...

The land is very high in relation to the river, but quite level. The little of it that is under cultivation produces very good grain and vegetables but is not fit for fruit trees that do not grow in clayey soil. There is eel fishing, but it is not plentiful. There are all types of wood, which are sold at Quebec ...

In relation to the great size of the settlement, there is not one-quarter of the workmen required to clear and cultivate the land.

Farmers do not cultivate the land with enough care. It is certain that one *minot* as sown in France would produce more than two as sown in Canada.

Since the seasons are too short and there is much bad weather, it would be desirable that the Church allow the performance of essential works on feast days. There are not ninety working days left from May, when sowing begins, to the end of September, after allowance is made for holy days and bad weather. Yet, the strength of the colony hinges on that period.

It would be necessary to compel neglectful habitants to labor on the land by depriving them of the right to go on voyages, which exempt them from work. They earn thirty or forty écus on a voyage of two or three months but waste the farming season, and land remains fallow as a result ...

Oblige the seigneurs, in order to facilitate the establishment of their seigneuries, to give sufficient common land at low prices and to build mills and other public conveniences. Many persons lose up to a third of their time traveling fifteen or twenty lieues to mill their flour ...

Order the grand voyer to apply himself to building the roads and bridges necessary for the public, which is something very essential ...

The subordination of the vassal to his seigneur is not observed. This error is the result of seigneuries being granted to commoners, who have not known how to maintain their rights over their tenants. Even the officers of militia, who are their dependents, have for the most part no consideration for their superiority and wish on occasions to be regarded as independent.

C) Memoir on Canada, 1673
Jean Talon

… It has appeared to me that one of the principal intentions of His Majesty was to form over the years a large and populous colony, full of men suited for all types of professions in the army, the navy, and the fisheries, and strong enough to engage in all types of work.

The girls sent from France by the king and the marriages they contracted with the soldiers who have voluntarily chosen to settle in the colony have so greatly increased the number of settlers that when taking the census in 1671 I found by the birth certificates that seven hundred children had been born in that year. At present I have reason to believe that one hundred marriages between young men and girls born in the colony are possible annually …

His Majesty further intended that the settlers of his colony of New France should enjoy the felicity of his reign to the same degree as his subjects of the old; that … the southern part of America should be supported by the northern part, which can produce clothing and the necessities of life of which the southern part finds itself deprived by its exposure to the sun and a tropical climate; that stationary fisheries be established, so that the kingdom may not only do without the fish it buys from foreign countries for considerable sums, but also send to the Levant the dried fish that is consumed there in great quantities …

He also had in view the support of his navy with the wood that grows in Canada, the iron that could be discovered there, the tar that could be manufactured, and the hemp that could be grown for the making of ships' riggings. With these four products, he would no longer have to obtain from the princes of the Baltic, with an appearance of dependence, what is necessary to sustain his navy, which is such an important element of his glory and of his state's support.

In all this Canada seems to have responded well enough to the hopes of His Majesty. Hemp is being cultivated with success, cloth is being woven, cable and rope are being produced. The tar which has been manufactured has been tested both here and in France and found to be as good as that drawn from the north. Iron has been discovered, which master forgers consider to be suitable for all purposes. Vessels, which have now been sailing for six years, have been built for individuals who opened up the trade of Canada with the islands. At present there is one of 450 tons and forty-two guns being built for the king, which will put to sea next summer, and there is almost enough material in the yards for another. Before leaving, I established two workshops. During the present winter the first, of twenty-eight men, should produce 1,000 to 1,200 pieces of lumber suitable for the construction of a vessel of 600 to 700 tons, of which his Majesty has seen the model; from the labors of the second, we may hope for 25,000 to 30,000 feet of sheathing ...

Stationary fisheries, which are so useful since dried cod is consumed almost everywhere in Europe, have been started before my departure ...

Opening a trade between Canada and the Antilles is no longer considered a difficult thing. It was done by me in 1668 with a vessel built in Canada which successfully carried a cargo of this country's products. From there it sailed to Old France with a load of sugar and then returned to the New with the products of the kingdom of which this country stands in need. Every year since, as a result of this example, this commerce has been carried out by two or more vessels ...

This commerce is made up of the excess quantities of peas, salmon, salted eels, green and dried cod, planks and cask wood, and will be increased by excess wheat which will be converted into flour. It is estimated that Canada could export 30,000 *minots* each year if the crops are not ruined by bad weather. Peas could amount to 10,000 *minots*, and salted beef and pork will not in the future make up the smaller portion of this trade. Sales in the islands being favorable, I expect that Canada could soon supply pork, since it now does without that of France from which it formerly drew up to 1,200 barrels annually. The inhabitants of Port Royal in Acadia could supply salted beef. I obtained sixty quintals at twenty-two deniers a pound from there two years ago, which was as good as that of Ireland.

Beer could also profitably enter into this trade. I can guarantee 2,000 barrels a year for the islands and more if the consumption is greater, without altering the supply to the colonists of New France. It is by these methods that His Majesty will succeed in his aim of destroying the trade of the Dutch with our islands, without depriving his subjects residing there of the support they derived from it.

With all the provisions, which Canada will be able to supply in proportionately greater quantities as she develops, the islands will be provided with the necessities of life and will only lack a few accessories like spices, olive oil, wine, and salt. There is even the possibility of establishing salt works in

Acadia if the king judges that it would not be prejudicial to Old France to make this new colony self-sufficient in this respect and to enable it to provide by itself for all its needs. I say all its needs not even excluding clothing which, we may hope, will be manufactured not only for the Canadians but in a few years for the islanders as well. For crafts have already been established for the fabrication of cloth, linen, and shoes; we already have enough leather to manufacture on the average 8,000 pairs of shoes annually; we will have as much hemp as we will care to grow; and the sheep which His Majesty sent have bred very well and will provide the material for the sheets and other cloths which we have begun to weave.

And all these things taken together will form the essence of a trade that will be useful to all His Majesty's subjects and will make for the happiness of those of New France. Thanks to the king's care and support, they live in peace and no longer suffer from those pressing needs which they felt for almost everything when his troops first landed in the colony.

Potash, which has successfully undergone a series of tests, can be used to wash linen or can be converted into a soft soap for bleaching or for cleaning silks and sheets. It can be produced in Canada in sufficient quantities to enable Paris to do without Spanish sodium, on which it spends a considerable sum. It could also enable Douay, Lille, Tournay, Courtrai, and other cities in Flanders and even in France where cloth is bleached to dispense with the potash of Muscovy and Poland, which increases the trade of the Dutch who accept this product in partial exchange for the beaver and spices they trade in those countries.

Potash should be received all the more favorably in Paris since all laundrywomen know very well that Spanish sodium is very acrid and wears out the cloth, something which potash does not do ...

Such, approximately, are the results of His Majesty's first attempt to make of a country that is crude, savage, and pagan the commencements of a province, and perhaps of a kingdom, that is refined, happy, and Christian.

D) To the Minister, November 10, 1679, Quebec
Jacques Duchesneau

... The greater part of the officers of the Sovereign Council and the inferior justices, although they ought to apply themselves principally to their vocation and to instructing themselves in it, are prevented by their poverty, the wages they are paid being very small, which makes them occupy themselves as much as possible with commerce and with improving their living.

Several of the *gentilhommes*, officers retired on half pay and owners of seigneuries, since they accustom themselves to what is called in France the life of a country gentleman which they have practised and wish to continue to practise, make their chief occupation that of hunting and fishing. Because their manner of life and clothing, and that of their wives and children, does not enable them to live on so little as the simple habitants, and since they do not apply themselves entirely to household work and to improving their lands, they mix themselves up in trade, running into debt on all sides, exciting young habitants to become *coureurs de bois*, and lastly sending their own children to trade in furs, in the Indian villages and in the depths of the forest, in spite of prohibitions of His Majesty, and yet nevertheless they are in great poverty.

The merchants living in the country, with the exception of five or six at the most, are poor. The artisans, if one excludes a small number who are inn-keepers, because of the social pretensions of the women among whom there is no class distinction here, and their own debauchery, spend everything they make. Consequently, their families are in great misery and are not settled down.

Whenever the labourers apply themselves assiduously to the land, they subsist not only more honestly but are without comparison happier than those who are called good peasants in France. But, in the spirit of this country of taking life easily, and having much of the savage temperament which is unsteady, fickle and opposed to hard work, seeing the liberty that is taken so boldly to run the woods, they debauch themselves with the others and go to look for furs as a means of living without working. This causes the land to be left uncleared and beasts not to multiply as they should and no industries can be established here.

To turn to those who come into the country for profits only with no intention of establishing themselves, and who are called foreign merchants, there is no doubt that their only interest is to fix up their affairs and afterwards return to live more comfortable in France with their families.

On all this you may observe, Monseigneur, if it pleases you, that among so many different interests, the chief and common interest of those who have chosen this country to live in, when they think seriously, must be to establish good order in the colony, to cultivate the soil, to raise and increase the number of livestock, to establish manufacturing and to attract the savages to trade in the French villages ...

In truth, Monseigneur, it is deplorable to see this country in its present state, when this colony which could become so important because of its advantages, of which I have so often informed you, is so little established.

E) Memoir Respecting Canada Prepared for the Marquis de Seignelay in January, 1690
Jacques-Rene de Brisay de Denonville

... Exclusive of the inability of the Governor-General to protect the country when obliged to act on the defensive, the great difficulty in controlling the people arises from the Colony being allowed to spread itself too much; and from every settler maintaining himself, isolated and without neighbours, in a savage independence. I see no remedy for this but to concentrate the Colony, and to collect the settlers, forming good inclosed villages. Whatever obstacle may be encountered herein, must be overcome if we would not hazard the destruction of the entire population ...

The weakness of that country arises from isolated settlements adjoining interminable forests. If under such circumstances it be desired to continue the occupation of remote forts, such as that of Cataracouy or Fort Frontenac, it will add to the weakness of the country and increase expenses which cannot be of any use to us, whatever may be alleged to the contrary; for those posts cannot do injury to hostile Indians but to ourselves, in consequence of the difficulty of reaching, and the cost of maintaining, them.

Nothing is more certain than that it was a great mistake to have permitted, in time past, the occupation of posts so remote that those who occupy them are beyond the reach of the Colony and of assistance. The garrisons have thus been necessitated to enter into the interests of those Tribes nearest to them, and in that way to participate in their quarrels in order to please and conciliate them. We have, thus, drawn down on ourselves the enmity of their enemies and the contempt of our friends, who not receiving the assistance they were made to expect or might desire, have on divers occasions embarrassed us more than even our enemies. This has been experienced more than once.

It had been much better not to have meddled with their quarrels, and to have left all the Indians to come to the Colony in quest of the merchandise they required, than to have prevented their doing so by carrying goods to them in such large quantities as to have been frequently obliged to sell them at so low a rate as to discredit us among the Indians and to ruin trade; for many of our Coureur de bois have often lost, instead of gained, by their speculations. Moreover, the great number of Coureurs de bois has inflicted serious injury on the Colony, by physically and morally corrupting the settlers, who are prevented marrying by the cultivation of a vagabond, independent and idle spirit. For the aristocratic manners they assume, on their return, both in their dress and their drunken revelries, wherein they exhaust all their gains in a very short time, lead them to despise the peasantry and to consider it beneath them to espouse their daughters, though they are themselves, peasants like them. In addition to this, they will condescend no more to cultivate the soil, nor listen, any longer, to anything except returning to the woods for the purpose of continuing the same avocations. This gives rise to the innumerable excesses that many among them are guilty of with the Squaws, which cause a great deal of mischief in consequence of the displeasures of the Indians at the seduction of their wives and daughters, and of the injury thereby inflicted on Religion, when the Indians behold the French practicing nothing of what the Missionaries represent as the law of the Gospel.

The remedy for this is, not to permit, as far as practicable, the return of any person to the Indian country except those who cannot follow any other business, nor to allow ill conducted persons to go thither; to oblige all to bring to the Governor and Intendant a certificate of good behaviour and good morals from the Missionaries; to find employment for the youth of the country; which is a very easy matter, for the cod and whale fisheries afford a sure commerce, if closely attended to and made a business of. There is reason to believe that the wisest and oldest merchants of the country are tired of sending into the bush, but there will be always too many new and ambitious petty traders, who will attempt to send ventures thither, both with and without license. It is very proper that an ordinance be enacted holding the merchants responsible for the fault of unlicensed Coureurs de bois, for did the merchants not furnish goods, there would not be any Coureurs de bois ...

As regards Acadia, that country is in great danger inasmuch as it has no fort of any value, and the settlers there are scattered and dispersed, as in

Canada. It would be desirable that the King had a good fort at La Heve for the security of ships. That post would be much more advantageous than Port Royal, which it is not easy to get out of to defend the Coast from pirates, and to be more convenient to the Islands of Cape Breton and Newfoundland as well as the Great Bank.

Fish is so abundant on all the coasts of the King's territory, that it is desirable that the King's subjects only should go there to catch them, and that his Majesty were sufficiently powerful in that Country to prevent Foreigners fishing on the Great Bank. They ought to be deprived, at least, of fishing on the King's coasts. The Spaniards go every year to those of Labrador adjoining the Straits of Belle Isle. The English trade there more than we.

Hitherto, all the people of Acadia as well as those of Canada have paid more attention to the Beaver trade and to the sale of Brandy than to the establishment of Fisheries, which, nevertheless, afford the most certain and most durable profit, and are best suited to the inhabitants of the country, and to the augmentation of the Colony. For what each settler might realize annually would supply him most abundantly with clothes; and as the fishing season being only after the sowing and terminates before the harvest, every individual of any industry would find means to drive a profitable business, without abandoning agriculture, as the Coureurs de bois do. The Canadians are adroit and would become in a short time as expert as the Basques in whaling, were they to apply themselves to it. If the establishment of this fishery be persevered in, there is reason to hope that they will turn their attention to it, being encouraged by the stimulus of gain. But he who is desirous of commencing it, is not wealthy, and will find it difficult to defray its expense ...

F) Memoir to His Royal Highness the Duc d'Orleans, Regent of France, December 12, 1715, Paris
Ruette d'Auteuil

Patriotism is such a common sentiment that all we can hope for is that those who read this memoir will appreciate the zeal of the Canadian ... who wrote it hoping to correct the erroneous, and publicly stated view, that Canada was worth nothing.

This vast stretch of country is immensely wealthy ... but restricting ourselves only to those areas actually inhabited by Frenchmen, and of the Gulf and Saint Lawrence River linked to the trade with the indigenous inhabitants, we can easily conclude that if the affairs of the country are in a poor condition it is not due to the nature of the land, but rather to the poor management of those who have directed the colony ...

Commercial endeavours in Canada ... may be divided into two sections: those involving the indigenous inhabitants and those carried on independently of them.

Since the first discovery of Canada the trade of European merchandise for beaver skins has been the most striking commercial endeavour because of the large profits that may be realized ... a commerce, that in some years, has had a value of 5 or 600,000 livres ...

As to the commercial endeavours which are carried on independently of the indigenous inhabitants they are divided as follows.

First there is agriculture, which produces maize, wheat, rye, barley, peas and other grains, meat, and wood, all of which are loaded on ships to be sent to the fishing grounds of the Gulf, and presently to Île Royale and to the French West Indies.

The second is that which is procured, and can be procured, from the River and Gulf of the Saint Lawrence ... cod, salmon, herring, mackerel, and other fish which can be salted ... and which can be said, without exaggeration, to be inexhaustible ...

To this must be added the construction of ships ... and forest products which can be sent to France for shipbuilding, masts, and planks ... for the forests of Canada can furnish all kinds of wood ... and the rivers emptying into the Saint Lawrence facilitate their transportation ...

To this may be added ... the exploitation of varied mineral reserves, for there are excellent iron ore deposits, and in a bay called Michigan and at Lake Huron almost pure copper mines have been found ...

No doubt it will be objected: 1 — that the country is very cold; 2 — that population growth has been slow; 3 — that commerce languishes ... The objections may be answered by saying that the first is not a drawback and that the inconvenience of the others cannot be blamed on the country or on the inhabitants, and that their remedy lies at hand ...

G) Journal of a Voyage to North America; Letter X, Montreal, April 22, 1721
P. F. X. de Charlevoix

... Thus it appears, Madam, that every one here is possessed of the necessaries of life; but there is little paid to the King; the inhabitant is not acquainted with taxes; bread is cheap; fish and flesh are not dear; but wine, stuffs, and all French commodities are very expensive. Gentlemen, and those officers who have nothing but their pay, and are besides encumbered with families, have the greatest reason to complain. The women have a great deal of spirit and good nature, are extremely agreeable, and excellent breeders; and these good qualities are for the most part all the fortune they bring their husbands; but God has blessed the marriages in this country ... There are a greater number of noblesse in New France than in all the other colonies put together.

The King maintains here eight and twenty companies of marines, and three *états-majors*. Many families have been ennobled here, and there still remain several officers of the regiment of Carignan-Salières, who have peopled this country with gentlemen who are not in extraordinary good circumstances, and would be still less so, were not commerce allowed them, and the right of hunting and fishing, which is common to everyone.

After all, it is a little their own fault if they are ever exposed to want; the land is good almost everywhere, and agriculture does not in the least derogate from their quality. How many gentlemen throughout all our provinces would envy the lot of the simple inhabitants of Canada, did they but know it? And can those who languish here in a shameful indigence, be excused for refusing to embrace a profession, which the corruption of manners and the most salutary maxims has alone degraded from its ancient dignity? There is not in the world a more wholesome climate than this; no particular distemper is epidemical here, the fields and woods are full of simples of a wonderful efficacy, and the trees distill balms of an excellent quality. These advantages ought at least to remain in it; but inconstancy, aversion to a regular and assiduous labour, and a spirit of independence, have ever carried a great many young people out of it, and prevented the colony from being peopled.

These, Madam, are the defects with which the French Canadians are, with the greatest justice, reproached. The same may likewise be said of the Indians. One would imagine that the air they breathe in this immense continent contributes to it; but the example and frequent intercourse with its natural inhabitants are more than sufficient to constitute this character. Our Creoles are likewise accused of great avidity in amassing, and indeed they do things with this view, which could hardly be believed if they were not seen. The journeys they undertake; the fatigues they undergo; the dangers to which they expose themselves, and the efforts they make, surpass all imagination ... Thus there is some room to imagine that they commonly undertake such painful and dangerous journeys out of a taste they have contracted for them. They love to breathe a free air, they are early accustomed to a wandering life; it has charms for them, which make them forget past dangers and fatigues, and they place their glory in encountering them often. They have a great deal of wit, especially the fair sex, in whom it is brilliant and easy; they are, besides, constant and resolute, fertile in resources, courageous, and capable of managing the greatest affairs. You, Madam, are acquainted with more than one of this character, and have often declared your surprise at it to me. I can assure you such are frequent in this country, and are to be found in all ranks and conditions of life.

I know not whether I ought to reckon amongst the defects of our Canadians the good opinion they entertain of themselves. It is at least certain that it inspires them with a confidence, which leads them to undertake and execute what would appear impossible to many others. It must however be confessed they have excellent qualities. There is not a province in the kingdom where the people have a finer complexion, a more advantageous stature, or a body better proportioned. The strength of their constitution is not always answerable, and if the Canadians live to any age, they soon look old and decrepit. This is not entirely their own fault, it is likewise that of their parents, who are not sufficiently watchful over their children to prevent their ruining their health at a time of life, when if it suffers it is seldom or never recovered. Their agility and address are unequalled; the most expert Indians themselves are not better marksmen, or manage their canoes in the most dangerous rapids with greater skill.

Many are of opinion that they are unfit for the sciences, which require any great degree of application, and a continued study. I am not able to say whether this prejudice is well founded, for as yet we have seen no Canadian who has endeavoured to remove it, which is perhaps owing to the dissipation in which they are brought up. But nobody can deny them an excellent genius for mechanics; they have hardly any occasion for the assistance of a master in order to excel in this science; and some are every day to be met with who have succeeded in all trades, without ever having served an apprenticeship.

Some people tax them with ingratitude, nevertheless they seem to me to have a pretty good disposition; but their natural inconstancy often prevents their attending to the duties required by gratitude. It is alleged they make bad servants, which is owing to their great haughtiness of spirit, and to their loving liberty too much to subject themselves willingly to servitude. They are however good masters, which is the reverse of what is said of those from whom the greatest part of them are descended. They would have been perfect in character, if to their own virtues they had added those of their ancestors. Their inconstancy in friendship has sometimes been complained of; but this complaint can hardly be general, and in those who have given occasion for it, it proceeds from their not being accustomed to constraint, even in their own affairs. If they are not easily disciplin'd, this likewise proceeds from the same principle, or from their having a discipline peculiar to themselves, which they believe is better adapted by carrying on war against the Indians, in which they are not entirely to blame. Moreover, they appear to me to be unable to govern a certain impetuosity, which renders them fitter for sudden surprises to hasty expeditions, than the regular and continued operations of a campaign. It has likewise been observed, that amongst a great number of brave men who distinguished themselves in the last wars, there were very few found capable of bearing a superior. This is perhaps owing to their not having sufficiently learned to obey. It is however true, that when they are well conducted, there is nothing which they will not accomplish, whether by sea or land, but in order to do this they must entertain a great opinion of their commander ...

There is one thing with respect to which they are not easily to be excused, and that is the little natural affection most of them shew to their parents, who for their part display a tenderness for them, which is not extremely well managed. The Indians fall into the same defect, and it produces amongst them the same consequences. But what above all things ought to make the Canadians be held in much esteem, is the great fund they have of piety and religion, and that nothing is wanting to their education upon this article. It is likewise true, that when they are out of their own country they hardly retain any of their defects. As with all this they are extremely brave and active, they might be of great service in war, in the marine and in the arts; and I am [of the] opinion that it would redound greatly to the advantage of the state, were they to be much more numerous than they are at present. Men constitute the principal riches of the Sovereign, and Canada, should it be of no other use to France, would still be, were it well peopled, one of the most important of all our colonies.

H) Memoir of the King to Serve as Instructions for Sr. Hocquart, Commissary General of the Marine and *Ordonnateur* in New France, March 22, 1729

... One of the greatest benefits that the Canadians can procure for France can come from the establishment of fisheries. Those of porpoises and seals that have been started in different places can provide the kingdom with an abundant quantity of fish oils, which are always in great demand but which for the most part are supplied by the Dutch. This commerce is likely to become very extensive and can never be too greatly encouraged. Besides oils it also provides sealskins, which can be used in a number of ways. In every respect, then, the commerce can only be most advantageous.

There are also masts and lumber to be drawn from Canada, not only for the royal shipyards, but also for private enterprise. In 1724 His Majesty sent the sr. de Tilly, a naval lieutenant, and a carpenter to Canada to inspect the forests and prepare wood for masts. This enterprise was beset by great difficulties and their efforts met with little success. The wood that was cut was of poor quality or wasted before being placed aboard the ships. As a result, there appeared reason to believe that obtaining masts from Canada would have to be deferred until the colony was more densely populated ...

Various crops can also be grown in Canada that will be of great utility to France, such as flax and hemp, which must be purchased in the north for considerable sums. In the past, His Majesty sent both types of seed to Quebec. The habitants, who were already in the habit of growing hemp, began to cultivate flax seven or eight years ago. In order to encourage them to increase this cultivation, His Majesty had set its price at sixty livres per quintal up to September 14 of last year and at forty livres after that date. He had ruled that this price would be maintained during the present year and lowered to twenty-five livres beginning on January 1, 1730, which is still higher than its cost in France. However, since this is a sizeable reduction, which might induce the habitants to discontinue this crop, His Majesty will approve if the sr. Hocquart sets the price at thirty-five livres or even at forty livres in 1730 ... His Majesty is prepared to incur this expense because of the future utility of this crop, but it would be in vain if the habitants continued to prepare their hemp as badly as they have done until now. Every year complaints have been received... The sr. Hocquart will do what he can to remedy this situation and will inform the habitants that His Majesty will not buy their hemp at any price if they are not more careful ...

Tar is also made in Canada from the pine trees that grow there in quantity. His Majesty recommends that he maintain the habitants in this habit so that in the future this produce may be available for the shipyards ...

His Majesty has been informed that sheep in Canada grow a good type of wool. Since there is a great consumption of this product in the kingdom, His Majesty wishes him to encourage as much as he can those who own suitable pastures to raise sheep. Eventually, this can procure considerable wealth for the colony and a more comfortable life for the habitants.

His Majesty recommends that he increase as much as possible the vegetable crops that have already been started in the colony. These not only procure abundance for the habitants but also give rise to a profitable trade with Île Royale and the West Indies, consisting of shipments of wheat, biscuit, and peas ...

Before concluding this article on cultivations, His Majesty will observe to him that the Canadians have not until now realized the progress that could have been expected. Long wars, verily, have hindered the growth of the colony. The habitants became accustomed to wielding weapons and to going on expeditions and felt no inclination to remain on the land after the return of peace, although this is what is most enduring and can best contribute to the concentration of strength which the colony requires as protection against the hostile enterprises of its neighbors. With this in mind, the sr. Hocquart must encourage and favor cultivation and the increase of the population as matters most important for the safety of the colony.

It is very important to prevent all manner of trade between the inhabitants of Canada and the English, since the latter would necessarily supply merchandise that can be drawn from the kingdom ...

l) Memoir to the Minister Containing a Characterization of the French-Canadian Population, November 8, 1737
Gilles Hocquart

The population of the colony of New France is about 40,000 people of all ages and sex among which there are 10,000 men capable of bearing arms. The Canadians are husky, well built, and of a vigorous temperament. As trades are not dominated by specialization, and since, at the establishment of the colony, tradesmen were rare, necessity has made them ingenious from generation to generation. The rural inhabitants handle the axe very adroitly. They make themselves most of the tools and utensils needed for farming, and build their own houses and barns. Many are weavers and make linen, and a large cloth which is called *droguet* which they use to clothe themselves and their families.

They love honours and praise, and pride themselves on their courage, and are extremely sensitive to criticism and the least punishment. They are self-seeking, vindictive, subject to drunkenness, make much use of liquor, and are not the most truthful people.

This characterization suits the majority, especially the rural inhabitants. Those in the cities have few faults. All are attached to religion. One sees few perfidious people. They are fickle, and have too high an opinion of themselves, which lessens their abilities to succeed in trade, agriculture, and commerce. Add to this the idleness occasioned by the long and rigorous winters. They love hunting, sailing, and travelling and are not as gross and rustic as our peasants of France. They are amenable enough when we flatter them and govern them with justice, but are by nature indocile.

It is more and more necessary to establish the respect due to authority especially amongst the people of the countryside. This aspect of administration has always been most important and the most difficult to implement. One means of achieving this is to choose the officers of the administration for the countryside from amongst the inhabitants who are wise and capable of commanding, and to give all the attention possible to supporting their authority. It can be said that a lack of firmness by the governments in the past has contributed to insubordination. For several years now crimes have been punished, disorders have been checked by suitable chastisements. Policing of public roads, cabarets, etc., has been better, and in general, the inhabitants have been controlled better than in the past. There are few noble families in Canada, but they are so large that there are many gentlemen.

4

"An Afflicted People"

The Acadian Dilemma

DOCUMENTS
A) Description Of Nova Scotia, 1720
   Paul Mascarene
B) Circular Letter to the Governors on the Continent,
   11 August 1755
   Governor Charles Lawrence
C) Journal, 1755
   Lt. Col. John Winslow
D) To the Board of Trade, Halifax, 18 October 1755
   Governor Charles Lawrence
E) A Relation of the Misfortunes of the French Neutrals,
   as laid before the Assembly of the Province of
   Pennsylvania, 1758
   John Baptiste Galerm, one of the said People

Religion and language bound the Acadians to France, but their geographical location compromised their political allegiance because their lands extended into the middle of a contentious area separating New England to the south from New France to the north. Prior to 1713 France concentrated its major efforts on the St. Lawrence valley, thus largely ignoring its Acadian citizens.

The Acadians, from force of circumstance and by choice, developed an independent spirit with political neutrality as the centerpiece. They could gain much by trading with both the English and French. Besides, France and England periodically squabbled over their land. Neutrality meant being left to their own devices, capitalizing on their location between two formidable trading empires, and never ending up on the wrong side after a military invasion.

A substantial part of Acadia changed hands in 1713. The Union Jack once again fluttered over the Nova Scotia peninsula, but Britain did not push the issue of allegiance. The Acadians viewed this change as yet another temporary changing-of-the-guard that would not impact their daily lives. And, indeed, they peacefully coexisted under their new English masters, always careful not to take sides, ever vigilant not to be drawn into allegiances that might haunt them. Time, however, caught them out, and their previous neutrality became a terrible liability. France and Britain stood poised for war by the 1740s, and both manoeuvred to get the Acadians on side. The Acadians lost control of their situation and became expendable pawns in a much bigger chess game. England concluded that "neutral" meant "enemy" in times of war. Britain could not simply evict the Acadians because their migration could strengthen those areas north of Nova Scotia. Instead they were rounded up and dispersed in small groups throughout the thirteen English colonies, where in theory they were to be integrated with the local population and eventually disappear.

Paul Mascarene (1684–1760) served with the British army, chiefly as a surveyor of Newfoundland and Massachusetts. He spent much of his time, however, settling disputes among Acadians after his arrival there in 1710. He was the right man for the job. Born in France, religious convictions saw him banished, but he retained his fluency in French and had considerable diplomatic talents. Mascarene genuinely believed in the Acadians' neutrality: he was one of the few English officers sympathetic to their plight. Even he, however, worried about the increased anti-British activities of the Catholic priests among their Acadian flock. There were other strategic problems: Britain kept relatively small garrisons of soldiers in Nova Scotia, and early British fortifications in Acadia were almost nonexistent — at a time when France had started to build its formidable fort at nearby Louisbourg on Cape Breton Island (Île Royale). Mascarene and Governor Philipps therefore used all their diplomatic skills to bring the Acadians on side in 1720, urging them to swear an oath of allegiance to the British crown. It did not work. The Acadians presumably weighed the odds and saw neutrality as their best bet. Mascarene eventually became Governor of Annapolis Royal in 1744 and tried a different tack: he set about encouraging immigration of English Protestants to the area. This, he believed, would eliminate the problem by assimilating the Acadians.

Major Charles Lawrence (1709–1760) arrived in Nova Scotia in 1749 as part of an English military buildup in preparation for war against France. He found so-called "neutral" Acadians aiding regular French forces at their forts on the Isthmus of Chignecto, the strip of land dividing French and English possessions in the area. He wanted them out and, like Mascarene, did what he could to encourage English immigrants to take their place. None came. Why would anyone settle on the borderlands between two old enemies? By July 1755 Lawrence demanded the Acadians swear an unconditional oath of loyalty to Britain, a threat that gained weight when he became Governor of Nova Scotia the following year. The Acadians once more hedged their bets: Could the British really enforce their will? Was the threat even genuine? And finally, if they did throw in their lot with the British, could they gain protection from French reprisals? The answers seemed negative. The Acadians once again refused to swear an unconditional oath of allegiance. Had it included provisions that exempted them from fighting against their mother country a compromise may have been reached, but the British were no longer prepared to accept anything short of complete compliance.

John Winslow (1703–1774) had the unpleasant task of enforcing Lawrence's orders. He and his men physically rounded up and deported the Acadian population to the eastern seaboard of New England. Winslow was born in the English Massachusetts Bay colony and rose through the ranks until he commanded a local regiment in Nova Scotia that saw action against French forts at Beausejour and Gaspereau.

We know nothing of John Baptiste Galerm, a displaced Acadian, except what can be pieced together from his address to the Assembly of the Province of Pennsylvania in 1758.

A) Description Of Nova Scotia, 1720
Paul Mascarene

The Boundaries having as yet not been agreed on between the British and French Governments in these parts as stipulated in the 10th Article of the treaty of Utrecht no just ones can be settled in this description. The extent of the province of Nova Scotia or Acadie, according to the notion the Britains have of it, is from the limits of the Government of Massachusetts Bay in New England, or Kennebeck River about the 44th degree North latitude, to Cape de Roziers on the South side of the entrance of the River of St. Lawrence in the 44th degree of the same latitude, and its breadth extends from the Easternmost part of the Island of Cape Breton to the South side of the River of St. Lawrence. Out of this large tract, the French had yielded to them at the above Treaty the Islands situated at the mouth of the River St. Lawrence and in the Gulph of the same with the Island of Cape Breton.

The climate is cold and very variable even in the southernmost part of this Country, and is subject to long and severe winters.

The soil notwithstanding this, may be easily made to produce all the supplies of life for the inhabitants which may more particularly appear when mention is made of each particular settlement. It produces in general, Wheat, Rye, Barley, Oats, all manner of pulse, garden roots and Herbs, it abounds in Cattle of all kinds, and has plenty of both tame and wild fowl. It is no less rich in its produce for what relates to trade. Its woods are filled with Oak, Fir, Pine of all sorts fit for masts, Pitch and Tar, Beach, Maple, Ash, Birch, Asp &c. There are also undoubtedly several Iron and Copper mines, the latter at Cape Doré have been attempted three different times, but the great expense which would attend the digging and thoroughly searching them has discouraged the undertakers, the whole Cape being of a vast height and an entire rock, through the crevices of which some bits of Copper are [spied]. There are good Coal mines and a quarry of soft stone near Chignecto, and at Musquash cove ten leagues from Annapolis Royal, as also in St. Johns River very good and plenty of white marble is found which burns into very good lime, feathers and furs are a considerable part of the trade of this Country, but the most material is the fishing of Cod which all the Coast abounds with, and seems to be inexhaustible. It is easy from hence to infer of how much benefit it is to Great Britain that two such considerable branches of trade as the supplies for Naval Stores, and the Fishery may remain in her possession, and if it should be objected that New England and Newfoundland are able to supply the demands of Great Britain on those two heads it may be easily replied, that the markets will be better, especially in relation to fish when Great Britain is almost the sole mistress of that branch of trade, and her competitors abridged of the large share they bear in it.

There are four considerable settlements on the south side of the Bay of Fundy, Annapolis Royal, Manis, Chignecto, and Cobequid which shall be treated on separately. Several families are scattered along the Eastern Coast which shall be also mentioned in their turn.

The Inhabitants of these Settlements are still all French and Indians; the former have been tolerated in the possession of the lands they possessed, under the French Government, and have had still from time to time longer time allowed them either to take the Oaths to the Crown of Great Britain, or to withdraw, which they have always found some pretence or other to delay, and to ask for longer time for consideration. They being in general of the Romish persuasion, can not be easily drawn from the French Interest, to which they seem to be entirely wedded tho' they find a great deal more sweetness under the English Government. They use all the means they can to keep the Indians from dealing with the British subjects, and by their mediation spreading among the Savages several false Notions tending to make them diffident, and frighten them from a free intercourse with them and prompting them now and then to some mischief which may increase that diffidence, and oblige them to keep more at a distance.

There are but two reasons which may plead for the keeping those French Inhabitants in this Country. 1st. The depriving the French of the addition of such a strength, which might render them too powerful neighbours, especially if these people on their withdrawing hence are received and settled at Cape Breton; and secondly, the use that may be made of them in providing necessaries for erecting fortifications, and for English Settlements and keeping on the stock of cattle, and the lands tilled, till the English are powerful enough of themselves to go on, which two last will sensibly decay if they withdraw before any considerable number of British subjects be settled in their stead, and it is also certain that they having the conveniency of saw mills (which it will not be in our power to hinder being destroyed by them, at their going away) may furnish sooner and cheaper the plank boards &c. requisite for building.

The reasons for not admitting these Inhabitants are many and strong, and naturally deriving from the little dependence on their allegiance. The free exercise of their religion as promised to them, implies their having missionaries of the Romish persuasion amongst them, who have that ascendance over that ignorant people, as to render themselves masters of all their actions, and to guide and direct them as they please in temporal as well as in spiritual affairs. These missionaries have their superiors at Canada or Cape Breton, from whom it is natural to think, they will receive such commands as will never square with the English interest being such as these, viz., Their forever inciting the Savages to some mischief or other, to hinder their corresponding with the English; their laying all manner of difficulties in the way when any English Settlement is proposed or going on by in citing underhand the Savages to disturb them, and making these last such a bugbear, as if they (the French) themselves durst not give any help to the English for fear of being massacred by them, when it is well known the Indians are but a handful in this country. And were the French Inhabitants (who are able to appear a thousand men under arms) hearty for the British Government, they could drive away, or utterly destroy the Savages in a very little time. The French Inhabitants besides are for the generality very little industrious, their lands not improved as might be expected, they living in a manner from hand to mouth, and provided they have a good field of Cabbages and Bread enough for their families with what fodder is sufficient for their cattle they seldom look for much further improvement.

It is certain that British Colonists would be far more advantageous to the settling this Province, and would besides the better improvement of it, for which their Industry is far superior to the French who inhabit it at present, lessen considerably the expense in defending of it, not only in regard to fortifications, but also in regard to Garrisons, because the English Inhabitants would be a strength of themselves, whereas the French require a strict watch over them. This would also reconcile the native Indians to the English, which the other as mentioned before, endeavour to keep at a distance.

The neighbouring Government of the French at Cape Breton is not very desirous of drawing the Inhabitants out of this Country so long as they remain in it under a kind of Allegiance to France, especially if they are not allowed to carry their cattle, effects, grain, &c., which last would be more welcome in the barren country than bare Inhabitants, but is opposing with all its might and by the influence of the Priests residing here, their taking the oaths of Allegiance to Great Britain, and if even that oath was taken by them, the same influence would make it of little or no effect. That Government is also improving by the same means the diffidence of the Indians, and will make them instruments to disturb the British Settlements on the Eastern Coast of this Government, or any other place, which might check the supplies they have from hence for their support on their barren territories besides the jealousy in trade and fear of this Government being too powerful in case of a War.

It would be therefore necessary for the interest of Great Britain, and in order to reap the benefit, which will accrue from the acquisition of this country, not to delay any longer the settling of it, but to go about it in good earnest to which it is humbly proposed, viz.:

That the French Inhabitants may not be tolerated any longer in their non-allegiance, but may have the test put to them without granting them any further delay, for which it is requisite a sufficient force be allowed to make them comply with the terms prescribed them, which force ought to be at least six hundred men to be divided to the several parts already inhabited by the French and Indians, and might be at the same time a cover to the British Inhabitants who would come to settle in the room of the French. For an encouragement to those new Inhabitants, should be given free transportation, free grants of land, and some stock of Cattle out of what such of the French who would rather choose to withdraw, than take the oaths, might be hindered to destroy or carry away.

The expense this project would cost the Government, would be made up by the benefit, which would accrue to trade, when the country should be settled with Inhabitants, who would promote it, and would be a security to it and in a little time a small force of regular troops would be able to defend it, with the help of loyal Inhabitants.

The great expense the Government has been at already on account of this country, and the little benefit that has accrued from it is owing for the most part, to its being peopled with Inhabitants that have been always enemies to the English Government, for it's evident from what has been said of the temper of the Inhabitants and the underhand dealings of the Government of Cape Breton, that what orders are or may be given out by the Governor of this Province, without they are backed by a sufficient force, will be always slighted and rendered of non effect.

It will be easy to judge how the number of Troops here proposed, ought to be disposed of by the description of every particular settlement and first.

Annapolis Royal is seated on the Southern side of the Bay of Fundy, about thirty leagues from Cape Sables ... On both sides of the British River are a great many fine farms Inhabited by about two hundred families. The tide flows that extent, but the river is not navigable above two leagues above the Fort, by any other than small boats. The Bank of this River is very pleasant and fruitful and produces wheat, rye and other grain, pulse, garden roots, herbs and the best cabbages of any place, here abounds also cattle and fowls of all kinds and if the several good tracts of land along this river were well improved they would suffice for a much greater number of Inhabitants than there is already.

The chief employment of the French Inhabitants now is farming and the time they have to spare they employ in hunting, and catching of Sable Martins. Their young men who have not much work at farming beget themselves to Fishing in the summer. The Fort is almost a regular square, has four Bastions, and on the side fronting the Point, which is formed by the junction of the two Rivers, it has a ravelin and a battery of large guns on the counterscarpe of the ravelin, which last with the battery, have been entirely neglected since the English had possession of this place and are entirely ruined. The works are raised with a sandy earth and were faced with sods, which being cut out of a sandy soil (the whole neck betwixt the two rivers being nothing else) soon mouldered away, and some part of the works needed repairing almost every spring. The French constantly repaired it after the same manner except part of the courtin, covered with the Ravelin, which they were obliged to face with pieces of timber some time before they quitted possession of this place. The English followed that last method in repairing of this Fort, reverting of it all round with pieces of round timber, of six or seven inches diameter, to the height of the Cordon, and raising a parapet of sod work, but whether by neglect of the workman, or those who had the overseeing of them, or their little thrift in carrying on these repairs, or some other reason, they put the Government to a prodigious deal of charge, and gave an entire disgust for any manner of repairs. Thus the fort laid for a great while tumbling down, till at the arrival of Governor Philipps, the orders from his Majesty signified by him to the French Inhabitants not pleasing them they shewed some forwardness to disturb the peace and to incite the Indians to some mischief, which made it necessary to put the fort into a posture of defence against the insults which might be offered to the Garrison which is too small of itself to encounter so great a number, as even the Inhabitants of this River, might make against it, they being able to arm and assemble four hundred men, in twenty four hours time. It is therefore humbly proposed in relation to this place, that till the Inhabitants are more loyal, two hundred men of regular Troops may remain garrisoned here, and that whilst a new projection for the fortifying of this place shall be agreed and carried, this fort may be next summer, thoroughly repaired, the sum demanded for these repairs, not exceeding eight hundred pounds sterling, by which this place will be put in a condition to last the time requisite for providing of materials, and building a stone redoubt &c., and may serve to secure the materials, and workmen, which otherwise will be much in danger. This project will be more particularly transmitted this fall to the Honorable Board of Ordnance.

Mannis called by the French Les Mines has its name from the Copper Mines which are said to be about it especially at one of the Capes, which divides the Bay of Fundy, and is called Cap Des Mines or Cape Doré ...

The houses which compose a kind of scattering Town, lies on a rising ground along two Cricks which run betwixt it and the meadow, and make of this last a kind of Peninsula. This place has great Store of Cattle, and other conveniences of life, and in the road they catch white porpoises, a kind of fish, the blubber of which turned into oil, yields a good profit.

The Inhabitants of this place and round about it are more numerous than those of the British River, besides the number of Indians which often resort here, and as they never had any force near them to bridle them, are less tractable, and subject to command. All the orders sent to them if not suiting to their humors, are scoffed and laughed at, and they put themselves upon the footing of obeying no Government. It will not be an easy matter to oblige these Inhabitants to submit to any terms which do not entirely Square to their humours unless a good force be landed there, and a Fort or redoubt of earth be thrown up, well ditched friezed and pallisaded, till a more durable may be built; this redoubt must have four pieces of cannon (sakers) and command the meadow, which is their treasure. The force sent for that purpose must be three or four hundred men, the reason of which will appear, when it is considered, when the wildness of the harbor will not make it safe for any Ship of force to remain there to give countenance to such an undertaking, and that even if she could anchor safely, it must be at the distance of near twelve miles from the place where the said redoubt is to be built and that any other vessels, which must be employed to carry the troops, and workmen must lie ashore dry, sixteen hours at least of the twenty four, and may be liable to be burned, and thereby cut off the retreat of those employed in this work unless they are able to defend themselves and to make head against the Inhabitants and the Indians; who will never suffer it to go on, if not kept in awe by a sufficient force. The redoubt ought to be capable of receiving a hundred and fifty men, which will be enough to curb the Inhabitants till they grow more loyal, or better be put in their stead.

Cobequid lies about twelve leagues North East of Manis, at the upper end of the Easternmost branch of the Bay of Fundy.

There are about fifty French Families settled in this place. The soil of which produces good grain, and abounds in cattle and other conveniences of life. By a River the Inhabitants have communication with Chibucto a harbor on the Eastern Coast and by a road across the woods at a distance of about twenty leagues they fall into the Bay of Vert, in the Gulph of St. Lawrence, by which they drive a trade to Cape Breton. The Indians resort much to this place.

Chignecto is seated upon the Westernmost branch of the Bay of Fundy almost at the upper end of it. The inhabitants are numerous having much increased of late years, and are about seventy or eighty families. This place is about twelve leagues distant from Manis having a communication by a river which discharges itself into Manis Road.

This place produces good store of grain and abounds in Cattle more than any other. Within seven leagues of Cape Chignecto (which with Cape Doré divides the Bay of Fundy in two branches) there are very good Coal Mines, and easily come at, but the want of shelter makes it dangerous for the vessels which come to receive it; they being forced to anchor in the open Bay. Near the town itself which lies four leagues beyond the coal mines, there is a small Island which has a good quarry of Soft Stone, it cuts in layers of four or six inches thick, and hardens soon after it is cut. The Inhabitants are more given to hunting and trading than those of the other settlements, which is partly occasioned by their being so conveniently seated for it. There being but a small neck of land of two leagues wide which parts the Bay of Fundy from the Gulph of St. Lawrence, by this last they have a continual intercourse with Cape Breton, carrying most of their Furs that way, and supplying it with provisions, of grain, cattle &c. and bringing for returns linens and other goods, to the prejudice of the British trade and manufactories. To put a stop to this, and to bring the Inhabitants of this place under obedience, who are the least subject to the English Government of any other here, it will be necessary that a small fort be built in some convenient place on this neck capable of containing one hundred and fifty men. This is the more so by reason the French have sent four Ships this Summer, with two hundred families with provisions stores and materials for the erecting a fort and making a settlement on the Island St. Johns, which lies in the Bay of Verte, part of the Gulph of St. Lawrence, part of which Island (which is near fifty leagues long) is but at three or four leagues distance from the main, and six in all from Chignecto. When this settlement is made by the French, they will from thence command all the Trade and carry a greater sway, over all the Bay of Fundy, than the English, who are the undoubted owners but have only the name of possessors of it, till such measures are taken as are here humbly proposed. For it is to be remembered, that each of these places have a French Popish Missionary, who is the real chief Commander of his flock, and receives and takes his commands from his superiors at Cape Breton.

The lesser settlements on this Bay, and other parts of this Government shall be referred to another opportunity and at this time, the most material of all shall only be touched upon, viz.

Cansoe is an Island with several other less ones adjoining, lying at a small distance from the Main, and at South East and North West from the Passage which bears the same name and separates the Island of Cape Breton from the main Continent. This place has been found so convenient and advantageous for catching and cureing Cod Fish that of late it has been the resort of numbers of English, as it was of French before the seizure made by Captain Smart in His Majesty's Ship Squirell. This stroke was so grevious to the French, who were concerned in this loss, amongst which were some of tho principal Officers of Cape Breton, that seeing they could not obtain the satisfaction they demanded, they have been all at work all this Spring, and incited the Indians to assemble at Canso and to surprise the English who were securely fishing there, (and did not expect such treatment) and having killed and wounded some and drove off the rest to Sea.

By means of this hurry and confusion whilst the Indians were plundering the dry goods, the French were robbing the fish and transporting of it away, till the English having recovered themselves sent after them, and seized several of their shallops and shareways, laden with English fish and other plunder, and made the robbers prisoners, and pursued the retreating Indians and took two of them also prisoners. Had it not been for this eruption twenty thousand Quintals of dry cod fish this season would have been exported out of this place, and the returns arising thereby, very considerable to Great Britain.

This is sufficient to show the necessity of supporting the British subjects, whom the advantage of the Fishery will draw every year, and induce to settle in this place, if they can be secured from the like insults by a Ship or armed Sloop countenancing them in summer, and a Fort and Garrison protecting them in winter. This if encouraged is very likely to be the chief place for Trade tho' not so conveniently situated for the chief seat of Government as Port Roseway, La-Have, Marligash, Chiboucto, or any other Harbor situated on the Eastern Coast of this Government; which by being near the centre may best hold communication with the whole. But as neither of these harbors, have been as yet narrowly surveyed, and no sufficient information can be had about them, further mention there of will be deferred to another opportunity.

B) Circular Letter to the Governors on the Continent,
11 August 1755
Governor Charles Lawrence

Sir: The success that has attended his Majesty's arms in driving the French from the Encroachments they had made in this province furnished me with a favorable Opportunity of reducing the French inhabitants of this Colony to a proper obedience to his Majesty's Government, or forcing them to quit the country. These Inhabitants were permitted to remain in quiet possession of their lands upon condition they should take the Oath of allegiance to the King within one year after the Treaty of Utrecht by which this province was ceded to Great Britain; with this condition they have ever refused to comply, without having at the same time from the Governor an assurance in writing that they should not be called upon to bear arms in the defence of the province; and with this General Philipps did comply, of which step his Majesty disapproved and the inhabitants pretending therefrom to be in a state of Neutrality between his Majesty and his enemies have continually furnished the French & Indians with Intelligence, quarters, provisions and assistance in annoying the Government; and while one part have abetted the French Encroachments by their treachery, the other have countenanced them by open Rebellion, and three hundred of them were actually found in arms in the French Fort at Beauséjour when it surrendered.

Notwithstanding all their former bad behaviour, as his Majesty was pleased to allow me to extend still further his Royal grace to such as would return to their Duty, I offered such of them as had not been openly in arms against us, a continuance of the Possession of their lands, if they would take the Oath of Allegiance, unqualified with any Reservation whatsoever; but this they have most audaciously as well as unanimously refused, and if they would presume to do this when there is a large fleet of Ships of War in the harbor, and a considerable land force in the province, what might not we expect from them when the approaching winter deprives us of the former, and when the Troops which are only hired from New England occasionally and for a small time, have returned home.

As by this behaviour the inhabitants have forfeited all title to their lands and any further favor from the Government, I called together his Majesty's Council, at which the Honble. Vice Adml. Boscawen and Rear Adml. Mostyn assisted, to consider by what means we could with the greatest security and effect rid ourselves of a set of people who would forever have been an obstruction to the intention of settling this Colony and that it was now from their refusal to the Oath absolutely incumbent upon us to remove.

As their numbers amount to near 7000 persons the driving them off with leave to go whither they pleased would have doubtless strengthened Canada with so considerable a number of inhabitants; and as they have no cleared land to give them at present, such as are able to bear arms must have been immediately employed in annoying this and neighbouring Colonies. To prevent such an inconvenience it was judged a necessary and the only practicable measure to divide them among the Colonies where they may be of some use, as most of them are healthy strong people; and as they cannot easily collect themselves together again it will be out of their power to do any mischief and they may become profitable and it is possible, in time, faithful subjects.

As this step was indispensably necessary to the security of this Colony, upon whose preservation from French encroachments the prosperity of North America is esteemed in a great measures dependent, I have not the least reason to doubt of your Excellency's concurrence and that you will receive the inhabitants I now send and dispose of them in such manner as may best answer our design in preventing their reunion.

C) Journal, 1755
Lt. Col. John Winslow

September 5th — At three in the afternoon the French inhabitants appeared agreeable to their citation at the church in Grand Pré, amounting to 418 of their best men. Upon which I ordered a table to be set in the centre of the church and, being attended with those of my officers who were off guard delivered them, by interpreters, the King's orders in the following words:
GENTLEMEN,
I have received from his Excellency, Governor Lawrence, the King's Commission which I have in my hand and by whose orders you are convened together to manifest to you His Majesty's final resolution to the French inhabitants of this, His Province of Nova Scotia ...

The part of duty I am now upon is what, though necessary, is very disagreeable to my natural make and temper, as I know it must be grievous to you ... but it is not my business to animadvert, but to obey such orders as I receive and, therefore, without hesitation, shall deliver to you His Majesty's orders and instructions ...

That your lands and tenements, cattle of all kinds and livestock of all sorts are forfeited to the Crown with all other of your effects, saving your money and household goods, and you yourselves to be removed from His Province ... I shall do everything in my power that all those goods be secured to you and that you are not molested in carrying off them and also that whole families shall go in the same vessel and make this remove, which I am sensible must give you a great deal of trouble, as easy as His Majesty's service will admit, and hope that in every part of the world you may fall you may be faithful subjects, a peaceable and happy people.

I must also inform you that it is His Majesty's pleasure that you remain in security under the inspection and direction of the troops

... and then declared them the King's prisoners.

After delivering these things, I returned to my quarters and they, the French inhabitants, soon moved by their elders that it was a great grief to them that they had incurred His Majesty's displeasure and that they were fearful that the surprise of their detention here would quite overcome their families, whom they had no means to apprise of these, their melancholy circumstances, and prayed that part of them might be retained as hostages for the appearance of the rest, and the bigger number admitted to go home to their families and that, as some of their men were absent, they would be obliged to bring them in. I informed them I would consider of their motion and report.

And immediately convened my officers to advise, who with me all agreed that it would be well that they, themselves, should choose twenty of their number for whom they would be answerable ...

The French people, not having any provisions with them and pleading for bread ... I ... ordered that, for the future, they be supplied from their respective families. Thus ended the memorable fifth of September, a day of great fatigue and trouble.

September 7th — the French remained in quiet. We mounted guard with half our party ... We all lay on our arms since detaining the French here.

September 10th — The French this morning discovered some uncommon motions among themselves which I do not like. Called my officers together and communicated to them what I had observed and, after debating matters, it was determined nemo contra dissent, that it would be best to divide the prisoners and that, as there was five transports idle which came from Boston, it would be good ... that fifty men of the French inhabitants be embarked on board of each of the five vessels, taking first all their young men ...

I sent for father Landry, their principal speaker who talks English, and told him the time has come for part of the inhabitants to embark and that the number concluded for this day was 250, and that we should begin with the young men and desired he would inform his brethren of it. He was greatly surprised. I told him it must be done ... and, as the tide in a very little time favoured my design, could not give them above an hour to prepare for going on board, and ordered our whole party to be under arms and post themselves between the two gates and the church ... which was obeyed ... I then ordered Capt. Adams with a lieutenant, 80 non-commission officers and private men to draw off from the main body to guard the young men ... and order the prisoners to march. They all answered they would not go without their fathers. I told them that was a word I did not understand, for that the King's command was to me absolute and should be absolutely obeyed, and that I did not love to use harsh means, but that the time did not admit of parleys or delays. And then ordered the whole troop to fix their bayonets and advance towards the French, and bid the four right hand files of the prisoners, consisting of 24 men ... to divide from the rest. One of whom I took hold on (who opposed the marching) and bid march. He obeyed and the rest followed, though slowly, and went off praying, singing, and crying being met by the women and children all the way (which is 1½ mile) with great lamentations, upon their knees, praying etc.

I then ordered the remaining French to choose out 109 of their married men to follow their young people (the ice being broke). They readily complied ... So that the number embarked was but 230 and thus ended this troublesome job, which was scene of sorrow. After this Capt. Adams with the transports fell down from Gaspereau and anchored in the mouth of that river ...

September 12th — I yesterday received a memorial in French from the Neutral inhabitants ... No. 1 is a petition from the inhabitants to General Philipps praying that all those who should take the oath of fidelity to His Majesty King George may be allowed the free exercise of their religion and that missionaries may be allowed them, praying also a guarantee of their estates and possessions on paying the customary quit rents. The answer signed by General Philipps is that the prayer of their petition is granted and accordingly follows the oath in these words:

> Dated April 25th, 1730
> I promise and swear sincerely by the faith of a Christian
> that I will be truly faithful and will submit myself to His

Majesty King George whom I acknowledge to be the Lord
and Sovereign of Nova Scotia.
So Help Me God.

Then follows a certificate from Monsieur de la Godalis and Alexandre
Nouville priests, who certify that General Philipps did promise to the inhabitants that they should be exempted from bearing arms against either
the French or Indians, and that they, on their part did promise that they
would not take up arms against the Kingdom of England or its government.
Dated April 29th, 1730.

No. 2 is a petition to John Winslow esq., Lieut. Col. of His Majesty's
troops commanding at Grand Pré, representing that the evils which seem to
threaten them on all sides oblige them to beg your protection on their behalf, and that you intercede with His Majesty to consider those who have
inviolably kept the fidelity and submission promised to his said majesty. And,
as you have given them to understand that the King has ordered them to be
transported of this province, they beg, at least, if they must quit their estates, that they may be permitted to go to such places where they will find
their kindred, and that at their own expense, allowing them a convenient
time for that purpose ... by that means they will be able to preserve their
religion which they have very much at heart, and for which they are content to sacrifice their estates, etc.

17th September, Letter to Lieut. Governor Charles Lawrence: ... having
convened the male inhabitants, I delivered them Your Excellency's orders ...
They were greatly struck at this determination, though I believe they did not
then nor to this day do imagine that they are actually to be removed.

September 29th, Letter to Governor Lawrence: ... I advise from Capt.
Lewis of the 25th instant that the inhabitants of Cobequid have entirely
deserted that country and that he began to burn and lay waste on the 23rd
... The French are constantly plying me with petitions and remonstrances.

October 6th — With the advice of my captains, made a division of the
villages and concluded that as many of the inhabitants of each as could be
commoded should proceed in the same vessel and that whole families go
together, and sent orders to several families to hold themselves in readiness
to embark with all their household goods, etc., but even now could not persuade the people I was in earnest.

October 7th — ... In the evening twenty-four of the French young men
deserted from on board Capts. Church and Stone ...

October 8th — began to embark the inhabitants who went off very solentarily and unwillingly, the women in great distress, carrying off their children in their arms. The others carrying their decrepit parents in their carts and all their goods moving in great confusion and appeared a scene of woe and distress. Filled up Church and Milbury with about eighty families, and also made the strictest inquiry I could how those young men made their escape ... found one François Hebert was either the contriver or abettor ... who I ordered ashore, carried to his own house and then, in his presence, burned both his house and barn. And gave notice to all the French that, in case these men did not surrender themselves in two days I should serve all their friends in the same manner and ... confiscate their household goods.

October 9th — ... Father Landry proposed to accommodate matters for the return of the young men deserted. This in case I would give under my hand that they should be not be punished upon their return, he imagined they might be induced to come in. I told him I had already passed my word of honour for it ...

October 12th — Our parties, being reconnoitring the country, fell in with one of the French deserters who endeavoured to make his escape on horseback. They hailed him and fired over him, but he persisted in riding off when one of our men shot him dead off his horse. And also meeting with a party of the same people, fired upon them, but they made their escape into the woods ...

October 13th — This evening came in and privately got on board the transports the ... twenty-two of the 24 deserters ...

October 19th, Letter to Messrs. Apthorp, Son and Hancock ... I have five hundred people more to embark than the nine mentioned can carry, which will fall some short of 1500. Have had two bad months placed in the centre of Nova Scotia without any fortification or cannon and only 360 men ... When parties are out had two Frenchmen to an Englishman within ... the difficulty is most over and be assured I am heartily tired of it ...

20th October, Letter to Governor Shirley: ... We are shipping off the inhabitants and should have been free of them a long time ago, but that we have wanted for transports. Have quite swept Grand Pré and River Gaspereau ...

D) To the Board of Trade, Halifax, 18th October 1755
Governor Charles Lawrence

My Lords,

Since the last letter I had the honor to write your Lordships of the 18th of July, the French deputys of the different districts have appeared before the Council to give a final answer to the proposal made them, of taking the Oath of Allegiance to his Majesty which they persisted in positively refusing; and tho' every means was used to point out to them their true interest, and sufficient time given them to deliberate maturely upon the step they were about to take, nothing would induce them to acquiesce in any measures that were consistent with his Majesty's honor or the security of his Province. Upon this behaviour the Council came to a resolution to oblige them to quit the Colony, and immediately took into consideration what might be the speediest, cheapest and easiest method of giving this necessary resolution its intended effect. We easily foresaw that driving them out by force of Arms to Canada or Louisbourg, would be attended with great difficulty, and if it had succeeded would have reinforced those settlements with a very considerable body of men, who were ever universally the most inveterate enemies to our religion and Government, and now highly enraged at the loss of their possessions.

The only safe means that appeared to us of preventing their return or their collecting themselves again into a large body, was distributing them among the Colonies from Georgia to New England. Accordingly the Vessels were hired at the cheapest rates: the embarkation is now in great forwardness, and I am in hopes some of them are already sailed, and that there will not be one remaining by the end of the next month. Herewith I transmit your Lordships a Copy of the Records of Council which contain a very particular account of this whole transaction.

I have taken all the care in my power to lessen the expense of the Transportation of the inhabitants, the vessels that have been taken up for that purpose, were most of them bound to the places where the inhabitants were destined, and by that means are hired greatly cheaper than the ordinary price. They have hitherto been victualled with their own provisions and will be supplied for the passage with the provisions that were taken in the French Forts at Chignecto as far as they will go.

In order to save as many of the French cattle as possible, I have given some of them among such of the Settlers as have the means of feeding them in the winter. As soon as the French are gone I shall use my best endeavours to encourage People to come from the continent to settle their lands, and if I succeed in this point we shall soon be in a condition of supplying ourselves with provisions, and I hope in time to be able to strike off the great expense of the Victualling the Troops. This was one of the happy effects I proposed to myself from driving the French off the Isthmus and the additional circumstance of the Inhabitants evacuating the Country will I flatter myself greatly hasten this event as it furnishes us with a large quantity of good land ready for immediate cultivation, renders it difficult for the Indians who cannot as formerly be supplied with provisions and intelligence, to make incursions upon our settlers, and I believe the French will not now be so sanguine in their hopes of possessing a province that they have hitherto looked upon as ready peopled for them the moment they would get the better of the English. I think it my duty to acquaint your Lordships that it will be highly necessary for the security of the province to fortify the Isthmus of Chignecto as early in the Spring as possible. The French Forts at Beauséjour and upon the Bay Verte are put into the best repair that the time would permit, but they are neither strong enough nor will they contain a sufficient number of men to resist any considerable force. It is also of the highest importance that there should be a Fort of some strength at St. John's River to prevent the French resettling there, as well as to awe the Indians of that district. I am very sensible that making these Fortifications will create a very considerable expense and therefore cannot be undertaken without orders, but if your Lordships should think it necessary to be done you may depend upon its being set about with the greatest economy ...

As the Three French Priests, Messrs. Chauvreulx, Daudin & Le Maire were of no further use in this Province after the removal of the French Inhabitants, Admiral Boscawen has been so good as to take them on board his fleet & is to give them a passage to England. I omitted in the paragraph about the French Inhabitants to mention to your Lordships my having wrote a circular letter to the Governors of the provinces to which they were destined, & directed one to be given to the master of each transport. In this Letter I have set forth the reasons which obliged us to take the measures we have done, and I enclose a copy of it for your Lordship's perusal. I am in hopes the provinces will make no difficulties about receiving them as they may in a short time become useful & beneficial subjects.

I have the Honour, &c. &c. .

CHARLES LAWRENCE

E)   A Relation of the Misfortunes of the French Neutrals, as laid before the Assembly of the Province of Pennsylvania, 1758
John Baptiste Galerm, one of the said People

About the Year 1713, when Annapolis Royal was taken from the French, our Fathers being then settled on the Bay of Fundi, upon the Surrender of that Country to the English, had, by Virtue of the Treaty of Utrecht, a Year granted to them to remove with their Effects; but not being willing to lose the Fruit of many Years Labour, they chose rather to remain there, and become Subjects of Great Britain, on Condition that they might be exempted from bearing Arms against France (most of them having near Relations and friends amongst the French, which they might have destroyed with their own Hands, had they consented to bear Arms against them). This Request they always understood to be granted, on their taking the Oath of Fidelity to her late Majesty Queen Anne; which Oath of Fidelity was by us, about 27 Years ago, renewed to his Majesty King George by General Philipse, who then allowed us an Exemption of bearing Arms against France; which Exemption, till lately (that we were told to the contrary) we always thought was approved of by the King. Our Oath of Fidelity, we that are now brought into this Province, as well at those of our Community that are carried late into the neighbouring Provinces, have always inviolably observed, and have, on all Occasions, been willing to afford all the Assistance in our Power to his Majesty's Governors in erecting Forts, making Roads, Bridges, &c., and providing Provisions for his Majesty's Service, as can be testified by the several Governors and Officers that have commanded in his Majesty's Province of Nova Scotia; and this notwithstanding the repeated Solicitations, Threats and Abuses which we have continually, more or less, suffered from the French and French Indians of Canada on that Account; particularly, about ten Years ago, when 500 French and Indians came to our Settlements, intending to attack Annapolis Royal, which, had their intention succeeded, would have made them Masters of all Nova Scotia, it being the only Place of Strength then in that Province, they earnestly solicited with us to join with, and aid them therein; but we persisting in our Resolution to abide true to our Oath of Fidelity, and absolutely refusing to give them any Assistance, they gave over their Intention and returned to Canada. And about seven Years past, at the Settling of Halifax, a body of 150 Indians came amongst us, forced some of us from our Habitations, and by Threats and blows would have compelled us to assist them in Way laying and destroying the English, then employed in erecting Forts in different parts of the Country; but we positively refusing, they left us, after having abused us, and made great Havock of our Cattle, &c. I myself was six Weeks before I wholly recovered of the blows I received from them at that time. Almost numberless are the Instances which might be given of the Abuses and Losses we have undergone from the French Indians, on Account of our steady Adhearance to our Oath of Fidelity; and yet notwithstanding our strict Observance thereof, we have not been able to prevent the grievous Calamity which is now come upon us, which we apprehend to be in a great Measure owing to the unhappy Situation and Conduct of some of our People settled at Chignecto, at the bottom of the Bay of Fundi, where the French, about four Years ago, erected a Fort; those of our People who were settled near it, after having had many of their Settlements burnt by the French; being too far from Halifax and Annapolis Royal to expect sufficient Assistance from the English, were obliged, as we believe, more through Compulsion and Fear than Inclination, to join with and assist the French; which also appears from the Articles of Capitulation agreed on between Colonel Monckton and the French Commander, at the Delivery of the said Fort to the English, which is expressly in the following Words.

"With regard to the Acadians, as they have been forced to take up Arms on Pain of Death, they shall be pardoned for the Part they have been taking." Notwithstanding this, as these People's Conduct had given just Umbrage to the Government and erected Suspicions, to the Prejudice of our whole Community, we were summoned to appear before the Governor and Council at Halifax, where we were required to take the Oath of Allegiance without any Exception, which we could not comply with because, as that Government is at present situate, we apprehend that we should have been obliged to take up Arms; but we are still willing to take the Oath of Fidelity, and to give the strongest Assurance of continuing peaceable and faithful to his Britannick Majesty, with that Exception. But this, in the present Situation of Affairs, not being satisfactory, we were made Prisoners, and our Estates, both real and personal, forfeited for the King's Use; and Vessels being provided, we were some time after sent off, with most of our Families, and dispersed amongst the English Colonies. The Hurry and Confusion in which we were embarked was an aggravating Circumstance attending our Misfortunes; for thereby many, who had lived in Affluence, found themselves deprived of every Necessary, and many Families were separated, Parents from Children, and Children from

Parents. Yet blessed be God that it was our Lot to be sent to Pennsylvania, where our Wants have been relieved, and we have in every Respect been received with Christian Benevolence and Charity. And let me add, that not withstanding the Suspicions and Fears which many here are possessed of on our Account, as tho' we were a dangerous People, who make little Scruple of breaking our Oaths. Time will manifest that we are not such a People: No, the unhappy situation which we are now in, is a plain Evidence that this is a false Claim, tending to aggravate the Misfortunes of an already too unhappy People; for had we entertained such pernicious Sentiments, we might easily have prevented our falling into the melancholy Circumstances we are now in, viz: Deprived of our Subsistance, banished from our native Country, and reduced to live by Charity in a strange Land; and this for refusing to take an Oath, which we are firmly persuaded Christianity absolutely forbids us to violate, had we once taken it, and yet an Oath which we could not comply with without being exposed to plunge our Swords in the Breasts of our Friends and Relations. We shall, however, as we have hitherto done, submit to what in the present Situation of Affairs may seem necessary, and with Patience and Resignation bear whatever God, in the course of his Providence, shall suffer to come upon us. We shall also think it our Duty to seek and promote the Peace of the Country into which we are transported, and inviolably keep the Oath of Fidelity that we have taken to his gracious Majesty King George, whom we firmly believe, when fully acquainted with our Faithfulness and Sufferings, will commiserate our unhappy Condition, and order that some Compensation be made us for our Losses. And may the Almighty abundantly bless his Honour the Governor, the Honourable Assembly of the Province, and the good People of Philadelphia, whose Sympathy, Benevolence and Christian Charity have been, and still are, greatly manifested and extended towards us, a poor distressed and afflicted People, is the sincere and earnest Prayer of John Baptiste Galerm.

5

"The Ruin of Canada"

Last Decades of New France

DOCUMENTS

A) Memoir on the French Colonies in North America, 1750
   Barrin de la Galissonière
B) To Marshal de Belle Isle, Quebec, 19 May 1758
   François Daine
C) Memoir, 1758
   M. de Capellis
D) To Marshal de Belle Isle, Montreal, 12 April 1759
   Louis-Joseph de Montcalm
E) Memoir on the Condition of Canada
   Michel-Jean-Hughes Péan
F) Mémoire sur le Canada, 1759
   M. de Beaucat
G) Memoir on Canada
   Unknown
H) Narrative of the Doings During the Siege of Quebec, and the Conquest of Canada
   Marie de la Visitation, Nun of the General Hospital of Quebec

N ew France capitulated to Britain in 1760, bringing almost two centuries of slow but steady French colonial development and settlement to the brink of oblivion. Most of the remaining French administrators, military people, and some clergy boarded ships under the watchful eye of British soldiers, and retreated to France.

The battles fought in North America during the 1740s and 1750s were important scenes in a world-wide conflict between Britain and France and their respective allies. As such, France chose its military and economic priorities, and New France unfortunately emerged toward the bottom of the list. Many French citizens shared Voltaire's view that New France was merely a "few acres of snow," so why pour in more resources? Thus soldiers, habitants, officials, and virtually everyone else in New France made do with less and bitterly begged France for more support. The only people who did well at the time were those involved with intendant Bigot's manipulation of colonial supplies. It was not an easy time, economically, militarily, or socially.

Barrin de la Galissonière (1693–1756) made a substantial and pragmatic contribution to the defense of New France, and maintained an optimism about the colony's future success. He used his connections to rise rapidly through the ranks, becoming captain in the French navy in 1738. Assigned to New France, he reluctantly agreed to act as interim governor from May to September of 1747. He wanted Acadians living in British Nova Scotia to withdraw to Isle Royale (Cape Breton Island), and to expand the network of forts deep in the Ohio country. Because networks of native allies were vital to the French, he ordered more generous trade with them to ensure their loyalty. He also worried about the strain on every facet of New France, and how badly the colony needed reinforcement and money. The French government in 1749 ordered him to begin secret settlement negotiations with the British — indicative of how much support he might get from the mother country. In preparation he wrote a report, including the following document, which recommended France retain all its North American possessions. The talks came to naught, but he continued his rise through the ranks to rear admiral in 1750, and then lieutenant general in 1755.

François Daine (1695?–1765) descended from a long line of bureaucrats and acted as subdelegate to the intendant of New France. Historians do not know when he arrived in New France, but by 1715 he was a local clerk, and became chief clerk to the Sovereign Council in 1722. A devoted civil servant, he remained loyal to his administration through the grimmest years of the war, not leaving until a year after France officially lost its colony in 1763.

Louis-Joseph de Montcalm (1712–1759) was born into the French aristocracy, and his close connections to the king won him a commission in the French army at age nine — without becoming an active soldier for another eleven years. He later distinguished himself in battle, and rose to the rank of brigadier by 1747. Few French aristocrats chose to serve in New France, unless they needed hideaways from creditors, but Montcalm obeyed when transferred and promoted to major-general on March 11, 1756. This title still made him subordinate to the governor, Pierre de Rigaud de Vaudreuil. The two had opposite personalities and bickered from the start. Montcalm, an arrogant and aloof European, insisted that New France fight according to gentlemanly European rules — offensively and defensively. He treated habitants and first nations people with contempt, though he took to calling the latter "my children." Vaudreuil, on the other hand, grasped the virtues of guerrilla warfare, of using natives and habitants in battle, and understood that an aggressive offensive campaign might make Britain think twice before tackling Canada.

Montcalm regularly disobeyed Vaudreuil and sent endless petitions to Paris. He demanded to be made governor general, or at least gain promotion. He wanted a raise to cover his expenses which were too high — although he and his professional soldiers received double the militia's salary. He even asked for a recall, citing poor health and financial ruin. Montcalm had valid complaints. As inflation reached epic proportions, the intendant Bigot and his associates filled their pockets with state funds just when New France needed every livre. All was not defeatist grumbling, however, and Montcalm did score important military victories against the British, particularly at Carillon in 1758. A combination of this and his persistent complaints presumably jarred France into promoting him to lieutenant general in 1758, the second highest rank in the French army. That helped little in his final field of battle: he died from wounds sustained on the Plains of Abraham.

Michel-Jean-Hughes Péan (1723?–1782) proved that justice occasionally occurs, even among the elite. He too rose rapidly through the ranks of the French army, and held an officer's commission in the colonial regular troops by the time of the Conquest. Born in New France, he quickly established himself as an opportunistic middleman on the crooked road to riches. He naturally sought a lucrative alliance with the intendant, Bigot. The two made fortunes by trading goods that France had sent as gifts for its native allies. He wisely fled for France in 1760 before life became too difficult, both militarily and as a result of numerous complaints against him. The law finally caught up with him after a long-overdue investigation. Arrested in 1761, he faced nine years of banishment and a restitution bill of 600,000 livres.

Capellis' life remains a mystery. We know only that he was a highly placed official in the French Ministry of the Marine. Nothing is known of the life of the French civil servant, M. de Beaucat, and an unknown author penned the document "Memoir on Canada." But from their reports one can see that French government officials were obviously sharply divided in their assessments of Canada.

The previous documents detail the military, economic, and political affairs of New France in the final years, but what of people living outside the military and bureaucratic sphere? How did the war affect their lives? Unfortunately, most habitants busied themselves staying alive and consequently left no record of their thoughts. Sister Marie de la Visitation, however, offers us at least a glimpse of this turbulent and very frightening time from a civilian perspective. No peasant, she did, however, come into regular contact with the general population of New France, and was sympathetic to their plight. Her father was a highly decorated soldier and seigneur, and her mother an outstanding business-woman in the colony. Historians know little of her life except that she was born before 1736, and that she served as mother superior of the general hospital for nine years. A published version of her account appeared in 1826.

A) Memoir on the French Colonies in North America, 1750
Barrin de la Galissonière

Article 1st. Of the Utility of Colonies and the Necessity
of Attending to their Preservation

It is not proposed to dwell on the Utility of Colonies. There are few persons at this day who do not admit that they are in some degree necessary to a great State.

If any doubt on this point still exists in men's minds, it would suffice, in order to remove it, to cast an eye on the accounts of the revenue of the King's farms, the immense quantity of all sorts of commodities and manu-factures sent to the Colonies, the returns which come from them, some whereof are necessary to manufactures, others to wants which have become habitual, and in some degree indispensable, in the Kingdom; finally, on the surplus exported to foreign countries, and which contribute essentially to make the balance of wealth incline in favor of France: objects which be-come daily more interesting, according as each State forms new projects in order to dispense with the products and manufactures of its neighbours ...

Article 2nd. Objections against the Preservation of Canada and Louisiana.

It may be objected that we must carefully preserve such of the Colonies as are a source of revenue to the State and of wealth to the Kingdom, as St. Domingo, Martinico and the other Tropical Islands; but that those Colonies, which, far from being productive of revenue or wealth, are, like Canada and Louisiana, an expense, ought to be abandoned to themselves ...

1st. Their immense extent often prevents their being ruled by the same mind, and able to afford each other that assistance they mutually stand in need of.

2nd. They cannot send nor receive anything except by sea, and by the mouths of two rivers more than nine hundred leagues distant, whatever course be taken. The interior of the country is liable to be exposed to great scarcity of goods from France and to be glutted with its own products should a maritime power, such as England, undertake to blockade the only two outlets of that vast Continent.

3rd. It is not even impossible for that power, or some other, to seize on the lower part of one, or of both, rivers, and erect forts there, which would, doubtless, most seriously jeopardize these two Colonies.

4th. Although these Colonies may be able to furnish Europe and the Islands of America with the same commodities as New England, we must not flatter ourselves that they can ever do so cheaply, especially those of great bulk which ordinarily constitute the principal and most certain objects of trade: the difference arising from the difficulty of navigating both rivers, from the length of the voyages, and from the inability of going to Canada except at a certain season of the year, whilst it prolongs the voyage and renders it more expensive and difficult, and increases its dangers, augments, at the same time, the rate of insurance.

5th. If this be not an inconvenience in time of peace, and on the contrary, it may, perhaps, be an advantage that these two Colonies should not be able to dispense with France as well for clothing and liquors as for powder and arms; such is not the case in time of war. The apprehension of a scarcity obliges a large stock to kept continually on hand; independent of the current expense, which is considerable, we are necessarily obliged to make very large advances.

6th. The expenses of the Colonies not only exceed, and will continue for a long time greatly to surpass, their revenue, but they are very unequal and subject to forced augmentations, especially in time of war, when the want of the Indians renders it necessary to gain these over by force of presents ...

Article 3rd. Of the Importance and Necessity of Preserving Canada and Louisiana.

Motives of honor, glory and religion forbid the abandonment of an established Colony; the surrender to themselves, or rather to a nation inimical by taste, education and religious principle, of the French who have emigrated thither at the persuasion of the Government with the expectation of its protection, and who eminently deserve it on account of their fidelity and attachment; in time, the giving up of so salutary a work as that of the conversion of the heathen who inhabit that vast Continent.

Yet we shall not insist on these motives; and how great soever may be the inconveniences set forth in the preceding article, neither will we object to them, the future and uncertain revenues both of Canada and Louisiana, although, nevertheless, these are extremely probable, since they have for basis an immense country, a numerous people, fertile lands, forests of mulberry trees, mines already discovered, &c.

... We ask if a country can be abandoned, no matter how bad it may be, or what the amount of expense necessary to sustain it, when by its position it affords a great advantage over its neighbours.

This is precisely the case of Canada: it cannot be denied that this Colony has been always a burden to France, and it is probable that such will be the case for a long while; but it constitutes, at the same time, the strongest barrier that can be opposed to the ambition of the English.

We may dispense with giving any other proofs of this than the constant efforts they have made, for more than a century, against that Colony.

We will add, however, that it alone is in a position to wage war against them in all their possessions on the Continent of America; possessions which are as dear to them as they are precious in fact, whose power is daily increasing, and which, if means be not found to prevent it, will soon absorb not only all the Colonies located in the neighbouring islands of the Tropic, but even all those of the Continent of America.

Long experience has proved that the preservation of the major portion of the settlements in the Tropical islands is not owing so much to their intrinsic strength, as to the difficulty of conveying troops thither from Europe in sufficient numbers to subjugate or keep them, and of supporting such troops there; but if the rapid progress of the English Colonies on the Continent be not arrested, or what amounts to the same thing, if a counterpoise capable of confining them within their limits, and of forcing them to the defensive, be not formed, they will possess, in a short time, such great facilities to construct formidable armaments on the Continent of America, and will require so little time to convey a large force either to St. Domingo or to the Island of Cuba, or to our Windward islands, that it will not be possible to hope to preserve these except at an enormous expense.

This will not be the case if we make a more energetic and generous effort to increase and strengthen Canada and Louisiana, than the English are making in favor of their Colonies; since the French Colonies, despite their destitute condition, have always waged war against the English of the Continent with some advantage, though the latter are, and always have been, more numerous; it is necessary to explain here the causes to which this has been owing.

The first is the great number of alliances that the French keep up with the Indian Nations. These people, who hardly act except from instinct, love us hitherto a little, and fear us a great deal, more than they do the English; but their interest, which some among them begin to understand, is that the strength of the English and French remain nearly equal, so that through the jealousy of these two nations those tribes may live independent of, and draw presents from, both.

The second reason of our superiority over the English is, the number of French Canadians who are accustomed to live in the woods like the Indians, and become thereby not only qualified to lead them to fight the English, but to wage war even against these same Indians when necessity oblige.

Hence 'twill be seen that this superiority of the French in America is in some sort accidental, and if they neglect to maintain it, whilst the English are making every effort to destroy it, 'twill pass into the hands of the latter. There is not doubt but such an event would be followed by the entire destruction of our settlements in that part of the Globe.

This, however serious it may seem, would not be our only loss; it would drag after it that of the superiority which France must claim over England.

If anything can, in fact, destroy the superiority of France in Europe, it is the Naval force of the English …

We must not flatter ourselves with being able long to sustain an expenditure equal to theirs; no other resource remains then but to attack them in their possessions; that cannot be effected by forces sent from Europe except with little hope of success, and at vast expense, whilst by fortifying ourselves in America and husbanding means in the Colonies themselves, the advantages we possess can be preserved, and even increased at a very trifling expense, in comparison with the cost of expeditions fitted out in Europe.

The utility of Canada is not confined to the preservation of the French Colonies, and to rendering the English apprehensive for theirs; that Colony is not less essential for the conservation of the Spanish possessions in America, especially of Mexico.

So long as that barrier is well secured; so long as the English will be unable to penetrate it; so long as efforts will be made to increase its strength, 'twill serve as a rampart to Louisiana, which hitherto sustains itself only under the shadow of the forces of Canada, and by the connection of the Canadians with the Indians ...

In fine, Canada, the fertility whereof is wonderful, can serve as the granary of the Tropical Colonies, which, in consequence of the men they destroy, sell their rich products very dear. It is proved that the number of Canadians who die in these Colonies that are admitted to be the most unhealthy, is much less than that of European French.

All that precedes sufficiently demonstrates that it is of the utmost importance and of absolute necessity not to omit any means, nor spare any expense to secure Canada, inasmuch as that is the only way to wrest America from the ambition of the English, and as the progress of their empire in that quarter of the globe is what is most capable of contributing to their superiority in Europe ...

Article 5th. Of the French Posts in the Gulf of St. Lawrence;
of Île Royale and Acadia.

The loss of Acadia has necessitated a very particular attention to be paid to Île Royale, where Louisbourg has been built and fortified. Acadia constituted, formerly, a part of Canada, and is doubtless one of the most serious losses we have experienced at the peace of Utrecht. The establishment of Louisbourg, with a view to repair that loss as much as possible, is but a feeble recompense.

'Tis universally admitted by all those acquainted with the locality, and cannot be too often repeated, that if Canada does not take Acadia at the beginning of the next war, Acadia will take, or cause the fall of Louisbourg.

It is not, however, to be concluded, as many seem to have done in the last war, that the preservation of Canada depends absolutely on Louisbourg. It has been proved that Canada could sustain herself without that place; but 'tis no less true that it is of great advantage to her in time of war.

The simple view of the position of Louisbourg dispenses with entering into any detail in this regard; but if it be evidently useful to New, it is no less so to Old, France both in time of war and of peace.

The harbours of Île Royale, especially that of Louisbourg, are most favourably situated as a place at which vessels may touch on their return from long voyages, also as a retreat for privateers and a point whence they can have an opportunity of destroying the enemy's trade, inasmuch as on leaving that port they are almost on the track of all the rich ships of the world.

In fine, it is, next to Acadia, the best adapted situation for the fishery; a branch of trade as useful on account of the money it saves to and brings in the Kingdom, as well as on account of the great number of seamen it employs, exercises, accustoms to labor without exposing them to acute and mortal diseases; an advantage not enjoyed by the rich Colonies of the Tropics ...

Nothing is more essential to the preservation of Île Royale than to secure for it the means of communication with Canada, and to spare no pains to establish entrepôts of provisions, and especially of cattle as well in Île Royale itself, though there cannot be either considerable or sufficient in the land of St. John (which is better adapted for that purpose), and in that part of Canada bordering on the Gulf of St. Lawrence.

There is a part of the year when there is no communication between Louisbourg and Canada by the River St. Lawrence, and no route practicable except by way of the River St. John ...

Article 6th. Of the Canadian Posts Inland.

The interior of Canada is traversed by the River St. Lawrence, and the Lakes which supply the waters of that great stream.

Its navigation and trade can be interrupted more easily than people suppose. That facility, which a powerful maritime enemy can possess, is one of the greatest misfortunes of Canada; a partial remedy only can be applied to it, by building one or two forts at Gaspé and the Seven Islands, under the cover of which vessels may retreat, but the true remedy would be, to place the Colony generally in a position to overawe those in the possession of England, and to make her fear war in America.

We shall not speak of the naval expedition the enemy might be able to make for the conquest of Canada. Though they should succeed, which could not be the case except by a very rare combination of circumstances in their favor, we do not think they would find it easy to retain that place even one minute.

But should they continue to increase the strength of their Colonies, and should the French Colonies not advance in the same proportion, 'tis not to be doubted but the former will soon be in a condition to lay Canada waste nearly to Montreal, and even to pillage the latter place, which would render the French as despicable in that country as they are now respected here, and terminate shortly in their entire ruin ...

What has been observed already in the course of this Memoir, when treating of the utility of Canada in regard to the preservation of Mexico, shows the absolute necessity of the free and certain communication from Canada to the Mississippi. This chain, once broken, would leave an opening of which the English would doubtless take advantage to get nearer the silver mines. Many of their writings are full of this project, which will never amount to anything but a chimera, if France retain her Canadian possessions ...

Continuing the same route and the same views, the post deserving of most attention next to Detroit, or concurrently with it, is that of Illinois.

Here the climate is almost altogether changed; we are no longer exposed to the rigors of a seven months' winter, nor obliged, as in the neighbourhood of Quebec, to make ruinous clearance for the purpose of improving very poor lands. Beyond the banks of the river, the entire country is open, and waiting only for the plough; there are, already, some settlers supplied with a pretty good stock of cattle, but nothing in comparison with what they could accommodate. Moreover, these vast prairies, which, in various directions, extend as far as several hundred leagues beyond the River Superior, and covered with an innumerable multitude of buffaloes, a species which will probably not run out for many centuries hence, both because the country is not sufficiently peopled to make their consumption perceptible, and because the hides, not being adapted to the same uses as those of the European race, it will never happen that the animals will be killed solely for the sake of their skins, as is the practice among the Spaniards of the River de la Plata.

If the Illinois buffaloes do not supply the tanneries with much, eventually, advantages at least equivalent may reasonably be expected, on which we cannot prevent ourselves dwelling for a moment.

1st These animals are covered with a species of wool, sufficiently fine to be employed in various manufactures, as experience has demonstrated.

2nd It can scarcely be doubted that by catching them young and gelding them, they would be adapted to ploughing; perhaps, even, they would possess the same advantage that horses have over domestic oxen, that is, superior swiftness; they appear to be as strong, but perhaps are indebted for this to wild breeding; in other respects, they do not seem difficult to tame; a 4 or 5 year old Bull and Cow have been seen that were extremely gentle.

3rd Were the Illinois country sufficiently well settled to admit of the people inclosing a great number of these animals in parks, some of them might be salted, a business susceptible of being extended very considerably, without Illinois possessing a large population for that purpose. This trade would perhaps enable us to dispense with Irish beef for Martinico, and even to compete with the English, and at a lower rate, for the supply of the Spanish Colonies ...

For this purpose the resolution ought to be adopted to send a great many people to New France, in order to enable those who have the administration thereof, to work at the same time at the different proposed posts.

These people ought to be principally soldiers, who can in a very short time be converted into good settlers ...

B) To Marshal de Belle Isle, Département de la Guerre, Paris, from Quebec, 19 May 1758
François Daine

My Lord,

Nothing is more melancholy or more afflicting than the actual condition of this Colony, after having passed a part of last autumn and winter on a quarter of a pound of bread per person a day, we are reduced, these six weeks past, to two ounces. This country has subsisted, up to the present time, only by the wise and prudent economy of our Intendant, but all resources are exhausted and we are on the eve of the most cruel famine, unless the succors which we are expecting from our monarch's bounty and liberality arrive within fifteen days at farthest.

I am at a loss for terms to describe our misfortunes. The supply of animals is beginning to fail; the butchers cannot furnish a quarter of the beef necessary for the subsistence of the inhabitants of this town, though they pay an exorbitant price for it; without fowls, vegetables, mutton or veal, we are on the eve of dying of hunger.

To make up for the want of bread, beef and other necessaries of life, our Intendant has ordered 12 or 1500 horses to be purchased; these he has had distributed among the poor of this town at a rate much below what they cost the King. He is now having distributed among the same poor, a quarter of a pound of pork, and half a pound of cod fish a day, but that cannot last long. The mechanics, artisans and day-laborers exhausted by hunger, absolutely cannot work any longer; they are so feeble that 'tis with difficulty they can sustain themselves.

We have not yet any news from Europe, and are ignorant of the projects of the English on this continent. We have learned only by 2 Indians belonging to the Five Nations, who have been to trade with the English near Fort Bull, that Mr. Jeanson, who was there, had told them that we were without provisions and would not receive any succors from France this year, in consequence of the measures adopted by the Court of London to intercept them; that a formidable fleet would blockade the river, and that none of our ships would be able to pass; they had last fall captured three of them from us richly laden; that as regarded themselves, they enjoyed abundance of everything and were preparing to visit their village for the purpose of conveying rich presents thither, and that the Indians should not want for anything if they would abandon the French ...

Our situation becomes more and more unfortunate and we are actually, my Lord, on the eve of perishing of hunger. Bread will cease to be furnished to the public on the first of June ...

C) Memoir, 1758
M. de Capellis

France is not able to populate a country as vast as Canada.

Until today, this colony has produced little for the state in time of peace, for reasons which I cannot go into in this memoir, and has cost enormous sums for more than ten years. The money spent on that colony which the King is about to lose represents the greater part of the funds allotted to the navy. If the money had been used to build vessels and to establish solidly our maritime forces, we would have been respected and even feared by our enemies, who seem inclined to flout us. We can, then, cede this land to England, but here is what we should ask for in return, and I dare say that the King will not lose in the exchange ...

The colony of St. Domingue has produced for the state in peacetime over twenty million livres annually. This amount can be doubled and some day may even exceed fifty million livres. Can we ever hope that Canada will sell that much to France? ... The island of Newfoundland will provide us with abundant fisheries ... France would derive an immense profit from the sale of salted fish for which she could find markets in Spain, Italy, and in part of Germany. The fisheries are also a nursery of seamen, and that is perhaps their greatest value. The more extensive our fisheries become, the more sailors we will have. This class of men can never become too numerous ... It has also been said that there are beavers in the interior of the island and I have no reason to doubt this ... It can also be assumed that the lands in the interior are covered by immense forests, which would provide wood for masts and planks ... We could also extract pitch, tar, and resin ... We might eventually draw from Newfoundland what we presently import from northern Europe ...

The advantages that the King's subjects would derive from the establishment of Newfoundland and from the cession of the Spanish part of St. Domingue would be far greater than those which the English would obtain from the cession of a part of Canada. I even dare advance that the island of Newfoundland and half of St. Domingue are worth much more than all of Canada; and I do not believe that we should hesitate to give it up entirely to obtain the other two establishments.

D) To Marshal de Belle Isle, Montreal, 12 April 1759
Louis-Joseph de Montcalm

Canada will be taken this campaign, and assuredly during the next, if there be not some unforeseen good luck, a powerful diversion by sea against the English Colonies, or some gross blunders on the part of the enemy.

The English have 60,000 men, we at most from 10 to 11,000. Our government is good for nothing; money and provisions will fail. Through want of provisions, the English will begin first; the farms scarcely tilled, cattle lack; the Canadians are dispirited; no confidence in M. de Vaudreuil or in M. Bigot. M. de Vaudreuil is incapable of preparing a plan of operations. He has no activity; he lends his confidence to empirics rather than to the General sent by the King. M. Bigot appears occupied only in making a large fortune for himself, his adherents and sycophants. Cupidity has seized officers, store-keepers; the commissaries also who are about the River St. John, or the Ohio, or with the Indians in the Upper country, are amassing astonishing fortunes. It is nothing but forged certificates legally admitted. If the Indians had a fourth of what is supposed to be expended for them, the King would have all those in America; the English none.

This interest has an influence on the war. M. de Vaudreuil, with whom men are equal, led by a knavish secretary and interested associates, would confide a vast operation to his brother, or any other Colonial officer, the same as to Chevalier de Levis. The choice concerns those who divide the cake; therefore has there never been any desire to send M. de Bourlamaque, or M. de Senezergues, commandant of the battalion of La Sarre, to Fort Duquesne. I did propose it; the King had gained by it; but what superintendents in a country, whose humblest cadet, a sergeant, a gunner, return with twenty, thirty thousand livres in certificates, for goods issued for the Indians on account of his Majesty.

This expenditure, which has been paid at Quebec by the Treasurer of the Colony, amounts to twenty-four millions. The year before, the expenses amounted only to twelve or thirteen millions. This year they will run up to thirty-six. Everybody appears to be in a hurry to make his fortune before the Colony is lost, which event many, perhaps, desire, as an impenetrable veil over their conduct. The craving after wealth has an influence on the war, and M. de Vaudreuil does not doubt it. Instead of reducing the expenses of Canada, people wish to retain all; how abandon positions which serve as a pretext to make private fortunes? Transportation is distributed to favorites. The agreement with the contractor is unknown to me as it is to the public. 'Tis reported that those who have invaded commerce participate in it. Has the King need of purchasing goods for the Indians? Instead of buying them directly, a favorite is notified, who purchases at any price whatever; then M. Bigot has them removed to the King's stores, allowing a profit of one hundred and even one hundred and fifty percent, to those who it is desired to favor. Is artillery to be transported, gun-carriages, carts, implements to be made? M. Mercier, commandant of the artillery, is the contractor under other people's names. Everything is done badly and at a high price. This officer, who came out twenty years ago a simple soldier, will be soon worth about six or seven hundred thousand livres, perhaps a million, if these things continue. I have often respectfully spoken to M. de Vaudreuil and M. Bigot of these expenses; each throws the blame on his colleague. The people alarmed at these expenses, fear a depreciation in the paper money of the country; the evil effect is, the Canadians who do not participate in those illicit profits, hate the Government. They repose confidence in the General of the French; accordingly, what consternation on a ridiculous rumor which circulated this winter that he had been poisoned ...

If the war continue, Canada will belong to the English, perhaps this very campaign, or the next. If there be peace, the Colony is lost, if the entire government be not changed ...

The general census of Canada has been at last completed. Though it has not been communicated to me, I think I'm correct, that there are not more than 82,000 souls in the Colony; of these, twelve thousand, at most, are men capable of bearing arms; deducting from this number those employed in works, transports, bateaux, in the Upper countries, no more than seven thousand Canadians will ever be collected together, and then it must not be either seed time or harvest, otherwise, by calling all out, the ground would remain uncultivated; famine would follow. Our eight battalions will make three thousand two hundred men; the Colonials, at most, fifteen hundred men in the field. What is that against at least fifty thousand men which the English have!

E) Memoir on the Condition of Canada
Michel-Jean-Hughes Péan

.... in the month of August last, the Colony remained in the most critical situation; the farmers, after having furnished the last bushel of their wheat for the subsistence of the troops which were marching against the enemy, were supporting themselves only by the aid of some vegetables and wild herbs; eighteen months ago the people, without excepting a single officer, had to be reduced to four ounces of bread a day; they have been reduced of late to two ounces only. During the winter it had become necessary to deprive the troops of bread, and to subsist them on beef, horseflesh and codfish.

The provisions brought by several ships during the year have been immediately forwarded to the armies, but Quebec has always remained in its melancholy situation.

Yet, people have to defend themselves at Carillon against thirty thousand men; against ten thousand at Fort Duquesne and against six thousand towards Chouaguen. The capture of Louisbourg, the settlements pretended to have been made by the English at Gaspé and on the Island of Anticosty, at the entrance of the Gulf of St. Lawrence, have rendered the situation of Canada much more afflicting, but the late misfortune experienced at Fort Frontenac by the Colony, is the most prejudicial of those it has been threatened with, and 'twill run the greatest risks if that fort be not retaken, as it served as an entrepôt for all the King's forts and Indian posts, and as the English will close all the passages. Then, the Indians, who constitute our principal force, finding themselves deprived of all they want, by failure of the succors the French would furnish them, will not fail to go over to the English, and will come and scalp at the very gates of the towns in which the people will be obliged to shut themselves up.

'Twill probably cost a great many men and much money to retake that fort, but it is of such great necessity for the preservation of Canada, that 'tis impossible to dispense with making every effort to retake it.

The harvest is reported very bad, and we must not be surprised at that, if we observe that all the farmers have been obliged to march to oppose the efforts of the enemy.

'Tis therefore to be presumed that this Colony is about to be exposed to much more serious suffering than it has experienced in preceding years, during which people have been under the necessity of consuming all the cattle.

Many persons have died of hunger, and the number would have been much greater had the King not subsisted a greater part of the people.

The land in Canada is in general, very good, and has often supplied in time of peace, provisions to other colonies, and almost always to Isle Royale; but not having had the good fortune to participate in the last peace, and being forced since fifteen years into continual war, which has employed almost all the farmers, the land could not be cultivated, and the failure of the crops which has ensued, has augmented so considerably the price of provisions and rendered them so excessively dear, that the officer can no longer subsist there without running considerably in debt; this is not the case with the soldier to whom too considerable an allowance, and one too expensive to the King has been made.

'Tis certain that Canada will, next year, have to fight more than sixty thousand men, as the English have just sent thither additional troops; no more than fifteen to eighteen thousand men can be employed in its defence, because many will be required for conveyance of provisions and ammunition, in consequence of the difficulty of the roads and the distance of the different posts.

Supposing the English are not yet at Gaspé, we may rest assured that they will seize it in the spring, and then they will be able to impede the navigation so much, that 'tis to be feared they will capture the greater portion of the succors which will be on the way to Quebec.

F) Mémoire sur le Canada, 1759
M. de Beaucat

There are about 60,000 inhabitants in Canada, 180,000 acres of farmland, and 20,000 of pasture. The annual crop, on the average, consists of 400,000 bushels of wheat, 5,000 of corn, 130,000 of oats, 3,000 of barley, 6,000 of peas, 100,000 quintals of tobacco, 120,000 of flax, and 5,000 of hemp.

The value of beaver and other types of pelts does not exceed 1,500,000 livres. The seal fisheries are of very little account.

Canada has very little timber that is suited for construction, and it is very greasy. A few frigates and vessels are built there at costs that are as great as those that prevail in France. Furthermore, those ships do not last half as long as those built in Europe.

In years of drought the crops fail and we are obliged to send flour to Canada. The trade of this colony is so slight that in 1755, when colonial commerce was in a most flourishing state, sixty vessels were dispatched from France and over half of these had to return by way of St. Domingue to find cargo for their return voyage. In passing, we might note that this island has only 18,000 settlers, but its trade is so great that it occupies 400 vessels of 500 tons.

The cost of maintaining troops in the Canadian forts is also very great.

... All of Canada is covered by a thick blanket of snow during half the year, and the Gulf of St. Lawrence is impassable during that time. The settlers are confined to their houses and only venture outdoors to hunt or to exchange a few pelts with the Indians. On this colony have we spent men and money in such great quantities! The Canadians are brave, vigorous, and active, but they lack the means of enriching themselves by commerce or agriculture. They live from day to day, so to speak, and in time of war are exposed either to dying of hunger or at least to doing without the most basic necessities of life.

G) Memoir on Canada
Unknown

First Question

Is it of importance to preserve Canada?

There have been, from all time, people who have thought, and perhaps there are some still who are of opinion, that the preservation of Canada is of little importance to France. Some allege that it costs the King a great deal, and that it will eventually cost more; that it yields nothing, or next to nothing; that, in 1755, 1756, 1757 and 1758, probably more than fifteen millions have been expended yearly, which might have been better employed in the centre of the Kingdom. Others say that the Kingdom, which is itself stripped of people, is being depopulated to settle a country which is extremely rough, full of lakes and forests, frequently subject to the greatest scarcities; that there are within the Kingdom good lands which remain uncultivated; that the Indian trade is little worth; that, so far from increasing, it will always diminish, as the trade in peltries cannot last a century; they add, that the Canadian voyages are long, fatiguing and dangerous.

Finally, the third pretend that, in all the wars we shall have with the English, Canada will be taken, at least in part; that t'will always be the cause of preventing France, at the peace, preserving European conquests. Besides, that when Canada will be well settled, it will be exposed to many revolutions; is it not natural that Kingdoms and Republics will be formed there, which will separate from France? ...

1st. It is certain that if France abandon Canada, heresy will establish itself there; Nations known and unknown, will remain in Paganism or adopt the religion of England. How many souls eternally lost! This reflection may strike a Christian Prince.

2nd. France possesses, in North America, more territory than is contained in the European continent. Its riches are not yet known; the best spots are not yet settled; the King's glory seems to require that so extensive a country be preserved notwithstanding the immense expenditure incurred there; it is always painful to behold the enemy aggrandizing themselves at our expense; besides, these expenses might considerably diminish; and, after all, this object is not so remarkable in times of peace; it would even be easy for those who are acquainted with finance to demonstrate that the trade and consumption of goods which is going on in Canada, produces for the King in time of peace, much more than is expended. This is the place where general reasons might be adduced to prove that it is of importance to a state to possess Colonies. 'Tis wrong to object, that it is depopulating the kingdom. One year of European war causes the loss of more men than would be required to people New France. It might be complained that no care has ever been taken to increase its population; that might be easily done now in a perceptible manner, because the Colony begins to grow in numbers. How many thousands of useless men within the heart of the Kingdom and in other states! Every year the English are transporting into foreign parts a great number of families whom they encourage to settle in New England. Were New France peopled, there is no country so easy of preservation; naval forces essentially necessary to Old France, would guard Acadia, Louisbourg; and it may be asserted that if Canada be lost to France the latter will require a larger naval force than ever, because the English will become absolute masters of the sea ...

3rd. Supposing, in fact, that Canada will never be of much use to France; that it will cost even a trifle, must it be reckoned as nothing, the preventing a rival nation aggrandizing itself, establishing, on the seas, a despotic empire and monopolizing all the trade?

The English, once masters of Canada, will necessarily take Louisiana and the Islands, because, being no longer disturbed by the Canadians, they will direct all their weight against the Islands, which are an object of importance for France. For the same reason it may be relied on, that the English will soon wrest New Mexico from Spain, and Portugal may truly be affected by it.

Our immense forests, our vast prairies, once in the hands of the English, will carry abundance everywhere, and facilitate forever the construction of all the ships they will desire.

Were it only the codfishery, this would be an object of infinite importance and which we should lose. Of all commerce, this is the richest, the easiest, the least expensive and the most extensive. As early as 1696, the trade of the Island of Newfoundland alone amounted yearly to 15 millions. Canada once taken, all the fishing ground must be renounced.

Without knowing all the branches of trade which is and can be carried on throughout New France, it may be said that if the King lose that country, the commerce of England will soon be augmented more than 150 millions.

A thousand other reflections present themselves to the mind, but it is unnecessary to abuse the patience of those who will read this Memoir.

Second Question

Should the war continue in 1759, will Canada be able to defend herself?

The number of men in that Colony bearing arms has perhaps been exaggerated. I dare assert that there are not fifteen thousand of them, but at least eleven thousand must be deducted from that number for the reasons following:

1. We must strike off 4,000, to wit: the old men, those necessary in the country, the sick, the husbands of sick women, the servants of the parish

priests, the sextons, those who hide themselves to avoid being called out, those who find means to be exempted, the pilots for navigating the river, sailors for a great many sloops and bateaux, those at outposts, who watch the signal fires day and night.

It is, in general, doing much to levy more than two-thirds of the men.

2. Of the eleven thousand men to be levied, nearly 1,000 must necessarily be deducted for the Upper and Lower posts, and usually these are the best; it would be easy to enumerate them.

3. 1,500 mechanics of different sorts, carpenters for bateaux, artillery work, blacksmiths, gate-keepers, cartmen in the towns, must also be deducted; again add to these, 1,500 domestics for the officers, the town's people, necessary couriers, clerks, writers.

4. Again, 3,000 men must be employed for the transportation of provisions, utensils and all the necessaries for the camps.

We have 4,000 leagues of country to preserve; we have scarcely 78 settled; the current must be surmounted, the wind is oftenest contrary; sloops are frequently a month going up to Montreal ...

Add to this, that we have in Canada scarcely 5 months of the year suitable for transportation.

It follows that, supposing eleven thousand men could be raised in Canada, 4,000 only of them will be fit to fight, the others being occupied elsewhere, and, in fact, they are perhaps never met in the camps.

The 8 battalions of French Regulars, the forty companies of the Marine, hardly form a corps of 6,000 men; 'tis a great deal, still, to add two thousand fighting Indians.

I ask now, if it be possible for twelve thousand men to resist the enemy's army, which certainly amount to sixty thousand men ...

I refer to the last question what regards our scarcity of provisions and liquors and presents for the Indians. I will not say that there is every prospect that no ploughing will be done this year, that the enemy will prevent this and the putting in seed the early part of spring.

Third Question

Is it easy for France to relieve Canada in 1759?

Troops and provisions are required; all must arrive in May; the examination of this article will point out the difficulty.

It is not too much to demand an augmentation of eight thousand troops. On arriving at Quebec, they will probably be reduced, by death or disease, to 6,000; consequently, we shall have only 18,000 to oppose against 60 thousand. Is this too much? Is it sufficient? The situation of the country must be relied on, and calculations made on the mistakes of the enemy.

Men-of-war or merchantmen are necessary for conveying 8,000 men; if the former be employed, 300 on board each, exclusive of the crew, is a liberal allowance; 27 ships will be required; if merchantmen, they will carry only 200, and 40 of them will be necessary; but will it be possible to dispense with having them convoyed by ships of the Line, Isle Royale and Gaspé being actually in the hands of the English?

The Contractor-General of Canada demands 40 ships for his share alone, but how many of these will be intercepted? 20 at least will be required by the merchants; here are at once 100 ships of 300 tons required, exclusive of those which are to carry the munitions of war; still more are necessary for the conveyance of provisions, for though the harvest be good, it is not sufficient for the Colony and for extra mouths. This has been proved in 1756.

The difficulty of transportation in Canada occasions a great consumption of provisions by pure loss, and it is impossible to remedy it; the necessity of employing Indians is another occasion of wasteful consumption. A party of Indians [is sent] to make prisoners, with 15 days' provisions; it returns at the end of 8 days victorious, or without striking a blow; it has consumed everything and demands provisions. How are they to be refused? Another inevitable abuse: Our domiciliated Indians are unwilling to go to fight unless we feed their women and children, so that if you have 2,000 Indians, it will require provisions at least for 6,000. It is not flour alone that is wanting, the Colony is very bare of oxen and sheep, and at the close of 1759, hardly any will be found for refreshments for the troops or the ships, and 'tis certain, if the war continue, the Colony will be obliged to live on salt meat, which will have to be imported from France, and in that case what a number of ships will be required. Finally, supposing France could furnish all those vessels, will they arrive in sufficient season? ... It is to be feared that they will meet the enemy on quitting France; some they will find about the roadsteads of Halifax; others will be about Louisbourg and Gaspé. Should those succors be sent altogether, a strong convoy will be required, and it will happen that many vessels will be separated by fogs and storms; it will happen that those ships will not be ready soon enough to sail together, and though they should be, their voyage will be a great deal longer. All these succors are necessary; can France furnish them? If an attempt be made to recover Louisbourg or Gaspé, or if any considerable diversion be made on the coasts of New England by a considerable fleet, then the whole of the succors I have enumerated may not be wanting; but has France ships and seamen? Enough for the seas of America and Europe.

Detached Thoughts

... It is almost impossible to retake Louisbourg; we possess no port in those seas; the enemy has, or will have, 8,000 men there, and doubtless after our example, will keep some ships of the line in that port.

Acadia is entirely ruined, stripped of all domestic animals; most of the inhabitants dead; 'twill cost immense sums to reestablish the few of them that remain ... Indeed, New England must be very weary of the wars our Indians are waging against it. It sees in its midst nearly 4,000 of its frontier families bewailing their kindred who have been massacred and whose properties have been laid waste. It knows that in taking Canada it will be rid of the cruelty of the Indians and enjoy forever the sweets of peace.

Quebec is not a strong place; all our hope depends on preventing the landing and having outside a flying camp of 4,000 men, to annoy the enemy in their march and during the siege; it is very improbable that the enemy is ignorant of the strength of the fleets which will be sent; 'tis natural that they will oppose stronger ones, especially as they can station them in the most advantageous ports.

To send succors in divisions is to run the risk of losing all in detail; to send them together, is to expose ourselves to a general action and to lose all at once; it is to expose oneself to a very long voyage ...

Canada has but one very narrow outlet, that is the gulf. If the English preserve Louisbourg and Acadia, 'twould be difficult to receive any relief by that way.

'Tis to be feared that the English will leave in New England 15 or 18 thousand Regulars, which they will, on declaring war, push suddenly into Canada; what means of resistance are there, if we do not keep up 8 or 10 thousand troops; but unfortunately the Colony will be unable to feed them except in the most abundant years, and supplies of provisions, all the implements and munitions of war necessary for 10,000 men, will be required from time to time from France. It will be necessary to think seriously of establishing granaries or magazines of reserve, on account of the scarcities which frequently overtake us.

The people of Canada must naturally be quite tired of the war, many have perished in it; they are burdened with the most harassing works, have not time to increase their property nor even to repair their houses; a portion of their subsistence has been wrested from them, many have been without bread for 3 months, the troops that incommode them are quartered on them, they have not throughout the year as much food as they think they need; they are told that the English will allow them freedom of religion, furnish them goods at a cheaper rate and pay liberally for the smallest service. These ideas are spreading. Some persons above the populace do not blush to speak in the same style; it is natural for the people to murmur and allow themselves to be seduced; the inhabitants of the cities will be the most easily debauched.

H) Narrative of the Doings During the Siege of Quebec, and the Conquest of Canada
Marie de la Visitation, Nun of the General Hospital of Quebec

My very reverend Mothers,

... The General Hospital is situated in the outer limits of Quebec, about half a mile from the walls.

The fire, from which our Sisters in Quebec have lately suffered, having rendered it impossible for them to continue their charge of the sick, Mr. Bigot, the Intendant of the country, proposed that we should receive them in our hospital. We readily agreed so to do; being desirous of rendering service and zealously fulfilling the duties of our calling, the Sisters lost no time in entering upon the sacred work. His Majesty, attentive to the wants of his subjects, and being informed of the preparations making by the English, did not fail to forward succour to the country, consisting in numerous vessels, laden with munitions of war and provisions, of which we were entirely destitute; and several regiments, who landed in a deplorable state, unfit for service, a great many men having died soon after. They were suffering from malignant fever. All the sick, officers and privates, were conveyed to our hospital, which was insufficient to contain them; we were therefore compelled to fill most parts of the building, even to the church, having obtained the permission of the late bishop Pontbriand, our illustrious prelate ...

Thereupon, the enemy, despairing of vanquishing us, ashamed to retreat, determined to fit out a formidable fleet, armed with all the artillery that the infernal regions could supply for the destruction of human kind. They displayed the British flag in the harbour of Quebec on the 24th May, 1759. On the receipt of intelligence of their arrival, our troops and militia came down from above. Our Generals left garrisons in the advanced posts, of which there is a great number above Montreal, in order to prevent the junction of their land forces, which it was understood were on the march, from Orange. Our Generals did not fail to occupy most points where the enemy might land; but they could not guard them all. The sickness suffered by our troops, lately from France, and the losses they sustained in two or three recent actions with the enemy, though victorious, weakened us considerably; and it became necessary to abandon Point Levi, directly opposite to and commanding Quebec. The enemy soon occupied it and constructed their batteries; which commenced firing on the 24th July, in a manner to excite the greatest alarm in our unfortunate Communities of religious ladies ...

The only rest we partook of, was during prayers, and still it was not without interruption from the noise of shells and shot, dreading every moment that they would be directed towards us. The red-hot shot and carcasses terrified those who attended the sick during the night. They had the affliction of witnessing the destruction of the houses of the citizens, many of our connexions being immediately interested therein. During one night, upwards of fifty of the best houses in the Lower Town were destroyed. The vaults containing merchandise and many precious articles, did not escape the effects of the artillery. During this dreadful conflagration, we could offer nothing but our tears and prayers at the foot of the altar at such moments as could be snatched from the necessary attention to the wounded.

In addition to these misfortunes, we had to contend with more than one enemy; famine, at all times inseparable from war, threatened to reduce us to the last extremity; upwards of six hundred persons in our building and vicinity, partaking of our small means of subsistence, supplied from the government stores, which were likely soon to be short of what was required for the troops. In the midst of this desolation, the Almighty, disposed to humble us, and to deprive us of our substance, which we had probably amassed contrary to his will, and with too great avidity, still mercifully preserved our lives, which were daily periled, from the present state of the country ...

The enemy, more cautious in their proceedings, on observing our army, hesitated in landing all their forces. We drove them from our redoubts, of which they had obtained possession. They became overwhelmed, and left the field strewed with killed and wounded. This action alone, had it been properly managed, would have finally relieved us from their invasion. We must not, however, attribute the mismanagement solely to our Generals; the Indian tribes, often essential to our support, became prejudicial to us on this occasion. Their hideous yells of defiance tended to intimidate our foes, who instead of meeting the onset, to which they had exposed themselves, precipitately retreated to their boats, and left us masters of the field. We charitably conveyed their wounded to our hospital, notwithstanding the fury and rage of the Indians, who, according [to] their cruel custom, sought to scalp them. Our army continued constantly ready to oppose the enemy. They dared not attempt a second landing; but ashamed of inaction, they took to burning the country places. Under shelter of darkness, they moved their vessels about seven or eight leagues above Quebec ...

After remaining in vain nearly three months at anchor in the Port, they appeared disposed to retire, despairing of success; but the Almighty, whose intentions are beyond our penetration, and always just, having resolved to subdue us, inspired the English Commander with the idea of making another attempt before his departure, which was done by surprise during the night. It was the intention, that night, to send supplies to a body of our troops forming an outpost of the heights near Quebec. A miserable deserter gave the information to the enemy, and persuaded them that it would be easy to surprise us, and pass their boats by using our countersign. They profited by the information, and the treasonable scheme succeeded. They landed on giving the password; our officer detected the deceit, but too late. He defended his post bravely with his small band, and was wounded. By this plan the enemy found themselves on the heights near the city. General de Montcalm, without loss of time, marched at the head of his army; but having to proceed about half a league, the enemy had time to bring up their artillery, and to form for the reception of the French. Our leading battalions did not wait the arrival and formation of the other forces to support them, they rushed with their usual impetuosity on their enemies and killed a great number; but they were soon overcome by the artillery. They lost their General and a great number of officers. Our loss was not equal to that of the enemy; but it was not the less serious. General De Montcalm and his principal officers fell on the occasion.

Several officers of the Canadian Militia, fathers of families, shared the same fate. We witnessed the carnage from our windows. It was in such a scene that charity triumphed, and caused us to forget self-preservation and the danger we were exposed to, in the immediate presence of the enemy. We were in the midst of the dead and the dying, who were brought in to us by hundreds, many of them our close connexions; it was necessary to smother our griefs and exert ourselves to relieve them. Loaded with the inmates of three convents, and all the inhabitants of the neighbouring suburbs, which the approach of the enemy caused to fly in this direction, you may judge of our terror and confusion. The enemy masters of the field, and within a few paces of our house; exposed to the fury of the soldiers, we had reason to dread the worst. It was then that we experienced the truth of the words of holy writ: "he who places his trust in the Lord has nothing to fear." ...

The loss we had just sustained, and the departure of that force, determined the Marquis De Vaudreuil, Governor General of the Colony, to abandon Quebec, being no longer able to retain it. The enemy having formed their entrenchments and their Camp, near the principal gate; their fleet commanding the Port, it was impossible to convey succour to the garrison ...

The principal inhabitants represented to him that they had readily sacrificed their property; but with regard to their wives and children, they could not make up their minds to witness their massacre, in the event of the place being stormed; it was therefore necessary to determine on capitulation.

The English readily accorded the articles demanded, religious toleration and civil advantages for the inhabitants. Happy in having acquired possession of a country, in which they had on several previous occasions failed, they were the most moderate of conquerors. We could not, without injustice, complain of the manner in which they treated us. However, their good treatment has not yet dried our tears ...

The reduction of Quebec, on the 18th September, 1759, produced no tranquillity for us, but rather increased our labours. The English Generals came to our Hospital and assured us of their protection, and at the same time, required us to take charge of their wounded and sick.

Although we were near the seat of war, our establishment had nothing to fear, as the well understood rights of nations protected Hospitals so situated, still they obliged us to lodge a guard of thirty men, and it was necessary to prepare food and bedding for them. On being relieved they carried off many of the blankets, &c. the officer taking no measures to prevent them. Our greatest misfortune was to hear their talking during divine service ...

Let us now return to the French. Our Generals not finding their force sufficient to undertake the recovery of their losses, proceeded to the construction of a Fort, about five leagues above Quebec, and left a garrison therein, capable of checking the enemy from penetrating into the country. They did not remain inactive, but were constantly on the alert, harassing the enemy. The English were not safe beyond the gates of Quebec. General Murray the commander of the place, on several occasions was near being made a prisoner; and would not have escaped if our people had been faithful. Prisoners were frequently made, which so irritated the Commander, that he sent out detachments to pillage and burn the habitations of the country people.

The desire to recover the country and to acquire glory, was attended with great loss to our citizens. We heard of nothing but combats throughout the winter; the severity of the season had not the effect of making them lay down their arms. Wherever the enemy was observed, they were pursued without relaxation; which caused them to remark, "they had never known a people more attached and faithful to their sovereign than the Canadians."

The English did not fail to require the oath of allegiance to their King; but, notwithstanding this forced obligation, which our people did not consider themselves bound to observe, they joined the flying camps of the French, whenever an opportunity offered.

The French forces did not spare the inhabitants of the country; they lived freely at the expense of those unfortunate people. We suffered considerable loss in a Seigneurie which we possessed below Quebec. The officer commanding seized on all our cattle, which were numerous, and wheat to subsist his troops. The purveyor rendered us no account of such seizures. Notwithstanding this loss, we were compelled to maintain upwards of three hundred wounded sent to us after the battle of the 13th September ...

Reverend Mothers, as I give you this account, merely from memory, of what passed under our eyes, and with a view to afford you the satisfaction of knowing that we sustained with fortitude and in an edifying manner the painful duties, imposed upon us by our vocation; I will not undertake to relate to you all the particulars of the surrender of the country. I could do it but imperfectly, and from hearsay. I will merely say that the majority of the Canadians were disposed to perish rather than surrender; and that the small number of troops remaining were deficient of ammunition and provisions, and only surrendered in order to save the lives of the women and children, who are likely to be exposed to the greatest peril where towns are carried by assault.

Alas! Dear Mothers, it was a great misfortune for us that France could not send, in the spring, some vessels with provisions and munitions; we should still be under her dominion. She has lost a vast country and a faithful people, sincerely attached to their sovereign; a loss we must greatly deplore, on account of our religion, and the difference of the laws to which we must submit. We vainly flatter ourselves that peace may restore us to our rights; and that the Almighty will treat us in a fatherly manner, and soon cease to humble us; we still continue to experience his wrath. Our sins, doubtless, are very great, which leads us to apprehend that we are doomed to suffer long; the spirit of repentance is not general with the people, and God is still offended. We, however, yet entertain the hope of again coming under the dominion of our former masters ...

6

"The Abundant Blessings of British Rule"

Quebec's New Administration

DOCUMENTS

A) Report of the State of the Government of Quebec in Canada, June 5th, 1762
   General James Murray

B) Mandate to Rebellious Subjects During the American War, 1776
   Jean-Olivier Briand, Bishop of Quebec

C) Sermon on Nelson's Victory at Aboukir, 1799
   Joseph-Octave Plessis, Bishop of Quebec

D) Travels Through Lower Canada, and the United States of North America, in the Years 1806, 1807, and 1808
   John Lambert

E) To Lord Liverpool, May 1, 1810
   Governor James Craig

The Conquest remains, for many French-Canadians, the single most important event in early Canada's history: an episode that shaped all subsequent developments. Was the Conquest a golden opportunity for those habitants left behind, or a bitter and humiliating defeat threatening to drown vibrant French-Canadian culture in a sea of Anglo domination? Englishmen at the time believed they offered the Québécois liberation from the yoke of tyranny. Today some historians accuse France of abandoning its colony: shirking its responsibility to its loyal subjects. Others accuse Britain of raping and looting Quebec, leaving its people as victims whose plight only independence can rectify. And then some remind French Canadians that although they were conquered, they received very generous treatment and should be content. It is therefore hardly surprising to find differing interpretations of the crisis, and not just among Québécois historians. Most early documentary evidence comes from English administrators and military people sent to govern their new colony. Their writings optimistically suggest that habitants could now enjoy far better lives than under the tyrannical thumb of the *fleur-de-lis*.

The only major French voice in the immediate post-Conquest period was the Catholic church, but even it stands accused of selling out to Britain. Why? Because clerics feared absorption into the new republican United States far more than they did England, and the French revolution of 1789 thrust them even further into the conservative folds of the Union Jack

James Murray (1721–1794) was a career soldier who fought his way from the West Indies, through France, and finally to North America where he battled the French at both Louisbourg and Quebec. Born into a Scottish noble family, Murray took over when Wolfe died on the Plains of Abraham. His first job as governor of the garrison of Quebec in 1759 was to immediately ensure stability. He declared martial law but allowed French Canadians their legal system and institutions, even though that was not in the terms of capitulation. Though deeply suspicious of the Catholic church and the Jesuits, Murray needed clergy support, as he believed that the local population was completely dominated by the church. Ironically, this led to a partnership between Quebec culture's greatest defender and its old enemy. No wonder the church later came in for derision from certain Quebec nationalists.

Murray, whom Wolfe accused of being "hot headed and impetuous," remained cool enough to keep the peace with his new citizens. Contrary to British tradition, he allowed Catholics to work in the civil service, gave latitude to local courts, and promoted several French Canadians to senior administrative posts. Even Québécois militia captains received new commissions! For these efforts he earned the wrath of the small Anglo business community intent upon exploiting the new colony. The powerful British merchants required careful handling, but Murray was arrogant, irascible, and not given to gentle diplomacy. He would not, for example, grant them an assembly. Thus he endured their complaints and accusations, but none stuck. In the end, he resumed his military career closer to home, as governor of Minorca. It was Murray's leniency for French Canadian cultural and legal attributes that eventually led Governor Carleton to enshrine these terms in the Quebec Act of 1774. Since then, the debate has continued over their motivation. Was this policy motivated by military considerations? Was it used to demonstrate British benevolence? Or did it hide the fact that continuity was the easiest form of administration?

Bishop Jean-Olivier Briand (1715–1794) rose from humble French origins through the ranks of the Catholic church to the highest clerical office in Quebec. That final appointment did not come easily, however, and required considerable political manipulation before it occurred in 1764. His biggest problem, one he struggled with for the rest of his tenure, was ensuring the Catholic church's survival now that Quebec was ruled by Protestants. He chose to steer a pragmatic course of guarded loyalty to Britain in exchange for support, and that loyalty deepened during the American revolution. Democracy and the excesses of republicanism to the south were anathema, and he commanded his habitant flock to shoulder muskets on behalf of the Union Jack when American rebels invaded in 1775. Few heeded his call.

Msgr. Joseph-Octave Plessis (1763–1825) was a consummate politician. As Bishop of Quebec betwen 1806 and 1825 he cemented the alliance between the Catholic church and its new political masters, preached deference and submission to British authority, and yet simultaneously eluded the English leash and maintained a remarkable degree of clerical independence. His relations with Governor Craig remained testy, but he worked well with the next senior administrator, George Prevost. This attitude of pragmatic compliance shines through the selected document: a sermon preached in 1799 during celebrations marking the great British victory over Napoleon. Plessis helped ensure French-Canadian loyalty during the War of 1812, and became an integral part of the new French-Canadian establishment, particularly after his appointment to Lower Canada's Legislative Council in 1817. No British sycophant, he interpreted French Canada's history to its people, explaining incidents like the Conquest and pointing the way for their future.

John Lambert (1775–?) arrived in Canada for the first time in 1806, on an official government mission to encourage hemp production after supplies dried up in northern Europe. He spent a year touring the Montreal and Quebec area, superficially exploring the land and its people by devoting himself exclusively to influential Québécois, not average habitants who would actually grow the crop. Returning in 1809, he combined a six-month trip to the United States with his visit to Canada. Lambert concluded that Great Britain really did not understand its new colony, an error he planned to correct. His ensuing volume offers many details of the conquered French Canadians and their lives but paints them in overly romantic and stereotypical hues. The book sold well, however, and his original publication of 1810 went through several later editions.

James Craig (1748–1812) also fought his way through the ranks of the British army, seeing action in the American revolution, India, and in the Mediterranean before he became Governor of Quebec in 1807. By then he was a versatile administrator with considerable experience, having run the Cape Colony (South Africa). British North America needed him, especially considering the fractious relations with the United States that eventually burst into flame in 1812. He busied himself with fortifications, with the militia, and with cementing alliances with native people. Though he did not initially show bias against French Canadians, he later tackled the newspaper *Le Canadien*, believing that it posed a security risk through its nationalist rhetoric. His stance simply made things worse, provoking Québécois wrath, both in and outside the Legislative Assembly. Action led to reaction in a downward spiral of antagonism as the two sides dug in, sniping through the press, the Legislature, and in parlors and public houses across the colony. Perhaps Britain was too arrogant and naive to see habitants as genuinely loyal subjects, considering their fundamental cultural differences and deep historical rivalry. These were certainly no longer Governor Murray's docile, passive, and malleable peasants, and now an educated professional class led them in their expressions of discontent. Craig might have trod more carefully, but his impetuous nature and strong ego made him react aggressively: he dissolved the Legislative Assembly in 1810, seized *Le Canadien's* press, and arrested many for "treacherous practices." Perhaps this permanently spoiled Britain's chance for a peaceful united colony, as it seems directly related to the birth and growth of French-Canadian nationalism.

A) Report of the State of the Government of Quebec in Canada, June 5th, 1762
General James Murray

The Canadians may be ranked under four different classes

    1st The Gentry or what they call Nobility
    2d The Clergy
    3d The Merchants or trading part
    4th The Peasantry or what is here stilled, Habitant.

1st The Gentry. These are descended from the Military and Civil officers, who have settled in the Country at different times and were usually provided for in the Colony Troops; These consisted formerly of 28 afterwards
30 and had been lately augmented to 40 Companys. They are in general
poor except such as have had commands in distant posts where they usually
made a fortune in three or four Years. The Croix de St Louis quite completed their happiness. They are extremely vain and have an utter contempt
for the trading part of the Colony, tho' they made no scruple to engage in
it, pretty deeply too, whenever a convenient opportunity served; They were
great Tyrants to their Vassals who seldom met with redress, let their grievances be ever so just.

This class will not relish the British Government from which they can
neither expect the same employments or the same douceurs, they enjoyed
under the French.

2d The Clergy. Most of the dignified among them are French, the rest
Canadians, and are in general of the lower class of People, the former no
doubt will have great difficulty to reconcile themselves to us, but must drop
off by degrees. Few of the latter are very clever ... they would soon become
easy and satisfied, their influence over the people was and is still very great,
but tho' we have been so short a time in the Country, a difference is to be
perceived, they [the people] do not submit so tamely to the Yoke, and under sanction of the capitulation they every day take an opportunity to dispute the tythes with their Curés.

These were moved from their respective parishes at the Bishop's pleasure, who thereby always kept them in awe, it may not be perhaps improper
to adopt the same Method, in case His Majesty should think right, for the
sake of keeping them in proper subjection, to nominate them himself or by
those who act under his authority ...

3d The Traders of this Colony under the French were either dealers in
gross or retailers, the former were mostly French and the latter in general
natives of this Country all of whom are deeply concerned in the letters of
Exchange; many are already gone to solicit payment and few of those who
have any fund of any consequence in France remain here.

4th ... The 4th Order is that of the Peasantry, these are a strong healthy
race, plain in their dress, virtuous in their morals and temperate in their
living: They are in general extremely ignorant, for the former government
would never suffer a printing press in the Country, few can read or write,

and all receive implicitly for truth the many arrant falsehoods and atrocious lies, industriously handed among them by those who were in power.

They took particular pains to persuade them, the English were worse than brutes, and that if they prevailed, the Canadians would be ruled with a rod of Iron, and be exposed to every outrage, this most certainly did not a little contribute, to make them so obstinate in their defence. However ever since the Conquest, I can with the greatest truth assert, that the Troops have lived with the Inhabitants in a harmony unexampled even at home. I must here, in justice to those under my command in this Government, observe to Your Lordship, that in the Winter which immediately followed the reduction of this Province, when from the Calamities of War, and a bad harvest, the inhabitants of these lowest parts were exposed to all the horrors of a famine, the Officers of every rank, even in the lowest generously contributed towards alleviating the distresses of the unfortunate Canadians by a large subscription, the British Merchants and Traders readily and cheerfully assisted in this good work, even the poor Soldiers threw in their mite, and gave a day's provisions, or a day's pay in the month, towards the fund, by this means a quantity of provisions was purchased and distributed with great care and assiduity to numbers of poor Families, who, without this charitable support, must have inevitably perished; such an instance of uncommon generosity towards the conquered did the highest honor to their conquerors and convinced these poor deluded people, how grossly they had been imposed upon; the daily instances of lenity, the impartial justice which has been administer'd, so far beyond what they had formerly experienced, have so alter'd their opinion with regard to us, I may safely venture to affirm for this most useful Order of the state, that far from having the least design to emigrate from their present habitations into any other of the French Colonies, their greatest dread is lest they should meet with the fate of the Acadians and be torn from their native Country.

Convinced that this is not to be their case and that the free exercise of their religion will be continued to them once Canada is irrecoverably ceded by a Peace the people will soon become faithful and good subjects to His Majesty, and the Country they inhabit within a short time prove a rich and most useful Colony to Great Britain ...

With a very slight cultivation all sorts of grain are here easily produced, and in great abundance, the inhabitants are inclinable enough to be lazy, and not much skilled in Husbandry, the great dependencies they have hitherto had on the Gun and fishing rod, made them neglect tillage beyond the requisites of their own consumption and the few purchases they needed, the Monopolies that were carried on here in every branch, made them careless of acquiring beyond the present use, and their being often sent on distant parties and detachments, to serve the particular purposes of greedy and avaricious Men without the least view to public utility, were circumstances under which no country could thrive; As they will not be subject to such Inconveniences under a British Government, and being necessarily deprived of arms they must of course apply more closely to the culture of their Lands.

The mines already discovered, and the mineral and sulphurous waters in many parts of this Country leave no room to doubt, nature has been bountiful to it in this respect, and that further discoveries and improvements are likely to be made with regard to these, whenever it becomes more populous. Notwithstanding the waste of war, which they have much more severely felt from pretended friends, than from their declared foes, the Country will abound in three or four Years with all kind of provisions, sufficient not only to answer their home consumption, but even to export if a Market can be procured ...

The present state of population may be easily seen for the annexed Account of the number of people in this Government taken about a twelve month ago.

There is great reason to believe this Colony has been upon the decrease in this respect for near twenty Years past, the Wars which they have been almost constantly carrying on, the strictness with which Marriages within a certain degree of consanguinity were forbidden except by dispensation, the obliging Strangers inclined to engage in that state, previously to prove their not being married before, and the prohibition of intermarriages between protestants and Roman Catholics were so many bars to the propagation of the Species, these difficulties are now in a good measure removed; the men are an active, strong, and healthy race, the Women are extremely prolifick and in all human probability the next twenty Years will produce a vast increase of People.

The French bent their whole attention in this part of the World to the Fur Trade, they never enter'd heartily or with any spirit into the fisheries: most of what was done in this way was by adventurers from the ports of France; some Fish indeed Lumber and provisions were exported to the French islands. Had this trade been opened and agriculture promoted here with any degree of warmth, this branch of Commerce must have become both valuable and extensive, but it was monopolized into the hands of a few, by the connivance and management of the Chiefs, the sole view of these being to enrich themselves by every means. The interest of the State could not fail to be sacrificed upon all occasions ...

The foregoing is an attempt to sketch the trade of Canada . . . but under the full enjoyment of His Majesty's mild and gentle administration, its commerce must flourish to a far greater extent.

1st A Most immense and extensive Cod Fishery can be established in the River and Gulph of St Laurence, and may in time prove an inexhaustible source of wealth and power to Great Britain; Settlements may be formed in the neighbourhood of the best fishing places to which the industrious and intelligent in that branch may be invited and encouraged to repair; a rich tract of country on the South side of the Gulph will in consequence be settled and improved, a Port or Ports established and furnished with every material requisite to repair Ships, that have suffer'd by stress of weather or the difficulties attending navigation in such narrow seas, a point much wanted which will lessen the risks, and considerably increase the profits of the Commerce of this Colony.

It is further to be observed that the Fish caught upon these coasts and in the bays, far exceed the bank Cod and fetch an advanced price in foreign markets; The fishermen being on the spot will commence fishing the very instant the season permits and will continue to the very last of it whereby at least two Months will be gained to the trade, which are just now a heavy expense to it, without producing the least profit to it.

2d Next to the Cod in importance is the Whale fishery which can be carried on to the greatest advantage in the River St Laurence with less risk and expence than in any other seas, where the animals resort; Under this head may be placed the seal and sea-Cow fisheries of which there is a prodigious abundance, and an immense (sic) of oil and Whale-bone may be annually exported to Great Britain.

3d ... There are several small rivers on the Coast of Labrador abounding with vast quantities of salmon; this if followed with spirit and industry, might very soon become a considerable object to the British Trader.

4th ... His Majesty's Yards may by the best accounts be supplied with masts from Chamblie, at a much cheaper and easier rate than from New England. By the latter a tedious Land carriage of several miles and the immense falls of a most rapid river over which they must be rafted and where many are lost must greatly enhance the value of this useful and necessary branch of Naval Stores; whereas by the former with little or no risk at a proper season there is an easy water carriage for them all the way to Quebec, the port for shipping them to Europe.

5th ... Tho' as has been before observed, this province must now share the Fur Trade, which she formerly possessed under the French Government, with the neighbouring Colonies, Yet that which was carried on with the different nations inhabiting the northern Coast of Canada, must still remain with her, she may likewise hereafter regain a great part of that with the upper Country, on account of the more easy conveyance.

It is likewise probable that this very branch may be much farther extended, than ever it was under the French, by reason of the superior diligence and application of the British Traders.

It must be allowed the French were laudable in restraining the vent of Spirituous Liquors to the Savages beyond a certain quantity: by this means many broils were avoided, for they are fond to excess of everything strong and are all mad in their intoxication.

6th ... Raising hemp and flax for which the lands are in many places extremely proper must be an object of the most serious consideration. And I must repeat here, how useful this must prove to the end of promoting agriculture, of employing the Women and Children during the tedious winter months, and of procuring in a short time a vast exportation of that useful commodity for which the returns will be made in British Manufactures.

7th ... As the Country abounds every where with oak, Ash, Hickory, Walnut, Birch, Beech, Maple and other hard woods, which by experience are known to Yield the most Salts, the article of Pot-ash so much demanded in our Manufactures, may be easily produced and soon become an object of consequence; The essais for this purpose which have been made in our other Colonies and have miscarried, ought not to discourage an attempt in this. The high price of Labor; the Woods being in many parts remote from Water carriage, and the greater encouragement for growing and exporting provisions to the West Indies, have been so many obstacles to the making of Pot-ash in our Colonies, whereas provisions here must be very cheap in a few Years, for the navigation being closed six months out of the twelve this Country can never vie with our Southern Provinces in the West India trade; besides the country being settled close to the River side, the conveyance of the Commodity to the Port where it is to be shipped, will be both cheap and easy it will likewise be a means to employ the men all Winter in the business of Felling and drawing of Wood which time they chiefly dedicate to idleness and smoking.

B) Mandate to Rebellious Subjects During the American War, 1776
Jean-Olivier Briand, Bishop of Quebec

To the people of this diocese, greeting and benediction in the name of our Lord.

… But if you persist in your rebellion, you will suffer the most rigorous punishment. What could save you from such sanctions? Do you suppose that an empire as powerful as the British Empire, whose navy can resist the united navies of Europe, will be denied, and that it will not accomplish the task which it has set itself? Only stubborn stupidity or great ignorance could harbour such an idea.

Your own interest then commands you to return forthwith to the path of duty. We exhort you, dear brethren, we beseech you, on the body of Jesus Christ, to do so. In this we propose no other goal than your own good, both spiritual and temporal. First, your temporal good; for, dear brethren, you cannot be unaware of the fatal effects of stubborn resistance. Your rebellion, which defied religion, good sense, and reason, deserved exemplary and rigorous punishment from a prince from whom until now you have received only signal marks of kindness. Kindness such as his is extremely rare in a powerful conqueror, and was quite unexpected; for you it has meant that a change of sovereignty resulted in greater well-being. Remember that when you joined the revolt no one was suffering from the effects of the late war. Not only had the losses which you had suffered been repaired, but your fortunes had greatly increased, and your property had become much more valuable. You should have praised and thanked Providence for your good fortune; duty and gratitude should have been ties binding you inseparably to the person, the authority, and the glory of your Sovereign. He had a right to expect such loyalty, and he was secure in the conviction that he could count upon it. Had you followed the rules of gratitude and the precepts of your religion, his hopes would not have been deceived.

Relying on this conviction, the King, faced with the necessity of using force in order to recall his rebellious provinces to their duty and obedience, did not fear to withdraw from ours troops no longer required here to ensure the submission which he was sure you felt in your minds and hearts. You should have been expected, and you were expected, to be ardent in support of the interests of a beneficent King, and of a court and Parliament devoted to you and busy with plans to make you a happy, rich, and flourishing people. With what surprise must England have learned of your defection, your disobedience, your revolt, and your union with rebels! How great must have been her anger and indignation! Have you not reason to fear that her kindness thus betrayed may change to fury, that she may mete out just punishment instead of the honours already lavished upon you, and of other very special favours which she had in store for you? If by a show of some part of her formidable strength your eyes had been opened to your duty, she would perhaps also have pardoned you in consideration of your ignorance and simplicity and of the tricks, ruses, lies, deceit, the threats, and false, unreasonable and unfounded promises with which your insidious enemies seduced and perverted you, involving you in their iniquitous designs, not for love of you or thought for your good, but out of envy and jealousy of the preference accorded to you.

No, no, dear brethren, the colonists did not seek your welfare; it was not brotherly love which brought them into this colony; it was not in order to procure for you the liberty which you already enjoyed and from which you were about to derive still greater advantages, that a handful of men, unskilled in military art, descended on the countryside and seized the defenceless towns of Montreal and Three Rivers. It was with a very different motive, a motive which, did you but comprehend it, would cover you with shame and disgrace, and which, if you plumbed all its depths of malice and treason, would fill you with rage and fury against the perfidious enemies whom you have been foolish enough to call brothers and friends of our people.

… These, dear brethren, are the crimes by which the southern colonies have betrayed you. Jealous, mad with jealousy, at the favours granted to you by the government, and which you did not sufficiently recognize, they went to London and bent all their efforts to prevent the granting of these honours. They have not yet relinquished those efforts; but, as their manoeuvres proved fruitless, they turned their attack against you. They knew that you had little instruction, and no knowledge of politics or your own interest; they considered you stupid and ignorant, and they concluded that they could not prevent the Court from being disposed in your favour nor shake its conviction of your loyalty and bravery and your sincere devotion to your religion. Your enemies, who understand the teachings and spirit of your religion better than you did yourselves, undertook to make you unworthy of the favours which had been granted to you. For your misfortune, as we shall point out to you, they succeeded, and you became guilty of revolt, cowardice, and a form of denial of the religion of your fathers ... they promised you exemption from seignorial dues, and you loved this injustice; they promised that you would pay no more tithes, and you were not moved with horror at such sacrilegious ingratitude towards the God without whose blessing your fields would remain infertile and your labour would be fruitless.

... [S]o that it was you who plunged the sword into your own hearts. Not only did you deprive yourselves of the favours already granted to you, but you destroyed and nullified the terms of capitulation, the peace treaty, and the other declarations by which the King had annexed you to the English nation, placed you on the same footing with his ancient subjects, and granted you the same rights and prerogatives. By your own act, you are now no more than a twice-conquered people, subject to the will of a conquering sovereign. All your possessions are justly liable to confiscation by the Crown and you yourselves are threatened with the harrowing prospect of exile, if the government should consider such a penalty necessary or useful for the conservation of its conquest.

This is the abyss, these are the misfortunes into which you have been cast by these false friends, these unnatural traitors, and barbarous brothers. So much for your temporal condition. Let us now consider your spiritual good, I mean your religion and your salvation.

To what dangers have you exposed that religion! What obstacles you have placed in the path of your salvation!

... You will perhaps say, and indeed you have said, that it is not the business of priests to make war or to concern themselves with it, and it is quite true that their ministry debars them from shouldering a musket or shedding blood; but is it not their duty to judge whether a war is just or unjust, as it is to give judgment on the obedience and the service which subjects owe to their sovereign? You must surely know that since swearing an oath is a religious act it concerns the Church. And when you have unwisely sworn oaths which you are unable to honour, do you not come to us to ask to be relieved of them, as you ask to be relieved of vows? You fall into gross error when you say that it is not for priests to meddle with war. Or alternatively, if, knowing that you were obliged to consult them, you did not do so, you have sinned with malice aforethought against the Holy Spirit and your own conscience.

The list of sins against God of which you have been guilty is a long one! First, the sin of disobedience to the lawful Sovereign; the sinner guilty of such resistance is damned. Secondly, the sin of perjury. You have also on your consciences the consequences of your forswearing: enormous expense to the Crown, and damage to private property. Thirdly, you are guilty of the thefts and murders which have been committed, of the fires which have been set ...

What can one think of these persons? They are all liable to excommunication, and especially those who committed acts of violence, or spoke insolently in churches, or advised or applauded such offenses ... The Americans themselves, deeply shocked, remarked that if ever they had a Canadian to roast, they would find a hundred others to turn the spit. And it is a fact that loyal subjects who have fallen into the enemy's hands have in all cases had more reason to complain of Canadians, their compatriots and brothers in the faith, than of foreigners. It was Canadians who robbed, looted, murdered, burned, kidnapped brother Canadians; it was Canadians who incited and spurred on the invaders to violence and depredation. If their urgings had always been followed, the toll of destruction would have been still greater than it was. Poor Canadians! Your name was covered with glory throughout Europe, and kingdoms rang with your praise! And now you will be known as the most traitorous, barbarous, and unworthy of peoples. I blush to think of it ...

C) Sermon on Nelson's Victory at Aboukir, 1799
Joseph-Octave Plessis, Bishop of Quebec

... What sort of government, Gentlemen, is the best suited for our happiness? Is it not the one marked by moderation, which respects the religion of those it rules, which is full of consideration for its subjects, and gives the people a reasonable part in its administration? Such has always been the British government in Canada. To say this is in no way to practise the flattery that cowards use to bless the powers that be. God forbid, my brothers, that I should profane this holy pulpit by base adulation or interested praise. This testimony is demanded by truth as well as gratitude, and I have no fear of being contradicted by anyone who knows the spirit of the English government. It always proceeds with wise deliberation; there is nothing precipitous in its methodical advance. Do you see in its operations any of the delusive enthusiasm, the thoughtless love of novelty, the liberty without limits or restraints that, before our very eyes, is destroying certain malconstituted states? What care it takes for the property of its subjects! What skillful efforts are made to arrange the public finances so that its subjects are scarcely aware of the burden! Have you heard any complaints, these past forty years under their rule, of the poll-taxes, the tariffs, the head taxes under which so many other nations groan? What of those arbitrary requisitions of immense sums that unjust conquerors arrogantly impose on the unhappy conquered? Have you been reduced, by their lack of foresight, to those famines that formerly afflicted our Colony, which we still recall with horror and shuddering? Have you not seen, on the contrary, that in years of scarcity the government wisely prohibits the export of grain until enough has been put aside for your own needs? Have you been subjected to military service since the Conquest, obliged to leave your wives and children destitute in order to go to some far-off place to attack or repulse some enemy of the State? Have you contributed a penny to the expenses of this costly war that Great Britain has been waging for almost six years? Almost the whole of Europe has been given over to carnage and destruction, the holiest cloisters have been violated, virgins dishonoured, mothers and children slaughtered in several places. Is it not evident, and can it not be said, that at the height of this war you enjoy all the advantages of peace? To whom, my brothers, aside from God, do you owe these favours, if not to the paternal vigilance of an Empire which, in peace as in war, I dare to say, has your interests closer to its heart than its own? In every field I see evidence of this partiality. Your criminal code, for example, was too severe; it provided no sufficiently reliable rule for distinguishing the innocent from the guilty, and it exposed the weak to the oppression of the strong. It has been replaced by the criminal law of England, that masterpiece of human intelligence, which checks calumny ... which convicts only those whose guilt is obvious, which gives the accused every means of legitimate defence, and which, leaving nothing to the discretion of the judge, punishes only in accordance with the precise provisions of the law. Finally, what about the common law? While in France all is in disorder, while every Ordonnance bearing the stamp of Royalty is proscribed, is it not wonderful to see a British Province ruled by the common law of Paris and by the Edicts and declarations of the kings of France? To what are we to attribute this gratifying peculiarity? To the fact that you wanted to maintain these ancient laws; to the fact that they seemed better adapted to the nature of real property in this country. There they are, then, preserved without any alterations except those that provincial Legislation is free to make. And in that Legislation you are represented to an infinitely greater degree than the people of the British Isles are in the Parliaments of England or Ireland.

Do such benefits, Gentlemen, not demand from us some return? A lively feeling of gratitude towards Great Britain; an ardent desire never to be separated from her; a deep conviction that her interests are no different from our own; that our happiness depends upon hers; and that if sometimes it has been necessary to grieve over her losses, we must, by the same principle, rejoice today in the glory she has won and regard her latest victory as an event no less consoling for us than it is glorious for her.

Where do we stand, Christians, if we add to these political considerations another that, above all else, makes this empire worthy of your gratitude and praise? I mean the liberty left our religion and guaranteed by law; the respect shown to those in our monasteries; the unbroken succession of Catholic Bishops, who have so far enjoyed the favour and confidence of the King's Representatives; the unfailing support our curés have enjoyed in the villages and countryside in their efforts to conserve faith and morals. If this faith is growing weaker among us, my brothers, if morality is becoming more lax, it is not because of any change of government; it is to you yourselves that this disorder must be attributed; to your lack of submission to the teaching of the Gospels; to your foolish pursuit of a liberty you already enjoy without knowing it; to the poisonous harangues of those dishonest and unprincipled men, those perpetual grumblers who are offended by order, humiliated by obedience, and outraged by the very existence of religion.

Alas! Where would we be, my brothers, if such men should ever get the upper hand, if their desires should be fulfilled, if this country, by a grievous misfortune, should return to its former masters? This house of God, this august temple, would soon be converted to a den of thieves! Ministers of religion — you would be displaced, banished, and perhaps decapitated! Fervent Christians — you would be deprived of the ineffable consolations you enjoy in the accomplishment of your religious duties! Your land, consecrated by the sweat and tears of so many virtuous missionaries who have planted the faith here, would, to a religious eye, display nothing but a vast, melancholy solitude. Catholic fathers and mothers, under your very eyes, in spite of yourselves, you would see your beloved children nursed on the poisoned milk of barbarism, impiety, and dissoluteness! Tender children, whose innocent hearts still manifest only virtue, your piety would become prey to these

vultures, and a savage education would soon obliterate the pleasing sentiments that humanity and religion have engraved on your souls!

Conclusion. — But what am I saying? Why dwell on such sad reflections on a day when all ought to be joy? No, no, my brothers. Fear not that
God will abandon us if we remain faithful. What he has just done for us
should inspire only comforting thoughts for the future. He has struck down
our perfidious enemies. Let us rejoice in this glorious event. Everything that
weakens France tends to draw us away from it. Everything that separates us
from her assures our lives, our liberty, our peace, our property, our religion,
and our happiness. Let us give everlasting thanks to the God of victories.
Let us pray that He will long preserve the bountiful and august Sovereign
who governs us, and that he will continue to lavish on Canada his most
abundant blessings.

D) Travels Through Lower Canada, and the United States of North America, in the Years 1806, 1807, and 1808
John Lambert

The French Canadians are an inoffensive, quiet people, possessed of little
industry, and less ambition. Yet from the love of gain, mere vanity, or that
restlessness which indolence frequently occasions, they will undergo the greatest hardships. There cannot be a stronger proof of this, than in those who
labour in the spring to collect the sap of the maple tree: their exertions for
five or six weeks while the snow is on the ground, are excessive. None also
undergo severer trials than those who are employed in the fur trade. They
penetrate the immense forests of the north-west for thousands of miles, exposed to all the severities of the climate, and often to famine and disease.
That vanity should be a predominant characteristic of the Canadians, is no
more than might be expected from the children of France, whose national
character is vanity.

The Habitans [*sic*] content themselves with following the footsteps of
their forefathers. They are satisfied with a little, because a little satisfies their
wants. They are quiet and obedient subjects, because they feel the value and
benefit of the government under which they live. They trouble themselves
not with useless arguments concerning its good or bad qualities, because
they feel themselves protected, and not oppressed by its laws. They are religious from education and habit, more than from principle. They observe its

ceremonies and formalities, not because they are necessary to their salvation, but because it gratifies their vanity and superstition. They live in happy mediocrity, without a wish or endeavour to better their condition, though many of them are amply possessed of the means. Yet they love money, and are seldom on the wrong side of a bargain. From poverty and oppression they have been raised, since the conquest, to independent affluence. They now know, and feel the value of money and freedom, and are not willing to part with either. Their parsimonious frugality is visible in their habitations, their dress, and their meals; and had they been as industrious and enterprizing, as they have been frugal and saving, they would have been the richest peasantry in the world.

Their houses are composed of logs slightly smoothed with the axe, laid upon each other, and dove-tailed at the corners ...

The roof is constructed with boards, and generally covered with shingles. Sometimes they are white-washed, but oftener allowed to remain in their natural state. In a few months the weather changes the colour of the wood, and gives the shingles the appearance of slate, which, with the white sides have a pleasing effect. The whole, however, falls very short of the neat wooden farm-houses in the United States, which are generally clapboarded over the rough logs, and neatly painted. They present a more complete and finished appearance, than the rough outsides of the Canadian farm-houses.

The Canadian habitations consist of only one story or ground floor, which is generally divided into four rooms. Over them, is a garret or loft formed by the sloping roof. Some of the small houses have only one or two apartments, according to the affluence, or poverty of their owners. The better sort of farmers have always four rooms ...

The chimney is built in the centre of the house; and the room which contains the fire-place, is the kitchen. The rest are bed rooms, for it matters not how many apartments a house consists of, they are seldom without one or two beds in each, according to the size of the family. This indispensable piece of furniture, which is always placed in one corner of the room, is a sort of four-post bedstead without the pillars, and raised three or four feet from the ground. At the head there is generally a canopy or tester fixed against the wall, under which the bed stands. Upon the bedstead is placed a feather or straw bed, with the usual clothes, and covered with a patchwork counterpane, or green stuff quilt. In winter, the men frequently lay themselves along the hearth, or by the stove, wrapped up in a buffalo robe. In the middle of the night, they will get up, stir the fire, smoke their pipe, and lie down again till morning ...

The furniture of the Habitans is plain and simple, and most commonly of their own workmanship. A few wooden chairs with twig or rush bottoms, and two or three deal tables, are placed in each room, and are seldom very ornamental; they, however, suffice, with a proper number of wooden bowls, trenchers, and spoons, for the use of the family at meals. A press, and two or three large chests, contain their wearing-apparel, and other property. A buffet in one corner, contains their small display of cups, saucers, glasses, and tea-pots, while a few broken sets may perhaps grace the mantle piece. A large clock is often found in their best apartment, and the sides of the room are ornamented with little pictures, or waxen images of saints and crucifixes; of the holy virgin and her son. An iron stove is generally placed in the largest apartment, with a pipe passing through the others into the chimney. The kitchen displays very little more than kettles of soup — tureens of milk — a table, a dresser, and a few chairs. The fire-place is wide, and large logs of wood are placed on old fashioned iron dogs. A wooden crane supports the large kettle of soup, which is forever on the fire.

Their chief article of food, is pork, as fat as they can procure it. They all keep a great number of swine, which they fatten to their liking. Peas-soup, with a small quantity of pork boiled in it, constitutes their breakfast, dinner, and supper, day after day, with very little alteration, except what is occasioned by a few sausages, and puddings made of the entrails, when a hog is killed; or during Lent, when fish and vegetables only, will suffice. They are extremely fond of thick sour milk, and will often treat themselves with a dish of it, after their pork. Milk, soup, and other spoon-meat, are eaten out of a general dish, each taking a spoonful after the other. Knives and forks are seldom in request.

The old people will sometimes treat themselves with tea or coffee, in which case, they generally have to boil their water in the frying-pan; for it rarely happens that they have a tea-kettle in the house ...

Milk and water is the usual drink of the females and younger part of the family. Rum is, however, the cordial balm which relieves the men from all their cares and anxieties. They are passionately fond of this pernicious liquor, and often have a debauch when they go to market with their commodities ...

Very few of the country people who frequent the markets in the towns, return home sober, and in winter time, when there is not room for more than one cariole on the road, without plunging the horse four or five feet deep in snow, these people, having lost their usual politeness by intoxication, do not feel inclined to make way for the gentry in carioles, and will often run their sleighs aboard, and upset them.

The Canadian country-people bake their own bread, which is made of wheat-flour and rye-meal; but for the want of yeast, it has a sour taste, and is coarse and heavy. Their ovens are built of wicker work, plastered inside and out with a thick coating of clay or mortar. Some are built of bricks or stones, but the former are more general ...

The dress of the Habitant is simple and homely; it consists of a long-skirted cloth coat or frock, of a dark gray colour, with a hood attached to it, which in winter time or wet weather he puts over his head. His coat is tied round the waist by a worsted sash of various colours ornamented with beads. His waistcoat and trousers are of the same cloth. A pair of moccasins, or swamp-boots, complete the lower part of his dress. His hair is tied in a thick long queue behind, with an eelskin; and on each side of his face a few straight locks hang down like what are vulgarly called "rat's tails." Upon his head is a bonnet rouge, or, in other words, a red nightcap. The tout ensemble of his figure is completed by a short pipe, which he has in his mouth from morning till night. A Dutchman is not a greater smoker than a French Canadian.

The visage of the Habitant is long and thin, his complexion sunburnt and swarthy, and not unfrequently of a darker hue than that of the Indian. His eyes, though rather small, are dark and lively; his nose prominent, and inclined to the aquiline or Roman form. His cheeks lank and meagre. His lips small and thin. His chin sharp and projecting.

Such is the almost invariable portrait of a Canadian Habitant, or countryman, and more or less of the lower order of French people in the towns. It is, in fact, a portrait of five-sixths of the male inhabitants of Lower Canada. It is very seldom that any alteration takes place in the dress of the men; unless in summer the long coat is exchanged for a jacket, and the bonnet rouge for a straw hat; but it oftener happens that the dress which I have described is worn the whole year round.

The dress of the women is old-fashioned; for the articles which compose it never find their way into Canada until they have become stale in England. I am now speaking of those who deck themselves out in printed cotton gowns, muslin aprons, shawls, and handkerchiefs; but there are numbers who wear only cloth of their own manufacture, the same as worn by the men. A petticoat and short jacket is the most prevailing dress; though some frequently decorate themselves in all the trappings of modern finery, but which, in point of fashion, are generally a few years behind those of Europe. The elderly women still adhere to long waists, full caps, and large clubs of hair behind. Some of the younger branches of the country women are becoming more modern, having imbibed a spirit for dress from the French girls who live in the towns as servants.

The Habitans have almost every resource within their own families. They cultivate flax, which they manufacture into linen; and their sheep supply them with the wool of which their garments are formed. They tan the hides of their cattle, and make them into moccasins and boots. From woollen yarn they knit their own stockings and bonnets rouges; and from straw they make their summer hats and bonnets. Besides articles of wearing apparel, they make their own bread, butter, and cheese; their soap, candles, and sugar; all which are supplied from the productions of their farm. They build their own houses, barns, stables, and ovens. Make their own carts, wheels, ploughs, harrows, and canoes. In short, their ingenuity, prompted as much by parsimony as the isolated situation in which they live, has provided them with every article of utility and every necessary of life. A Canadian will seldom or never purchase that which he can make himself; and I am of opinion that it is this saving spirit of frugality alone, which has induced them to follow the footsteps of their fathers, and which has prevented them from profiting by the modern improvements in husbandry, and the new implements of agriculture introduced by the English settlers ...

The manners of the Habitans are easy and polite. Their behaviour to strangers is never influenced by the cut of a coat, or a fine periwig. It is civil and respectful to all, without distinction of persons. They treat their superiors with that polite deference which neither debases the one nor exalts the other. They are never rude to their inferiors because they are poor, for if they do not relieve poverty they will not insult it. Their carriage and deportment are easy and unrestrained; and they have the air of men who have lived all their days in a town rather than in the country.

They live on good terms with each other; parents and children to the third generation residing frequently in one house. The farm is divided as long as there is an acre to divide; and their desire of living together is a proof that they live happy, otherwise they would be anxious to part.

They are universally modest in their behaviour; the women from natural causes, the men from custom. The latter never bathe in the river without their trousers, or a handkerchief tied round their middle.

They marry young, and are seldom without a numerous family. Hence their passions are kept within proper bounds, and seldom become liable to those excesses which too often stigmatize and degrade the human character.

The men are possessed of strong natural genius and good common sense; both of which are however but seldom improved by education, owing to the paucity of schools in Canada. The women are better instructed, or at least better informed, for they are more attended to by the priests. Hence they generally acquire an influence over their husbands, which those who are gay and coquettish know how to turn to their own advantage.

The general deficiency of education and learning among the great body of the people in Canada has long been a subject of newspaper-complaint in that country. But it is extremely doubtful whether the condition of the people would be meliorated, or the country benefited, by the distribution of learning and information among them. The means of obtaining instruction, at present, are undoubtedly very limited; but it is occasioned, in a great measure, by their own parsimonious frugality; for, if they were willing to spare a sufficient sum for the education of their children, plenty of masters would be found, and plenty of schools opened. The British or American settlers in the back townships teach their own children the common rudiments of education; but the Canadians are themselves uneducated, and ignorant even of the smallest degree of learning; therefore they have it not in their power to supply the want of a school in their own family, and thus do they propagate from age to age the ignorance of their ancestors ...

With respect to their obtaining a knowledge of the English language, I agree with those who are of opinion that so desirable an object might, to a certain extent, be attained by the interference of the government, and the establishing of parochial Sunday schools. The number who understand, or speak, English in Lower Canada does not amount to one-fifth of the whole population, including the British subjects. Few of the French clergy understand it; for in the seminary at Quebec, where it ought to form an indispensable part of the student's education, it is totally neglected; in consequence of which, a great many French children who are educated there, besides those that are designed for the church, lose a favourable opportunity of becoming acquainted with it; and that which is omitted in youth is neither easily nor willingly ac-

quired in manhood. It is possible that the French clergy may look with jealousy upon the diffusion of the English language among their parishioners; they
may think that, as the intercourse between the British and French Canadians
will be facilitated by such a measure, the eyes of the latter would be opened
to many of the inconsistencies and defects of their religion; and that, in consequence, they may be induced to change their faith, and throw off the dominion of their priests. These, however, are but groundless fears; for as long
as vanity retains its hold in the breast of the Canadians, and while the clergy
continue that indefatigable perseverance in their ministry, and that unblem-
ished character and reputation, which distinguish them at present, it is not
probable that their parishioners will depart from the religion of their forefathers. The instruction of the French children in the English language is therefore neither difficult nor liable to any serious objection. That it is a desirable
object, and highly necessary for political as well as private reasons, is without
doubt: that it is necessary for the dispatch of business, and for the impartial
administration of justice, every man who has been in a Canadian court of law
must acknowledge without hesitation ...

In Canada, as well as in some parts of the United States, it is a custom
among the people to drive on the right side of the road, which to the eye of
an Englishman has a very awkward appearance ... From what cause the custom originated in America I cannot say; but I have observed that in the
winter season the driver frequently jumps out of the cariole on the right
side, in order to prevent it from upsetting in places where the road is narrow and the snow uneven: this may possibly have given rise to their driving
on the right side of the road, though I think the same thing might be accomplished as easily on the left. That which from necessity had become a
habit in the winter, was not easily laid aside in the summer; and consequently
settled into a general custom, which was afterwards fully established by law.
Acts of the legislature in the United States, as well as in Canada, now compel people to drive on the right hand side of the road ...

Sometimes I have seen the men kiss each other on the cheek; but the
practice is not in general use. They are extremely civil and polite to strangers, and take off their cap to every person, indifferently, whom they pass
on the road. They seldom quarrel but when intoxicated; at other times they
are good-humoured, peaceable, and friendly.

They are fond of dancing and entertainments at particular seasons and
festivals, on which occasions they eat, drink, and dance in constant succes-

sion. When their long fast in Lent is concluded, they have their "jours gras," or days of feasting. Then it is that every production of their farm is presented for the gratification of their appetites; immense turkey-pies; huge joints of pork, beef and mutton; spacious tureens of soup, or thick milk; besides fish, fowl, and a plentiful supply of fruit-pies, decorate the board. Perhaps fifty or a hundred sit down to dinner; rum is drunk by the half-pint, often without water; the tables groan with their load, and the room resounds with jollity and merriment. No sooner however does the clash of the knives and forks cease, than the violin strikes up and the dances commence. Minuets, and a sort of reels or jigs, rudely performed to the discordant scrapings of a couple of vile fiddlers, conclude the festival, or "jour gras."

On Sundays and festivals every one is dressed in his best suit, and the females will occasionally powder their hair and paint their cheeks. In this respect they differ but little from their superiors, except that they use beet-root instead of rouge. Even the men are sometimes vain enough to beautify their cheeks with that vegetable. A young fellow who had enlivened his swarthy complexion by a fine glow from the beet-root, most probably to captivate the heart of some fair nymph on a "jour gras," was unfortunately so jeered and laughed at by several of his companions, that the next day he went to his priest, to inquire if it was a sin to paint his face; thinking, no doubt, to obtain the sanction of his confessor. The priest however told him that though it was no sin, yet it was a very ridiculous vanity, and advised him to discontinue it ...

The Habitans are said to have as little rusticity in their language as in their deportment. The colony was originally peopled by so many of the noblesse, disbanded officers and soldiers, and persons of good condition, that correct language and easy and unembarrassed manners were more likely to prevail among the Canadian peasantry than among the common rustics of other countries. Previous to the conquest of the country by the English, the inhabitants are said to have spoken as pure and correct French as in old France; since then they have adopted many anglicisms in their language, and have also several antiquated phrases, which may probably have arisen out of their intercourse with the new settlers. For *froid* (cold) they pronounce *frête*. For *ici* (here) they pronounce *icite*. For *prêt* (ready) they pronounce *parré*; besides several other obsolete words which I do not at present recollect.

Another corrupt practice is very common among them, of pronouncing the final letter of their words, which is contrary to the custom of the European French. This perhaps may also have been acquired in the course of fifty years communication with the British settlers; if not, they never merited the praise of speaking pure French.

Upon a review of the preceding sketch of the character and manners of the Habitans, who constitute the great body of the Canadian people, it will be found that few peasantry in the world are blest with such a happy mediocrity of property, and such a mild form of government as they universally enjoy. They possess every necessary of life in abundance, and, when inclined, may enjoy many of its luxuries. They have no taxes to pay, but such as their religion demands. The revenues of the province are raised, in an indirect manner, upon those articles which are rather pernicious than beneficial to them; and therefore it is their own fault if they feel the weight of the impost. They are contented and happy among themselves, and protected by a well regulated government. The laws are severe, but tempered in their administration with so much lenity and indulgence for human failings, that it has occasioned a singular proverbial saying among the people, that "it requires great interest for a man to be hung in Canada;" so few in that country ever meet with such an ignominious fate.

They have now enjoyed an almost uninterrupted peace for half a century, for they were so little disturbed in the American war, that that event can hardly be considered as an interruption. This has increased the population, agriculture, commerce, and prosperity of the country; and while it has raised the people to all the comforts of moderate possessions, of freedom, and independence, it has strengthened their attachment to the constitution and government under which they have thus prospered ...

E) To Lord Liverpool, May 1, 1810
Governor James Craig

My Lord,

... [T]he particular situation in which this Province stands, as being a conquered Country may never be put out of view ... the population of which ... I myself believe to exceed 250,000. Of these 250,000 souls about 20,000 or 25,000 may be English or Americans, the remainder are French. I use the term designedly My Lord, because I mean to say that they are in Language, in religion, in manner and in attachment completely French — bound to us by no one tie, but that of a Common Government, and on the contrary viewing us with sentiments or mistrust & jealousy, with envy, and I believe I should not go too far, were I to say with hatred.

So compleat do I consider this alienation to be, that on the most careful review of all that I know in the Province there are very few whom I could venture to point out as [not] being tainted with it; the line or distinction between us is completely drawn. Friendship [and] Cordiality are not to be found — even common intercourse scarcely exists — the lower class of people to strengthen a term of contempt add Anglois — and the better sort with whom there formerly did exist some interchange or the common civilities of Society have of late entirely withdrawn themselves — the alleged reason is that their circumstances have gradually declined in proportion as ours have increased in affluence; this may have had some effect, but the observation has been made also, that this abstraction has taken place exactly in proportion as the power of the French in England has become more firmly established ...

Among the objects which I deem it necessary to bring to your Lordship's view, it is impossible for me to overlook the Clergy, and the Religious establishments of the Country ...

This Bishop tho' unknown to our Constitution and confirmed, if not appointed by a Foreign Power, has been suffered to exercise every Jurisdiction incident to the episcopal functions, he nominates to all the benefices of the Province, and removes at his pleasure from one living, to another, and it is not an unfrequent circumstance, for an offence, or a supposed offence, to be punished by a degradation from a good Cure to one of lesser emolument. His Patronage is at least equal to that of the Government, & it is so perfectly at his pleasure, that Government has no other notice of it, than that he usually once a year delivers to the Governor a list of such changes as have taken place during the preceding twelve months, so complete does the Bishop consider his independence, & so cautious is he not to perform any act which might be construed into an acknowledgement of His Majesty's Rights that if a Proclamation is issued for a Fast, or thanksgiving or any other object which involves it in an Act of the Church, He will not obey it as an emanation from the King, but He issues a mandate of his own to the same purpose, indeed, but without the least allusion to His Majesty's authority or the Proclamation which the Government has issued. In truth the Catholic Bishop tho' unacknowledged as such, exercises now a much greater degree or authority than he did in the time of the French Government, because he has arrogated to himself every power which was then possessed by the Crown; The arms of England are nowhere put up in the Churches.

With the Curés themselves, no direct communication from the Government exists in any shape, a numerous and powerful body, dispersed in every corner of the Country and certainly possessing a very considerable weight, and influence with the people, scarcely know, and are hardly known to the Government, no one Act or Government since it has been under my direction has ever been addressed to a Curé, nor has any one instance of communication from a Curé ever reached me, perhaps an exception to the first part of this observation might be brought in my having in the desire of circulating the Speech I made to the Parliament when I dissolved it, directed a Copy to be sent to each of the Curés, the circumstance however will furnish no exception to the second part, for there did not occur a single instance of a Curé even acknowledging the receipt of it ...

To a people circumstanced as I have described these to be, ignorant and credulous in the extreme, having no one common tie of affection, or union, viewing us with Jealousy, mistrust, and hatred, having separate & distinct Interests, it has been thought proper to give a share in the Government of the Country, by a House of Representatives, in which they must ever have the Majority. It is very far from my intention to question the liberal views on which the measure was originally founded, but it is my business to point out the consequences that have ensued from it.

Your Lordship is aware that tho' the Constitutional Act has established a qualification for the Electors, there is none required in the Representation, I mean with respect to Property. The Numbers of English in the House has never exceeded 14 or 15, in the two last parliaments there have been 12, in the present there are ten, some of these have of late come from a pretty low step in the scale of society, but in general they are composed of two, or three Avocats, about the same number of Gentlemen possessing Landed property, and the remainder of Merchants of Character & estimation; Upon the first establishment of the House, the few Canadian Gentlemen that existed in the Country stepped forward, and some were elected, but they soon found that nothing was to be gained by it, on the contrary, that their absence from home and their attendance at Quebec, during three months of the year, was given at an expense that very few of them could afford, and they gradually withdrew: now that some of them have attempted to resume the stations they abandoned, they have found it impossible; but at all times, their num-

bers were inconsiderable: the House has ever been as it is now, in great proportion as to the Canadian part, filled up with Avocats, and Notaries, shopkeepers, and with the Common Habitants, as they are called, that is, the
most ignorant of Labouring farmers, some of these, can neither read nor
write. In the last parliament there were two who actually signed the Roll by
marks, and there were five more, whose signatures were scarcely legible, and
were such as to shew that to be the extent of their ability in writing.

I know not whether the excessive ignorance of those people, be not more
prejudicial than even any malevolence could be with which they could be
supposed to be actuated ...

Of the Party who had the House, I have already had occasion to speak
in a former dispatch, and have been induced to enter into the Characters of
a few of them; They consist mostly of a set of unprincipled Avocats, and
Notaries totally uninformed as to the Principles of the British Constitution
or parliamentary proceedings, which they profess to take for their Model,
with no property of any sort, having everything to gain, and nothing to lose
by any change they can bring about, only any state of Confusion into which
they may throw the Province: — That these people have gradually advanced
in audacity, in proportion as they have considered the power of France as
more firmly established by the Successes of Bonaparte in Europe is obvious
to everyone, and that they are using every endeavour to pave the way for a
change of Dominion, and a Return under that Government, is the general
opinion of all ranks with whom it is possible to converse on the Subject;
Even the very few of the better sort of Canadians themselves who have sufficient information to be aware of the misery that would ensue on such an
event, while the present Government exists in that Country, and who notwithstanding their natural affection towards what they still consider as their
Mother Country, would shrink from a Return under its rule at the moment,
nevertheless confess the obvious tendency of the proceedings that are going
on here; Unfortunately the great Mass of the people are completely infected,
they look forward to the event, they whisper it among themselves, and I am
assured that they have even a song among them, which points out Napoleon as the person who is to expel the English: with them the expectation is
checked by no sort of apprehension. They are completely ignorant of the
nature of the French System, they have not an idea that a change of Rulers
would produce any alteration in their situation, and tho' if you argue with
them they are ready to admit that they are happy, and in a State of prosper-

ity as they are, they do not conceive that they would not have been equally so had they remained Subjects of France.

... [T]hey have been taught however to look to His Majesty's Government with the utmost Jealousy, and distrust, they avow it, and they publickly declare, that no officer of the Crown is to be trusted, or to be Elected into the House.

... The great vehicle of communication between the leaders & the people has been a paper called the Canadian, which has been published & industriously circulated in the Country for these three or four years past; the avowed object of this paper has been to vilify and degrade the officers of Government ... and to bring into contempt His Majesty's Government itself ...

Every topic that is calculated to mislead & inflame the people has at times occupied the pages of this paper ...

In considering the probability of these people having in view their return to their own Government, it may be urged that they have been hitherto quiet & faithful subjects, during the long lapse of 50 years, in which it would rather be to be supposed that their old attachment should have gradually decreased, so that there should be the less likelihood of their assuming now a disposition, of which they have hitherto shown no indication; to all this however it may be replied, that no circumstance whatever has occurred to awaken their attachment to their Mother Country, nor have any pains ever been taken to produce such a change, their habits, language and religion, have remained as distinct from ours as they were before the Conquest. Indeed it seems to be a favourite object with them to be considered as [a] separate Nation; *La Nation Canadienne* is their constant expression, and with regard to their having been hitherto quiet & faithful subjects, it need only be observed that no opportunity has presented them an encouragement to shew themselves otherwise. From 1764 to 75 the Country was in a state of poverty and Misery, that would not for a moment admit of a thought or revolt in which they could expect no assistance, but even during that period there was a constant intercourse with France; Young Men who sought to advance themselves went to France, not to England, and some are now in the Province who during that period served in the French Army: during the American Rebellion it was a contest whether they should remain attached to the Crown of England, or become a part of the American Republic, and to say the best for them, their conduct did not manifest a very strong affection for the former, tho' the force the Americans had in the Province was never such as to encourage them in an open display of any predilection for the latter, which however, I do not believe they entertained: their object was to remain quiet ...

The great object of their jealousy at this moment is, the progress of the Townships — that is, in fact the introduction of Settlers of any denomination but Canadians, as having a tendency, which of all others, they are most anxious to assert, to impede the complete Establishment of a Canadian Nation; These Townships are generally settled by Americans, a proportion of whom are Loyalists who were under the necessity of quitting their Country on the peace of 1784, but by far the greater Number are of Americans who have come in and settled upon those lands since that event. How far it may be good policy to admit of settlers of this description is another question, the Canadians however are loud in their Clamours against it ...

... [A] summary of the various objects ...

2d. That the great Mass of this population ... so far from being united to us by any bond of affection, views us with mistrust, jealousy and hatred.

3d. That they are, and consider themselves as French, attached to that nation from identity of religion, laws, language, and manners. This is general, and runs thro' all Ranks and descriptions, the exceptions as I believe being very few.

4th. That this people immersed in a degree of ignorance that is scarcely to be exceeded, and credulous in the extreme are particularly open to the arts and delusions that may be practised on them by factious, and designing Men.

5th. That they are at this moment compleatly in the hands of a party of such factious and designing Men.

6th. That the whole Proceedings of this Party are calculated to alienate the people from any attachment they might be supposed to entertain for a Government under which they cannot but confess they have enjoyed the most perfect security, liberty and prosperity, and to pave the way for their return to their ancient connection with that which they esteem their Mother Country ...

8th. That the Clergy under the general influence of attachment to France are further from religious motives decidedly our Enemies ...

12th. That the Government is equally destitute of all influence over the Clergy with whom it has scarcely a connection, and that this influence is entirely in the hands of an individual who holds his power under the confirmation at least of a foreign authority, which authority is now under the compleat direction of our inveterate Enemy.

The first and most obvious remedy that presents itself, is to deprive them of the constitution, as they term it, that is of that representative part of the Government which was unquestionably prematurely given them — neither from habits, information or assimilation, with the Government of England, were they prepared for it, nor was this circumstance of their unprepared state unforeseen by many of the best informed of the Canadians themselves, who opposed its being granted to them. It was in fact brought about by the English part of the Inhabitants, who in their Enthusiasm for the Constitution which they so justly Esteemed as it exists in their own Country, could not conceive that any inconvenience, or any thing but happiness, and prosperity, could result from its establishment elsewhere ... Catholic Bishop Denaud a very worthy Man, observed at the time to an English Gentleman who was very warm on the subject ... "You do not know my Countrymen, they are not at all prepared for the Constitution you wish to give them, once let the rein loose, and be assured they will never know when to stop." ...

Short of the decisive step of taking away the House altogether, one or other of these two measures either of reuniting the Provinces, or of forming a new division of the Counties seems to offer the only option, from which a hope can be entertained of rendering that House less capable of doing mischief when I say this, I mean as offering the only expectation of ever effecting a Balance, to the Canadian Party, but under any shape in which it may be thought proper to continue the House, the enactment of a qualification with respect to the Representatives seems to be indispensably necessary. It really My Lord appears to be an absurdity, that the Interests of certainly not an unimportant Colony involving in them those also of no inconsiderable portion of the Commercial concerns of the British Empire should be in the hands of six petty shopkeepers, a Blacksmith, a Miller, and 15 ignorant peasants who form part of our present House, a Doctor or Apothecary, twelve Canadian Avocats, and Notaries, and four, so far respectable people that at least they do not keep shops, together with ten English members compleat the List; there is not one person coming under the description of a Canadian Gentleman among them ...

I have the Honor to be, My Lord,
Your Lordship's most obedient humble Servant.
J. H. CRAIG.

7

"For the Sake of Humanity"

Newfoundland and the Beothuk

DOCUMENTS

A) Report of Committee Appointed to Inquire into the State of the Trade to Newfoundland in March, April and June, 1793
   Parliamentary Papers

B) To the Editor of the *Liverpool Mercury*
   E.S.

C) Narrative, St. John's, Newfoundland, May 27, 1819
   John Peyton Jr.

D) Royal Gazette, November 13, 1827
   W. E. Cormack, Esq.

Of the many mysteries in Canada's early history, few are more controversial than the tragic disappearance of the Beothuk, Newfoundland's indigenous people. No one refutes their disappearance: we know the last survivor, Shawnadithit, died of tuberculosis in 1829. But why? Did they lose a tribal rivalry with the Micmac? Or was it losing the brutal competition for limited resources on Newfoundland's harsh terrain? Theories certainly abound. One critical factor was the unique relationship, or lack of one, between European and Beothuk. In fishing outposts, Europeans living in Newfoundland could go about their business without local native assistance. Such was obviously not the case in areas concentrating on the fur trade where indigenous people provided most of the pelts. Being rendered superfluous to European needs perhaps increased the Beothuks' vulnerability.

The Beothuk, on the other hand, developed a dependency upon European goods, especially iron items such as fish hooks, knives, and cooking utensils. They had little to barter or sell, and therefore "stole" what they needed. This inevitably led to reprisals from frustrated settlers and fishers, and may have accelerated their demise. The British government knew fishers harassed the Beothuk and occasionally hunted them, but Britain barely controlled this land and lacked the will to do so. There was a plan to forbid harassment, and the government did call an inquiry into the fishery in 1793, but it was too little, too late. In the end, British officials offered bounties for Beothuk captives in a strange plan that intended to turn these prisoners into mediators and translators for future dealings with other Beothuk bands.

John Jeffrey was a well known entrepreneur associated with the West Country Merchants, the group which all but ran Newfoundland, often with scant regard for British common law.

George Cartwright (1739–1819), a former army officer, visited Newfoundland in 1766. He returned in 1768 with a mandate to explore the interior of the island and establish friendly contact with the Beothuk. He was far more sympathetic toward different cultures than most of his contemporaries, and even sponsored a tour of England for an Inuit family. Cartwright made his living as a fish, seal, and fur trader, but American privateers eventually ruined his business. He left Newfoundland in 1787, and spent the rest of his life in England.

Peter Ougier (?–1803) was a member of the West Country Merchants who dominated Newfoundland society at this time. By 1788 he owned eight ships and annually employed between 600 and 800 fishers. Complaining about over-fishing is not a recent phenomenon: Ougier wrote and spoke about it. Nor did his complaints fall on deaf ears. His vociferous concerns about the cod trade helped spark the 1793 inquiry.

Richard Edwards (1715–1795) had a distinguished career in the Royal Navy and served two terms as governor of Newfoundland. His chief concern, on both occasions, was with defense, not the Beothuk.

John Reeves (1752–1829) was a Newfoundland maverick. He vigorously opposed the autocratic rule of the West Country Merchants, calling for greater local control over colonial affairs. This stance presumably gained him enemies in high places and friends among the ordinary folk eking out lives on "The Rock." His Eton and Oxford education, plus a legal practice, became invaluable in the brutal thrust and parry of Newfoundland politics. The British government made him a judge for the island in 1791, and he wrote the first comprehensive history of the colony.

Nothing is known of "E.S.," whose letter to the *Liverpool Mercury* appears in this volume.

No one enjoyed a more legendary reputation for brutality against the Beothuk than John Peyton Sr. (1749–1829). He came from England as a young man and took up residence as an independent trader in the middle of a key Beothuk migration route. There he apparently considered the Beothuk lowly enough to hunt. His son, John Peyton Jr. (1793–1879) was Newfoundland born but educated in England. He, thankfully, seemed more civilized than his father, and Britain appointed him Justice of the Peace upon his return to the island. Peyton Jr. and his father set out, in 1818, to find the Beothuk allegedly responsible for several thefts of family property. They managed to capture one Beothuk, a woman named Demasduwit.

W.E. Cormack (1796–1863) came from Newfoundland but enjoyed the rare opportunity of a university education in Glasgow and Edinburgh. There he studied natural history and developed his keen interest in what is today called anthropology. A party of immigrant Scots later followed him to Prince Edward Island, but he did not tarry. He wanted to return to Newfoundland, explore the interior, and establish settlements, which required friendly relations with the Beothuk. Though he set out to make contact, each of several attempts failed. In 1827, however, he did establish the Beothuk Institute, which collected lore, artifacts, and information on Beothuk language, beliefs, and movements. Surprisingly, Cormack eventually concluded that the Beothuk originated from Scandinavia.

A) Report of Committee Appointed to Inquire into the State of the Trade to Newfoundland in March, April and June, 1793
Parliamentary Papers

Examination of Mr Jeffrey, merchant of Newfoundland.

On being asked if he knew anything respecting the conduct of the inhabitants towards the Indians, he said, "He has heard in many instances of very inhuman treatment of individuals towards them in the North part of the island; he thinks it requires investigation."

George Cartwright Esq., being examined, informed your Committee, that he was an Officer of Foot in His Majesty's service. And being asked whether he has been in Newfoundland? he said, "Yes; several times." And being asked in what capacity? he said, "Twice on pleasure, five times on business, on his way backwards and forwards to Labrador; the last time he was there was in 1786; he has been much in that part of Newfoundland inhabited by the native Indians, he has reason to believe that their numbers are considerable, but he cannot state what the numbers are, as they have been so much chased and driven away by the Fishermen and Furriers."

And being asked, How near to any of our settlements do the Indians come? he said, "They frequently come in the night into the harbours to pilfer what they can get, to supply their necessities."

And being asked, What were the articles which they mostly steal? he said, "Sails, hatchets, boats, kettles and such other things as they think will be of use; they use the sails as covering for their wigwams or tents."

And being asked, could he state any particulars respecting the condition of the Indians in Newfoundland? he said, "He thinks their condition is very wretched and forlorn indeed; our fishermen and furriers shooting at the Indians for their amusement." He said, "He has heard many say they had rather have a shot at an Indian than at a deer: A few years ago there two men, one of whom he knew personally, went up the Great River Exploits in the winter, on purpose to murder and plunder such Indians as they could meet with; when they got to the head of the river where it comes out of a great lake, they met with an Indian town, containing above one hundred inhabitants; they immediately fired upon them with long guns loaded with buckshot; they killed and wounded several, the rest made their escape into the woods, some naked, others only half clothed; none of them provided with implements to procure either food or fuel; they then plundered their houses or wigwams of what they thought worth bringing away, and burnt the rest, by which they must necessarily have destroyed the remainder, as they could not exist in the snow." And being asked, If he meant to state that the conduct of the Fishermen and Furriers towards the Indians was in general of that cruel nature, or that these were only particular instances? he said, "He has reason to believe from the conversations he has had with the fishermen of these parts, that there are very few who would not have done the same thing."

The witness having stated, that the Indians sometimes come down into the ports where our cod-fishery is carried on, and steal various articles, he was asked, Whether he believes that was in consequence of any provocation or molestation that they might have received from the Fishermen and Furriers? he said, "Most certainly, and also from the impossibility of their ever getting anything they want by any other means; he has been well assured, that formerly a very beneficial barter was carried on between our people and the Indians, somewhere near the port of Bonavista, by our people leaving goods at a certain place, and the Indians taking what they wanted and leaving furs in return: but that barter was at length put a stop to by one of our fishermen hiding himself near the place of deposit, and shooting a woman dead upon the spot as she was suiting herself to what she wanted."

And being asked, Whether he believes, from what he has seen of the Indians, that any intercourse could be again established between them and the British Fishermen and Furriers in Newfoundland? he said, "He thinks it very possible and practicable that he gave in a plan several years ago to the administration for that purpose, and then stated generally these circumstances, and he offered to undertake the execution of it himself."

And being asked, from what he has seen of the Indians, did they seem to be of a more sanguinary and savage disposition than people in that state of society generally are? he said, "By no means, for he has heard many instances of their saving the lives of our people, when they might very easily have put them to death; he heard one man tell his master, that a few days before he left the Bay of Exploits, as he was going to land out of his boat to look at a trap that he had set for an otter, he was surprised by the voice of an Indian; and on turning his head, saw an Indian standing on the shore with an arrow in his bow ready to shoot him; the Indian made a motion with his hand for him to retire; he was then not above four or five yards from the Indian; he immediately pulled his boat round and made off as fast as he could; the Indian remained in the same posture until he had got some distance from the shore, and then retired into the woods; the Fisherman then added, that he regretted not having his gun with him, as he would have shot him dead upon the spot."

And being asked, Whether the Indians are large and stout men? he said, "From what few he had seen of them, he believes they are."

And being asked, Did the cruelties which he mentioned to be exercised by the Fishermen and Furriers to the Indians happen in summer as well as in winter? he said, "Yes, in both, but more opportunities happen in summer than in winter." — And being asked, Did the merchants and persons who go out from this country to Newfoundland use their influence and endeavours to prevent such practices? he said, "He did not recollect an instance of it."

And being asked, Had the Magistrates used any exertions to prevent those outrages? he said, "There are no Magistrates within that district, that he knew of, he means the district between Cape St John and Cape Freels."

And being asked, Whether the Magistrates resident within any of the other districts were capable of preventing these horrors if they exerted themselves for that purpose? he said, "He does not believe they could, because they reside at too great a distance."

And being asked, Did he conceive that those horrors could be prevented without the establishment of a regular Court of Judicature in Newfoundland? he said, "He thinks that if his plan, or something similar to it, was adopted, it would effectually prevent every thing of the kind and the offender might be carried to St John's to be tried by any Court of Judicature established there for the trial of criminal offences."

And being asked, Whether there is not a trade at present carried on with the Indians? he said, "No: he knew not when the intercourse was interrupted; it was twenty-seven years ago that he first heard of it."

And being asked, Whether there is any English merchant that carries on a Fishery North of Cape John? he said, "Not now he believes."

And being asked, Whether the people that he states to have committed those enormities were annual Fishermen from England or residents in Newfoundland? he said, "Generally the resident Fishermen."

And being asked, If that residence was prohibited, would not these enormities be in a great measure prevented? he said, "If residency within the district he alludes to was not permitted, it would in a great measure have that effect;" he means the district between Cape Freels and Cape St. John.

And being asked, Whether he thinks that the disposition of the Indians is such as to lead them to live upon good terms with our people, provided there were only a sufficient number left to take care of the fishing materials? he said, "He thinks our people would be in danger, unless some intercourse was first established."

And being asked, In what year did the enormities he represents happen, and who were the Officers of the Navy commanding in those parts at the time? he said, "He could not recollect."

And being asked, if he was conversant with the Coast of Labrador? he said, "Yes."

And being asked Whether there is not an annual Fishery carried on there from Great Britain, without any residence? he said, "No, there are very few who go out for the summer there."

And being asked, How is justice administered in Labrador? he said, "There has been neither law, justice, nor equity there for many years."

And being asked, Whether there is not a more flourishing Fishery carried on there than in Newfoundland? he said, "He could not tell how flourishing it is, but he knew that numbers of people have suffered there for want of justice."

And being desired to state any instances he might have heard while he resided in Newfoundland, which might make a new Court of Judicature necessary, he said, "He could not pretend to say; he knew of none."

And being desired to state the outlines of his plan, he said, "It was to appropriate that part of the Coast from North Head to Dog Creek, including Chapel Island, and all other islands within that line, to the use of the Indians, and to have some person stationed there with a schooner and a sufficient number of people to protect them; by which means some acquaintance and connection might be formed betwixt the Indians and the English, and beyond all doubt a traffic would be established." There is no intercourse or barter between those native Indians he speaks of and our people. There are parts of the island where some intercourse is maintained with the Mickmack Indians, and in other parts with the Nescopite Indians.

And being asked, If he meant that all the residents should be removed from that part he has described, and that no person should land or go there without permission? he said, "He does."

And being asked, Whether he ever knew more than one man residing upon the River Exploits? he said, "He knew but of one."

And being asked, Whether the same cruelties were exercised against the Indians of the Coast of Labrador, as against the Red Indians? he said, "Not since the year 1770, since he went amongst them, and learned their language, and got upon terms of friendship with them; previous to that period the cruelties were just as numerous as those exercised in Newfoundland. It appears to him that the Indians wish to be on terms of friendship with the English."

And being asked, Whether the inveteracy of the Indians towards the Europeans is not so great that they murder every European they are able? he said, "Yes."

And being asked, Whether he conceives that, if the traders, going in the summer to Newfoundland, use their influence to prevent the horrors that have been described, that they might not in some degree be prevented? he said, "He believes it would have a good effect, but in general they do not trouble their heads about the matter, for fear it should affect their own interests."

And being asked, Whether those Indians are not universally afraid of an Englishman? he said, "They are."

And being asked, Would they venture to come within sight of an European? he said, "They conceal themselves in the woods as much as possible, and very seldom show themselves."

And being asked, Did not the merchants going to Newfoundland receive the furs that are taken from the Indians without making any enquiry? he said, "Yes."

And being asked, Whether our trade and intercourse with Labrador was not very insignificant before the year 1770? he said, "Yes." ...

Mr. Ougier, merchant, examined, said, "A grand jury would at this time have readily found a bill against the murderer of an Indian, and the Petty Jury on proof would have convicted him."

On being asked whether he knew anything of the Island of Newfoundland, or the coast of Labrador? he said, "He knows there is at present a beneficial traffic with the Indians, both Esquimaux and Micmacs, which has been acquired from the humane treatment of His Majesty's subjects towards them; there are instances of two or three hundred coming together to traffic with the English merchants, and that there is no apprehension of fear between one party and the other. It has been doubted whether there are any Newfoundland Indians or not; they are supposed to be of the other two descriptions, only who, at certain seasons of the year, inhabit Newfoundland. Some Esquimaux have been in the service of English merchants as boat-masters in the Cod Fishery, in which they have been very excellent: he has known an Indian who lived in Dartmouth some years; he returned to Labrador, and joined with his countrymen; he is now the cause of a considerable traffic between them.

Vice-Admiral Edwards, examined, said, "He was Governor of Newfoundland in 1757, 1758, 1759, and in 1789 and 1790."

And being asked, Whether he knew anything of the manner in which the Indians are treated? he said, "He knew one instance, in 1758, of a murder committed by some Irish hunters on the north part of the island; they fired into a wigwam, killed a woman with a child, and brought away a girl of nine years old. Complaint was made to him by the Justices, and pains taken to catch the culprits, but without effect. The girl was brought home to England. If they had been found he would have tried them at the Court of Oyer and Terminer. Mr Cartwright never made any complaints to him of the cruel treatment of the Indians by the inhabitants, and he knows of no other instance of it."

John Reeves, Esq., Chief Justice of Newfoundland, being examined, said, "Another subject is the state of the Wild Indians in the interior parts of the island.

"At a time when the Legislature is manifesting so much anxiety for the protection and welfare of a people who do not belong to us I make no doubt of being heard while I say a few words in behalf of these poor people, who are a part of the King's subjects. These Indians inhabit a country the sovereignty of which is claimed and exercised by His Majesty. Unlike the wandering tribes upon the continent, who roam from place to place, these people are more peculiarly our own people than any other of the savage tribes; they and everything belonging to them is in our power; they can be benefitted by none others; they can be injured by none others: in this situation they are entitled the protection of the King's government, and to the benefit of good neighborhood from his subjects; but they enjoy neither; they are deprived of the free use of the shores and the rivers, which should entitle them to some compensation from us; but they receive none; instead of being traded with, they are plundered, instead of being taught, they are pursued with outrage and murder.

"It seems very extraordinary, but it is a fact known to hundreds in the northern part of the island, that there is no intercourse or connection whatsoever between our people and the Indians but plunder, outrage and murder. If a wigwam is found it is plundered of the furs it contains, and is burnt; if an Indian is discovered he is shot at exactly as a fox or bear. This has gone on for years in Newfoundland, while Indians in all other parts of the King's dominions have received benefit from their connection with us, either in the supply of their worldly necessities by traffic, or in being initiated in the principles of morality and religion; but such has been the policy respecting this island, that the residents for many years had little benefit of a regular government for themselves, and when they were so neglected, it is not to be wondered that the condition of the poor Indians was never mended.

"When the Indians show themselves, it is in the Bay of Exploits and in Gander Bay, to the northward. They come down to get what the seashore affords for food. This is a lawless part of the island, where there are no Magistrates resident for many miles, nor any control, as in other parts, from the short visit of a man-of-war during a few days in the summer; so that people do as they like, and there is hardly any time of account for their actions. The persons who are best acquainted with the resort of the Indians, and who are deepest in the outrages that have been committed upon them, are the furriers of the bays I have just mentioned, and of the places thereabouts. Some of these men have been conversed with last summer, and I understand, if they were relieved from the danger of enquiry into what is past, they would open upon the subject, and make themselves useful in commencing any new system of treatment and conduct.

"What then do I propose to be done for these Indians, and what is the manner in which I propose it should be accomplished? In the first place, it seems they ought to be protected from violence, and that ought to be done by executing the present laws against offenders. I hope something is already begun towards attaining this, by what I said to the Grand Jury, last year, and the apprehension expressed, as I understand by some furriers, who feared they should be brought to justice; but in so distant a part of the island the fear of the law is little security, and if it is really to be executed, I hardly know the means of doing it in the present circumstances of the island and its government.

"But supposing this attained, does our bare duty towards these people end here? Separated as they are from all the world but us, is it not incumbent upon us to use the means in our power to impart to them the rights of religion and civil society? or at least, does not our interest suggest an advantage that might be derived by a free and unrestrained trade with them, in which furs and other produce might be exchanged for British manufactures? Should any or all of these considerations be thought sufficient for endeavouring to conciliate the confidence of these people, and to open a friendly intercourse with them, there seems no difficulty or hazard in the undertaking. It is similar to what has already been done on the Labrador coast with a race of savages said to be more untractable, and under circumstances much less favourable. It is only to choose between holding out encouragement to the Moravians to send a Missionary, as they now do to Labrador, or employing the present furrier under the direction of some person who has a talent for such enterprises. In both cases, there should be some small force; and if one of the sloops of war upon that station were to winter in the Bay of Exploits, or Gander Bay, for protecting such a project in the season that is most favourable to it, it would be as much force as would be needed; but the mode and manner of carrying into execution such a scheme is for the consideration of the Committee."

B) To the Editor of the *Liverpool Mercury*
E.S.

Sir,

Observing among the deaths in the Mercury of September 18th that of "Shanawdithit" supposed to be the last of the "Red Indians" or aborigines of Newfoundland, I am tempted to offer a few remarks on the subject, convinced as I am that she cannot be the last of the tribe by many hundreds. Having resided a considerable time in that part of the north of Newfoundland which they most frequented, and being one of the party who captured Mary March in 1819, I have embodied into a narrative the events connected with her capture, which I am confident will gratify many of your readers.

Proceeding northward, the country gradually assumes a more fertile appearance; the trees, which in the south are, except in a few places, stunted in their growth, now begin to assume a greater height and strength till you reach the neighbourhood of Exploits River and Bay; here the timber is of a good size and quality, and in sufficient quantity to serve the purposes of the inhabitants: — both here and at Trinity Bay some very fine vessels have been built. — To Exploits Bay it was that the Red Indians came every summer for the purpose of fishing, the place abounding with salmon. No part of the Bay was inhabited; the islands at the mouth consisting of Twillingate, Exploits island, and Burnt islands, had a few inhabitants. There were also several small harbours in a large island, the name of which I now forget, including Herring Neck and Morton. In 1820 the population of Twillingate amounted to 720, and that of all the other places might perhaps amount to as many more; — they were chiefly the descendants of West England settlers; and having many of them been for several generations without religious or moral instruction of any kind, were immersed in the lowest state of ignorance and vice. Latterly, however, churches have been built and schools established, and I have been credibly informed that the moral and intellectual state of the people is much improved. While I was there the church was opened, and I must say that the people came in crowds to attend a place of worship, many of them coming 15 and 20 miles purposely to attend. On the first settlement of the country, the Indians naturally viewed the intruders with a jealous eye, and some of the settlers having repeatedly robbed their nets &c., they retaliated and stole several boats, sails, implements of iron &c. The settlers in return mercilessly shot all the Indians they could meet with: — in fact so fearful were the latter of fire arms, that in an open space one person with a gun would frighten a hundred; when concealed among the bushes, however, they often made a most desperate resistance. I have heard an old man named Rogers, living on Twillingate Great Island boast that he had shot at different periods above sixty of them. So late as 1817, this wretch, accompanied by three others, one day discovered nine unfortunate Indians lying asleep on a small island far up the bay. Loading their guns very heavily, they rowed up to them and each taking aim fired. One only rose, and rushing into the water, endeavored to swim to another island, close by, covered with wood: but the merciless wretch followed in the boat, and butchered the poor creature in the water with an axe, then took the body to the shore and piled it on those of the other eight, whom his companions had in the meantime put out of their misery. He minutely described to me the spot, and I afterwards visited the place, and found their bones in a heap, bleached and whitened with the winters blast.

I have now I think said enough to account for the shyness of the Indians towards the settlers, but could relate many other equally revolting scenes, some of which I shall hereafter touch upon. In 1815 or 1816, Lieutenant, now Captain Buchan, set out on an expedition to endeavour to meet with the Indians, for the purpose of opening a friendly communication with them. He succeeded in meeting with them, and the intercourse seemed firmly established, so much so, that two of them consented to go and pass the night with Capt. Buchan's party he leaving two of his men who volunteered to stop. On returning to the Indians' encampment in the morning, accompanied by the two who had remained all night, on approaching the spot, the two Indians manifested considerable disquietude, and after exchanging a few glances with each other, broke from their conductors and rushed into the woods. On arriving at the encampment, Capt. Buchan's poor fellows lay on the ground a frightful spectacle, their heads being severed from their bodies, and almost cut to pieces.

In the summer of 1818 a person who had established a salmon fishery at the mouth of the Exploits River, had a number of articles stolen by the Indians; they consisted of a gold watch, left accidently in the boat, the boats, sails, some hatchets, cordage and iron implements. He therefore resolved on sending an expedition into the country, in order to recover his property.

... Mr ——— instructed the men in which way he wished them to act, informing them that his object was to open a friendly communication with the Indians, rather than act on the principle of intimidating them by revenge; that if they avoided him, he should endeavour to take one or two prisoners and bring them with him, in order that by the civilization of one or two an intercourse might be established that would end in their permanent civilization. He strictly exhorted them not to use undue violence; everyone was strictly enjoined not to fire on any account. About three o'clock in the afternoon two men, who then led the party were about two hundred yards before the rest; three deer closely followed by a pack of wolves, issued from the woods on the left, and bounded across the lake, passing very near the men, whom they totally disregarded. The men incautiously fired at them. We were then about half a mile from the point of land that almost intersected the lake, and in a few minutes we saw it covered with Indians, who instantly retired. The alarm was given; we soon reached the point; about five hundred yards on the other side we saw the Indians' houses, and the Indians, men, women and children rushing from them, across the lake, here about a mile broad. Hurrying on we quickly came to the houses; when within a short distance from the last house, three men and a woman carrying a child issued forth. One of the men took the infant from her, and their speed soon convinced us of the futility of pursuit; the woman however, did not run so fast. Mr —— loosened his provision bag from his back and let it fall, threw away his gun and hatchet and set off at a speed that soon overtook the woman. One man and myself did the same, except our guns. The rest, picking up our things followed. On overtaking the woman, she instantly fell on her knees, and tearing open the cossack (a dress composed of deerskin bound with fur), showing her breasts to prove she was a woman, and begged for mercy. In a few moments we were by Mr ——'s side. Several of the Indians, with the three who had quitted the house with the woman, now advanced, while we retreated towards the shore. At length we stopped and they did the same. After a pause three of them laid down their bows, with which they were armed, and came within two hundred yards. We then presented our guns, intimating that not more than one would be allowed to approach. They retired and fetched their arms, when one, the ill fated husband of Mary March, our captive, advanced with a branch of a fir tree (spruce) in his hand. When about ten yards off he stopped and made a long oration. He spoke at least ten minutes, towards the last his gesture became very animated and his eye "shot fire." He concluded very mildly, and advancing, shook hands with many of the party — then he attempted to take his wife from us; being opposed in this he drew from beneath his cossack, an axe, the whole of which was finely polished, and brandished it over our heads.

On two or three pieces being presented, he gave it up to Mr —— who then intimated that the woman must go with us, but that he might go also if he pleased, and that in the morning both should have their liberty. At the same time two of the men began to conduct her towards the houses. On this being done he became infuriated, and rushing towards her strove to drag her from them; one of the men rushed forward and stabbed him in the back with a bayonet; turning round, at a blow he laid the fellow at his feet; the next instant he knocked down another and rushing on (Mr) — like a child laid him on his back, and seizing his dirk from his belt brandished it over his head; the next instant it would have been buried in him had I not with both hands seized his arm; he shook me off in an instant, while I measured my length on the ice; Mr —— then drew a pistol from his girdle and fired. ... While the scene which I have described was acting, and which occurred in almost less space than the description can be read, a number of Indians had advanced within a short distance, but seeing the untimely fate of their chief haulted. Mr. —— fired over their heads, and they immediately fled. The banks of the lake, on the other side, were at this time covered with men women and children, at least several hundreds; but immediately being joined by their companions all disappeared in the woods. We then had time to think. For my part I could scarcely credit my senses, as I beheld the remains of the noble fellow stretched on the ice, crimsoned with his already frozen blood. One of the men then went to the shore for some fir tree boughs to cover the body, which measured as it lay, 6 feet 7 1/2 inches. The fellow who first stabbed him wanted to strip off his cossack (a garment made of deer skin, lined with beaver and other skins, reaching to the knees), but met with so stern a rebuke that he instantly desisted, and slunk abashed away.

After covering the body with boughs, we proceeded towards the Indian houses — the woman often required force to take her along ...

A watch was set outside; and having partaken of the Indian's fare, we began to talk over the events of the day. Both —— and myself bitterly reproached the man who first stabbed the unfortunate native; for though he acted violently, still there was no necessity for the brutal act, — besides, the untaught Indian was only doing that which every man ought to do, — he came to rescue his wife from the hands of her captors, and nobly lost his life in his attempt to save her. —— here declared that he would rather have defeated the object of his journey a hundred times than have sacrificed the life of one Indian. The fellow merely replied, "it was only an Indian, and he wished he had shot a hundred instead of one." The poor woman was now tied securely, we having, on consideration, deemed it for the best to take her with us, so that by kind treatment and civilization she might, in the course of time, be returned to the tribe, and be the means of effecting a lasting reconciliation between them and the settlers ...

C) Narrative, St. John's, Newfoundland, May 27, 1819
John Peyton Jr.

Sir,

I beg leave to lay before Your Excellency the following statements by which it will appear to what extent I have been a sufferer by depredation committed on my property by the Native Indians, and which at last drove me to the necessity of following them to endeavour to recover some part of it again.

In April 1814, John Morris, a furrier of mine, came out from one of my furrier's tilts in the country on business to me, leaving in the tilt his provisions, some fur, and his clothes. On his return to the tilt again he found that some persons had been there in his absence, and carried away and destroyed the provisions, and all the fur with many other little things but yet valuable to a furrier; the distance being 20 miles from the tilt to my residence he was obliged to sleep there that night, but the next day Morris came out and told me what had happened, and that he had every reason to suspect that it had been done by the Red Indians. On the following morning I, with Thomas Taylor, another of my furriers, and John Morris, went to Morris's tilt and found what he had told me to be correct, and near the tilt I found part of an Indian's snow racket and a hatchet, which convinced me that the depredation had been committed by them. We, after this, followed their tracks to Morris's different beaver houses and found that they had carried away seven of my traps. The damage done and loss I sustained on this occasion cannot be estimated at less than £15 independent of losing the season for catching fur.

In June 1814 Mathew Huster and John Morris were sent by me to put out a new fleet of salmon nets consisting of two nets 60 fathoms long. On going the following morning to haul them, they were cut from the moorings and nothing but a small part of the Head Rope left. From the manner the moorings were cut and hackled, and the marks of Red Ochre on the Buoys, we were satisfied that it was done by the Indians, no other persons being near us at that season. In the following August some of my people had an occasion to land on a point often frequented by the Indians, they saw there had been two wigwams built there that summer, but the Indians had left it some time, there they found the cork and part of the head rope of the nets, which convinced us who it was had cut away the nets in June. The damage done me by the loss of the nets was £20 independent of the fish that might have been caught by them that summer.

In August 1815 the Red Indians came into the harbour of Exploits Burnt Island in the night, and cut adrift from my stage a fishing boat, carried away her sails and fishing tackle; they also the same night cut a boat adrift belonging to Geo. Luff, of the same harbour. The loss I sustained here was full £10. In October 1817 I sent Edward Rogers, an apprentice, to set a number of traps for catching marten cats, they being apparently very plenty at that time. On going to visit his traps he found that fourteen of his best traps were carried away, and an Indian's arrow driven through the roof of the cat-house, at the end of the path were two Indian paddles, the loss here, independent of the fur, was £4. 18s.

In September 1818 the Indians came to my wharf at Sandy Point, and cut adrift a large boat of mine which I had in the day loaded with salmon, &c., for St John's market, and was only waiting for a fair wind to sail. On my missing her at half past one in the morning, I took a small boat, and with a servant went in search of her. About seven o'clock in the evening I discovered her ashore in a most dangerous situation. With great difficulty I boarded her, and found that the Indians had cut away her sails and part of her rigging, and had plundered her of almost every thing moveable. Her hull being much damaged, it was impossible to get her off without assistance. I proceeded to Exploits Burnt Island for a crew, and brought her into the harbour, the damage done to the boat and some part of her cargo, and the property stolen cannot be replaced under £140 or £150. Having so frequently suffered such heavy losses, on my arrival I waited on Your Excellency requesting permission to follow the property and regain it if possible, I made deposition of the truth of what I had asserted, and obtained Your Excellency's permission to go into the country during the winter.

On the first of March, 1819, I left my house accompanied by my father and eight of my own men with a most anxious desire of being able to take some of the Indians and thus through them open a friendly communication with the rest, everyone was ordered by me not upon any account to commence hostilities without my positive orders. On the 2nd March we came up with a few wigwams frequented by the Indians during the spring and autumn for the purpose of killing deer. On the 3rd we saw a fireplace by the side of the brook where some Indians had slept a few days before. On the 4th, at 10 o'clock we came to a storehouse belonging to the Indians. On entering it I found five of my cat traps, set, as I supposed, to protect their venison from the cats, and part of my boat's jib, from the fireplace and tracks on the snow, we were convinced the Indians had left it the day before in the direction SW. We therefore followed their footing with all possible speed and caution ... I could not tell at this time whether the Indian I saw was a male or female. I showed myself on the point openly, when the Indian discovered me she for a moment was motionless. She screamed out as soon as she appeared to make me out and ran off. I immediately pursued her, but did not gain on her until I had taken off my rackets and Jacket, when I came up with her fast, she kept looking back at me over her shoulder, I then dropped my gun on the snow and held up my hands to show her I had no gun, and on my pointing to my gun which was then some distance behind me, she stopped. I did the same and endeavoured to convince her I would not hurt her. I then advanced and gave her my hand, she gave hers to me and to all my party as they came up. We then saw seven or eight Indians repeatedly running off and on the pond, and as I imagined from their wigwams. Shortly after three Indians came running towards us — when they came within about 200 or 300 yds. from us they made a halt. I advanced towards them with the woman, and on her calling to the Indians two of their party came down to us, the third halted again about 100 yards distant. I ordered one of the men to examine one of the Indians that did come to us, having observed something under his cassock, which proved to be a hatchet, which the man took from him, — the two Indians came and took hold of me by the arms endeavouring to force me away. I cleared myself as well as I could still having the woman in my hand. The Indian from whom the hatchet was taken attempted to lay hold of three different guns, but without effect, he at last succeeded in getting hold of my father's gun, and tried to force it from him, and in the attempt to get his gun he and my father got off nearly fifty yards from me and in the direction of the woods, at the same time the other Indian was continually endeavouring to get behind our party. The Indian who attacked my father grasped him by the throat. My father drew a bayonet with the hope of intimidating the Indian. It had not the desired effect, for he only made a savage grin at it. I then called for one of the men to strike him, which he did across the hands with his gun; he still held on my father till he was struck on the head, when he let my father go, and either struck at or made a grasp at the man who struck him, which he evaded by falling under the hand, at the same time this encounter was taking place, the third Indian who had halted about 100 yards, kept at no great distance from us, and there were seven or eight more repeatedly running out from the woods on the look out, and no greater distance from us than 100 yards. The Indian turned again on my father and made a grasp at his throat — my father extricated himself and on his retreat the Indian still forcing on him, fired. I ordered one of the men to defend my father, when two guns were fired, but the guns were all fired so close together that I did not know till some time after that more than one had been fired. The rest of the Indians fled immediately on the fall of the unfortunate one. Could we have intimidated or persuaded him to leave us, or even have seen the others go off, we should have been most happy to have spared using violence, but when it was remembered that our small party were in the heart of the Indians country, one hundred miles from any European settlement, and that there were in our sight at times as many Indians as our party amounted to, and we could not ascertain how many were in the woods that we did not see, it could not be avoided with safety to ourselves. Had destruction been our object we might have carried it much further. Nor should I have brought this woman to the capital to Your Excellency, nor should I offer my services for the ensuing summer, had I wantonly put an end to the unfortunate man's existence, as in the case of success in taking any more during the summer and opening a friendly intercourse with them, I must be discovered.

My object was and still is to endeavour to be on good terms with the Indians for the protection of my property, and the rescuing of that tribe of our fellow-creatures from the misery and persecution they are exposed to in the interior from Micmacs, and on the exterior by the Whites. With this impression on my mind I offer my services to the Government for the ensuing summer and I implore Your Excellency to lend me any assistance you may think proper. I cannot afford to do much at my own expense, having nothing but what I work for, the expenses of doing anything during the summer would be less than the winter, as it will not be safe ever to attempt going into their country with so small a crew as I had with me last winter. Still these expenses are much greater than I can afford, as nothing effectual can be expected to be done under £400. Unless Your Excellency should prefer sending an expedition on the service out of the fleet, in which case I would leave the woman at Your Excellency's disposal, but should I be appointed to cruise the summer for them, and which I could not do and find men and necessaries under £400, I have not the least doubt but that I shall, through the medium of the woman I now have, be enabled to open an intercourse with them, nor is it all improbable but that she will return with us again, if she can, to procure an infant child she left behind her. I beg to assure Your Excellency from my acquaintance with the bays and the place of resort for the Indians during the summer, that I am most confident of succeeding in the plan here laid down.

D) Royal Gazette, November 13, 1827
W. E. Cormack, Esq.

Every man who has common regard for the welfare of his fellow beings, and who hears of the cause for which we are now met, will assuredly foster any measures that may be devised to bring within the protection of civilization that neglected and persecuted tribe — the Red Indians of Newfoundland. Every man will join us, except he be callous to the misfortunes or regardless of the prosperity of his fellow creatures. Those who by their own merits, or by the instrumentality of others, become invested with power and influence in society, are bound the more to exert themselves — to do all the good they can, in promoting the happiness of their fellow men: and if there be such men in Newfoundland, who say there is no good to be gained by reclaiming the aborigines from their present hapless condition, let them not expose their unvirtuous sentiments to the censure of this enlightened age. — Is there no honest pride in him who protects man from the shafts of injustice? — nay, is there not an inward monitor approving of all our acts which shall have the tendency to lessen crime and prevent murder?

We now stand on the nearest part of the New World to Europe — of Newfoundland to Britain; and at this day, and on this sacred spot, do we form the first assembly that has ever yet collected together to consider the condition of the invaded and ill-treated first occupiers of the country. — Britons have trespassed here, to be a blight and a scourge to a portion of the human race; under their (in other respects) protecting power, a defenceless, and once independent, proud tribe of men, have been nearly extirpated from the face of the earth — scarcely causing an enquiry how, or why. Near this spot is known to remain in all his primitive rudeness, clothed in skins, and with a bow and arrow only to gain his subsistence by, and to repel the attacks of his lawless and reckless foes: there on the opposite approximating point, is man improved and powerful: — Barbarity and civilization are this day called upon to shake hands.

The history of the original inhabitants of Newfoundland, called by themselves Beothuck, and by Europeans, the Red Indians, can only be gleaned from tradition, and that chiefly among the Micmacs. It would appear that about a century and a half ago, this tribe was numerous and powerful — like their neighbouring tribe, the Micmacs: — both tribes were then on friendly terms, and inhabited the western shores of Newfoundland, in common with the other parts of the island, as well as Labrador. A misunderstanding with the Europeans (French) who then held the sway over those parts, led, in the result, to hostilities between the two tribes; and the sequel of the tale runs as follows.

The European authorities, who we may suppose were not over scrupulous in dealing out equity in those days, offered a reward for the persons or heads of certain Red Indians. Some of the Micmacs were tempted by the reward, and took off the heads of two of them. Before the heads were delivered for the award, they were by accident discovered, concealed in the canoe that was to convey them, and recognized by some of the Red Indians as the heads of their friends. The Red Indians gave no intimation of their discovery to the perpetrators of the unprovoked outrage, but consulted amongst themselves, and determined on having revenge. They invited the Micmacs to a great feast, and arranged their guests in such order that every Beothuck had a Micmac by his side, at a preconcerted signal each Beothuck slew his guest. They then retired quickly from those parts bordering on the Micmac country. War of course ensued. Firearms were little known to the Indians at this time, but they soon came into more general use amongst such tribes as continued to hold intercourse with Europeans. This circumstance gave the Micmacs an undisputed ascendancy over the Beothucks, who were forced to betake themselves to the recesses of the interior, and retired parts of the island, alarmed, as well they might be, at every report of the fire-lock.

Since that day European weapons have been directed, from every quarter, (and in latter times too often) at the open breasts and unstrung bows of the unoffending Beothucks. Sometimes these unsullied people of the chase have been destroyed wantonly, because they have been thought more fleet, and more evasive, than men ought to be. At other times, at the sight of them, the terror of the ignorant European has goaded him on to murder the innocent, — at the bare mention of which civilization ought to weep. Incessant and ruthless persecution, continued for many generations, has given these sylvan people an utter disregard and abhorrence of the very signs of civilization. Shawnawdithit, the surviving female of those who were captured four years ago, by some fishermen, will not now return to her tribe, for fear they should put her to death; a proof of the estimation in which we are held by that persecuted people.

The situation of the unfortunate Beothuck carries with it our warmest sympathy and loudly calls on us all to do something for the sake of humanity. — For my own satisfaction, I have for a time, released myself from all other avocations, and am here now, on my way to visit that part of the country which the surviving remnant of the tribe have of late years frequented, to endeavour to force a friendly interview with some of them, before they are entirely annihilated: but it will most probably require many such interviews, and some years, to reconcile them to the approaches of civilized man ...

8

"A Place Where Rum Is as Cheap as Beer"

Maritime Colonies

DOCUMENTS

A) Historical and Descriptive Sketches of the Maritime
Colonies of British America, 1828
J. McGregor

Various governments and agencies in Canada have, over time, spent considerable sums and gone to great lengths to lure prospective settlers to our shores. Many of those efforts were, in fact, far more seductive than accurate. A number of earlier writings, however, were balanced in their appraisal. Some authors attempted to educate prospective immigrants, not just lure them across the Atlantic. Immigrants who knew what to expect, so the argument went, should succeed far more readily than those arriving without any forewarning, or worse, with inaccurate or false information.

J. McGregor (1797–1857), like John Lambert in Chapter 6, sought to popularize immigration to British North America among people in the British Isles without sugar-coating it. He knew how loudly the American siren called to his fellow countrymen, but believed that settling in the Maritimes was far superior to the United States. And he knew his subject. He and his family arrived in Nova Scotia in 1803, then three years later moved to Prince Edward Island where they farmed the rich red soil. McGregor was ambitious, becoming a merchant, land agent, attorney, sheriff, and finally, in 1824, a member of the Legislative Assembly. There was, however, a minor scandal when he apparently pilfered the library fund. This made life in tightly knit Prince Edward Island too uncomfortable, and he moved back to England in 1827. There he began a prolific writing career, churning out some thirty volumes, none with much commercial success. No literary giant, he could write well when the subject, such as the Maritimes, suited him. The British government certainly saw merit in his talents and hired him to negotiate various commercial treaties on their behalf. Ever ambitious and restless, he successfully ran for the British House of Commons in 1847. Then his rising star crashed. Charged with fraud, he once again sought exile in 1856, fleeing to France.

A) Historical and Descriptive Sketches of the Maritime Colonies of British America, 1828
J. McGregor

New Brunswick.

The timber trade has no doubt been one, if not the principal, cause of the rapid growth of St. John. Great gains were at first realized, both by it and ship-building; and although the merchants and others immediately concerned in these pursuits were nearly ruined afterwards by the extent of their undertakings and engagements; yet, it must be recollected, that each of those trades has enabled New Brunswick to pay for her foreign imports, and with the timber trade she has built St. John, Fredericton, and St. Andrew. To the settler on new lands it presented a ready resource; and if he only engaged in it for a few winters it was wise to do so; as by the gains attending it, he was put in possession of the means of stocking his farm and clothing himself and family. The province, therefore, gained great advantage by this trade; and, although it is not less certain that it has been prosecuted to more than double the extent of the demand for timber, it would, notwithstanding, be extreme folly to abandon it altogether. Two-thirds of the people engaged in the timber trade and ship-building have only to give their industry another direction, and the remainder may work to advantage. In this view agriculture offers the most alluring, and at the same time most certain, source of employment. The fisheries follow next. Let the industry of the inhabitants be but divided between agriculture, the timber trade, and the fisheries, and this beautiful and fertile province will probably flourish beyond any precedent. But the farmer must adhere to agriculture alone; the lumberer will do better, or at least he will realize more money, by following his own business, and those engaged in the fisheries will find it best to confine themselves chiefly to this pursuit ...

   The principal settlements are along the River St. John, and its lakes; on the north banks of the St. Croix; on the Gulf of St. Lawrence; on the River

Miramichi; and on the shores of the Bay de Chaleur. The spirit of agriculture is beginning to diffuse itself rapidly through all, even the most north-
erly and coldest, parts of the province. Hitherto the timber trade and
shipbuilding, by engaging a great part of the labour of a population so very
small in proportion to the extent of the country, have retarded the cultivation of the soil and the improvement of the country. None of the North
American colonies are more in want of settlers of steady and rural habits.

The roads in this colony are few, and those in bad condition; and although its numerous rivers open in almost all directions channels of intercourse with the interior; yet without good roads, the mode of travelling or
of conveyance is more uncertain, and generally less expeditious. Great leading roads are an essential desideratum in New Brunswick. There is, it is true,
a tolerably good carriage road between St. John and Fredericton, and another from opposite St. John to St. Andrew.

An object of paramount importance would be to accomplish a continu-
ation of the road between Nova Scotia and Fredericton, to Quebec. The
best line for this route has been examined, and it has already engaged the
attention of the legislature of Canada. It should be accomplished at the joint
expense of Nova Scotia, New Brunswick and Canada; all would derive great
advantage from opening a direct line of communication, which might then
be said to extend from Great Britain to the upper countries of British America.
The course of this line would be across the Atlantic, either by the packets or
merchant ships, to Halifax; or, by the trading vessels to New Brunswick; or,
if steam packets should be established to the Gut of Canso from whence a
road must be opened to join the road from Halifax to Fredericton. The road
from Fredericton should then be continued to the lake Timisquata, and from
thence to the banks of the St. Lawrence; along which the Canadian inhabitants keep the main road always in a fair state of repair for carriages.

The town of St. Andrew, on the north side of the River St. Croix, is a
thriving place, in which a brisk trade has been carried on for some years. It
has a Commercial Bank; and it will, from its situation at the mouth of a
river which spreads over an extensive country, be always a place of considerable importance; but much of its prosperity will depend on the final settlement of the boundary line between New Brunswick and the United States.
The Americans have on the opposite side a small town called Lubec. The
revenue collected at St. Andrew's is considerable; but smuggling on a great
scale has long been carried on.

From the views which the Government of the United States entertain respecting the limits of the British possessions the adjustment of the boundary line of New Brunswick, if not soon agreed upon, will in all probability give birth to disputes, the settlement of which may be attended with more than ordinary difficulty ...

A little above Newcastle, and a short distance below the confluence of the two great arms of the river, the south west and north west branches, there is a small Island, on which there are stores and a mercantile establishment. On the banks of the three branches of this river there is a very thinly scattered population, who employ themselves chiefly in hewing timber during winter in the woods, and in rafting it down the river, in summer, to where the ships load. On the various branches of this beautiful and majestic river, fertile tracts of intervale land abound, which might be cultivated to profitable advantage, if the country were once settled with people of steady rural habits. The lumberers, who compose probably more than half the population, never will become industrious farmers; and the cultivation of the soil is consequently neglected.

The timber trade, which, in a commercial as well as political point of view, is of more importance in employing our ships and seamen, than it is generally considered to be, employs also a vast number of people in the British Colonies, whose manner of living, owing to the nature of the business they follow, is entirely different from that of the other inhabitants of North America.

Several of these people form what is termed a "lumbering party," composed of persons who are all either hired by a master lumberer, who pay them wages, and finds them in provisions; or, of individuals, who enter into an understanding with each other, to have a joint interest in the proceeds of their labour. The necessary supplies of provisions, clothing, &c., are generally obtained from the merchants on credit, in consideration of receiving the timber which the lumberers are to bring down the river the following summer. The stock deemed requisite for a "lumbering party," consists of axes, a cross-cut saw, cooking utensils; a cask of rum; tobacco and pipes; a sufficient quantity of biscuit, pork, beef, and fish; pease and pearl barley for soup, with a cask of molasses to sweeten a decoction usually made of shrubs, or of the tops of the hemlock tree, and taken as tea. Two or three yokes of oxen, with sufficient hay to feed them, are also required to haul the timber out of the wood.

When thus prepared, these people proceed up the rivers, with the provisions, &c., to the place fixed on for their winter establishment; which is selected as near a stream of water, and in the midst of much pine timber, as possible. They commence by clearing away a few of the surrounding trees, and building a camp of round logs; the walls of which are seldom more than four or five feet high; the roof is covered with birch bark, or boards ... These men are enormous eaters, and they also drink great quantities of rum, which they scarcely ever dilute. Immediately after breakfast, they divide into three gangs; one of which cuts down the trees, another hews them, and the third is employed with the oxen in hauling the timber, either to one general road leading to the banks of the nearest stream, or at once to the stream itself: fallen trees and other impediments in the way of the oxen are cut away with an axe.

The whole winter is thus spent in unremitting labour: the snow covers the ground from two to three feet from the setting in of winter until April; and, in the middle of fir forests, often till the middle of May. When the snow begins to dissolve in April, the rivers swell, or, according to the lumberers' phrase, the "freshets come down." At this time all the timber cut during winter is thrown into the water, and floated down until the river becomes sufficiently wide to make the whole into one or more rafts. The water at this period is exceedingly cold; yet for weeks the lumberers are in it from morning till night, and it is seldom less than a month and a half, from the time that floating the timber down the streams commences, until the rafts are delivered to the merchants. No course of life can undermine the constitution more than that of a lumberer and raftsman. The winter snow and frost, although severe, are nothing to endure in comparison to the extreme coldness of the snow water of the freshets; in which, the lumberer is day after day, wet up to the middle, and often immersed from head to foot. The very vitals are thus chilled and sapped; and the intense heat of the summer sun, a transition, which almost immediately follows, must further weaken and reduce the whole frame.

To stimulate the organs, in order to sustain the cold, these men swallow immoderate quantities of ardent spirits, and habits of drunkenness are the usual consequence. Their moral character, with few exceptions, is dishonest and worthless. I believe there are few people in the world, on whose promises less faith can be placed, than on those of a lumberer. In Canada, where they are longer bringing down their rafts, and have more idle time, their character, if possible, is of a still more shuffling and rascally description. Premature old age, and shortness of days, form the inevitable fate of a lumberer. Should he even save a little money, which is very seldom the case, and be enabled for the last few years of life to exist without incessant labour, he becomes the victim of rheumatisms and all the miseries of a broken constitution.

But notwithstanding all the toils of such a pursuit, those who once adopt the life of a lumberer seem fond of it. They are in a great measure as independent, in their own way, as the Indians. In New Brunswick, and particularly in Canada, the epithet " lumberer" is considered synonymous with a character of spendthrift habits, and villainous and vagabond principles. After selling and delivering up their rafts, they pass some weeks in idle indulgence; drinking, smoking, and dashing off, in a long coat, flashy waistcoat and trousers, Wellington or hessian boots, a handkerchief of many colours round the neck, a watch with a long tinsel chain and numberless brass seals, and an umbrella. Before winter they return again to the woods, and resume the pursuits of the preceding year. Some exceptions, however, I have known to this generally true character of lumberers. Many young men of steady habits, who went from Prince Edward Island, and other places, to Miramichi, for the express purpose of making money, have joined the lumbering parties for two or three years; and, after saving their earnings, returned and purchased lands, &c. on which they now live very comfortably.

From 800 to 1,000 cargoes of timber have been imported annually for some years from British America, and this trade employs about 6,000 seamen, who are exposed to every variety of climate. The timber trade is very important as a nursery for sailors, and it is besides of great value to England, in the value of freights and timber, which are principally paid for by the production of British labour. On the most convenient streams, there are several saw mills, from which the quantity of boards and deals required are brought down the river for shipping. Ship building has also occupied the attention of the merchants, about twenty large vessels having been built on the river.

In October, 1825, upwards of a hundred miles of the country, on the north side of Miramichi river, became a scene of the most dreadful conflagration that has perhaps ever occurred in the history of the world. In Europe, we can scarcely form a conception of the fury and rapidity with which the fires rage through the American forests during a dry hot season; at which time, the underwood, decayed vegetable substances, fallen branches, bark, and withered trees, are as inflammable as a total absence of moisture can render them. When these tremendous fires are once in motion, or at least when the flames extend over a few miles of the forest, the surrounding air becomes highly rarefied, and the wind naturally increases to a hurricane. It appears that the woods had been, on both sides of the North West branch, partially on fire for some time but not to an alarming extent, until the 7th of October, when it came on to blow furiously from the north-west, and the inhabitants on the banks of the river were suddenly alarmed by a tremendous roaring in the woods, resembling the incessant rolling of thunder; while at the same time, the atmosphere became thickly darkened with smoke. They had scarcely time to ascertain the cause of this phenomenon before all the surrounding woods appeared in one vast blaze, the flames ascending more than a hundred feet above the tops of the loftiest trees, and the fire, like a gulf in flames, rolling forward with inconceivable celerity. In less than an hour Douglastown and Newcastle were enveloped in one vast blaze, and many of the wretched inhabitants, unable to escape, perished in the midst of this terrible fire.

The following account is taken from a Miramichi paper of the 11th October: "More than a hundred miles of the shores of Miramichi are laid waste, independent of the north west branch, the Baltibog, and the Nappan settlements. From one to two hundred people have perished within immediate observation, and thrice that number are miserably burnt or otherwise wounded; and, at least two thousand of our fellow creatures are left destitute of the means of subsistence, and thrown at present upon the humanity of the Province of New Brunswick.

"The number of lives that have been lost in the remote parts of the woods, among the Lumbering Parties, cannot be ascertained for some time to come, for it is feared that few were left to tell the tale.

"It is not in the power of language to describe the unparalleled scene of ruin and devastation which the Parish of Newcastle at this moment presents; out of upwards of two hundred and fifty houses and stores, fourteen of the least considerable only remain. The Court House, Gaol, Church, and Barracks; Messrs. Gilmour, Rankin and Co.'s, and Messrs. William Abrams and Co's Establishments, with two Ships on the stocks are reduced to ashes.

"The loss of property is incalculable, for the fire, borne upon the wings of a hurricane, rushed upon the wretched inhabitants with such inconceivable rapidity, that the preservation of their lives could be their only care ...

"At Douglastown scarcely any kind of property escaped the ravages of the fire, which swept off the surface every thing coming in contract with it, leaving but time for the unfortunate inhabitants to fly to the shore; and there by means of boats, canoes, rafts of timber, timber-logs, or any article however ill calculated for the purpose, they endeavoured to escape from the dreadful scene, and reach the town of Chatham, numbers of men, women, and children, perishing in the attempt.

"In some parts of the country the cattle have all been destroyed, or suffered greatly, and the very soil in many places has been parched and burnt up, and no article of provisions to speak of has been rescued from the flames.

"The hurricane raged with such dreadful violence, that large bodies of timber on fire, as also trees from the forest, and parts of the flaming houses and stores, were carried to the rivers with amazing velocity, to such an extent, and affecting the water in such a manner, as to occasion large quantities of salmon and other fish to resort to land; hundreds of which were scattered on the shores of the north and south west branches.

"Chatham at present contains about three hundred of the unfortunate sufferers, who have resorted to it for relief, and are experiencing some partial assistance, and almost every hour brings with it great number from the back settlement, burnt, wounded, or in a most abject state of distress; and it is reported that nearly two hundred bodies have been actually destroyed."

The ravages of the fire extended as far as Fredericton, on the River St. John, where it destroyed the Governor's residence, and about eighty other houses; and to the northward, as far as the Bay de Chaleur. At the lowest computation, five hundred lives were lost.

If the benevolence and charity of mankind were ever manifested in a more than common degree of feeling for their fellow-men, it was assuredly on this memorable occasion. Clothing and provisions were sent from the neighbouring colonies immediately on the accounts of the distress arriving. Sir Howard Douglas, the Governor, crossed the country at once, to ascertain the full extent of the calamity. Subscriptions for the relief of the sufferers were raised to an amount hitherto unexampled, in Great Britain, in the United States, and in all the British American Colonies.

Miramichi may now be said to have completely surmounted the misery and loss occasioned by the ravages of so terrible a calamity. Newcastle is again rising from its ashes, and will in a few years likely contain as many houses, and as large a population as formerly. The country laid waste by the insatiate element is of little value, it is true, in comparison with its former worth. The timber has been destroyed, and the land impoverished, on which, trees common to sterile soils are springing up. I have often heard it observed by people unacquainted with America, that the land would become valuable by being cleared of the woods by fire, and that immense labour in reclaiming the forest lands would thus be saved; but no opinion can be more erroneous. Settlers who know the value of wilderness lands always choose those covered with the heaviest and largest trees; and the strongest objection that can be made to a piece of land, is its having been subjected to fire, which withers the trees, and effectually exhausts the soil, in consequence of its producing afterwards two or three crops of tall weeds, which require more nourishment than the same number of corn crops would. If the land were, immediately after a fire, brought under cultivation, they would then be equally valuable to those cleared in the usual way; but as these great fires seldom level the large trees, they are in consequence of losing the sap, much harder and more difficult to cut down than green wood; and, by being all charred, exceedingly disagreeable to work among. The clearing of ground, on which the trees are all in a fresh growing state, is therefore preferred to that which has been subjected to fires, which seldom consume effectually more than the underwood, decayed fragments, and the branches of the large trees. The trees cut down for the timber of commerce, are not of the smallest importance in respect to clearing the lands; although I have heard it urged in England as an argument in favour of the timber trade. The lumberers choose the trees that they consider the most suitable, and not one in ten thousand is esteemed so. Almost every description of forest trees would be valuable for different purposes, if once landed in the United Kingdoms; but the principal part of the cost is the freight across the Atlantic, and in order, therefore, that a ship may carry the greatest possible quantity, the largest and straightest trees are hewn square, and not brought round to market as the trees cut down in England are. The timber trade of America has been attended with loss to almost every merchant engaged in it. The causes of which are numerous, but principally arising, first, from the low price of labour and naval stores in the northern kingdoms of Europe, enabling the people of those countries to export timber to Great Britain at extremely low prices; and secondly, from the lumberers not being able, or indeed willing, to pay the debts they contracted with the merchants, in consequence of the depreciated value of timber. Many adventurers, also, without any capital, from witnessing extraordinary gains having been occasionally made by the merchants, entered into this business, and who, having nothing to lose, ventured into daring speculations, which were exceedingly injurious to regularly established merchants ...

Newfoundland.

... The population of St. John's fluctuates so frequently, that it is very difficult to state its numbers, even at any one period. Sometimes, during the fishing season, the town appears full of inhabitants; at others, it seems half deserted. At one time they depart for the seal fishery; at another, to different fishing stations. In the fall of the year the fishermen arrive from all quarters, to settle with the merchants, and procure supplies for winter. At this period St. John's is crowded with people, swarms of whom depart for Prince Edward Island, Nova Scotia, and Cape Breton, to procure a livelihood in those places among the farmers during winter. Many of them never return again to the fisheries, but remain in those colonies; or often, if they have relations in the United States, and sometimes when they have not, find their way thither.

Society in St. John's, particularly when we consider its great want of permanency, is in a much more respectable condition than might be expected; and the moral and social habits of the inhabitants are very different from the description of lieutenant Chappell (whom I very strongly suspect of arrogating more respect for himself than the best class of society would willingly acknowledge), when he represents the principal inhabitants as having risen from the lowest fishermen, and the rest composed of turbulent Irishmen — both alike destitute of literature. The fishermen, who are principally Irishmen, are by no means altogether destitute of education: there are few of them but who can read and write; and they are, in general, neither turbulent nor immoral. That they soon become, in Newfoundland as well as in all the other colonies, very different people to what they were before they left Ireland, is very certain. The cause is obvious — they are more comfortable, and they work cheerfully. When, after a fishing season of almost incredible fatigue and hardship, they return to St. John's, and meet their friends and acquaintances, they indulge, it is true, in drinking and idleness for a short time; and, when the life they follow is considered, we need scarce be surprised that they do so, especially in a place where rum is as cheap as beer is in England.

For many years, the officers of government, and the merchants, returned before winter to England; but, since the appointment of a resident governor, there has been also a more permanent state of society. It must be acknowledged, that some of the inhabitants who have made fortunes in the country, were, and it is much to their credit, formerly fishermen, and these men are fully as polished in their manners, and are equally intelligent as many of the principal merchants in London, or in any of the other great trading towns in the United Kingdom, who did not in early life receive a liberal education. A great majority of the merchants at St. John's, as well as the agents who represent the principal houses, are men who received a fair education, in the mother country, for all the purposes of utility and the general business of life; and, are certainly as intelligent as any merchants in the world. This observation will be found perfectly just, if applied to the merchants and principal inhabitants in all the British colonies. The amusements of St. John's are much the same as in the colonies already described.

There are three weekly newspapers published at St. John's; and there is also a book society. A seminary of education was established in 1802, for educating the poor, where about three hundred children, Protestants and Roman Catholics, are educated. It was established, I believe, principally through Lord Gambier, then the admiral on the station.

The benevolent Irish society, established in 1806, by the present secretary of state for the colonies, then colonel Murray, and James M'Braire, Esq. then a merchant of eminence a St. John's, but since retired to the banks of the Tweed, has extended the most beneficial relief to the aged and infirm; and has also diffused the benefits of education among the children of the poorer classes, by supporting a school in which from two hundred to three hundred of both sexes are instructed. A respectable school-house is now erecting by the society, to contain 700 to 800 children.

The leading features of the character of the inhabitants of Newfoundland, both at St. John's and all the out harbours, are, honesty, persevering industry, hardy contempt of fatigue, and a laudable sense of propriety in moral and religious duties.

There are places of public worship at St. John's, and in each of the out harbours, in which there is an adequate population. The religious professions are members of the Church of England, Roman Catholics, Presbyterians, and Methodists, each of whom have clergymen among them. In the principal out harbours, also, there are schools, where the rudiments of education may be acquired.

The inhabitants are employed, the majority wholly, and the rest occasionally, in the fisheries. Feeding cattle and a few sheep, and cultivating small spots of land, are, also, partial sources of occupation. The women, besides affording great assistance to the men, during the process of curing fish, make themselves useful in planting gardens and gathering the productions of the soil. In all domestic duties they are correct and attentive; and they manufacture the small quantity of wool they have among them into strong worsted stockings, mittens, and socks.

Capital offences are exceedingly rare, and petty thefts are scarcely known, while property is seldom secured by locked doors, as in the United Kingdom.

In the winter season much of the time of the inhabitants is occupied in bringing home fuel. Boats for the fishery are also constructed at this time; and poles, &c. for fish flakes, are, or should be provided ...

Nova Scotia.

... The population of the province was, in 1817, according to a census taken by order of the Earl of Dalhousie, 78,345; but this account has been considered extremely inaccurate, and the population at present (1827) is rated, exclusive of Cape Breton, at 126,000 to 130,000, consisting of English, Scotch, Irish, Germans, Dutch, French Acadians, American loyalists, and the descendants of those who have settled at different periods in the colony. The Scotch, in a numerical scale, predominate, and are principally settled in the district of Pictou, at the Gut of Canso, Antigonishe Bay, and along the coast and harbours of the straits of Northumberland, and also more or less in every part of the province. The principal part of the English population is in Halifax; a small proportion only is to be found in the settlements. The Irish settlers are mingled among the others all over the country. The American loyalists, with the exception of their first settlement, at Shelburne, appear to have selected the best spots in the colony: they certainly had the advantage, at the time, of making a choice of situation, and they understood doing so better than emigrants from Europe. The Germans are not numerous, but are always distinguished by their industry and economy ...

Slavery does not exist in Nova Scotia: the number of free negroes may be equal to 1500; part of whom came from the West India Islands, others from the United States, and the residue were born in the province. A settlement was laid out, a few miles from Halifax, for these people, and every facility afforded them, by the provincial government, yet they are still in a state of miserable poverty; while Europeans, who have settled on wood-lands, under circumstances scarcely so favourable, thrive with few exceptions.

Whether the wretchedness of these negroes may be attributed to servitude and degradation having extinguished in them the spirit that endures present difficulties and privations, in order to attain future advantages; or to the consciousness that they are an unimportant and distinct race, in a country where they feel that they must ever remain a separate people; or, that they find it more congenial to their habits to serve others, either as domestic servants, or labourers, by which they make sure of the wants of the day, certain it is that they prefer servitude, and generally live more comfortably in this condition, than they usually do when working on their own account. I do not, by this observation, mean to inculcate the revolting doctrine, that slavery is the most happy state in which the unfortunate negroes in the West Indies and America can live; but I am certainly of opinion, that, unless they are gradually prepared for personal liberty, they will, on obtaining their freedom, become objects of greater commiseration than they now are in a state of bondage; and the condition of the free negroes in Nova Scotia will fully substantiate this assertion ...

The Church of England in this province is supported by the Society for propagating the Christian Religion. The clergy, about thirty in number, are under the control of a bishop, styled the bishop of Nova Scotia, who has also under his jurisdiction the clergy of New Brunswick, Prince Edward Island, Newfoundland, and Bermuda. One-fourth of the population are Roman Catholics, who are likewise under the care of a bishop. The Church of Scotland properly so called, has only a few clergymen in the colony; but the Presbyterian seceders, the great body of which are settled in the district of Pictou, have a provincial church government of their own. Methodists are numerous all over the province, and a few other sects are also met with. Religious or fanatical animosities never interfere with the peace of society; nor is the neighbourly kindness so general among the inhabitants ever disturbed by spiritual discord.

What, more than any other circumstance, places Nova Scotia in the most meritorious point of view, is, that the benefits of education are established on a sure and liberal foundation. Amidst all the active engagements of the inhabitants, in occupations of which wealth is the sole object, they have not neglected to cultivate the field of learning. It is a matter of doubt, whether more general and useful knowledge, among a whole people, can be discovered in any country, than is found to prevail in this province: many of those born and educated in it have distinguished themselves in different parts of the world; and the young men of the present day possess, in an eminent degree, a ready power of comprehension, a remarkably clear knowledge of the general business of life, and the art of adapting themselves to the circumstances of any situation in which chance or direction may place them.

Much of the prosperity of this colony is certainly due to the careful provision that has been made for the education of youth. At the bar, and in the pulpit; as merchants, or as private gentlemen; we discover the nativea of Nova Scotia with few exceptions to be men of superior attainments.

The seminaries of education are on a more respectable footing than in any of the British American colonies. On an elevated and beautiful spot of ground, a short distance from Windsor, and 40 miles by a good carriage road, west from Halifax, stands the University of King's College. It has a royal charter, dated 1802, which gives to it all the privileges that are enjoyed by the Universities of Great Britain and Ireland ...

The state of society in Halifax is highly respectable; and in proportion to the population, a much greater number of well-dressed and respectable-looking persons are observed, than in a town of the same size in the United Kingdoms. This is indeed peculiar to all the towns in America, and may readily be accounted for, from there being few manufacturers, or few people out of employment, and the labouring classes living principally in the country. The officers of the Government, and of the Army and Navy, mix very generally with the Merchants and Gentlemen of the learned professions; and from this circumstance, the first class of society is doubtless more refined than might otherwise be expected. The style of living, the hours of entertainment, and the fashions, are the same as in England. Dress is fully as much attended to as in London; and many of the fashionable sprigs who exhibit themselves in the streets of Halifax, and indeed in lesser towns in America, might even in Bond Street, be said to have arrived at the ne plus ultra of dandyism.

The amusements of Halifax are such as are usual in the other towns in the North American provinces; in all which, assemblies, picnics, amateur theatricals, riding, shooting, and fishing, form the principal sources of pleasure.

The markets are abundantly supplied with all kinds of butcher's meat and other eatables; vegetables alone are scarce during winter, and, with the exception of potatoes, cabbages, turnips and carrots, are not to be had. The fish market is the best supplied of any in America: I have heard it said, of any in the world. Fishes of different kinds, and of excellent quality, are brought by the boats fresh every morning from sea, and none else is suffered to be exposed ...

Prince Edward Island.

... When travelling through the settlements, we discover the inhabitants of Prince Edward Island to consist of Englishmen from almost every county in the kingdom; Scotchmen, who it is true predominate, from the Highlands, Hebrides, and the southern counties; Irishmen from different parts of the Emerald Isle; Acadian French, American loyalists, and a few Dutch, Germans, and Swedes.

In the English farmer will be observed the dialect of his county, the honest John Bull bluntness of his style, and the other characteristics that mark his character. His house or cottage is distinguished by cleanliness and neatness, his agricultural implements, and utensils are always in order, and where an English farmer is industrious and persevering, he is sure to do well. He does not, however, reconcile himself so readily as the Scotch settler does, to the privations necessarily connected for the first few years, with being set down in a new country, where the habits of those around him, and almost every thing else attached to his situation, are somewhat different from what he has been accustomed to, and it is not till he is sensibly assured of succeeding and bettering his condition, that he becomes fully reconciled to the country.

The Scotchman, habituated to greater privations in his native country, has probably left it with the full determination of undergoing any hardships that may lead to the acquisition of solid advantages; he acts with great caution and industry, subjects himself to many inconveniences, neglects the comforts for some time, which the Englishman considers indispensable, and in time certainly succeeds in surmounting all difficulties; and then, and not till then, does he willingly enjoy the comfort of life. The Irish peasant may be easily distinguished by his brogue, his confidence, readiness of reply, seeming happiness, although often describing his situation as worse than it is. The Irish emigrants are more anxious in general to gain a temporary advantage, by working sometime for others, than by beginning immediately on a piece of land for themselves: and this, by procuring the means, leads them too frequently into the habit of drinking, a vice to which a great number of English and Scotch become also unfortunately addicted. The American loyalists came here during the American revolutionary war: they are in general industrious and independent in their circumstances, extremely ingenious, building their own houses, doing their own joiner work, mason work, glazing and painting. The men make their own shoes, their ploughs, harrows, and carts, as well as their sledges and cabriolles; the women spin, knit, and weave linens and coarse woollen cloths for domestic use. A division of labour does not answer well in a new country, and all other settlers are obliged to adopt the plans which necessity first taught the Americans.

Few people find themselves sooner at their ease than the Highland Scotch; no class can encounter difficulties, or suffer privations with more hardihood, or endure fatigue with less repining. They acquire what they consider an independence in a few years; but they remain in too many instances contented with their condition, when they find themselves in possession of more ample means than they possessed in their native country. This observation is however more applicable to those who settled from thirty to forty years ago in the country, and who retain many of the characteristics which prevailed at that time in the Highlands and Isles of Scotland. I have observed, that wherever the Highlanders form distinct settlements, their habits, their system of husbandry, disregard for comfort in their houses, their ancient hospitable customs and their language, undergo no sensible change. There are but few indeed that I ever met with in any part of America, who do not, in a greater or less degree, feel a lingering wish to see their native country; and, although prudence or necessity forbids their doing so, yet nothing appears to destroy the warm affection they retain for the land where they first drew breath. This feeling even descends to their children who are born in America, and all call the United Kingdoms by the endearing name of "Home."

Various circumstances connected with Scotland makes the attachment which her children retain for a country to which destiny allows but few of them to return, more strongly apparent than is usually observed among the natives of England or Ireland. Among the latter, indeed, both the recollection of their country, and an affection for relatives are strong; but the distress to which they were inured, by the oppressive system under which they lived, extinguished an attachment which would otherwise have been warmly cherished.

The honest pride of an Englishman makes him consider every country inferior to his own, nor can he on earth discover a nation so eminently blessed as England is with comforts and advantages; but when abroad he seems rather to value it for its many sources of enjoyment, and to sigh for the society of friends left behind, than to regard it from the sentiments which at first inspire a spirit of adventure. All these feelings are just, but they check the ardour which conquers difficulties ...

The amusements of the farmers and other inhabitants settled in different parts of the island, are much the same as they have been accustomed to before leaving the countries they came from. Dances on many occasions are common, families visit each other at Christmas and New Year's Day, and almost all that is peculiar to Scotland at the season of "Halloween" is repeated here. Among the young men, feats of running, leaping, and gymnastic exercises are common; but that which they most delight in is galloping up and down the country on horseback. Indeed many of the farmers' sons who could make a certain livelihood by steady labour, acquire a spirit for bargain-making, dealing in horses, timber, old watches, &c. in order to become what they consider (by being idle) gentlemen: those who lead this course of life seldom do any good, and generally turn out lazy, drunken, dishonest vagabonds.

The term frolic is peculiar, I believe, to America, in the different senses in which it is there used. If a good wife has a quantity of wool or flax to spin, she invites as many of her neighbours as the house can well accommodate; some bring their spinning wheels, others their cards; they remain all day at work, and after drinking abundance of tea, either go home or remain to dance for some part of the night: this is called a spinning frolic. They are on these occasions as well as at other frolics, joined by the young men of the settlement, and in this way many of their love matches are made up. When a farmer or new settler wants a piece of wood cut down, he procures a few gallons of rum to drink on the occasion, and sends for his neighbours to assist him in levelling the forest: this is again called a chopping frolic ...

The Indians, who are of the once numerous Micmac tribe, profess the Roman Catholic religion, and have a chapel and burying place on Lennox Island, in Richmond Bay, where their chief has a house. This is their principal rendezvous, where they assemble about midsummer, on which occasion they meet their priest, or the bishop, who hears confessions, administers baptisms, marries those who are inclined to enter into that state, and makes other regulations for their conduct during the year. After remaining here a few weeks, the greater number resume their accustomed and favorite roving life, and wander along the shores, and through the woods of the neighbouring countries. This tribe, like all those in the vicinity of civilization, has diminished in number more than two-thirds during the recollection of the present settlers. The wild beasts and game having become scarce, they are subjected to a precarious subsistence; and small pox, fevers, &c. to which they were strangers previous to their acquaintance with Europeans, have often swept away whole families; and when we add their fondness of spirituous liquors, the vagabond life they are compelled to lead, and the determination they evince not to become stationary, or to follow agriculture as a means of subsistence, we need not be surprised at their numbers decreasing rapidly …

The descendants of the French, who settled in the colonies now possessed by Great Britain, are distinguished by the appellations of Acadians and Canadians. The former were principally settled during the French government in Nova Scotia, then called Acadia: the latter in Canada. The Acadians are now to be found (as before mentioned) in Nova Scotia, New Brunswick, Prince Edward Island, and Cape Breton, always by themselves in distinct settlements. They are averse from settling among other people; and I have not been able to discover more than four instances of their intermarrying with strangers. They profess the Roman Catholic faith, and observe the most rigid adherence to all the forms of their Church. Their general character is honest and inoffensive. Religiously tenacious of their dress, and all the habits of their forefathers, they have no ambition to rise in the world above the condition in which they have lived since their first settling in America. The dread of being exposed to the derision of the rest, or attempting to imitate the English inhabitants, is one, if not the principal cause that prevents individuals among them, who would willingly alter their dress and habits from doing so.

In Prince Edward Island, the Acadian women dress nearly in the same way as the Bavarian broom-girls. On Sundays their clothes and linen look extremely clean and neat; and they wear over their shoulders a small blue cloth cloak, reaching only half way down the body, and generally fastened at the breast with a brass broach. On week days they are more carelessly dressed, and they usually wear sabots (wood shoes). The men dress in round blue cloth jackets, with strait collars, and metal buttons set close together; blue or scarlet waistcoats, and blue trousers. Among all the Acadians in Prince Edward Island, I never knew but one person who had the hardihood to dress differently from what they call "notre façon." On one occasion he ventured to put on an English coat, and he has never since, even among his relations, been called by his proper name, Joseph Gallant, which has been supplanted by that of "Joe Peacock" …

There are about 4000 Acadian French on the island, who are principally the descendants of the French, who were settled in Nova Scotia, before the taking of Cape Breton. They retain with a kind of religious feeling, the dress and habits of their ancestors. With few exceptions, they are harmless, honest, and inoffensive, and have not at all times received the kindest treatment from their neighbours. The industry of their wives and daughters is wonderful: they are at work during the spring and harvest on their farms: they cook and wash, make their husbands' as well as their own clothes; they spin, knit, and weave, and are scarcely an hour idle during their lives. The Acadian French profess the Roman Catholic religion, and adhere more rigidly to all its forms than the Catholics in Europe do; and indeed more so than the Scotch and Irish Catholics. Their priests are educated in Canada, and by their examples as well as precepts, teach morals and propriety to their flocks.

These people are not in such easy circumstances as the other inhabitants of the island. Those that confine themselves to agriculture, are it is true more independent, perhaps sufficiently so for people in their station, when one considers that few of them can either read or write. At the villages of Rustico, they follow so many different pursuits, that it is impossible for them to succeed: at one time they are employed in building vessels, at another for a few weeks farming, then fishing, and again cutting timber. It follows that they are poor, while the Acadians in other parts of the island (although their system of husbandry, from which the force of example will not prevail on them to depart, is rude and tardy) acquire what renders their condition independent. On Sundays one observes a decorum and simplicity in the appearance of the Acadians, men, women, and children, that remind us of what we read of the correct unassuming manners of primitive times.

The farmers are employed during winter in attending to their cattle, threshing out their corn, cutting and hauling home firewood for winter use, and a stock of fuel for summer; all these, with many other little matters immediately connected with his farm and house, require the constant attention of a managing industrious man. Those however who imprudently think they will succeed better by attempting more, go into the woods to hew timber for exportation, or neglect their farms for ship-building, and other speculations which have ruined many. The low price of rum, and the vast numbers of houses along all the roads which retail it, form the most baneful evil connected with the country, and is the grand cause of any wretchedness that may be met with. Hitherto almost all the farmers have caught the fish required for their own consumption, and it is generally wise for new settlers to do so; but those who have been any time on the island, will find it much more advantageous to purchase what fish they may want, in exchange for the overplus produce of the soil. Formerly a considerable quantity of sugar was made from the sap of the maple tree. In the spring of the year, not earlier than March, a small notch or incision is cut (making an angle across the grain in the tree), out of which the juice oozes, and is conveyed by a thin piece of wood let in at the lower end of the cut, to a wooden trough, or a dish made of bark placed on the ground. This liquor is collected once or twice a day, and carried to a large kettle or pot, where it is reduced by boiling into a very agreeable sugar. Scarcely any but the Acadians and Indians make any at present ...

At Arichat, the Acadians, both men and women, sometimes depart in their dress from the fashions of the Acadians, and wear coats and gowns. At Caraquette, I observed also a partial deviation from their usual dress. Some of the men wearing coats, and a few of the women wearing gowns. The head dress of the women on the south side of the Bay de Chaleur, is, I believe, peculiar to themselves: instead of the Bavarian-like small caps, worn by all the other Acadians, they delight in immense muslin caps, in shape like a balloon.

The women in all the fishing settlements are perfect drudges. The men, after splitting the fish, leave the whole labour of curing to the women, who have also to cook, nurse their children, plant their gardens, gather what little corn they raise, and spin and weave coarse cloth. The old worn clothes, they either cut into small stripes, and weave as waft into coarse bed covers; or they untwist the threads into wool, which they again spin and make into cloth. The Acadians are nearly destitute of education: scarcely any of the women, and few of the men, can read or write, and, like all ignorant people, it matters not of what religion, are exceedingly bigoted and superstitious. They labour under the impression, that justice is not, under the British Government, administered impartially to them, in the courts of law; and this has arisen perhaps entirely from the conduct of the justices of the peace; many of whom, appointed in the settlements, are stupid ignorant men; and I regret to say, that I have often known them to make iniquitous and unjust decisions against the Acadians.

The descendants of the French, settled on the north side of the Bay de Chaleur, are mostly Acadians; but, from their intimate intercourse with Quebec, and the Canadians, are a more intelligent and respectable people than the other Acadians, whom they, as well as the Canadians, denominate "Les Sauvages" ...

9

"Our Robinson Crusoe
Sort of Life"

Three Women in Upper Canada

DOCUMENTS
A) Roughing It in the Bush
    Susanna Moodie
B) Winter Studies and Summer Rambles in Canada
    Anna Brownell Jameson
C) The Backwoods of Canada
    Catherine Parr Trail

F ew pioneer women left written records of their lives. They were too busy carving out existences from the harsh Canadian landscape, or too exhausted for anything but sleep at the end of their long days. Many women were also illiterate, or could not waste precious cents on frivolous luxuries like pen and paper. Regardless of why they did not write, historians examining past women's lives face the frustration of doing so through glasses blurred by lack of evidence.

Historians can, however, join a few tantalizing pieces to create an incomplete picture of their lives. Women like Susanna Moodie (née Strickland, 1803–1885) and her older sister Catherine Parr Trail provide us with these rare fragments. Though they had little spare money or time, ink flowed through their veins, which compelled them to write both for personal satisfaction and to provide cautionary tales to others contemplating immigration to the "backwoods of Canada." Their accounts were, naturally, directed toward their own kind: the upper and upper middle class English family unable to keep up with the Joneses and anxious to avoid social humiliation. That, after all, was why Moodie and her husband immigrated. Her brother sent glowing reports of economic prosperity and high social status from Upper Canada, and they followed him in 1832. Susanna's husband must have been a stock promoter's delight: he invested much of their precious money on dubious stocks that inevitably crashed. That plus limited farming experience lost them two farms and made them all but destitute in a land that Susanna increasingly called her "prison house." She was not happy.

Susanna Moodie eventually petitioned the Lieutenant Governor of Upper Canada for help, and in 1839 he secured her husband an appointment as sheriff. She probably wrote *Roughing It in the Bush* during the depths of their troubles, but it was not published until 1852, by which time the Moodies enjoyed modest prosperity. They owned a stone house instead of their earlier crude log structures, they had access to schools for their children, bought a piano, and hired several servants. This was not the genteel England Susanna always pined for, but it was a far cry from the grim days when there was not enough money to provide shoes for their children, let alone hire servants.

Anna Brownell Jameson was already a well-established author by the time she arrived in Toronto for an eight-month stay in 1836. She had little wish to come, but did so to save her marriage to a husband who arrived three years earlier and was by then Attorney General for Upper Canada. She failed in her primary objective, but did leave an invaluable study of society in Upper Canada during the early part of the nineteenth century. Brownell Jameson visited several communities in the area, found few attractions, and hated the unsophisticated pretensions of Upper Canada's urban upstarts. This was not pure snobbery on her part: she clearly sympathized with ordinary settlers creating new lives in tough environments. Her book on Upper Canada is generally bleak and probably discouraged a number of would-be immigrants. It sold well in England after publication in 1838, perhaps to people willing to move anywhere but Canada.

Catherine Parr Trail (1802–1899) could have been writing about a different colony altogether. She arrived in Upper Canada in the same year as her sister Susanna and established a bush farm close by. She came from the same upper class background, and had similar financial worries. She too was a writer, with several published children's books to her credit. Her husband, Thomas, also had little practical farming experience. Repeated crop failures brought them, like the Moodies, to the precipice of bankruptcy. Through it all, Catherine maintained a sense of wonder at her new world, and remained enthusiastic about life in the backwoods, especially the natural beauty of the countryside. But it was not easy. Her husband hated the isolation of the backwoods and suffered from acute depression. This left her to sustain the family, which she did with aplomb: she lived and wrote into her nineties, and gave birth to nine children. Though she never made much from her writing, her many articles and books did establish her as a distinguished naturalist. The following account, published in 1836, comes from a series of eighteen letters describing her initial experiences in the backwoods of Upper Canada.

A) Roughing It in the Bush
Susanna Moodie

In most instances, emigration is a matter of necessity, not of choice; and this is more especially true of the emigration of persons of respectable connections, or of any station or position in the world. Few educated persons, accustomed to the refinements and luxuries of European society, ever willingly relinquish those advantages, and place themselves beyond the protective influence of the wise and revered institutions of their native land, without the pressure of some urgent cause. Emigration may, indeed, generally be regarded as an act of severe duty, performed at the expense of personal enjoyment, and accompanied by the sacrifice of those local attachments which stamp the scenes amid which our childhood grew, in imperishable characters upon the heart. Nor is it until adversity has pressed sorely upon the proud and wounded spirit of the well-educated sons and daughters of old but impoverished families, that they gird up the loins of the mind, and arm themselves with fortitude to meet and dare the heart-breaking conflict.

The ordinary motives for the emigration of such persons may be summed up in a few brief words — the emigrant's hope of bettering his condition, and of escaping from the vulgar sarcasms too often hurled at the less wealthy by the purse-proud, commonplace people of the world. But there is a higher motive still, which has its origin in that love of independence which springs up spontaneously in the breasts of the high-souled children of a glorious land. They cannot labour in a menial capacity in the country where they were born and educated to command. They can trace no difference between themselves and the more fortunate individuals of a race whose blood warms their veins, and whose name they bear. The want of wealth alone places an impassable barrier between them and the more favoured offspring of the same parent stock; and they go forth to make for themselves a new name and to find another country, to forget the past and to live in the future, to exult in the prospect of their children being free and the land of their adoption great.

The choice of the country to which they devote their talents and energies depends less upon their pecuniary means than upon the fancy of the
emigrant or the popularity of a name. From the year 1826 to 1829, Australia
and the Swan River were all the rage. No other portions of the habitable globe
were deemed worthy of notice. These were the El Dorados and lands of Goshen
to which all respectable emigrants eagerly flocked. Disappointment, as a matter
of course, followed their high-raised expectations. Many of the most sanguine
of these adventurers returned to their native shores in a worse condition than
when they left them. In 1830, the great tide of emigration flowed westward.
Canada became the great landmark for the rich in hope and poor in purse.
Public newspapers and private letters teemed with the unheard-of advantages
to be derived from a settlement in this highly favoured region.

Its salubrious climate, its fertile soil, commercial advantages, great water
privileges, its proximity to the mother country, and last, not least, its almost
total exemption from taxation — that bugbear which keeps honest John Bull
in a state of constant ferment — were the theme of every tongue, and lauded
beyond all praise. The general interest, once excited, was industriously kept
alive by pamphlets, published by interested parties, which prominently set
forth all the good to be derived from a settlement in the Backwoods of Canada;
while they carefully concealed the toil and hardship to be endured in order to
secure these advantages. They told of lands yielding forty bushels to the acre,
but they said nothing of the years when these lands, with the most careful
cultivation, would barely return fifteen; when rust and smut, engendered by
the vicinity of damp over-hanging woods, would blast the fruits of the poor
emigrant's labour, and almost deprive him of bread. They talked of log houses
to be raised in a single day, by the generous exertions of friends and neighbours, but they never ventured upon a picture of the disgusting scenes of riot
and low debauchery exhibited during the raising, or upon a description of the
dwellings when raised — dens of dirt and misery, which would, in many instances, be shamed by an English pig-sty. The necessaries of life were described
as inestimably cheap; but they forgot to add that in remote bush settlements,
often twenty miles from a market town, and some of them even that distance
from the nearest dwelling, the necessaries of life which would be deemed indispensable to the European, could not be procured at all, or, if obtained, could
only be so by sending a man and team through a blazed forest road — a process
far too expensive for frequent repetition.

Oh, ye dealers in wild lands — ye speculators in the folly and credulity of
your fellow-men — what a mass of misery, and of misrepresentation produc-

tive of that misery, have ye not to answer for! You had your acres to sell, and what to you were the worn-down frames and broken hearts of the infatuated purchasers? The public believed the plausible statements you made with such earnestness, and men of all grades rushed to hear your hired orators declaim upon the blessings to be obtained by the clearers of the wilderness.

Men who had been hopeless of supporting their families in comfort and independence at home, thought that they had only to come out to Canada to make their fortunes; almost even to realize the story told in the nursery, of the sheep and oxen that ran about the streets, ready roasted, and with knives and forks upon their backs. They were made to believe that if it did not actually rain gold, that precious metal could be obtained, as is now stated of California and Australia, by stooping to pick it up.

The infection became general. A Canada mania pervaded the middle ranks of British society; thousands and tens of thousands, for the space of three or four years, landed upon these shores. A large majority of the higher class were officers of the army and navy, with their families — a class perfectly unfitted by their previous habits and education for contending with the stern realities of emigrant life. The hand that has long held the sword, and been accustomed to receive implicit obedience from those under its control, is seldom adapted to wield the spade and guide the plough, or try its strength against the stubborn trees of the forest. Nor will such persons submit cheerfully to the saucy familiarity of servants, who, republicans in spirit, think themselves as good as their employers. Too many of these brave and honourable men were easy dupes to the designing land-speculators. Not having counted the cost, but only looked upon the bright side of the picture held up to their admiring gaze, they fell easily into the snares of their artful seducers.

To prove their zeal as colonists, they were induced to purchase large tracts of wild land in remote and unfavourable situations. This, while it impoverished and often proved the ruin of the unfortunate immigrant, possessed a double advantage to the seller. He obtained an exorbitant price for the land which he actually sold, while the residence of a respectable settler upon the spot greatly enhanced the value and price of all other lands in the neighbourhood ...

Many a hard battle had we to fight with old prejudices, and many proud swellings of the heart to subdue, before we could feel the least interest in the land of our adoption, or look upon it as our home.

All was new, strange, and distasteful to us; we shrank from the rude, coarse familiarity of the uneducated people among whom we were thrown;

and they in turn viewed us as innovators, who wished to curtail their independence by expecting from them the kindly civilities and gentle courtesies of a more refined community ... The semi-barbarous Yankee squatters, who had "left their country for their country's good," and by whom we were surrounded in our first settlement, detested us, and with them we could have no feeling in common. We could neither lie nor cheat in our dealings with them; and they despised us for our ignorance in trading and our want of smartness.

The utter want of that common courtesy with which a well-brought-up European addresses the poorest of his brethren, is severely felt at first by settlers in Canada. At the period of which I am now speaking, the titles of "sir," or "madam," were very rarely applied by inferiors ...

Why they treated our claims to their respect with marked insult and rudeness, I never could satisfactorily determine, in any way that could reflect honour on the species, or even plead an excuse for its brutality, until I found that this insolence was more generally practised by the low, uneducated emigrants from Britain, who better understood your claims to their civility, than by the natives themselves. Then I discovered the secret.

The unnatural restraint which society imposes upon these people at home forces them to treat their more fortunate brethren with a servile deference which is repugnant to their feelings, and is thrust upon them by the dependent circumstances in which they are placed. This homage to rank and education is not sincere. Hatred and envy lie rankling at their heart, although hidden by outward obsequiousness. Necessity compels their obedience; they fawn, and cringe, and flatter the wealth on which they depend for bread. But let them once emigrate, the clog which fettered them is suddenly removed; they are free; and the dearest privilege of this freedom is to wreak upon their superiors the long-locked-up hatred of their hearts. They think they can debase you to their level by disallowing all your claims to distinction; while they hope to exalt themselves and their fellows into ladies and gentlemen by sinking you back to the only title you received from Nature — plain "man" and "woman" ...

But from this folly the native-born Canadian is exempt; it is only practised by the low-born Yankee, or the Yankeefied British peasantry and mechanics. It originates in the enormous reaction springing out of sudden emancipation from a state of utter dependence into one of unrestrained liberty ...

And here I would observe, before quitting this subject, that of all follies, that of taking out servants from the old country is one of the greatest, and is sure to end in the loss of the money expended in their passage, and to become the cause of deep disappointment and mortification to yourself.

They no sooner set foot upon the Canadian shores than they become possessed with this ultra-republican spirit. All respect for their employers, all subordination is at an end; the very air of Canada severs the tie of mutual obligation which bound you together. They fancy themselves not only equal to you in rank, but that ignorance and vulgarity give them superior claims to notice. They demand the highest wages, and grumble at doing half the work, in return, which they cheerfully performed at home. They demand to eat at your table, and to sit in your company, and if you refuse to listen to their dishonest and extravagant claims, they tell you that "they are free; that no contract signed in the old country is binding" ...

When we consider the different position in which servants are placed in the old and new world, this conduct, ungrateful as it then appeared to me, ought not to create the least surprise ...

The serving class, comparatively speaking, is small, and admits of little competition. Servants that understand the work of the country are not easily procured, and such always can command the highest wages ...

The Canadian women, while they retain the bloom and freshness of youth, are exceedingly pretty; but these charms soom fade, owing perhaps, to the fierce extremes of their climate ...

The early age at which they marry and are introduced into society takes from them all awkwardness and restraint ...

To the benevolent philanthropist, whose heart has bled over the misery and pauperism of the lower classes in Great Britain, the almost entire absence of mendicity from Canada would be highly gratifying. Canada has few, if any, native beggars; her objects of charity are generally imported from the mother country, and these are never suffered to want food or clothing. The Canadians are a truly charitable people; no person in distress is driven with harsh and cruel language from their doors; they not only generously relieve the wants of suffering strangers cast upon their bounty, but they nurse them in sickness, and use every means in their power to procure them employment. The number of orphan children yearly adopted by wealthy Canadians, and treated in every respect as their own, is almost incredible.

It is a glorious country for the labouring classes, for while blessed with health, they are always certain of employment, and certain also to derive from it ample means of support for their families ...

It has often been remarked to me by people long resident in the colony, that those who come to the country destitute of means, but able and willing to work, invariably improve their condition and become independent; while the gentleman who brings out with him a small capital is too often tricked and cheated out of his property, and drawn into rash and dangerous speculation which terminate in his ruin. His children, neglected and uneducated, but brought up with ideas far beyond their means, and suffered to waste their time in idleness, seldom take to work, and not infrequently sink down to the lowest class ...

The clouds of the preceding night, instead of dissolving in snow, brought on a rapid thaw. A thaw in the middle of winter is the most disagreeable change that can be imagined. After several weeks of clear, bright, bracing, frosty weather, with a serene atmosphere and cloudless sky, you awake one morning surprised at the change in the temperature; and, upon looking out of the window, behold the woods obscured by a murky haze — not so dense as an English November fog, but more black and lowering — and the heavens shrouded in a uniform covering of leaden-coloured clouds, deepening into a livid indigo at the edge of the horizon. The snow, no longer hard and glittering, has become soft and spongy, and the foot slips into a wet and insidiously-yielding mass at every step. From the roof pours down a continuous stream of water, and the branches of the trees, collecting the moisture of the reeking atmosphere, shower it upon the earth from every dripping twig. The cheerless and uncomfortable aspect of things without never fails to produce a corresponding effect upon the minds of those within, and casts such a damp upon the spirits that it appears to destroy for a time all sense of enjoyment. Many persons (and myself among the number) are made aware of the approach of a thunderstorm by an intense pain and weight about the head; and I have heard numbers of Canadians complain that a thaw always made them feel bilious and heavy, and greatly depressed their animal spirits.

I had a great desire to visit our new location, but when I looked out upon the cheerless waste, I gave up the idea, and contented myself with hoping for a better day on the morrow; but many morrows came and went before a frost again hardened the road sufficiently for me to make the attempt.

The prospect from the windows of my sister's log hut was not very prepossessing. The small lake in front, which formed such a pretty object in summer, now looked like an extensive field covered with snow, hemmed in from the rest of the world by a dark belt of sombre pine-woods. The clearing round the house was very small, and only just reclaimed from the wilderness, and the greater part of it was covered with piles of brush-wood, to be burnt the first dry days of spring.

The charred and blackened stumps on the few acres that had been cleared during the preceding year were everything but picturesque; and I concluded, as I turned, disgusted, from the prospect before me, that there was very little beauty to be found in the backwoods. But I came to this decision during a Canadian thaw, be it remembered, when one is wont to view every object with jaundiced eyes.

Moodie had only been able to secure sixty-six acres of his government grant upon the Upper Katchawanook Lake, which, being interpreted, means in English, the "Lake of the Waterfalls," a very poetical meaning, which most Indian names have. He had, however, secured a clergy reserve of two hundred acres adjoining; and he afterwards purchased a fine lot, which likewise formed part of the same block, one hundred acres, for £150. This was an enormously high price for wild land; but the prospect of opening the Trent and Otonabee for the navigation of steamboats and other small craft, was at that period a favourite speculation, and its practicability, and the great advantages to be derived from it, were so widely believed as to raise the value of the wild lands along these remote waters to an enormous price; and settlers in the vicinity were eager to secure lots, at any sacrifice, along their shores.

Our government grant was upon the lake shore, and Moodie had chosen for the site of his log house a bank that sloped gradually from the edge of the water, until it attained to the dignity of a hill. Along the top of this ridge, the forest road ran, and midway down the hill, our humble home, already nearly completed, stood, surrounded by the eternal forest. A few trees had been cleared in its immediate vicinity, just sufficient to allow the workmen to proceed, and to prevent the fall of any tree injuring the building, or the danger of its taking fire during the process of burning the fallow.

A neighbour had undertaken to build this rude dwelling by contract, and was to have it ready for us by the first week in the new year. The want of boards to make the divisions in the apartments alone hindered him from fulfilling his contract. These had lately been procured, and the house was to be ready for our reception in the course of a week. Our trunks and baggage had already been conveyed thither by Mr D——; and, in spite of my sister's kindness and hospitality, I longed to find myself once more settled in a home of my own ...

The snow had been so greatly decreased by the late thaw, that it had been converted into a coating of ice, which afforded a dangerous and slippery footing. My sister, who had resided for nearly twelve months in the woods, was provided for her walk with Indian moccasins, which rendered her quite independent; but I stumbled at every step. The sun shone brightly, the air was clear and invigorating, and, in spite of the treacherous ground and my foolish fears, I greatly enjoyed my first walk in the woods. Naturally of a cheerful, hopeful disposition, my sister was enthusiastic in her admiration of the woods. She drew such a lively picture of the charms of a summer residence in the forest, that I began to feel greatly interested in her descriptions, and to rejoice that we, too, were to be her near neighbours and dwellers in the woods; and this circumstance not a little reconciled me to the change.

Hoping that my husband would derive an income equal to the one he had parted with from the investment of the price of his commission in the steamboat stock, I felt no dread of want. Our legacy of £700 had afforded us means to purchase land, build our house, and give out a large portion of land to be cleared, and, with a considerable sum of money still in hand, our prospects for the future were in no way discouraging ...

The house was made of cedar logs, and presented a superior air of comfort to most dwellings of the same kind. The dimensions were thirty-six feet in length, and thirty-two feet in breadth, which gave us a nice parlour, a kitchen, and two small bedrooms, which were divided by plank partitions. Pantry or storeroom there was none; some rough shelves in the kitchen, and a deal cupboard in a corner of the parlour, being the extent of our accommodations in that way ...

The first spring we spent in comparative ease and idleness. Our cows had been left upon our old place during the winter. The ground had to be cleared before it could receive a crop of any kind, and I had little to do but to wander by the lake shore, or among the woods, and amuse myself.

These were the halcyon days of the bush. My husband had purchased a very light cedar canoe, to which he attached a keel and a sail: and most of our leisure hours, directly the snows melted, were spent upon the water.

These fishing and shooting excursions were delightful. The pure beauty of the Canadian water, the sombre but august grandeur of the vast forest that hemmed us in on every side and shut us out from the rest of the world, soon cast a magic spell upon our spirits, and we began to feel charmed with the freedom and solitude around us. Every object was new to us. We felt as if we were the first discoverers of every beautiful flower and stately tree that attracted our attention, and we gave names to fantastic rocks and fairy isles, and raised imaginary houses and bridges on every picturesque spot which we floated past during our aquatic excursions. I learned the use of the paddle, and became quite a proficient in the gentle craft.

It was not long before we received visits from the Indians, a people whose beauty, talents, and good qualities have been somewhat overrated, and invested with a poetical interest which they scarcely deserve. Their honesty and love of truth are the finest traits in characters otherwise dark and unlovely. But these are two God-like attributes, and from them spring all that is generous and ennobling about them.

There never was a people more sensible of kindness, or more grateful for any little act of benevolence exercised towards them. We met them with confidence; our dealings with them were conducted with the strictest integrity; and they became attached to our persons, and in no single instance ever destroyed the good opinion we entertained of them.

The tribes that occupy the shores of all these inland waters, back of the great lakes, belong to the Chippewa or Missasagua Indians, perhaps the least attractive of all these wild people, both with regard to their physical and mental endowments.

The men of this tribe are generally small of stature, with very coarse and repulsive features. The forehead is low and retreating, the observing faculties large, the intellectual ones scarcely developed; the ears large, and standing off from the face; the eyes looking towards the temples, keen, snake-like, and far apart; the cheek bones prominent; the nose long and flat, the nostrils very round; the jaw-bone projecting, massy, and brutal; the mouth expressing ferocity and sullen determination; the teeth large, even, and dazzlingly white. The mouth of the female differs widely in expression from that of the male; the lips are fuller, the jaw less projecting, and the smile is simple and agreeable. The women are a merry, light hearted set, and their constant laugh and incessant prattle form a strange contrast to the iron taciturnity of their grim lords ...

The summer of '35 was very wet; a circumstance so unusual in Canada that I have seen no season like it during my sojourn in the country. Our wheat crop promised to be both excellent and abundant; and the clearing and seeding sixteen acres, one way or another, had cost us more than fifty pounds; still we hoped to realize something handsome by the sale of the produce; and, as far as appearances went, all looked fair. The rain commenced about a week before the crop was fit for the sickle, and from that time until nearly the end of September was a mere succession of thunder showers; days of intense heat, succeeded by floods of rain. Our fine crop shared the fate of all other fine crops in the country; it was totally spoiled; the wheat grew in the sheaf, and we could scarcely save enough to supply us with bad sickly bread; the rest was exchanged at the distillery for whiskey, which was the only produce which could be obtained for it. The storekeepers would not look at it, or give either money or goods for such a damaged article.

My husband and I had worked hard in the field; it was the first time I had ever tried my hand at field-labour, but our ready money was exhausted, and the steamboat stock had not paid us one farthing; we could not hire, and there was no help for it. I had a hard struggle with my pride before I would consent to render the least assistance on the farm, but reflection convinced me that I was wrong — that Providence had placed me in a situation where I was called upon to work — that it was not only my duty to obey that call, but to exert myself to the utmost to assist my husband and help to maintain my family.

Ah, poverty! thou art a hard taskmaster, but in thy soul-ennobling school I have received more god-like lessons, have learned more sublime truths, than ever I acquired in the smooth highways of the world!

The independent in soul can rise above the seeming disgrace of poverty, and hold fast their integrity, in defiance of the world and its selfish and unwise maxims. To them, no labour is too great, no trial too severe; they will unflinchingly exert every faculty of mind and body before they will submit to become a burden to others ...

The misfortunes that now crowded upon us were the result of no misconduct or extravagance on our part, but arose out of circumstances which we could not avert nor control. Finding too late the error into which we had fallen, in suffering ourselves to be cajoled and plundered out of our property by interested speculators, we braced our minds to bear the worst, and determined to meet our difficulties calmly and firmly, nor suffer our spirits to sink under calamities which energy and industry might eventually repair. Having once come to this resolution, we cheerfully shared together the labours of the field. One in heart and purpose, we dared remain true to ourselves, true to our high destiny as immortal creatures, in our conflict with temporal and physical wants.

We found that manual toil, however distasteful to those unaccustomed to it, was not after all such a dreadful hardship; that the wilderness was not without its rose, the hard face of poverty without its smile. If we occasionally suffered severe pain, we as often experienced great pleasure, and I have contemplated a well-hoed ridge of potatoes on that bush farm with as much delight as in years long past I had experienced in examining a fine painting in some well-appointed drawing-room.

I can now look back with calm thankfulness on that long period of trial and exertion — with thankfulness that the dark clouds that hung over us, threatening to blot us from existence, when they did burst upon us, were full of blessings. When our situation appeared perfectly desperate, then were we on the threshold of a new state of things, which was born out of that very distress.

In order more fully to illustrate the necessity of a perfect and childlike reliance upon the mercies of God — who, I most firmly believe, never deserts those who have placed their trust in Him — I will give a brief sketch of our lives during the years 1836 and 1837.

Still confidently expecting to realize an income, however small, from the steamboat stock, we had involved ourselves considerably in debt, in order to pay our servants and obtain the common necessaries of life; and we owed a large sum to two Englishmen in Dummer, for clearing ten more acres upon the farm. Our utter inability to meet these demands weighed very heavily upon my husband's mind. All superfluities in the way of groceries were now given up, and we were compelled to rest satisfied upon the produce of the farm. Milk, bread, and potatoes during the summer became our chief, and often, for months, our only fare. As to tea and sugar, they were luxuries we would not think of, although I missed the tea very much; we rang the changes upon peppermint and sage, taking the one herb at our breakfast, the other at our tea, until I found an excellent substitute for both in the root of the dandelion ...

Necessity has truly been termed the mother of invention, for I contrived to manufacture a variety of dishes almost out of nothing, while living in her school. When entirely destitute of animal food, the different varieties of squirrels supplied us with pies, stews, and roasts. Our barn stood at the top of the hill near the bush, and in a trap set for such "small deer," we often caught from ten to twelve a day.

The flesh of the black squirrel is equal to that of the rabbit, and the red, and even the little chipmunk, is palatable when nicely cooked. But from the lake, during the summer, we derived the larger portion of our food. The children called this piece of water "Mamma's pantry", and many a good meal has the munificent Father given to his poor dependent children from its well-stored depths. Moodie and I used to rise by daybreak, and fish for an hour after sunrise, when we returned, he to the field, and I to dress the little ones, clean up the house, assist with the milk, and prepare the breakfast.

Oh, how I enjoyed these excursions on the lake; the very idea of our dinner depending upon our success added double zest to our sport!

One morning we started as usual before sunrise; a thick mist still hung like a fine veil upon the water when we pushed off, and anchored at our accustomed place. Just as the sun rose, and the haze parted and drew up like a golden sheet of transparent gauze, through which the dark woods loomed out like giants, a noble buck dashed into the water ...

That winter of '36, how heavily it wore away! The grown flour, frosted potatoes, and scant quantity of animal food rendered us all weak, and the children suffered much from the ague ...

On the 21st of May of this year, my second son, Donald, was born. The poor fellow came in hard times. The cows had not calved, and our bill of fare, now minus the deer and Spot, only consisted of bad potatoes and still worse bread. I was rendered so weak by want of proper nourishment that my dear husband, for my sake, overcame his aversion to borrowing, and procured a quarter of mutton from a friend. This, with kindly presents from neighbours — often as badly off as ourselves — a loin of a young bear, and a basket containing a loaf of bread, some tea, some fresh butter, and oatmeal, went far to save my life.

Shortly after my recovery, Jacob — the faithful, good Jacob — was obliged to leave us, for we could not longer afford to pay wages. What was owing to him had to be settled by sacrificing our best cow, and a great many valuable articles of clothing from my husband's wardrobe. Nothing is more distressing than being obliged to part with articles of dress which you know that you cannot replace. Almost all my clothes had been appropriated to the payment of wages, or to obtain garments for the children, excepting my wedding dress, and the beautiful baby-linen which had been made by the hands of dear and affectionate friends for my first-born. These were now exchanged for coarse, warm flannels, to shield him from the cold.

Moodie and Jacob had chopped eight acres during the winter, but these had to be burnt off and logged up before we could put in a crop of wheat for the ensuing fall. Had we been able to retain this industrious, kindly English lad, this would have been soon accomplished; but his wages, at the rate of thirty pounds per annum, were now utterly beyond our means ...

Reader! it is not my intention to trouble you with the sequel of our history. I have given you a faithful picture of a life in the backwoods of Canada, and I leave you to draw from it your own conclusions, To the poor, industrious working man it presents many advantages; to the poor gentleman, none!

The former works hard, puts up with coarse, scanty fare, and submits, with a good grace, to hardships that would kill a domesticated animal at home. Thus he becomes independent, inasmuch as the land that he has cleared finds him in the common necessaries of life; but it seldom, if ever, in remote situations, accomplishes more than this. The gentleman can neither work so hard, live so coarsely, nor endure so many privations as his poorer but more fortunate neighbour. Unaccustomed to manual labour, his services in the field are not of a nature to secure for him a profitable return. The task is new to him, he knows not how to perform it well; and, conscious of his deficiency, he expends his little means in hiring labour, which his bush-farm can never repay. Difficulties increase, debts grow upon him, he struggles in vain to extricate himself, and finally sees his family sink into hopeless ruin.

If these sketches should prove the means of deterring one family from sinking their property, and shipwrecking all their hopes, by going to reside in the backwoods of Canada, I shall consider myself amply repaid for revealing the secrets of the prison-house, and feel that I have not toiled and suffered in the wilderness in vain.

B) Winter Studies and Summer Rambles in Canada
Anna Brownell Jameson

... Their deportment was taciturn and self-possessed, and their countenances melancholy; that of the chief was by far the most intelligent. They informed me that they were Chippewas from the neighborhood of Lake Huron; that the hunting season had been unsuccessful; that their tribe was suffering the extremity of hunger and cold; and that they had come to beg from their Great Father the Governor rations of food, and a supply of blankets for their women and children. They had walked over the snow, in their snow-shoes, from the lake, one hundred and eighty miles, and for the last forty-eight hours none of them had tasted food. A breakfast of cold meat, bread, and beer, was immediately ordered for them; and though they had certainly never beheld in their lives the arrangement of an European table, and were besides half-famished, they sat down with unembarrassed tranquillity, and helped themselves to what they wished, with the utmost propriety — only, after one or two trials, using their own knives and fingers in preference to the table knife and fork. After they had eaten and drunk sufficiently, they were conducted to the government-house to receive from the governor presents of blankets, rifles, and provisions, and each, on parting, held out his hand to me, and the chief, with grave earnestness, prayed for the blessing of the Great Spirit on me and my house. On the whole, the impression they left, though amusing and exciting from its mere novelty, was melancholy. The sort of desperate resignation in their swarthy countenances, their squalid, dingy habiliments, and their forlorn story, filled me with pity, and, I may add, disappointment; and all my previous impressions of the independent children of the forest are for the present disturbed.

These are the first specimens I have seen of that fated race, with which I hope to become better acquainted before I leave the country. Notwithstanding all I have heard and read, I have yet but a vague idea of the Indian character; and the very different aspect under which it has been represented by various travellers, as well as writers of fiction, adds to the difficulty of forming a correct estimate of the people, and more particularly of the true position of their women. Colonel Givins, who has passed thirty years of his life among the north-west tribes, till he has become in habits and language almost identified with them, is hardly an impartial judge. He was their interpreter on this occasion, and he says that there is as much difference between the customs and language of different nations, the Chippewas and Mohawks, for instance, as there is between any two nations of Europe.

January 16

... The cold is at this time so intense, that the ink freezes while I write, and my fingers stiffen round the pen; a glass of water by my bed-side, within a few feet of the hearth (heaped with logs of oak and maple kept burning all night long), is a solid mass of ice in the morning. God help the poor emigrants who are yet unprepared against the rigor of the season! — yet this is nothing to the climate of the lower province, where, as we hear, the thermometer has been thirty degrees below zero. I lose all heart to write home, or to register a reflection or a feeling; — thought stagnates in my head as the ink in my pen — and this will never do! — I must rouse myself to occupation; and if I cannot find it without, I must create it from within. There are yet four months of winter and leisure to be disposed of. How? — I know not; but they *must* be employed, not wholly lost ...

February 17

"There is no *society* in Toronto," is what I hear repeated all around me — even by those who compose the only society we have. "But," you will say, "what could be expected in a remote town, which forty years ago was an uninhabited swamp, and twenty years ago only began to exist?" I really do not know what I expected, but I will tell you what I did not expect. I did not expect to find here in this new capital of a new country, with the boundless forest within half a mile of us on almost every side — concentrated as it were the worst evils of our old and most artificial social system at home, with none of its *agrémens*, and none of its advantages. Toronto is like a fourth- or fifth-rate provincial town with the pretensions of a capital city. We have here a petty colonial oligarchy, a self-constituted aristocracy, based upon nothing real, nor even upon anything imaginary; and we have all the mutual jealousy and fear, and petty gossip, and mutual meddling and mean rivalship, which are common in a small society of which the members are well known to each other, a society composed, like all societies, of many heterogeneous particles; but as these circulate within very confined limits, there is no getting out of the way of what one most dislikes: we must necessarily hear, see, and passively endure much that annoys and disgusts anyone accustomed to the independence of a large and liberal society, or the ease of continental life. It is curious enough to see how quickly a new fashion, or a new folly, is imported from the old country, and with what difficulty and delay a new idea finds its way into the heads of the people, or a new book into their hands. Yet, in the midst of all this, I cannot but see that good spirits and corrective principles are at work; that progress is making: though the march of intellect be not here in double quick time, as in Europe, it does not absolutely stand stock-still.

There reigns here a hateful factious spirit in political matters, but for the present no public or patriotic feeling, no recognition of general or generous principles of policy: as yet I have met with none of these. Canada is a colony, not a *country*; it is not yet identified with the dearest affections and associations, remembrances, and hopes of its inhabitants: it is to them an adopted, not a real mother. Their love, their pride, are not for poor Canada, but for high and happy England; but a few more generations must change all this.

We have here Tories, Whigs, and Radicals, so called; but these words do not signify exactly what we mean by the same designations at home.

You must recollect that the first settlers in Upper Canada were those who were obliged to fly from the United States during the revolutionary war, in consequence of their attachment to the British government, and the soldiers and non-commissioned officers who had fought during the war. These were recompensed for their losses, sufferings, and services, by grants of land in Upper Canada. Thus the very first elements out of which our social system was framed, were repugnance and contempt for the new institutions of the United States, and a dislike to the people of that country — a very natural result of foregoing causes; and thus it has happened that the slightest tinge of democratic, or even liberal principles in politics, was for a long time a sufficient impeachment of the loyalty, a stain upon the personal character, of those who held them. The Tories have therefore been hitherto the influential party; in their hands we find the government patronage, the principal offices, the sales and grants of land, for a long series of years.

Another party, professing the same boundless loyalty to the mother country, and the same dislike for the principles and institutions of their Yankee neighbors, may be called the Whigs of Upper Canada; these look with jealousy and scorn on the power and prejudices of the Tory families, and insist on the necessity of many reforms in the colonial government. Many of these are young men of talent, and professional men, who find themselves shut out from what they regard as their fair proportion of social consideration and influence, such as, in a small society like this, their superior education and character ought to command for them.

Another set are the Radicals, whom I generally hear mentioned as "those scoundrels," or "those rascals," or with some epithet expressive of the utmost contempt and disgust. They are those who wish to see this country erected into a republic, like the United States. A few among them are men of talent and education, but at present they are neither influential nor formidable.

There is among all parties a general tone of complaint and discontent — a mutual distrust — a languor and supineness — the causes of which I cannot as yet understand. Even those who are enthusiastically British in heart and feeling, who sincerely believe that it is the true interest of the colony to remain under the control of the mother country, are as discontented as the rest: they bitterly denounce the ignorance of the colonial officials at home, with regard to the true interests of the country: they ascribe the want of capital for improvement on a large scale to no mistrust in the resources of the country, but to a want of confidence in the measures of the government, and the security of property.

In order to understand something of the feelings which prevail here, you must bear in mind the distinction between the two provinces of Upper and Lower Canada. The project of uniting them once more into one legislature, with a central metropolis, is most violently opposed by those whose personal interests and convenience would suffer materially by a change in the seat of government. I have heard some persons go so far as to declare, that if the union of the two provinces were to be established by law, it were sufficient to absolve a man from his allegiance. On the other hand, the measure has powerful advocates in both provinces. It seems, on looking over the map of this vast and magnificent country, and reading its whole history, that the political division into five provinces, each with its independent governor and legislature, its separate correspondence with the Colonial office, its local laws, and local taxation, must certainly add to the amount of colonial patronage, and perhaps render more secure the subjection of the whole to the British crown; but may it not also have perpetuated local distinctions and jealousies — kept alive divided interests, narrowed the resources, and prevented the improvement of the country on a large and general scale?

But I had better stop here, ere I get beyond my depth. I am not one of those who opine sagely, that women have nothing to do with politics. On the contrary; but I do seriously think, that no one, be it man or woman, ought to talk, much less write, on what they do not understand. Not but that I have my own ideas on these matters, though we were never able to make out, either to my own satisfaction or to yours, whether I am a Whig, or Tory, or Radical …

February 18

Toronto is, as a residence, worse and better than other small communities — worse in so much as it is remote from all the best advantages of a high state of civilization, while it is infected by all its evils, all its follies; and better, because, besides being a small place, it is a *young* place; and in spite of this affectation of looking back, instead of looking up, it must advance — it may become the thinking head and beating heart of a nation, great, wise, and happy; who knows? And there are moments when, considered under this point of view, it assumes an interest even to me; but at present it is in a false position, like that of a youth aping maturity; … With the interminable forests within half a mile of us — the haunt of the red man, the wolf, the bear — with an absolute want of the means of the most ordinary mental and moral development, we have here conventionalism in its most oppressive and ridiculous forms. If I should say, that at present the people here want cultivation, want polish, and the means of acquiring either, *that* is natural — is intelligible — and it were unreasonable to expect it could be otherwise; but if I say they want honesty, you would understand me, *they* would not; they would imagine that I accused them of false weights and cheating at cards. So far they are certainly "indifferent honest" after a fashion, but never did I hear so little truth, nor find so little mutual benevolence. And why is it so? — because in this place, as in other small provincial towns, they live under the principle of fear — they are afraid of each other, afraid to be themselves; and where there is much fear, there is little love, and less truth ...

February 21

... Fires are not uncommon in Toronto, where the houses are mostly wood; they have generally an alarum once or twice a week, and six or eight houses burned in the course of the winter; but it was evident this was of more fearful extent than usual. Finding, on inquiry, that all the household had gone off to the scene of action, my own maid excepted. I prepared to follow, for it was impossible to remain here idly gazing on the flames, and listening to the distant shouts in ignorance and suspense. The fire was in the principal street (King-street), and five houses were burning together. I made my way through the snow-heaped, deserted streets, and into a kind of court or garden at the back of the blazing houses. There was a vast and motley pile of household stuff in the midst, and a poor woman keeping guard over it, nearly up to her knees in the snow. I stood on the top of a bedstead, leaning on her shoulder, and thus we remained till the whole row of buildings had fallen in. The Irishmen (God bless my countrymen! for in all good — all mischief — all frolic — all danger — they are sure to be the first) risked their lives most ...

March 28

There is yet no indication as the approach of spring, and I find it more than ever difficult to keep myself warm. Nothing in myself or around me feels or looks like *home*. How much is comprised in that little word! May it please God to preserve to me all that I love! But, O absence! how much is comprised in *that* word too! it is death of the heart and darkness of the soul; it is the ever springing, ever-dying hope; the ever-craving, never-having wish; it is fear, and doubt, and sorrow, and pain; — a state in which the past swallows up the present, and the future becomes the past before it arrives! ...

April 1

So, there is another month gone; and the snows are just beginning to disappear, and the flocks of snow-birds with them; and the ice is breaking up at the entrance of the bay, and one or two little vessels have ventured as far as the King's Wharf; and the wind blows strong to dry up the melting snow, and some time or other, perhaps, spring will come, and this long winter's imprisonment will be at an end ...

This is the worst season in Canada. The roads are breaking up, and nearly impassable; lands are flooded, and in low situations there is much sickness, particularly ague. We have still sixteen square miles of ice within the bay.

The market at Toronto is not well supplied, and is at a great distance from us. The higher class of people are supplied with provisions from their own lands and farms, or by certain persons they know and employ. With a little management and forethought, we now get on very well; but at first we had to suffer great inconvenience. Quantities of salted provisions are still imported into the country for the consumption of the soldiers and distant settlers, and at certain seasons — at present, for example — there is some difficulty in procuring anything else.

Our table, however, is pretty well supplied. Beef is tolerable, but lean; mutton bad, scarce, and dearer than beef; pork excellent and delicate, being fattened principally on Indian corn. The fish is of many various kinds, and delicious. During the whole winter we had black-bass and white-fish, caught in holes in the ice, and brought down by the Indians. Venison, game, and wild fowl are always to be had; the quails, which are caught in immense numbers near Toronto, are most delicate eating; I lived on them when I could eat nothing else. What they call partridge here is a small species of pheasant, also very good; and now we are promised snipes and woodcocks in abundance. The wild goose is also excellent eating when well cooked, but the old proverb about Heaven sending meat, &c. &c. is verified here. Those who have farms near the city, or a country establishment of their own, raise poultry and vegetables for their own table. As yet I have seen no vegetables whatever but potatoes; even in the best seasons they are not readily to be procured in the market. Every year, however, as Toronto increases in population and importance, will diminish these minor inconveniences.

The want of good servants is a more serious evil. I could amuse you with an account of the petty miseries we have been enduring from this cause, the strange characters who come to offer themselves, and the wages required. Almost all the servants are of the lower class of Irish emigrants, in general honest, warm-hearted, and willing; but never having seen anything but want, dirt, and reckless misery at home, they are not the most eligible persons to trust with the cleanliness and comfort of one's household. Yet we make as many complaints, and express as much surprise at their deficiencies, as though it were possible it could be otherwise. We give to our man-servant eight dollars a month, to the cook six dollars, and to the housemaid four; but these are lower wages than are usual for good and experienced servants, who might indeed command almost any wages here, where all labor is high priced ...

Apropos to newspapers — my table is covered with them. In the absence or scarcity of books, they are the principal medium of knowledge and communication in Upper Canada. There is no stamp-act here — no duty on paper; and I have sometimes thought that the great number of local newspapers which do not circulate beyond their own little town or district, must, from the vulgar, narrow tone of many of them, do mischief; but on the whole, perhaps, they do more good. Paragraphs printed from English or American papers, on subjects of general interest, the summary of political events, extracts from books or magazines, are copied from one paper into another, till they have travelled round the country. It is true that a great deal of base, vulgar, inflammatory party feeling is also circulated by the same means; but, on the whole, I should not like to see the number or circulation of the district papers checked. There are about forty published in Upper Canada; of these, three are religious, viz. the "Christian Guardian," "The Wesleyan Advocate," and "The Church;" a paper in the German language is published at Berlin, in the Gore district, for the use of the German settlers; "The Correspondent and Advocate" is the leading radical, "The Toronto Patriot," the leading Conservative paper. The newspapers of Lower Canada and the United States are circulated in great numbers; and as they pay postage, it is no inconsiderable item in the revenue of the post-office. In some of these provincial papers I have seen articles written with considerable talent; amongst other things, I have remarked a series of letters signed Evans, addressed to the Canadians on the subject of an education fitted for an agricultural people, and written with infinite good sense and kindly feeling; these have been copied from one paper into another, and circulated widely; no doubt they will do good. Last year the number of newspapers circulated through the post-office, and paying postage, was

Provincial papers 178,065
United States and foreign papers 149,502

... There is a commercial news-room in the city of Toronto, and this is absolutely the only place of assembly or amusement, except the taverns and low drinking-houses. An attempt has been made to found a mechanics' institute and a literary club; but as yet they create little interest, and are very ill supported.

If the sympathy for literature and science be small, that for music is less. Owing to the exertions of an intelligent musician here, some voices have been so far drilled that the psalms and anthems at church are very tolerably performed; but this gentleman receives so little general encouragement, that he is at this moment preparing to go over to the United States. The archdeacon is collecting subscriptions to pay for an organ which is to cost a thousand pounds; if the money were expended in aid of a singing-school, it would do more good.

The interior of the episcopal church here is rather elegant, with the exception of a huge window of painted glass which cost £500, and is in a vile, tawdry taste.

Besides the episcopal church, the Presbyterians, Methodists, Roman Catholics, and Baptists have each a place of worship. There is also an African church for the negroes.

The hospital, a large brick building, is yet too small for the increasing size of the city. The public grammar-school, called the "Upper Canada College," forms a cluster of ugly brick-buildings; and although the system of education there appears narrow and defective, yet it is a *beginning*, and certainly productive of good.

The physician I have mentioned to you, Dr. Rees, entertains the idea of founding a house of reception for destitute female emigrants on their arrival in Canada — a house, where, without depending on *charity*, they may be boarded and lodged at the smallest possible cost, and respectably protected till they can procure employment. You may easily imagine that I take a deep interest in this design ...

I have not often in my life met with contented and cheerful-minded women, but I never met with so many repining and discontented women as in Canada. I never met with *one* woman recently settled here, who considered herself happy in her new home and country: I *heard* of one, and doubtless there are others, but they are exceptions to the general rule. Those born here, or brought here early by their parents and relations, seemed to me very happy, and many of them had adopted a sort of pride in their new country, which I liked much. There was always a great desire to visit England, and some little airs of self-complacency and superiority in those who had been there, though for a few months only; but all, without a single exception, returned with pleasure, unable to forego the early habitual influences of their native land ...

C) The Backwoods of Canada
Catherine Parr Trail

November the 20th, 1832

... We begin to get reconciled to our Robinson Crusoe sort of life, and the consideration that the present evils are but temporary goes a great way towards reconciling us to them.

One of our greatest inconveniences arises from the badness of our roads, and the distance at which we are placed from any village or town where provisions are to be procured.

Till we raise our own grain and fatten our own hogs, sheep, and poultry, we must be dependent upon the stores for food of every kind. These supplies have to be brought up at considerable expense and loss of time, through our beautiful bush-roads; which, to use the words of a poor Irish woman, "can't be no worser" ...

This is now the worst season of the year — this, and just after the breaking up of the snow. Nothing hardly but an ox-cart can travel along the roads, and even that with difficulty, occupying two days to perform the journey to and fro, and the worst of the matter is, that there are times when the most necessary articles of provisions are not to be procured at any price. You see, then, that a settler in the bush requires to hold himself pretty independent, not only of the luxuries and delicacies of the table, but not unfrequently even of the very necessaries.

One time no pork is to be procured; another time there is a scarcity of flour, owing to some accident that has happened to the mill, or for the want of proper supplies of wheat for grinding; or perhaps the weather and bad roads at the same time prevent a team coming up, or people from going down. Then you must have recourse to a neighbour, if you have the good fortune to be near one, or fare the best you can on potatoes. The potato is indeed a great blessing here; new settlers would otherwise be often greatly distressed, and the poor man and his family who are without resources, without the potato must starve ...

November the 2nd, 1833

... We had a glorious burning this summer after the ground was all logged up; that is, all the large timbers chopped into lengths, and drawn together in heaps with oxen. To effect this the more readily we called a logging-bee. We had a number of settlers attend, with yokes of oxen and men to assist us. After that was over, my husband, with the menservants, set the heaps on fire; and a magnificent sight it was to see such a conflagration all around us. I was a little nervous at first on account of the nearness of some of the log-heaps to the house, but care is always taken to fire them with the wind blowing in a direction away from the building. Accidents have sometimes happened, but they are of rarer occurrence than might be expected when we consider the subtlety and destructiveness of the elements employed on the occasion.

If the weather be very dry, and a brisk wind blowing, the work of destruction proceeds with astonishing rapidity; sometimes the fire will communicate with the forest and run over many hundreds of acres. This is not considered favourable for clearing, as it destroys the underbrush and light-timbers, which are almost indispensable for ensuring a good burning. It is, however, a magnificent sight to see the blazing trees and watch the awful progress of the conflagration, as it hurries onward, consuming all before it, or leaving such scorching mementos as have blasted the forest growth for years.

When the ground is very dry the fire will run all over the fallow, consuming the dried leaves, sticks, and roots. Of a night the effect is more evident; sometimes the wind blows particles of the burning fuel into the hollow pines and tall decaying stumps; these readily ignite, and after a time present an appearance that is exceedingly fine and fanciful. Fiery columns, the bases of which are hidden by the dense smoke wreaths, are to be seen in every direction, sending up showers of sparks that are whirled about like rockets and fire-wheels in the wind. Some of these tall stumps, when the fire has reached the summit, look like gas lamps newly lit. The fire will sometimes continue unextinguished for days ...

Our crops this year are oats, corn, and pumpkins, and potatoes, with some turnips. We shall have wheat, rye, oats, potatoes and corn next harvest, which will enable us to increase our stock. At present we have only a yoke of oxen (Buck and Bright, the names of three-fourths of all the working oxen in Canada), two cows, two calves, three small pigs, ten hens, and three ducks, and a pretty brown pony ...

A small farmer at home would think very poorly of our Canadian possessions, especially when I add that our whole stock of farming implements consists of two reaping-hooks, several axes, a spade, and a couple of hoes. Add to these a queer sort of harrow that is made in the shape of a triangle for the better passing between the stumps: this is a rude machine compared with the nicely painted instruments of the sort I have been accustomed to see used in Britain. It is roughly hewn, and put together without regard to neatness; strength for use is all that is looked to here. The plough is seldom put into the land before the third or fourth year, nor is it required; the general plan of cropping the first fallow with wheat or oats, and sowing grass-seeds with the grain to make pastures, renders the plough unnecessary till such time as the grasslands require to be broken up. This method is pursued by most settlers while they are clearing bushland; always chopping and burning enough to keep a regular succession of wheat and spring crops, while the former clearings are allowed to remain in grass ...

On first coming to this country nothing surprised me more than the total absence of trees about the dwelling-houses and cleared lands; the axe of the chopper relentlessly levels all before him. Man appears to contend with the trees of the forest as though they were his most obnoxious enemies; for he spares neither the young sapling in its greenness nor the ancient trunk in its lofty pride; he wages war against the forest with fire and steel.

There are several sufficient reasons to be given for this seeming want of taste. The forest-trees grow so thickly together that they have no room for expanding and putting forth lateral branches; on the contrary, they run up to an amazing height of stem, resembling seedlings on a hot-bed that have not duly been thinned out. Trees of this growth when unsupported by others are tall, weak, and entirely divested of those graces and charms of outline and foliage that would make them desirable as ornaments to our grounds ...

Lake Cottage, March 14, 1834.

... You say you fear the rigours of the Canadian winter will kill me. I never enjoyed better health, nor so good, as since it commenced. There is a degree of spirit and vigour infused into one's blood by the purity of the air that is quite exhilarating. The very snow seems whiter and more beautiful than it does in your damp, vapoury climate. During a keen bright winter's day you will often perceive the air filled with minute frozen particles, which are quite dry, and slightly prick your face like needle-points, while the sky is blue and bright above you. There is a decided difference between the first snow-falls and those of mid-winter; the first are in large soft flakes, and seldom remain long without thawing, but those that fall after the cold has regularly set in are smaller, drier, and of the most beautiful forms, sometimes pointed like a cluster of rays, or else feathered in the most exquisite manner ...

The swarthy complexions, shaggy black hair and singular costume of the Indians formed a striking contrast with the fair-faced Europeans that were mingled with them, seen as they were by the red and fitful glare of the wood-fire that occupied the centre of the circle ...

The hymn was sung in the Indian tongue, a language that is peculiarly sweet and soft in its cadences, and seems to be composed with many vowels. I could not but notice the modest air of the girls; as if anxious to avoid observation that they felt was attracted by their sweet voices, they turned away from the gaze of the strangers, facing each other and bending their heads down over the work they still held in their hands. The attitude, which is that of the Eastern nations; the dress, dark hair and eyes, the olive complexion, heightened colour, and meek expression of face, would have formed a study for a painter, I wish you could have witnessed the scene; I think you would not easily have forgotten it. I was pleased with the air of deep reverence that sat on the faces of the elders of the Indian family as they listened to the voices of their children singing praise and glory to the God and Saviour they had learned to fear and love.

The Indians seem most tender parents; it is pleasing to see the affectionate manner in which they treat their young children, fondly and gently caressing them with eyes overflowing and looks of love ...

September 20, 1843

... Canada is the land of hope; here everything is new; everything going forward; it is scarcely possible for arts, sciences, agriculture, manufactures, to retrograde; they must keep advancing; though in some situations the progress may seem slow, in others they are proportionately rapid.

There is a constant excitement on the minds of emigrants, particularly in the partially settled townships, that greatly assists in keeping them from desponding. The arrival of some enterprising person gives a stimulus to those about him: profitable speculation is started, and lo, the value of the land in the vicinity rises to double and treble what it was thought worth before; so that, without any design of befriending his neighbours, the schemes of one settler being carried into effect shall benefit a great number. We have already felt the beneficial effect of the access of respectable emigrants locating themselves in this township, as it has already increased the value of our own land in a three-fold degree ...

Our society is mostly military or naval; so that we meet on equal grounds, and are, of course, well acquainted with the rules of good breeding and polite life; too much so to allow any deviation from those laws that good taste, good sense, and good feeling have established among persons of our class.

Yet here it is considered by no means derogatory to the wife of an officer or gentleman to assist in the work of the house, or to perform its entire duties, if occasion requires it; to understand the mystery of soap, candle, and sugar-making; to make bread, butter, and cheese, or even to milk her own cows, to knit and spin, and prepare the wool for the loom. In these matters we bush-ladies have a wholesome disregard of what Mr and Mrs So-and-so think or say. We pride ourselves on conforming to circumstances; and as a British officer must needs be a gentleman and his wife a lady, perhaps we repose quietly on that incontestable proof of our gentility, and can afford to be useful without injuring it.

Our husbands adopt a similar line of conduct: the officer turns his sword into a ploughshare, and his lance into a sickle; and if he be seen ploughing among the stumps in his own field, or chopping trees on his own land, no one thinks less of his dignity, or considers him less of a gentleman, than when he appeared upon parade in all the pride of military etiquette, with sash, sword, and epaulette. Surely this is as it should be in a country where independence is inseparable from industry; and for this I prize it.

Among many advantages we in this township possess, it is certainly no inconsiderable one that the lower or working-class of settlers are well disposed, and quite free from the annoying Yankee manners that distinguish many of the earlier-settled townships. Our servants are as respectful, or nearly so, as those at home; nor are they admitted to our tables, or placed on an equality with us, excepting at "bees," and such kinds of public meetings; when they usually conduct themselves with a propriety that would afford an example to some that call themselves gentlemen, viz., young men who voluntarily throw aside those restraints that society expects from persons filling a respectable situation.

Intemperance is too prevailing a vice among all ranks of people in this country; but I blush to say it belongs most decidedly to those that consider themselves among the better class of emigrants. Let none such complain of the airs of equality displayed towards them by the labouring class, seeing that they degrade themselves below the honest, sober settler, however poor. If the sons of gentlemen lower themselves, no wonder if the sons of poor men endeavour to exalt themselves above him in a country where they all meet on equal ground and good conduct is the distinguishing mark between the classes ...

November the 28th, 1834

You will have been surprised, and possibly distressed, by my long silence of several months, but when I tell you it has been occasioned by sickness, you will cease to wonder that I did not write.

My dear husband, my servant, the poor babe, and myself, were all at one time confined to our beds with ague. You know how severe my sufferings always were at home with intermittents, and need not marvel if they were no less great in a country where lake-fevers and all kinds of intermittent fevers abound.

Few persons escape the second year without being afflicted with this weakening complaint; the mode of treatment is repeated doses of calomel, with castor-oil or salts, and is followed up by quinine. Those persons who do not choose to employ medical advice on the subject dose themselves with ginger-tea, strong infusion of hyson, or any other powerful green tea, pepper, and whiskey, with many other remedies that have the sanction of custom or quackery.

I will not dwell on this uncomfortable period further than to tell you that we considered the complaint to have had its origin in a malaria, arising from a cellar below the kitchen. When the snow melted, this cellar became half full of water, either from the moisture draining through the spongy earth, or from the rising of a spring beneath the house; be it as it may, the heat of the cooking and Franklin stoves in the kitchen and parlour caused a fermentation to take place in the stagnant fluid before it could be emptied; the effluvia arising from this mass of putrefying water affected us all. The female servant, who was the most exposed to its baneful influence, was the first of our household that fell sick, after which we each in turn became unable to assist each other ...

I lost the ague in a fortnight's time — thanks to calomel and quinine; so did my babe and his nurse: it has, however, hung on my husband during the whole of the summer, and thrown a damp upon his exertions and gloom upon his spirits. This is the certain effect of ague, it causes the same sort of depression on the spirits as a nervous fever. My dear child has not been well ever since he had the ague, and looks very pale and spiritless ...

I have stood of a bright winter day looking with infinite delight on the beautiful mimic waterfalls congealed into solid ice along the bank of the river; and by the mill-dam, from contemplating these pretty frolics of Father Frost, I have been led to picture to myself the sublime scenery of the arctic regions.

In spite of its length and extreme severity, I do like the Canadian winter: it is decidedly the healthiest season of the year; and it is no small enjoyment to be exempted from the torments of the insect tribes, that are certainly great drawbacks to your comfort in the warmer months ...

Not to regret my absence from my native land, and one so fair and lovely withal, would argue a heart of insensibility: yet I must say, for all its roughness, I love Canada, and am as happy in my humble log-house as if it were courtly hall or bower; habit reconciles us to many things that at first were distasteful. It has ever been my way to extract the sweet rather than the bitter in the cup of life, and surely it is best and wisest so to do. In a country where constant exertion is called for from all ages and degrees of settlers, it would be foolish to a degree to damp our energies by complaints, and cast a gloom over our homes by sitting dejectedly down to lament for all that was so dear to us in the old country. Since we are here, let us make the best of it, and bear with cheerfulness the lot we have chosen. I believe that one of the chief ingredients in human happiness is a capacity for enjoying the blessings we possess.

Though at our first outset we experienced many disappointments, many unlooked-for expenses, and many annoying delays, with some wants that to us seemed great privations, on the whole we have been fortunate, especially in the situation of our land, which has increased in value very considerably; our chief difficulties are now over, at least we hope so, and we trust soon to enjoy the comforts of a cleared farm.

My husband is becoming more reconciled to the country, and I daily feel my attachment to it strengthening. The very stumps that appeared so odious, through long custom seem to lose some of their hideousness; the eye becomes familiarized even with objects the most displeasing till they cease to be observed. Some century hence how different will this spot appear! I can picture it to my imagination with fertile fields and groves of trees planted by the hand of taste. All will be different; our present rude dwellings will have given place to others of a more elegant style of architecture, and comfort and grace will rule the scene which is now a forest wild ...

10

"The Long and Heavy Chain of Abuses"

Calls for Political Reform

DOCUMENTS

A) The Six Counties Address, Montreal, October 31, 1837
   The Vindicator

B) The Declaration of the Reformers of the City of Toronto to their Fellow-Reformers in Upper Canada, Toronto, August 2, 1837
   The Constitution

C) Letters to Lord John Russell, Halifax, Nova Scotia, 1839
   Joseph Howe

Canadians pride themselves on their "peaceable kingdom" that, according to Canadian mythology, resists the level of political and social violence of the United States. This was not always the case. 1837 was a turbulent year that saw both Upper and Lower Canada erupt in violence as bands of desperate men sought to overthrow the British administration in favour of an American-style republican structure. Rebel support was far from unanimous, and their attempts ultimately failed. There was, however, widespread dissatisfaction with colonial rule, and many called for the type of democratic changes sweeping through Parliament in London.

The "Six Counties Address" was Lower Canada's equivalent to the American Declaration of Independence and captures the rebel spirit. It remains a critical document for understanding the event. The Address won mass support at a meeting in St. Charles, a farming community outside Montreal, on October 24th, 1837. Flushed with the heat of political passion, the leaders then prepared for open battle against the British colonial government. Their leader, Louis Joseph Papineau, expressed grave doubts about open rebellion and ultimately fled to the United States before the shooting began.

Wolfred Nelson (1791–1861), the primary author of the "Six Counties Address," had no such qualms, and bravely led his rebel followers in the initially successful defense of St. Denis. How did this doctor, with his Loyalist mother and London father, end up a hero to the cause of French-Canadian nationalism? He entered the British army as a young man and trained as a surgeon. He was, in his own words, "a hot Tory inclined to detest all that was Catholic and French-Canadian, but a more intimate knowledge of these people changed [his] views." He served as a military surgeon during the War of 1812, and subsequently started a private practice before entering politics in 1827. Though a Justice of the Peace, distiller, and prominent member of the community, Nelson's social prestige did not tame his strident opposition to what he perceived as abuses of local government. A close friend's death at the hands of British troops further inflamed his wrath, and put him on a collision course with the authorities. First his support for the Patriotes cost him his job as Justice of the Peace. Then, after the Address, Nelson and other Patriotes resisted arrest and set about procuring arms. The die was cast. British troops found and arrested Nelson as the rebellion disintegrated. Charged with treason, he spent seven months in a Montreal prison before the courts banished him to Bermuda. He slipped through a legal loophole, however, and returned to his Montreal medical practice in 1842. There he won a seat in the Legislative Assembly from where he continued to champion French-Canadian rights. This country doctor, ever passionate for his cause, always put medicine before politics and cared for the wounded of both sides during the rebellion. He also reputedly performed Canada's first operation using anesthetics. Some say that Nelson demonstrated more ability as a doctor than a rebel.

Amury Girod (?–1837), a Swiss rebel and intellectual, supposedly fought with Simon Bolivar's independence forces in South America and with the Mexican cavalry before he arrived in Lower Canada in 1831. He attempted to farm and write about farming, but he was a far better tiller of the mind than the soil and quickly concentrated on organizing reform forces in the Montreal region instead. Girod and others formed the radical *Fils de la Liberté*, the vanguard of radicalism in Lower Canada. He took charge of a group of Patriote habitants after skirmishing broke out with the British army, but could not assert his authority. He disappeared in the ensuing confusion and critics say he, like

Papineau, panicked and fled. In his defence, he maintained that he had sought reinforcements. Rather than fall into the hands of the British, Girod committed suicide on December 18th, 1837.

Jean-Philippe Boucher-Belleville (1800–1874) also signed the Address, but not as a diehard rebel. Formerly a teacher, newspaper owner, and editor, he later became a civil servant and linguist after writing extensively about education and agriculture in the colony. He took the politically incorrect stance of blaming the 1836–37 agricultural slump on outdated and unenterprising French-Canadian farming techniques. British forces captured Boucher-Belleville early in the rebellion, and he languished in jail until his release, penniless, in 1838. Eventually, as a leading Montreal editor, he promoted reconciliation between English and French Canadians.

Many from Upper Canada signed the Resolutions of the Toronto Union, but its chief author was likely the leading reformer and radical republican, William Lyon MacKenzie (1795–1861). Growing up in a large and impoverished Scottish family in Dundee marked the mercurial young MacKenzie for the rest of his life. Forever restless and a voracious but undisciplined reader, he came to hate hereditary authority and had difficulty getting along with people. He understood the power of the pen, however, and quickly established himself as a journalist and publisher after immigrating to Upper Canada in 1820. Using his *Colonial Advocate*, he soon gained notoriety across the colony as a reformer and harsh critic of the Family Compact, so much so that a group of conservative youths, dressed as natives, broke into his office one night and dumped his press into Lake Ontario. MacKenzie could write, but he could not handle money, and he fled to America in 1826 to avoid arrest for debt. From there he successfully prosecuted the young vandals, receiving enough compensation to return to Toronto. A subsequent trip to the United States convinced him that its system of government was superior to England's constitutional monarchy. That, combined with a growing frustration with Upper Canada's political process, led him into the seductive arms of republicanism. The *Colonial Advocate* dripped with vitriolic attacks against the Upper Canadian establishment, and his own aggressive crusade in the Legislative Assembly saw him ejected on numerous occasions. Always he bounced back, propelled by support from average citizens who took him as their reform champion. Not everyone supported MacKenzie, however, and his tantrums and often contradictory diatribes against established authority lost him many potential allies. He enjoyed limited success in the Legislature, and therefore shifted to municipal politics, first as alderman, then as mayor of Toronto in 1834. Most of his ideas came to naught and the electorate ejected him from office the following year. From then on, the ideas of violent revolution and armed resistance slowly crept into his newspaper and the cause gathered its own momentum. Unfortunately for the rebels, the rebellion lacked effective leadership and organization, and MacKenzie's plans remained veiled. The British army consequently crushed it with little difficulty and the rebels either fled across the border, went to jail, or disassociated themselves from the movement. MacKenzie tried to rally his forces from his hideaway in the United States, but that violated American neutrality laws and landed him in jail. Pardoned in 1840, a disillusioned MacKenzie wrote: "the more I see [the United States] the more bitterly I regret the attempt at revolution at Toronto." And yet he became an American in 1843 and worked briefly as a federal customs clerk. British authorities granted him amnesty in 1849, and he returned to Upper Canada the following year. MacKenzie had few political allies after his electoral victory to the Legislature in 1851, and he eventually resigned, demoralized, in 1858. He continued to campaign for independence from British rule for the rest of his life.

Other names on the Upper Canadian document include John Doel (1790–1871) a businessman and politician. Though openly opposed to rebellion, he may have known some of the plans. Arrested on three occasions, he was never charged with treason and never played an active part in the rebellion. Thomas D. Morrison (1796–1856) was a respected physician, clerk, and politician who distinguished himself in the cholera epidemics of 1832 and 1834. He also served a term as mayor of Toronto in 1836. Like Doel, he was arrested but acquitted of high treason and then fled to the United States rather then face other charges. A surveyor and public servant, David Gibson (1804–1864) took prisoners during the fighting and spent ten years in exile until he returned to Canada to resume his surveying career. William J. O'Grady (?–1840) was an ordained Catholic priest who came to Upper Canada in 1828. Quarrels within the church led him to a career in journalism, but like many of the others on this list he took no active part in the rebellion. Nor did John Montgomery (1788–1879), a prominent tavern keeper, John Tims, a doctor, or James Hervey Price (1797–1882), an attorney. Wright was a tailor, Gilbert a cabinet maker, Ketchum a tanner, Reynolds a printer, MacKay a grocer, and Armstrong owned an axe-making firm.

Joseph Howe (1804–1873) was the best known voice of reform in Atlantic Canada. His parents were loyalists who fled the conflagration of the American Revolution, and fierce loyalty to Britain shaped Howe for the rest of his life. Self-taught, he started work with his father, who was Nova Scotia's Postmaster General and King's Printer. As with so many other politicians, Howe, too, started in journalism. He purchased the *Novascotian* in 1827, and turned it into an influential newspaper. It also became a vehicle for his political ideas, which set him on a collision course with Nova Scotia's establishment. He hated the systemic corruption among colonial officials and members of the legislative council. His attacks on both led to charges of seditious libel. No lawyer dared defend him, so he did it himself and convinced a jury, over the course of six hours, of his innocence. He left the courtroom a free man, a hero, and a champion of reform. Howe then successfully ran for the Legislative Assembly, taking his seat in 1836. His strident opposition to universal suffrage and his deep loyalty to Britain made him appear an arch conservative, not a reformer. Accepting a seat in the Executive Council in 1840 lost him many of his more radically minded followers, who by then thought he had completely sold out.

A) The Six Counties Address, Montreal, October 31, 1837
The Vindicator

Fellow Citizens:

When a systematic course of oppression has been invariably harassing a People, in despite of their wishes expressed in every manner recognized by constitutional usage; by popular assemblies, and by their Representatives, in Parliament, after grave deliberation; when their rulers, instead of redressing the various evils produced by their own misgovernment, have solemnly enregistered and proclaimed their guilty determination to sap and subvert the very foundations of civil liberty, it becomes the imperative duty of the People to betake themselves to the serious consideration of their unfortunate position — of the dangers by which they are surrounded — and by well-concerted organization, to make such arrangements as may be necessary to protect, unimpaired, their rights as Citizens and their dignity as Freemen.

The wise and immortal framers of the American Declaration of Independence, embodied in that document the principles on which alone are based the Rights of Man; and successfully vindicated and established the only institutions and form of government which can permanently secure the prosperity and social happiness of the inhabitants of this Continent, whose education and habits, derived from the circumstances of their colonization, demand a system of government entirely dependent upon, and directly responsible to, the People.

In common with the various nations of North and South America who have adopted the principles contained in that Declaration, we hold the same holy and self-evident doctrines: that God created no artificial distinctions between man and man; that government is but a mere human institution formed by those who are to be subject to its good or evil action, intended for the benefit of all who may consent to come, or remain under, its protection and control; and therefore, that its form may be changed whenever it ceases to accomplish the ends for which such government was established; that public authorities and men in office are but the executors of the lawfully-expressed will of the community, honoured because they possess public confidence, respected only so long as they command public esteem, and to be removed from office the moment they cease to give satisfaction to the People, the sole legitimate source of all power.

In conformity with these principles, and on the faith of treaties and capitulations entered into with our ancestors, and guaranteed by the Imperial Parliament, the People of this Province have for a long series of years complained by respectful petitions, of the intolerable abuses which poison their existence and paralyse their industry. Far from conceding our humble prayers, aggression has followed aggression, until at length we seem no longer to belong to the British Empire for our own happiness or prosperity, our freedom or the honour of the British Crown or people, but solely for the purpose of fattening a horde of useless officials, who not content with enjoying salaries enormously disproportioned to the duties of their offices, and to the resources of the country, have combined as a faction, united by private interest alone, to oppose all reforms in the Province, and to uphold the iniquities of a Government inimical to the rights and liberties of this colony.

Notwithstanding the universally admitted justice of our demands, and the wisdom and prudence of remedying our complaints, we still endure the misery of an irresponsible Executive, directed by an ignorant and hypocritical Chief; our Judges, dependent for the tenure of their office on the mere will and pleasure of the Crown, for the most part the violent partisans of a corrupt administration, have become more completely the tools and mercenaries of the Executive, by accepting the wages of their servility, in gross violation of every principle of Judicial independence, from foreign authority, without the intervention of the people to whom, through their Representatives, belongs the sole right of voting the salaries of their public servants; the office-holders of the Province devour our revenues, in salaries so extravagant as to deprive us of the funds requisite for the general improvement of the Country, whereby our public works are arrested, and the navigation of our rivers obstructed; a Legislative Council appointed by men resident three thousand miles from this country, and systematically composed so as to thwart and oppose the efforts of our freely-chosen Representatives in all measures for the promotion of the public good, after continuing unchanged during the present administration, thereby depriving the country of the advantages of domestic legislation, has at length been modified in a manner insulting to all classes of society, disgraceful to public morality, and to the annihilation of the respect and confidence of all parties in that branch of the Legislature, by the introduction of men for the most part notorious only for their incapacity, and remarkable alone for their political insignificance, thus making evident, even to demonstration, to all, whatever may be their preconceived ideas, the propriety and urgent necessity of introducing the principle of election into that body, as the only method of enabling the Provincial Legislature to proceed beneficially to the despatch of public business.

Our municipalities are utterly destroyed; the country parts of the Province, as a disgraceful exception to the other parts of this Continent, are totally deprived of all power of regulating, in a corporate capacity, their local affairs, through freely elected Parish and Township Officers; the rising generation is deprived of the blessings of education, the primary schools, which provided for the instruction of 40,000 children, having been shut up by the Legislative Council, a body hostile to the progress of useful knowledge, and instigated to this act by an Executive inimical to the spread of general information among the people — the Jesuits' College founded and endowed by the provident government which colonized this Province for the encouragement and dissemination of learning and the sciences therein, has, with a barbarism unworthy the rulers of a civilized state, disgraceful to the enlightened age in which we live ... , been converted into, and is still retained, as a barrack for soldiery, whilst the funds and property devoted to the support of this and similar institutions have been, and continue to be, squandered and maladministered for the advantage of the favourites, creatures and tools of the Government; our citizens are deprived of the benefits of impartially chosen juries, and are arbitrarily persecuted by Crown officers, who to suit the purposes of the vindictive Government of which they are the creatures, have revived proceedings of an obsolete character, precedents for which are to be found only in the darkest pages of British history. Thus our Judiciary being sullied by combined conspiracies of a wicked Executive, slavish Judges, partizan Law Officers, and political Sheriffs, the innocent and patriotic are exposed to be sacrificed, whilst the enemies of the country, and the violators of all law, are protected and patronized, according as it may please the administration to crush and destroy; to save and protect. Our commerce and domestic industry are paralysed; our public lands alienated, at a nominal price, to a company of speculators, strangers to the country, or bestowed upon insolent favourites, as a reward for their sycophancy; our money is extorted from us without our consent, by taxes unconstitutionally imposed by a foreign Parliament, to be afterwards converted into an instrument of our degradation by being distributed among a howling herd of officials, against our will, without our participation and in violation of all principles of constitutional law.

In the midst of their honest and unwearied efforts to procure a redress of the foregoing grievances, our fellow citizens have been insolently called on to give an account of their public conduct, for which they were responsible to no individual, least of all to the person whom chance or ministerial patronage may place for a season at the head of our Provincial Government. They have been harassed and annoyed by dismissals from offices of mere honour, held for the benefit and at the request of their own immediate neighbours, because they vindicated the rights of their country, like American Freemen; and as an index of further intended aggression, armed troops are being scattered in time of profound peace throughout the country, with the presumptuous and wicked design of restraining by physical force the expression of public opinion, and of completing by violence and bloodshed our slavery and ruin, already determined upon beyond the seas.

Such an aggression as this might justify the recourse, on the part of an outraged people, to all and every means to preserve the last of their insulted privileges — the right to complain. But, thanks to the blindness of the aggressors, the wickedness of the measure will be providentially neutralized by its folly. The regiments about to be quartered among us are composed of men sprung from, and educated with, the Democracy of their country. They, for the most part, entered on their present profession, not from choice, but because they could not find any other employment in their native land. Instead of being stimulated to good conduct by the hope of promotion, too poorly paid, they are exposed to every sort of petty tyranny, and if a murmur escape their lips, they are subjected, like the bonded slave, to the ignoble punishment of the lash. [Contrast] this hard fate with the freedom, content, employment and high wages to be obtained in the United States ...

The long and heavy chain of abuses and oppressions under which we suffer, and to which every year has only added a more galling link, proves that our history is but a recapitulation of what other Colonies have endured before us. Our grievances are but a second edition of their grievances. Our petitions for relief are the same. Like theirs, they have been treated with scorn and contempt, and have brought down upon the petitioners but additional outrage and persecution. Thus the experience of the past demonstrates the folly of expecting justice from European authorities.

Dark, however, and unpromising as may be the present prospects of this our beloved country, we are encouraged by the public virtues of our fellow citizens to hope that the day of our regeneration is not far distant. Domestic manufactures are springing up amongst us, with a rapidity to cheer us in the contest. The impulse given but a few short months ago by the example of generous and patriotic minds, of wearing domestic cloths, has been generally followed, and will shortly be universally adopted. The determination not to consume duty-paying merchandise, and to encourage Free Trade with our neighbours, matters of vital importance, is daily becoming more general, resolute and effective. The people are everywhere being duly impressed with the conviction that the sacrifices to be made must bear some proportion to the glorious object to be achieved, and that personal inconvenience for the good cause must therefore be not only freely, but readily, endured.

Fellow-countrymen! Brothers in affliction! Ye, whatsoever be your origin, language or religion, to whom Equal Laws and the Rights of Man are dear; whose hearts have throbbed with indignation whilst witnessing the innumerable insults to which your common country has been exposed, and who have often been justly alarmed whilst pondering over the sombre futurity [being prepared] by misgovernment and corruption for this Province and for your posterity; in the name of that country, and of the rising generation, now having no hope but in you, we call upon you to assume, by systematic organization in your several Townships and Parishes, that position which can alone procure respect for yourselves and your demands. Let Committees of Vigilance be at once put in *active* operation throughout your respective neighbourhoods. Withdrawing all confidence from the present administration, and from such as will be so base as to accept office under it, forthwith assemble in your Parishes and elect Pacificator Magistrates, after the example of your brother

Reformers of the County of Two Mountains, in order to protect the people at once from useless and improvident expense, and from the vengeance of their enemies. Our Young Men, the hope of the country, should everywhere organize themselves, after the plan of their brothers, 'The Sons of Liberty' in Montreal, in order that they may be prepared to act with promptitude and effect as circumstances may require; and the brave Militiamen, who by their blood and valour have twice preserved this country for ungrateful rulers, should at once associate together, under officers of their own choice, for the security of good order and the protection of life and property in their respective localities. Thus prepared, Colonial Liberty may haply be yet preserved.

In this hope, and depending, for a disenthralment from the misrule under which we now groan, on the Providence of God, whose blessing on our disinterested labours we humbly implore; relying on the love of liberty which the free air and impregnable fastnesses of America should inspire in the hearts of the People at large, and upon the sympathy of our Democratic neighbours who in the establishment of arbitrary rule on their borders, wisely and clearly [will foresee] the uprearing of a system which might be made a precedent and instrument for the introduction of the same arbitrary rule into other parts of the American Continent, and who can never consent that the principles for which they successfully struggled in the Eighteenth, shall, in our persons, be trampled in the dust in the Nineteenth century, We, the Delegates of the Confederated Counties of Richelieu, St Hyacinthe, Rouville, L'Acadie, Chambly and Verchères, hereby publicly register the solemn and determined resolution of the People whom we represent, to carry into effect, with the least delay possible, the preceding recommendations, and never to cease their patriotic exertions until the various grievances of which they now complain shall have been redressed; and We hereby invite our fellow-citizens throughout the Province to unite their efforts to ours to procure a good, cheap and responsible system of government for their common country.

Signed for, and on behalf of, the Confederation of the Six Counties, this 24th day of October, 1837.

WFD. Nelson, President

J. T. Drolet,

F. C. Duvert, Vice Presidents

A. Girod,

J. P. Boucher-Belleville, Secretaries

B) The Declaration of the Reformers of the City of Toronto to their Fellow-Reformers in Upper Canada, Toronto, August 2, 1837
The Constitution

... The time has arrived, after nearly half a century's forbearance under increasing and aggravated misrule, when the duty we owe our country and posterity requires from us the assertion of our rights and the redress of our wrongs.

Government is founded on the authority and is instituted for the benefit of a people; when, therefore, any government long and systematically ceases to answer the great ends of its foundation, the people have a natural right given them by their Creator to seek after and establish such institutions as will yield the greatest quantity of happiness to the greatest number.

Our forbearance heretofore has only been rewarded with an aggravation of our grievances; and our past inattention to our rights has been ungenerously and unjustly urged as evidence of the surrender of them. We have now to choose on the one hand between submission to the same blighting policy as has desolated Ireland, and on the other hand, the patriotic achievement of cheap, honest, and responsible government.

The right was conceded to the present United States at the close of a successful revolution, to form a constitution for themselves; and the loyalists with their descendants and others, now peopling this portion of America, are entitled to the same liberty without the shedding of blood — more they do not ask; less they ought not to have. — But, while the revolution of the former has been rewarded with a consecutive prosperity, unexampled in the history of the world, the loyal valor of the latter alone remains amidst the blight of misgovernment to tell them what they might have been as the not less valiant sons of American Independence ...

The affairs of this country have been ever against the spirit of the Constitutional Act, subjected in the most injurious manner to the interferences and interdictions of a succession of Colonial Ministers in England who have never visited the country, and can never possibly become acquainted with the state of parties, or the conduct of public functionaries, except through official channels in the province, which are illy calculated to convey the information necessary to disclose official delinquencies and correct public abuses. — A painful experience has proved how impracticable it is for such a succession of strangers beneficially to direct and control the affairs of the people four thousand miles off; and being an impracticable system, felt to be intolerable by those for whose good it was professedly intended, it ought to be abolished, and the domestic institutions of the province so improved and administered by the local authorities as to render the people happy and contented. — This system of baneful domination has been uniformly furthered by a Lieutenant Governor sent amongst us as an uninformed, unsympathising stranger, who, like Sir Francis, has not a single feeling in common with the people, and whose hopes and responsibilities begin and end in Downing Street. And this baneful domination is further cherished by a Legislative Council not elected and therefore responsible to people for whom they legislate, but appointed by the ever changing Colonial Minister for life, from pensioners on the bounty of the Crown, official dependents and needy expectants.

Under this mockery of human Government we have been insulted, injured and reduced to the brink of ruin. The due influence and purity of all our institutions have been utterly destroyed. Our Governors are the mere instruments for effecting domination from Downing Street; Legislative Councillors have been intimidated into executive compliance, as in the case of the late Chief Justice Powell, Mr. Baby, and others; the Executive Council has been stript of every shadow of responsibility, and of every shade of duty; the freedom and purity of elections have lately received, under Sir Francis Head, a final and irretrievable blow; our revenue has been and still is decreasing to such an extent as to render heavy additional taxation indispensable for the payment of the interest of our public debt incurred by a system of improvident and profligate expenditure; our public lands, although a chief source of wealth to a new country, have been sold at a low valuation to speculating companies in London, and resold to the settlers at very advanced rates, the excess being remitted to England to the serious impoverishment of the country; the ministers of religion have been corrupted by the prostitution of the casual and territorial revenue to salary and influence them; our clergy reserves, instead of being devoted to the purpose of general education, though so much needed and loudly demanded, have been in part sold to the amount of upwards of 300,000 dollars, paid into the military chest and sent to England; numerous rectories have been established, against the almost unanimous wishes of the people, with certain exclusive, ecclesiastical and spiritual rights and privileges, according to the Established Church of England, to the destruction of equal religious rights; public salaries, pensions and sinecures, have been augmented in number and amount, notwithstanding the impoverishment of our revenue and country; and this parliament have, under the name of arrearages, paid the retrenchments made in past years by reform parliaments; our Judges have, in spite of our condition, been doubled, and wholly selected from the most violent political partisans against our equal, civil and religious liberties, and a court of chancery suddenly adopted by a subservient parliament, against the long cherished expectations of the people against it, and its operation fearfully extended into the past so as to jeopardize every title and transaction from the beginning of the Province to the present time. A law has been passed enabling Magistrates, appointed during pleasure, at the representation of a Grand Jury selected by a Sheriff holding office during pleasure, to tax the people at pleasure, without their previous knowledge or consent, upon all their rateable property to build and support work-houses for the refuge of the paupers invited by Sir Francis from the parishes in Great Britain; thus unjustly and wickedly laying the foundation of a system which must result in taxation, pestilence and famine. Public loans have been authorized by improvident legislation to nearly 8 millions of dollars, the surest way to make the people both poor and dependent; the parliament, subservient to Sir Francis Head's blighting administration, has, by an unconstitutional act sanctioned by him, prolonged their duration after the demise of the crown, thereby evading their present responsibility to the people, depriving them of the exercise of their elective franchise on the present occasion, and extending the period of their unjust, unconstitutional and ruinous legislation with Sir Francis Head; our best and most worthy citizens have been dismissed from the bench of Justice, from the militia, and other stations of honour and usefulness, for exercising their rights as freemen in attending public meetings for the regeneration of our condition, as instanced in the case of Dr. Baldwin, Messrs. Scatchard, Johnson, Small, Ridout, and others; those of our fellow subjects who go to England to represent our deplorable condition are denied a hearing, by a partial, unjust and oppressive government, while the authors and promoters of our wrongs are cordially and graciously received, and enlisted in the cause of our further wrongs and misgovernment; our public revenues are plundered and misapplied without redress, and unavailable securities make up the late defalcation of Mr. P. Robinson the Commissioner of Public Lands to the amount of 80,000 dollars. Interdicts are continually sent by the colonial minister to the Governor, and by the Governor to the Provincial Parliament, to restrain and render futile their legislation, which ought to be free and unshackled ...

The British Government, by themselves and through the Legislative Council of their appointment, have refused their assent to laws the most wholesome and necessary for the public good, among which we may enumerate the Intestate Estate equal distribution Bill, the Bill to sell the Clergy Reserves for educational purposes; the Bill to remove the corrupt influence of the executive in the choosing of juries, and to secure a fair and free trial by jury; the several bills to encourage emigration from foreign parts; the bills to secure the independency of the Assembly; the bill to amend the law of libel; the bills to appoint commissioners to meet others appointed by Lower Canada, to treat on matters of trade and other matters of deep interest; the bills to extend the blessings of Education to the humbler classes in every township, and to appropriate annually a sum of money for that purpose; the bill to dispose of the school lands in aid of education; several bills for the improvement of the highways; the bill to secure independence to voters by establishing the vote by ballot; the bill for the better regulation of elections of members of the Assembly, and to provide that they be held at places convenient for the people; the bills for the relief of Quakers, Menonists and Tunkers; the bill to amend the present obnoxious courts of requests laws, by allowing the people to choose the commissioners, and to have a trial by jury if desired; with other bills to improve the administration of justice and diminish unnecessary costs; the bills to amend the Charter of King's College University so as to remove its partial and arbitrary system of government and education; and the bill to allow free competition in Banking.

The King of England has forbidden his governors to pass laws of immediate and pressing importance, unless suspended in their operation till his assent should be obtained; and when so suspended, he has utterly neglected to attend to them. He has interfered with the freedom of elections, and appointed elections to be held at places dangerous, unconvenient and unsafe for the people to assemble at, for the purpose of fatiguing them into his measures, through the agency of pretended representatives; and has through his legislative council, prevented provision from being made for quiet and peaceable elections ...

He has dissolved the late House of Assembly for opposing with manly firmness Sir Francis Head's invasion of the right of the people to a wholesome control over the revenue, and for insisting that the persons conducting the government should be responsible for their official conduct to the country through its representatives.

He has endeavoured to prevent the peopling of this province and its advancement in wealth; for that purpose obstructing the laws for the naturalization of foreigners, refusing to pass others to encourage their migration hither, and raising the conditions of new appropriations of the public lands, large tracts of which he has bestowed upon unworthy persons his favorites, while deserving settlers from Germany and other countries have been used cruelly.

He has rendered the administration of Justice liable to suspicion and distrust, by obstructing laws for establishing a fair trial by Jury, by refusing to exclude the chief criminal judge from interfering in political business, and by selecting as the judiciary violent and notorious partisans of his arbitrary power.

He has sent a standing army into the sister province to coerce them to his unlawful and unconstitutional measures, in open violation of their rights and liberties, and has received with marks of high approbation military officers who interfered with the citizens of Montreal, in the midst of an election of their representatives, and brought the troops to coerce them, who shot several persons dead wantonly in the public streets.

Considering the great number of lucrative appointments held by strangers to the country, whose chief merit appears to be their subservience to any and every administration, we may say with our brother colonists of old — "He has sent hither swarms of new officers to harass our people and eat out their substance."

The English Parliament have interfered with our internal affairs and regulations, by the passage of grievous and tyrannical enactments, for taxing us heavily without our consent, for prohibiting us to purchase many articles of the first importance at the cheapest European or American markets, and compelling us to buy such goods and merchandise at an exorbitant price in markets of which England has a monopoly ...

In every stage of these proceedings we have petitioned for redress in the most humble terms; our repeated petitions have been answered only by repeated injuries.

Nor have we been wanting in attention to our British brethren. We have warned them from time to time of attempts by their legislature to extend an unwarrantable jurisdiction over us. We have reminded them of the circumstances of our emigration and settlement here, we have appealed to their native justice and magnanimity, and we have conjured them by the ties of our common kindred to disavow these usurpations which would inevitably interrupt our connection and correspondence. They too have been deaf to the voice of justice and consanguinity.

We, therefore, the Reformers of the City of Toronto, sympathizing with our fellow citizens here and throughout the North American Colonies, who desire to obtain cheap, honest, and responsible government, the want of which has been the source of all their past grievances, as its continuance would lead to their utter ruin and desolation, are of opinion,

1. That the warmest thanks and admiration are due from the Reformers of Upper Canada to the Honorable Louis Joseph Papineau, Esq., Speaker of the House of Assembly of Lower Canada, and his compatriots in and out of the Legislature, for their past uniform, manly, and noble independence, in favour of civil and religious liberty; and for their present devoted, honorable and patriotic opposition to the attempt of the British Government to violate their constitution without their consent, subvert the powers and privileges of their local parliament, and overawe them by coercive measures into a disgraceful abandonment of their just and reasonable wishes.

2. And that the Reformers of Upper Canada are called upon by every tie of feeling, interest, and duty, to make common cause with their fellow citizens of Lower Canada, whose successful coercion would doubtless be in time visited upon us, and the redress of whose grievances would be the best guarantee for the redress of our own.

To render this co-operation the more effectual, we earnestly recommend to our fellow citizens that they exert themselves to organize political associations; that public meetings be held throughout the province; and that a convention of delegates be elected, and assembled at Toronto, to take into consideration the political condition of Upper Canada, with authority to its members to appoint commissioners to meet others to be named on behalf of Lower Canada and any of the other colonies, armed with suitable powers as a Congress, to seek an effectual remedy for the grievances of the colonists.

T. D. Morrison, Chairman of Com.	John Elliot, Secretary
Committee:	
David Gibson,	James H. Price,
John Macintosh,	John Doel,
Wm. J. O'Grady,	M. Reynolds,
Edward Wright,	James Armstrong,
Robert McKay,	James Hunter,
Thomas Elliott,	John Armstrong,
E.B. Gilbert,	William Ketchum,
John Montgomery,	Wm. L. Mackenzie,
John Edward Tims	

C) Letters to Lord John Russell, Halifax, Nova Scotia, 1839
Joseph Howe

Howe's First Letter, September 18, 1839

My Lord,

... It appears to me that a very absurd opinion has long prevailed among many worthy people, on both sides of the Atlantic; that the selection of an Executive Council, who, upon most points of domestic policy, will differ from the great body of the inhabitants and the majority of their representatives, is indispensable to the very existence of colonial institutions; and that if it were otherwise, the colony would fly off, by the operation of some latent principle of mischief, which I have never seen very clearly defined ...

I have ever held, my Lord, and still hold to the belief, that the population of British North America are sincerely attached to the parent State; that they are proud of their origin, deeply interested in the integrity of the empire and not anxious for the establishment of any other form of government here than that which you enjoy at home ... Why should we desire a severance of old ties that are more honourable than any new ones we can form? Why should we covet institutions more perfect than those which have worked so well and produced such admirable results? Until it can be shown that there are forms of government, combining stronger executive power with more of individual liberty; offering nobler incitements to honourable ambition, and more security to unaspiring ease and humble industry; why should it be taken for granted, either by our friends in England or our enemies elsewhere, that we are panting for new experiments; or are disposed to repudiate and cast aside the principles of that excellent Constitution, cemented by the blood and the long experience of our fathers and upon which the vigorous energies of our brethren, driven to apply new principles to a field of boundless resources, have failed to improve? ... [B]ut surely none of these distinguished men would wish to deny the Constitution itself to large bodies of British subjects on this side of the water, who have not got it, who are anxious to secure its advantages to themselves and their children; who, while they have no ulterior designs that can by any possibility make the concession dangerous, can never be expected to be contented with a system the very reverse of that they admire; and in view of the proud satisfaction with which, amidst all their manly struggles for power, their brethren at home survey the simple machinery of a government, which we believe to be, like the unerring principles of science, as applicable to one side of the Atlantic as to the other, but which we are nevertheless denied.

... [B]ut it must fade if the system be not changed, and our children, instead of exhibiting the bold front and manly bearing of the Briton, must be stamped with the lineaments of low cunning and sneaking servility, which the practical operation of colonial government has a direct tendency to engender.

From some rather close observation of what has occurred in Nova Scotia and in the adjoining colonies, I am justified in the assertion, that the English rule is completely reversed on this side of the Atlantic. Admitting that in Lower Canada ... such a policy may have been necessary; surely there is no reason why the people of Upper Canada, Nova Scotia, New Brunswick, Prince Edward Island, and Newfoundland, should, on that account, be deprived of the application of a principle which is the corner-stone of the British Constitution — the fruitful source of responsibility in the Government, and of honourable characteristics in the people. If the Frenchmen in one Province do not understand, or cannot be entrusted with this valuable privilege, why should we, who are all Britons or of British descent, be deprived of what we do understand and feel that we can never be prosperous and happy without? ...

Looking at all the British North American Colonies, with one single exception, so far as my memory extends, although it has sometimes happened that the local administration has secured a majority in the Lower House, I never knew an instance in which a hostile majority could displace an Executive Council, whose measures it disapproved; or could, in fact, change the policy or exercise the slightest influence upon administrative operations of the Government ... Let us suppose that a general election takes place in the Province next year and that the great body of the people are dissatisfied with the mode in which the patronage of the Government has been distributed and the general bearing of the internal policy of its rule. If that colony were an English incorporated town, the people would have the remedy in their own hands; if they were entrusted with the powers which as British subjects of right belongs to them, they would only have to return a majority of their own way of thinking; a few men would change places; the wishes of the majority would be carried out, and by no possibility could anything occur to bring the people and their rulers into such a state of collision as was exhibited in that fine Province [New Brunswick] for a long series of years. But under the existing system, if a hostile majority is returned, what can they do? Squabble and contend with an executive whom they cannot influence; see the patronage and favour of Government lavished upon the minority who annoy but never outvote them; and, finally, at the expiration of a further period of ten years, appeal by delegation to England ...

To give your Lordship an idea of the absurd anomalies and ridiculous wretchedness of our system up to that time [1836], it is only necessary to state, that a Council of twelve persons administered the government, and at the same time formed the upper branch of the Legislature [of Nova Scotia], sitting invariably with closed doors. Only five of these twelve gentlemen were partners in one private bank, five of them were relations, two of them were heads of departments, and one was the Chief Justice, who in one capacity had to administer the law he had assisted to make, and then in a third to advise the Governor as to its execution. To heighten the absurdity of the whole affair, it is hardly necessary to add, that only nine of these twelve were members of a particular Church, which, however useful or respectable, only embraced one-fifth of the whole population of the Province. To the passage of certain measures for the regulation of our currency, the derangement of which was supposed to be profitable to those who dealt in money, the bankers were said to have opposed their influence. Any attempt at reduction of the expense of the revenue departments, the heads of which sat at the board, was not likely to prevail; while the patronage of the Government was of course distributed by the nine Churchmen, in a way not very satisfactory to the four-fifths of the people who did not happen to belong to that communion. Such a combination as this never could have grown up in any colony where the English principle of responsibility had been in operation ...

You ask me for the remedy ... [T]he Colonial Governors must be commanded to govern by the aid of those who possess the confidence of the people and are supported by a majority of the representative branch. Where is the danger? Of what consequence is it to the people of England whether half-a-dozen persons, in whom that majority have confidence, but of whom they know nothing and care less, manage our local affairs; or the same number selected from the minority and whose policy the bulk of the population distrust? Suppose there was at this moment a majority in our Executive Council who think with the Assembly, what effect would it have upon the funds? Would the stocks fall? Would England be weaker, less prosperous or less respected because the people of Nova Scotia were satisfied and happy?

But, it is said, a colony being part of a great empire must be governed by different principles from the metropolitan state; that unless it be handed over to the minority it cannot be governed at all; that the majority, when they have things their own way, will be discontented and disloyal; that the very fact of their having nothing to complain of will make them desire to break the political compact and disturb the peace of the empire. Let us fancy that this reasoning were applied to Glasgow or Aberdeen or to any other town in Britain which you allow to govern itself. And what else is a Province like Nova Scotia than a small community, too feeble to interfere with the general commercial and military arrangements of the Government; but deeply interested in a number of minor matters, which only the people to be affected by them can wisely manage; which the ministry can never find leisure to attend to and involve in inextricable confusion when they meddle with them? ...

[T]he principle of responsibility to the popular branch must be introduced into all the colonies without delay. It is the only simple and safe remedy for an inveterate and very common disease. It is mere mockery to tell us that the Governor himself is responsible. He must carry on the government by and with the few officials whom he finds in possession when he arrives. He may flutter and struggle in the net, as some well-meaning Governors have done, but he must at last resign himself to his fate; and like a snared bird be content with the narrow limits assigned him by his keepers. I have known a Governor bullied, sneered at, and almost shut out of society, while his obstinate resistance to the system created a suspicion that he might not become its victim; but I never knew one who, even with the best intentions and the full concurrence and support of the representative branch, backed by the confidence of his Sovereign, was able to contend, on anything like fair terms, with the small knot of functionaries who form the Councils, fill the Offices, wield the powers of the Government. The plain reason is, because, while the Governor is amenable to his Sovereign, and the members of Assembly are controlled by their constituents, these men are not responsible at all; and can always protect and sustain each other, whether assailed by the representatives of the Sovereign or the representatives of the people ...

The planets that encircle the sun, warmed by its heat and rejoicing in its effulgence, are moved and sustained, each in its bright but subordinate career, by the same laws as the sun itself. Why should this beautiful example be lost upon us? Why should we run counter to the whole stream of British experience; and seek, for no object worthy of the sacrifice, to govern on one side of the Atlantic by principles the very reverse of those found to work so admirable on the other. The employment of steamers will soon bring Halifax within a ten days' voyage of England. Nova Scotia will then not be more distant from London than the north of Scotland and the west of Ireland were a few years ago. No time should be lost, therefore, in giving us the rights and guards to which we are entitled; for depend upon it the nearer we approach the mother country the more we shall admire its excellent constitution and the more intense will be the sorrow and disgust with which we must turn to contemplate our own.

Howe's Fourth Letter, September 1839

My Lord — ...
THE COLONIAL OFFICE
The Colonial Secretary's duties should be narrowed to a watchful supervision over each colony to see that the authority of the Crown was not impaired and that Acts of Parliament and public treaties were honestly and firmly carried out; but he should have no right to appoint more than two or three officers in each Province and none to intermeddle in any internal affair, so long as the Colonial Government was conducted without conflict with the Imperial Government and did not exceed the scope of its authority. This would give him enough to do, without heaping upon him duties so burdensome and various that they cannot be discharged with honour by any man, however able; nor with justice or safety to the millions whose interests they affect. His responsibility should be limited to the extent of his powers; and as these would be familiar to every Englishman, exposure and punishment would not be difficult, in case of ignorance, incapacity or neglect.
THE GOVERNOR
I have shown that most Governors come out to colonies so ignorant of their geography and topography, climate, productions, commerce, resources and wants, and above all, of the parties, passions and prejudices which divide them, and of the character, talents and claims of the men by whom the population are influenced and led, that for the first six or twelve months they are like overgrown boys at school ...

Now let us suppose, that when a Governor arrives in Nova Scotia, he finds himself surrounded, not by this irresponsible Council, who represent nothing except the whims of his predecessors and the interests of a few families (so small in point of numbers, that but for the influence which office and the distribution of patronage give them, their relative weight in the country would be ridiculously diminutive), — but by men who say to him: "May it please your Excellency, there was a general election in the Province last month or last year, or the year before last, and an administration was formed upon the results of that election. We, who compose the Council, have ever since been steadily sustained by a majority of the Commons and have reason to believe that our conduct and policy have been satisfactory to the country at large." A Governor thus addressed would feel that at all events he was surrounded by those who represented a majority of the population, who possessed the confidence of an immense body of the electors, and who had been selected by the people who had the deepest interest in his success, to give him advice and conduct the administration. If he had doubts on this point — if he had reason to believe that any factious combination had obtained office improperly and wished to take the opinions of the country; or if the Executive Council sought to drive him into measures not sanctioned by the charter, or exhibited a degree of grasping selfishness which was offensive and injurious he could at once dissolve the assembly and appeal to the people: who here as in England, would relieve him from doubt and difficulty, and, fighting out the battle on the hustings, rebuke the councillors if they were wrong. This would be a most important point gained in favour of the Governor; for now he is the slave of an irresponsible Council which he cannot shake off; and is bound to act by the advice of men who, not being accountable for the advice they give and having often much to gain and nothing to lose by giving bad advice, may get him into scrapes every month, and lay the blame on him. The Governor's responsibility would also be narrowed to the care of the Queen's prerogative, the conservation of treaties, the military defence, and the execution of the imperial Acts; the local administration being left in the hands of those who understood it and who were responsible ...

THE EXECUTIVE COUNCIL

... The heads of departments are always very well paid for their trouble in governing the country by the enormous official salaries they receive; their colleagues either are looking for office, or have means of providing for their relatives and friends; while if it should so happen, that such a thing as a colonial Executive Councillor can be found for any length of time in office, who has not served himself or his friends, the title and the consciousness of possessing for life the right to approach and advise every Governor and give a vote upon every important act of administration, without a possibility of being displaced or called to account for anything said or done, is no mean reward for the small amount of labour and time bestowed. Formerly these people, in addition to other benefits, obtained for themselves and their friends immense tracts of Crown land. This resource is now cut off by the substitution of sales for free grants; but looking at the Executive Council or Cabinet, as it exists in any of the North American Provinces at present, we find a small knot of individuals, responsible neither to the Queen, the Secretary of State, the Governor nor the people; who owe their seats to neither, but to their relatives and friends through whose influence and intrigue they have been appointed; and who, while they possess among them some of the best salaries and nearly all the patronage of the country, have a common interest in promoting extravagance, resisting economy, and keeping up the system exactly as it stands. It will be perceived that such a body as this may continue to govern a colony for centuries ... To understand more clearly how un-English, how anti-constitutional, how dangerous this body is, it is only necessary to contrast it with what it ought to resemble, but never does. In England, the government of the country is invariably carried on by some great political party, pledged to certain principles of foreign or domestic policy which the people for the time approve; but the Cabinet in a colony is an official party who have the power forever to keep themselves and their friends in office and to keep all others out, even though nineteen out of every twenty of the population are against them ...

Now for this body I propose to substitute one sustained by at least a majority of the electors; whose general principles are known and approved; whom the Governor may dismiss, whenever they exceed their powers; and who may be discharged by the people whenever they abuse them, who, instead of laying the blame when attacked, upon the Governor, or Secretary of State, shall be bound as in England, to stand up and defend, against all comers, every appointment made and every act done under their administration. One of the first results of this change would be to infuse into every department of administration a sense of accountability which now is nowhere found — to give vigorous action to every vein and artery now exhibiting torpidity and languor — and to place around the Governor and at the head of every department of public affairs the ablest men the colony could furnish; men of energy and talent instead of the brainless sumphs, to whom the task of counselling the Governor or administering the affairs of an extensive department, is often committed under the present system ...

THE LEGISLATIVE COUNCIL

The colonies, having no hereditary peerage, this body has been constructed to take its place. From the difficulty of making it harmonize with the popular branch, some politicians in Lower Canada ... thought it might be abolished. I think there is no necessity for this; first, because it would destroy the close resemblance which it is desirable to maintain between our institutions and those of the mother country; and again, because a second legislative chamber, not entirely dependent upon popular favour, is useful to review measures and check undue haste or corruption in the popular branch. Besides, I see no difficulty in maintaining its independence ...

The main object of the Executive Council being the preservation of a system by which they enjoy honours, office and patronage, uncontrolled and uninfluenced by the people, and they having the nomination of Legislative Councillors, of course they have always selected a majority of those whose interests and opinions were their own and who could help them to wrestle with and fight off the popular branch. Hence the constant collision and the general outcry against the second chamber. The simple remedy for all this appears to be to introduce the English practice: let the people be consulted in the formation of the Executive Council; and then the appointments to the Legislative will be more in accordance with public sentiment and the general interest, than they are now. I should have no objection to the Legislative Councillors holding their seats for life, by which their independence of the Executive and of the people would be secured, provided they were chosen fairly by those to whom, from time to time, the constituency, as at home, entrusted the privilege; and not as they are now selected, to serve a particular purpose and expressly to wrangle rather than to harmonize with the popular branch. The House of Lords includes men selected by all the administrations which the people of Britain have called into power. The House of Lords, in the colonies, have been created by all the administrations which the people never could influence or control ...

THE COMMONS

One of the first effects of a change of system would be a decided improvement in the character of all the Colonial Assemblies. The great centre of political power and influence would in the Provinces, as at home, be the House of Commons. Towards that body the able, the industrious, the eloquent and the wealthy, would press with ten times the ardour and unanimity which are now evinced; because then, like its great prototype in Britain, it would be an open and fair arena, in which the choice spirits of the country would battle for a share in its administration, a participation in its expenditure and in the honour and influence which public employment confers ...

Another improvement would be the placing of the government of a colony, as it always is in England, in a majority in the Commons ... Of course, an Executive Council in the colonies should not be expected to resign upon every incidental and unimportant question connected with the details of government; but, whenever a fair and decisive vote, by which it was evident that they had lost the confidence of the country, was registered against them, they should either change their policy, strengthen their hands by an accession of popular talents and principles, or abandon their seats and assume the duties and responsibilities of opposition ...

APPOINTMENTS, INTERNAL IMPROVEMENTS, ETC.

One of the greatest evils of the present form of government is that nothing like system or responsibility can be carried into any one branch of the public service. There are, exclusive of militia and road commissions, nearly nine hundred offices to be filled, in the Province of Nova Scotia alone; all essential to the administration of internal affairs, not one of them having anything to do with imperial interests. And will it be believed in England that the whole of this patronage is in the hands of a body whom the people can never displace — that the vast majority in the Commons have not the slightest influence in its distribution — while the greatest idiot who gives his silent and subservient vote in the minority is certain of obtaining his reward? But the evil does not stop here. It is utterly impossible for the people either to bring to punishment or to get rid of a single man of the whole nine hundred if the local government chooses to protect him.

Perhaps the most cruel injury that the system inflicts upon the colonists, arises from the manner in which they are compelled to conduct their internal improvements ...

But make the Governor's advisers responsible to the Assembly and the representatives would at once resign to them the management of such affairs. It would then be the business of the Executive, instead of leaving the road service to the extemporaneous zeal or corrupt management of individuals, to come prepared, at the commencement of each session, with a general review of the whole system; and supported by its majority, to suggest and to carry a comprehensive and intelligible scheme, embracing the whole of this service, accounting for the previous year's expenditure and appointments, and accepting the suggestions of members as to the plans of the current year. We should then have an Executive to which every commissioner would be directly accountable; to which he could apply for instructions from January to December; and which, being itself responsible, would be careful of its proceedings; and yet, being more independent than individual members are in dealing with their own constituents, would be more firm and unyielding where it was right.

This is the simple and I am satisfied the only safe remedy for the abuses of the road system. To take the distribution of commissions from fifty men, possessed of much local knowledge and partially responsible, to give it to twelve others having less information and subject to no control, would be an act of madness. Fortunately, in this, as in all other cases, we have no occasion to seek for new theories or try unsafe experiments; let us adopt the good old practices of our ancestors and of our brethren; let us "keep the old paths," in which, while there is much facility, there is no danger ...

... [T]hose who fancy that Nova Scotians are an inferior race to those who dwell upon the ancient homestead or that they will be contented with a less degree of freedom, know little of them. A country that a century ago was but a wilderness and is now studded with towns and villages, and intersected with roads, even though more might have been done under a better system, affords some evidence of industry. Nova Scotian ships, bearing the British flag into every quarter of the globe, are some proofs of enterprise; and the success of the native author ... more than contradicts the humorous exaggeration by which, while we are stimulated to higher efforts, others may be for a moment misled. If then our right to inherit the constitution be clear, if our capacity to maintain and enjoy it cannot be questioned, have we done anything to justify the alienation of our birthright? Many of the original settlers of this Province emigrated from the old colonies when they were in a state of rebellion — not because they did not love freedom, but because they loved it under the old banner and the old forms; and many of their descendants have shed their blood, on land and sea, to defend the honour of the Crown and the integrity of the empire ... All suspicion of disloyalty we cast aside, as the product of ignorance or cupidity; we seek for nothing more than British subjects are entitled to; but we will be contented with nothing less ...

Then look at the United States, in which the son of a mechanic in the smallest town, of a squatter in the wildest forest, may contend, on equal terms, with the proudest, for an office in twenty-eight different States; and having won as many as contents him, may rise, through the national grades, to be President of the Union. There are no family compacts to exclude these aspirants; no little knots of irresponsible and self-elected councillors, to whom it is necessary to sell their principles, and before whom the manliness of their nature must be prostrated, before they can advance ...

11

"To the Barren Grounds"

Samuel Hearne's Odyssey

DOCUMENTS

A) A Journey from Prince of Wales's Fort in Hudson's Bay
   to the Northern Ocean [1770–1771]
   Samuel Hearne

Well into the twentieth century Canada's far north remained our final frontier. Indigenous people lived there for millennia and knew it well, and European explorers cruised through parts of the eastern arctic as early as the 12th century. Generally, however, it remained an unknown land: a glaring blank on the increasingly annotated maps of the world. Weather alone made the area very difficult to explore. Why go north into certain adversity, and with very uncertain returns, when gentler southern latitudes seemed to offer so much more with far less misery? Just the same, limited exploration of the "barren grounds" did continue, however haltingly, and organizations like the Hudson's Bay Company hoped to eventually capitalize on it.

How can someone with little education, who joined the British navy at age eleven, produce marvelous literature? That is what historians would like to ask Samuel Hearne (1745–1792). The literary quality of his narrative, published in 1795, is so high that the authorship is suspect. Was the work his, or did he hire a competent ghost writer? Does that matter? Does it challenge the report's authenticity? Whether he had help or not will likely remain a mystery. Hearne was, however, one of the few who offered tantalizing glimpses of the unknown world of Canada's far north in the 18th century.

Hearne served the Royal Navy until 1763, then either hired on immediately with the Hudson's Bay Company or did so in 1766. His naval experience made him an obvious choice for the little fleet sailing out of Churchill, hunting whales along the west coast of Hudson's Bay. Young, tough, and intelligent, Hearne was also a born adventurer who snowshoed from Churchill to York and back in the dead of winter during 1767–68. This stamina and spirit, plus knowledge and ability, likely made him the leading candidate for an expedition into the far north. The Hudson's Bay Company wanted to address critics who accused it of reneging on its mandate to explore, and Hearne also sought copper deposits rumoured to be found among the Chipewyan Indians. The expedition also hoped to locate distant northern native people, who could be encouraged to trade with the Company.

Off they went, guided by natives who soon abandoned Hearne. He tried again, and this time they robbed him and he lost his way. Undaunted, he began for the third time in December 1770, now guided by a Chipewyan named Matonabbee who demanded that native women come along. They all had a tough time. Matonabbee insisted they travel light, obtaining their food by shadowing the seasonal movement of the buffalo and caribou. Thus Hearne complained that provisions were "either all feasting, or all famine." The weather, too, plagued them, and they only found one small lump of copper during the expedition's two-year duration. They finally returned to Fort Prince of Wales in late June, 1772. The trip, by offering little other than an important view of tribal relationships at the time, perhaps earned more gratitude from subsequent historians than from his immediate superiors.

Hearne then gained command of Fort Prince of Wales at Churchill in 1776. He was a successful fur trader and brought significant profits into the Bay's coffers, but his career almost ended in humiliation when he surrendered his fort to the French in 1782. His faithful friend, Matonabbee, hanged himself in shame. Hearne returned later that same year, however, to found a new fort at Churchill, but retired to England in 1787, plagued by ill health.

There he began writing the manuscript describing his years in Canada's north, working very slowly, apparently wary of his critics. Some accused him of geographical inaccuracies which, they said, threatened the accuracy of his depiction. And they had grounds. Hearne never claimed to be a geographer and guessed at his daily directions. His latitudes and longitudes were often inaccurate, and he did get lost periodically. Nonetheless, he acquired an unsurpassed knowledge of local conditions and the northern indigenous people by immersing himself in native culture while on the march. He was one of the very few Europeans who observed and reported on the lives of indigenous women. He was also a fine naturalist who recorded animals like the muskox for the first time. Perhaps his fear of criticism stalled publication. It was not until 1795, many years after the initial journey, that a published account finally appeared.

A) A Journey from Prince of Wales's Fort in Hudson's Bay to the Northern Ocean [1770–1771]
Samuel Hearne

In the evening of the twentieth, we were joined from the Westward by a famous Leader, called Matonabbee, mentioned in my instructions; who, with his followers, or gang, was also going to Prince of Wales's Fort, with furs, and other articles for trade. This Leader, when a youth, resided several years at the above Fort, and was not only a perfect master of the Southern Indian language, but by being frequently with the Company's servants, had acquired several words of English, and was one of the men who brought the latest accounts of the Coppermine River; and it was on his information, added to that of one I-dot-le-ezey (who is since dead) that this expedition was set on foot.

The courteous behaviour of this stranger struck me very sensibly. As soon as he was acquainted with our distress, he got such skins as we had with us dressed for the Southern Indians, and furnished me with a good warm suit of otter and other skins: but, as it was not in his power to provide us with snowshoes, being then on the barren ground, he directed us to a little river which he knew, and where there was a small range of woods, which, though none of the best, would, he said, furnish us with temporary snow-shoes and sledges, that might materially assist us during the remaining part of our journey. We spent several nights in company with this Leader, though we advanced towards the Fort at the rate of ten or twelve miles a day; and as provisions abounded, he made a grand feast for me in the Southern Indian style, where there was plenty of good eating, and the whole concluded with singing and dancing, after the Southern Indian style and manner. In this amusement my homeguard Indians bore no inconsiderable part, as they were both men of some consequence when at home, and well known to Matonabbee: but among the other Northern Indians, to whom they were not known, they were held in no estimation; which indeed is not to be wondered at, when we consider that the value of a man among those people, is always proportioned to his abilities in hunting; and as my two Indians had not exhibited any great talents that way, the Northern Indians shewed them as much respect as they do in common to those of very moderate talents among themselves ...

He attributed all our misfortunes to the misconduct of my guides, and the very plan we pursued, by the desire of the Governor, in not taking any women with us on this journey, was, he said, the principal thing that occasioned all our wants: "for," said he, "when all the men are heavy laden, they can neither hunt nor travel to any considerable distance; and in case they meet with success in hunting, who is to carry the produce of their labour? Women," added he, "were made for labour; one of them can carry, or haul, as much as two men can do. They also pitch our tents, make and mend our clothing, keep us warm at night; and, in fact, there is no such thing as travelling any considerable distance, or for any length of time, in this country, without their assistance. Women," said he again, "though they do every thing, are maintained at a trifling expense; for as they always stand cook, the very licking of their fingers in scarce times, is sufficient for their subsistence." This, however odd it may appear, is but too true a description of the situation of women in this country: it is at least so in appearance; for the women always carry the provisions, and it is more than probable they help themselves when the men are not present.

Early in the morning of the twenty-third, I struck out of the road to the Eastward, with my two companions and two or three Northern Indians, while Matonabbee and his crew continued their course to the Factory, promising to walk so slow that we might come up with them again; and in two days we arrived at the place to which we were directed. We went to work immediately in making snow-shoe frames and sledges; but notwithstanding our utmost endeavours, we could not complete them in less than four days. On the first of November we again proceeded on our journey toward the Factory; and on the sixth, came up with Matonabbee and his gang: after which we proceeded on together several days; when I found my new acquaintance, on all occasions, the most sociable, kind, and sensible Indian I had ever met with. He was a man well known, and, as an Indian, of universal knowledge, and generally respected ...

Having a good stock of dried provisions, and most of the necessary work for canoes all ready, on the eighteenth we moved about nine or ten miles to the North North West, and then came to a tent of Northern Indians who were tenting on the North side of Thelewey-aza River. From these Indians Matonabbee purchased another wife; so that he had now no less than seven, most of whom would for size have made good grenadiers. He prided himself much in the height and strength of his wives, and would frequently say, few women would carry or haul heavier loads; and though they had, in general, a very masculine appearance, yet he preferred them to those of a more delicate form and moderate stature. In a country like this, where a partner in excessive hard labour is the chief motive for the union, and the softer endearments of a conjugal life are only considered as a secondary object, there seems to be great propriety in such a choice; but if all the men were of this way of thinking, what would become of the greater part of the women, who in general are but of low stature, and many of them of a most delicate make, though not of the exactest proportion, or most beautiful mould? Take them in a body, the women are as destitute of real beauty as any nation I ever saw, though there are some few of them, when young, who are tolerable; but the care of a family, added to their constant hard labour, soon make the most beautiful among them look old and wrinkled, even before they are thirty; and several of the more ordinary ones at that age are perfect antidotes to love and gallantry. This, however, does not render them less dear and valuable to their owners, which is a lucky circumstance for those women, and a certain proof that there is no such thing as any rule or standard for beauty. Ask a Northern Indian, what is beauty? he will answer, a broad flat face, small eyes, high cheekbones, three or four broad black lines a-cross each cheek, a low forehead, a large broad chin, a clumsy hook-nose, a tawny hide, and breasts hanging down to the belt. Those beauties are greatly heightened, or at least rendered more valuable, when the possessor is capable of dressing all kinds of skins, converting them into the different parts of their clothing, and able to carry eight or ten stone in Summer, or haul a much greater weight in Winter. These, and other similar accomplishments, are all that are sought after, or expected, of a Northern Indian woman. As to their temper, it is of little consequence; for the men have a wonderful facility in making the most stubborn comply with as much alacrity as could possibly be expected from those of the mildest and most obliging turn of mind; so that the only real difference is, the one obeys through fear, and the other complies cheerfully from a willing mind; both knowing that what is commanded must be done. They are, in fact, all kept at a great distance, and the rank they hold in the opinion of the men cannot be better expressed or explained, than by observing the method of treating or serving them at meals, which would appear very humiliating, to an European woman, though custom makes it sit light on those whose lot it is to bear it. It is necessary to observe, that when the men kill any large beast, the women are always sent to bring it to the tent: when it is brought there, every operation it under-goes, such as splitting, drying, pounding, &c. is performed by the women. When any thing is to be prepared for eating, it is the women who cook it; and when it is done, the wives and daughters of the greatest Captains in the country are never served, till all the males, even those who are in the capac-ity of servants, have eaten what they think proper; and in times of scarcity it is frequently their lot to be left without a single morsel. It is, however, natu-ral to think they take the liberty of helping themselves in secret; but this must be done with great prudence, as capital embezzlements of provisions in such times are looked on as affairs of real consequence, and frequently subject them to a very severe beating. If they are practised by a woman whose youth and inattention to domestic concerns cannot plead in her favour, they will for ever be a blot in her character, and few men will chuse to have her for a wife ...

Having finished such wood-work as the Indians thought would be nec-essary, and having augmented our stock of dried meat and fat, the twenty-first was appointed for moving; but one of the women having been taken in labour, and it being rather an extraordinary case, we were detained more than two days. The instant, however, the poor woman was delivered, which was not until she had suffered all the pains usually felt on those occasions for near fifty-two hours, the signal was made for moving when the poor creature took her infant on her back and set out with the rest of the company; and though another person had the humanity to haul her sledge for her (for one day only) she was obliged to carry a considerable load beside her little charge, and was frequently obliged to wade knee-deep in water and wet snow. Her very looks, exclusive of her moans, were a sufficient proof of the great pain she endured, insomuch that although she was a person I greatly disliked, her distress at this time so overcame my prejudice, that I never felt more for any of her sex in my life; indeed her sighs pierced me to the soul, and rendered me very miser-able, as it was not in my power to relieve her.

When a Northern Indian woman is taken in labour, a small tent is erected for her, at such a distance from the other tents that her cries cannot easily be heard, and the other women and young girls are her constant visitants: no male, except children in arms, ever offers to approach her. It is a circumstance perhaps to be lamented, that these people never attempt to assist each other on those occasions, even in the most critical cases. This is in some measure owing to delicacy, but more probably to an opinion they entertain that nature is abundantly sufficient to perform every thing required, without any external help whatever. When I informed them of the assistance which European women derive from the skill and attention of our midwives, they treated it with the utmost contempt; ironically observing, "that the many humpbacks, bandy-legs, and other deformities, so frequent among the English, were undoubtedly owing to the great skill of the persons who assisted in bringing them into the world, and to the extraordinary care of their nurses afterwards."

A Northern Indian woman after child-birth is reckoned unclean for a month or five weeks; during which time she always remains in a small tent placed at a little distance from the others, with only a female acquaintance or two; and during the whole time the father never sees the child. Their reason for this practice is, that children when first born are sometimes not very sightly, having in general large heads, and but little hair, and are, moreover, often discoloured by the force of the labour; so that were the father to see them in such great disadvantage, he might probably take a dislike to them, which never afterward could be removed ...

During our stay at Clowey we were joined by upward of two hundred Indians from different quarters, most of whom built canoes at this place; but as I was under the protection of a principal man, no one offered to molest me, nor can I say they were very clamorous for any thing I had. This was undoubtedly owing to Matonabbee's informing them of my true situation; which was, that I had not, by any means, sufficient necessaries for myself, much less to give away. The few goods which I had with me were intended to be reserved for the Copper and Dog-ribbed Indians, who never visit the Company's Factories. Tobacco was, however, always given away; for every one of any note, who joined us, expected to be treated with a few pipes, and on some occasions it was scarcely possible to get off without presenting a few inches to them; which, with the constant supplies which I was obliged to furnish my own crew, decreased that article of my stock so fast, that notwithstanding I had yet advanced so small a part of my journey, more than one half of my store was expended. Gunpowder and shot also were articles commonly asked for by most of the Indians we met; and in general these were dealt round to them with a liberal hand by my guide Matonabbee. I must however, do him the justice to acknowledge, that what he distributed was all his own, which he had purchased at the Factory; to my certain knowledge he bartered one hundred and fifty martens' skins for powder only, besides a great number of beaver, and other furs, for shot, ball, iron-work, and tobacco, purposely to give away among his countrymen; as he had certainly as many of these articles given to him as were, in his opinion, sufficient for our support during our journey out and home ...

In the night, one of Matonabbee's wives and another woman eloped: it was supposed they went off to the Eastward, in order to meet their former husbands, from whom they had been sometime before taken by force. This affair made more noise and bustle than I could have supposed; and Matonabbee seemed entirely disconcerted, and quite inconsolable for the loss of his wife. She was certainly by far the handsomest of all his flock, of a moderate size, and had a fair complexion; she apparently possessed a mild temper, and very engaging manners. In fact, she seemed to have every good quality that could be expected in a Northern Indian woman, and that could render her an agreeable companion to an inhabitant of this part of the world. She had not, however, appeared happy in her late situation; and chose rather to be the sole wife of a sprightly young fellow of no note (though very capable of maintaining her) than to have the seventh or eighth share of the affection of the greatest man in the country. I am sorry to mention an incident which happened while we were building the canoes at Clowey, and which by no means does honour to Matonabbee: it is no less a crime than that of having actually stabbed the husband of the above-mentioned girl in three places; and had it not been for timely assistance, would certainly have murdered him, for no other reason than because the poor man had spoken disrespectfully of him for having taken his wife away by force. The cool deliberation with which Matonabbee committed this bloody action, convinced me it had been a long premeditated design; for he no sooner heard of the man's arrival, than he opened one of his wives' bundles, and, with the greatest composure, took out a new long box-handled knife, went into the man's tent, and, without any preface whatever, took him by the collar, and began to execute his horrid design. The poor man anticipating his danger, fell on his face, and called for assistance; but before any could be had he received three wounds in the back. Fortunately for him, they all happened on the shoulder-blade, so that his life was spared. When Matonabbee returned to his tent, after committing this horrid deed, he sat down as composedly as if nothing had happened, called for water to wash his bloody hands and knife, smoked his pipe as usual, seemed to be perfectly at ease, and asked if I did not think he had done right? ...

Notwithstanding the Northern Indians are so covetous, and pay so little regard to private property as to take every advantage of bodily strength to rob their neighbours, not only of their goods, but of their wives, yet they are, in other respects, the mildest tribe, or nation, that is to be found on the borders of Hudson's Bay: for let their affronts or losses be ever so great, they never will seek any other revenge than that of wrestling. As for murder, which is so common among all the tribes of Southern Indians, it is seldom heard of among them. A murderer is shunned and detested by all the tribe, and is obliged to wander up and down, forlorn and forsaken even by his own relations and former friends ... The cool reception he meets with by all who know him, occasions him to grow melancholy, and he never leaves any place but the whole company say, "There goes the murderer!" The women, it is true, sometimes receive an unlucky blow from their husbands for misbehaviour, which occasions their death; but this is thought nothing of: and for one man or woman to kill another out of revenge, or through jealousy, or on any other account, is so extraordinary, that very few are now existing who have been guilty of it. At the present moment I know not one, beside Matonabbee, who ever made an attempt of that nature; and he is, in every other respect, a man of such universal good sense, and, as an Indian, of such great humanity, that I am at a loss how to account for his having been guilty of such a crime, unless it be by his having lived among the Southern Indians so long, as to become tainted with their blood-thirsty, revengeful, and vindictive disposition ...

It should have been observed, that during our stay at Clowey a great number of Indians entered into a combination with those of my party to accompany us to the Copper-mine River; and with no other intent than to murder the Esquimaux, who are understood by the Copper Indians to frequent that river in considerable numbers. This scheme, notwithstanding the trouble and fatigue, as well as danger, with which it must be obviously attended, was nevertheless so universally approved by those people, that for some time almost every man who joined us proposed to be of the party. Accordingly, each volunteer, as well as those who were properly of my party, prepared a target, or shield, before we left the woods of Clowey. Those targets were composed of thin boards, about three quarters of an inch thick, two feet broad, and three feet long; and were intended to ward off the arrows of the Esquimaux. Notwithstanding these preparations, when we came to leave the women and children, as has been already mentioned, only sixty volunteers would go with us; the rest, who were nearly as many more, though they had all prepared targets, reflecting that they had a great distance to walk, and that no advantage could be expected from the expedition, very prudently begged to be excused, saying that they could not be spared for so long a time from the maintenance of their wives and families; and particularly, as they did not see any then in our company, who seemed willing to encumber themselves with such a charge. This seemed to be a mere evasion, for I am clearly of opinion that poverty on one side, and avarice on the other, were the only impediments to their joining our party; had they possessed as many European goods to squander away among their countrymen as Matonabbee and those of my party did, in all probability many might have been found who would have been glad to have accompanied us.

When I was acquainted with the intentions of my companions, and saw the warlike preparations that were carrying on, I endeavoured as much as possible to persuade them from putting their inhuman design into execution; but so far were my entreaties from having the wished-for effect, that it was concluded I was actuated by cowardice; and they told me, with great marks of derision, that I was afraid of the Esquimaux. As I knew my personal safety depended in a great measure on the favourable opinion they entertained of me in this respect, I was obliged to change my tone, and replied, that I did not care if they rendered the name and race of the Esquimaux extinct; adding at the same time, that though I was no enemy to the Esquimaux, and did not see the necessity of attacking them without cause, yet if I should find it necessary to do it, for the protection of any one of my company, my own safety out of the question, so far from being afraid of a poor defenceless Esquimaux, whom I despised more than feared, nothing should be wanting on my part to protect all who were with me. This declaration was received with great satisfaction; and I never afterwards ventured to interfere with any of their war-plans. Indeed, when I came to consider seriously, I saw evidently that it was the highest folly for an individual like me, and in my situation, to attempt to turn the current of a national prejudice which had subsisted between those two nations from the earliest periods, or at least as long as they had been acquainted with the existence of each other ...

Whether it was from real motives of hospitality, or from the great advantages which they expected to reap by my discoveries, I know not; but I must confess that their civility far exceeded what I could expect from so uncivilized a tribe, and I was exceedingly sorry that I had nothing of value to offer them. However, such articles as I had, I distributed among them, and they were thankfully received by them. Though they have some European commodities among them, which they purchase from the Northern Indians, the same articles from the hands of an Englishman were more prized. As I was the first whom they had ever seen, and in all probability might be the last, it was curious to see how they flocked about me, and expressed as much desire to examine me from top to toe, as an European Naturalist would a non-descript animal. They, however, found and pronounced me to be a perfect human being, except in the colour of my hair and eyes: the former, they said, was like the stained hair of a buffaloe's tail, and the latter, being light, were like those of a gull. The whiteness of my skin also was, in their opinion, no ornament, as they said it resembled meat which had been sodden in water till all the blood was extracted. On the whole, I was viewed as so great a curiosity in this part of the world, that during my stay there, whenever I combed my head, some or other of them never failed to ask for the hairs that came off, which they carefully wrapped up, saying, "When I see you again, you shall again see your hair" ...

As Matonabbee and the other Indians thought it advisable to leave all the women at this place, and proceed to the Copper-mine River without them, it was thought necessary to continue here a few days, to kill as many deer as would be sufficient for their support during our absence. And notwithstanding deer were so plentiful, yet our numbers were so large, and our daily consumption was so great, that several days elapsed before the men could provide the women with a sufficient quantity; and then they had no other way of preserving it, than by cutting it in thin slices and drying it in the Sun. Meat, when thus prepared, is not only very portable, but palatable; as all the blood and juices are still remaining in the meat, it is very nourishing and wholesome food; and may, with care, be kept a whole year without the least danger of spoiling. It is necessary, however, to air it frequently during the warm weather, otherwise it is liable to grow mouldy: but as soon as the chill air of the fall begins, it requires no farther trouble till next Summer ...

To do Matonabbee justice on this occasion, I must say that he endeavoured as much as possible to persuade his countrymen from taking either furs, clothing, or bows, from the Copper Indians, without making them some satisfactory return; but if he did not encourage, neither did he endeavour to hinder them from taking as many women as they pleased. Indeed, the Copper Indian women seem to be much esteemed by our Northern traders; for what reason I know not, as they are in reality the same people in every respect; and their language differs not so much as the dialects of some of the nearest counties in England do from each other.

It is not surprising that a plurality of wives is customary among these people, as it is so well adapted to their situation and manner of life. In my opinion no race of people under the Sun have a greater occasion for such an indulgence. Their annual haunts, in quest of furs, is so remote from any European settlement, as to render them the greatest travellers in the known world; and as they have neither horse nor water carriage, every good hunter is under the necessity of having several persons to assist in carrying his furs to the Company's Fort, as well as carrying back the European goods which he receives in exchange for them. No persons in this country are so proper for this work as the women, because they are inured to carry and haul heavy loads from their childhood and to do all manner of drudgery; so that those men who are capable of providing for three, four, five, six, or more women, generally find them humble and faithful servants, affectionate wives, and fond and indulgent mothers to their children. Though custom makes this way of life sit apparently easy on the generality of the women, and though, in general, the whole of their wants seem to be comprised in food and clothing only, yet nature at times gets the better of custom, and the spirit of jealousy makes its appearance among them: however, as the husband is always arbitrator, he soon settles the business, though perhaps not always to the entire satisfaction of the parties.

Much does it redound to the honour of the Northern Indian women when I affirm, that they are the mildest and most virtuous females I have seen in any part of North America; though some think this is more owing to habit, custom, and the fear of their husbands, than from real inclination. It is undoubtedly well known that none can manage a Northern Indian woman so well as a Northern Indian man; and when any of them have been permitted to remain at the Fort, they have, for the sake of gain, been easily prevailed on to deviate from that character; and a few have, by degrees, become as abandoned as the Southern Indians, who are remarkable throughout all their tribes for being the most debauched wretches under the Sun. So far from laying any restraint on their sensual appetites, as long as youth and inclination last, they give themselves up to all manner of even incestuous debauchery; and that in so beastly a manner when they are intoxicated, a state to which they are peculiarly addicted, that the brute creation are not less regardless of decency. I know that some few Europeans, who have had little opportunity of seeing them, and of enquiring into their manners, have been very lavish in their praise: but every one who has had much intercourse with them, and penetration and industry enough to study their dispositions, will agree, that no accomplishments whatever in a man, is sufficient to conciliate the affections, or preserve the chastity of a Southern Indian woman.

The Northern Indian women are in general so far from being like those I have above described, that it is very uncommon to hear of their ever being guilty of incontinency, not even those who are confined to the sixth or even eighth part of a man ...

It may appear strange, that while I am extolling the chastity of the Northern Indian women, I should acknowledge that it is a very common custom among the men of this country to exchange a night's lodging with each other's wives. But this is so far from being considered as an act which is criminal, that it is esteemed by them as one of the strongest ties of friendship between two families; and in case of the death of either man, the other considers himself bound to support the children of the deceased. Those people are so far from viewing this engagement as a mere ceremony, like most of our Christian god-fathers and god-mothers, who, notwithstanding their vows are made in the most solemn manner, and in the presence of both God and man, scarcely ever afterward remember what they have promised, that there is not an instance of a Northern Indian having once neglected the duty which he is supposed to have taken upon himself to perform. The Southern Indians, with all their bad qualities, are remarkably humane and charitable to the widows and children of departed friends; and as their situation and manner of life enable them to do more acts of charity with less trouble than falls to the lot of a Northern Indian, few widows or orphans are ever unprovided for among them ...

Soon after our arrival at the river-side, three Indians were sent off as spies, in order to see if any Esquimaux were inhabiting the river-side between us and the sea. After walking about three quarters of a mile by the side of the river, we put up, when most of the Indians went a hunting, and killed several musk-oxen and some deer. They were employed all the remainder of the day and night in splitting and drying the meat by the fire. As we were not then in want of provisions, and as deer and other animals were so plentiful, that each day's journey might have provided for itself, I was at a loss to account for this unusual economy of my companions; but was soon informed, that those preparations were made with a view to have victuals enough ready-cooked to serve us to the river's mouth, without being obliged to kill any in our way, as the report of the guns, and the smoke of the fire, would be liable to alarm the natives, if any should be near at hand, and give them an opportunity of escaping ...

When we arrived on the West side of the river, each painted the front of his target or shield; some with the figure of the Sun, others with that of the Moon, several with different kinds of birds and beasts of prey, and many with the images of imaginary beings, which, according to their silly notions, are the inhabitants of the different elements, Earth, Sea, Air, &c.

On enquiring the reason of their doing so, I learned that each man painted his shield with the image of that being on which he relied most for success in the intended engagement. Some were contented with a single representation; while others, doubtful, as I suppose, of the quality and power of any single being, had their shields covered to the very margin with a group of hieroglyphics quite unintelligible to every one except the painter. Indeed from the hurry in which this business was necessarily done, the want of every colour but red and black, and the deficiency of skill in the artist, most of those paintings had more the appearance of a number of accidental blotches, than "of anything that is on the earth, or in the water under the earth"; and though some few of them conveyed a tolerable idea of the thing intended, yet even these were many degrees worse than our country sign-paintings in England.

When this piece of superstition was completed, we began to advance toward the Esquimaux tents; but were very careful to avoid crossing any hills, or talking loud, for fear of being seen or overheard by the inhabitants; by which means the distance was not only much greater than it otherwise would have been, but, for the sake of keeping in the lowest grounds, we were obliged to walk through entire swamps of stiff marly clay, sometimes up to the knees. Our course, however, on this occasion, though very serpentine, was not altogether so remote from the river as entirely to exclude me from a view of it the whole way: on the contrary, several times (according to the situation of the ground) we advanced so near it, as to give me an opportunity of convincing myself that it was as unnavigable as it was in those parts which I had surveyed before, and which entirely corresponded with the accounts given of it by the spies.

It is perhaps worth remarking, that my crew, though an undisciplined rabble, and by no means accustomed to war or command, seemingly acted on this horrid occasion with the utmost uniformity of sentiment. There was not among them the least altercation or separate opinion; all were united in the general cause, and as ready to follow where Matonabbee led, as he appeared to be ready to lead, according to the advice of an old Copper Indian, who had joined us on our first arrival at the river where this bloody business was first proposed ...

The land was so situated that we walked under cover of the rocks and hills till we were within two hundred yards of the tents. There we lay in ambush for some time, watching the motions of the Esquimaux; and here the Indians would have advised me to stay till the fight was over, but to this I could by no means consent; for I considered that when the Esquimaux came to be surprised, they would try every way to escape, and if they found me alone, not knowing me from an enemy, they would probably proceed to violence against me when no person was near to assist. For this reason I determined to accompany them, telling them at the same time, that I would not have any hand in the murder they were about to commit, unless I found it necessary for my own safety. The Indians were not displeased at this proposal; one of them immediately fixed me a spear, and another lent me a broad bayonet for my protection, but at that time I could not be provided with a target; nor did I want to be encumbered with such an unnecessary piece of lumber.

While we lay in ambush, the Indians performed the last ceremonies which were thought necessary before the engagement. These chiefly consisted in painting their faces; some all black, some all red, and others with a mixture of the two; and to prevent their hair from blowing into their eyes, it was either tied before and behind, and on both sides, or else cut short all round. The next thing they considered was to make themselves as light as possible for running; which they did, by pulling off their stockings, and either cutting off the sleeves of their jackets, or rolling them up close to their armpits; and though the muskettoes at that time were so numerous as to surpass all credibility, yet some of the Indians actually pulled off their jackets and entered the lists quite naked, except their breech-cloths and shoes. Fearing I might have occasion to run with the rest, I thought it also advisable to pull off my stockings and cap, and to tie my hair as close up as possible.

By the time the Indians had made themselves thus completely frightful, it was near one o'clock in the morning of the seventeenth; when finding all the Esquimaux quiet in their tents, they rushed forth from their ambuscade, and fell on the poor unsuspecting creatures, unperceived till close at the very eves of their tents, when they soon began the bloody massacre, while I stood neuter in the rear.

In a few seconds the horrible scene commenced; it was shocking beyond description; the poor unhappy victims were surprised in the midst of their sleep, and had neither time nor power to make any resistance; men, women, and children, in all upward of twenty, ran out of their tents stark naked, and endeavoured to make their escape; but the Indians having possession of all the land-side, to no place could they fly for shelter. One alternative only remained, that of jumping into the river; but, as none of them attempted it, they all fell a sacrifice to Indian barbarity!

The shrieks and groans of the poor expiring wretches were truly dreadful; and my horror was much increased at seeing a young girl, seemingly about eighteen years of age, killed so near me, that when the first spear was stuck into her side she fell down at my feet, and twisted round my legs, so that it was with difficulty that I could disengage myself from her dying grasps. As two Indian men pursued this unfortunate victim, I solicited very hard for her life; but the murderers made no reply till they had stuck both their spears through her body, and transfixed her to the ground. They then looked me sternly in the face, and began to ridicule me, by asking if I wanted an Esquimaux wife; and paid not the smallest regard to the shrieks and agony of the poor wretch, who was twining round their spears like an eel! Indeed, after receiving much abusive language from them on the occasion, I was at length obliged to desire that they would be more expeditious in dispatching their victim out of her misery, otherwise I should be obliged, out of pity, to assist in the friendly office of putting an end to the existence of a fellow creature who was so cruelly wounded. On this request being made, one of the Indians hastily drew his spear from the place where it was first lodged, and pierced it through her breast near the heart. The love of life, however, even in this most miserable state, was so predominant, that though this might justly be called the most merciful act that could be done for the poor creature, it seemed to be unwelcome, for though much exhausted by pain and loss of blood, she made several efforts to ward off the friendly blow. My situation and the terror of my mind at beholding this butchery, cannot easily be conceived, much less described; though I summed up all the fortitude I was master of on the occasion, it was with difficulty that I could refrain from tears; and I am confident that my features must have feelingly expressed how sincerely I was affected at the barbarous scene I then witnessed; even at this hour I cannot reflect on the transactions of that horrid day without shedding tears.

The brutish manner in which these savages used the bodies they had so cruelly bereaved of life was so shocking, that it would be indecent to describe it; particularly their curiosity in examining, and the remarks they made, on the formation of the women; which, they pretended to say, differed materially from that of their own …

When the Indians had completed the murder of the poor Esquimaux, seven other tents on the East side the river immediately engaged their attention: very luckily, however, our canoes and baggage had been left at a little distance up the river, so that they had no way of crossing to get at them. The river at this part being little more than eighty yards wide, they began firing at them from the West side. The poor Esquimaux on the opposite shore, though all up in arms, did not attempt to abandon their tents; and they were so unacquainted with the nature of fire-arms, that when the bullets struck the ground, they ran in crowds to see what was sent them, and seemed anxious to examine all the pieces of lead which they found flattened against the rocks. At length one of the Esquimaux men was shot in the calf of his leg, which put them in great confusion. They all immediately embarked in their little canoes, and paddled to a shoal in the middle of the river, which being somewhat more than a gun-shot from any part of the shore, put them out of reach of our barbarians.

When the savages discovered that the surviving Esquimaux had gained the shore above mentioned, the Northern Indians began to plunder the tents of the deceased of all the copper utensils they could find; such as hatchets, bayonets, knives, &c. after which they assembled on the top of an adjacent high hill, and standing all in a cluster, so as to form a solid circle, with their spears erect in the air, gave many shouts of victory, constantly clashing their spears against each other, and frequently calling out "tima! tima!" by way of derision to the poor surviving Esquimaux, who were standing on the shoal almost knee-deep in water …

It ought to have been mentioned in its proper place, that in making our retreat up the river, after killing the Esquimaux on the West side, we saw an old woman sitting by the side of the water, killing salmon, which lay at the foot of the fall as thick as a shoal of herrings. Whether from the noise of the fall, or a natural defect in the old woman's hearing, it is hard to determine, but certain it is, she had no knowledge of the tragical scene which had been so lately transacted at the tents, though she was not more than two hundred yards from the place. When we first perceived her, she seemed perfectly at ease, and was entirely surrounded with the produce of her labour. From her manner of behaviour, and the appearance of her eyes, which were as red as blood, it is more than probable that her sight was not very good; for she scarcely discerned that the Indians were enemies, till they were within twice the length of their spears of her. It was in vain that she attempted to fly, for the wretches of my crew transfixed her to the ground in a few seconds, and butchered her in the most savage manner. There was scarcely a man among them who had not thrust at her with his spear; and many in doing this, aimed at torture, rather than immediate death, as they not only poked out her eyes, but stabbed her in many parts very remote from those which are vital ...

When the Indians had plundered the seven tents of all the copper utensils, which seemed the only thing worth their notice, they threw all the tents and tent-poles into the river, destroyed a vast quantity of dried salmon, musk-oxen flesh, and other provisions; broke all the stone kettles; and, in fact, did all the mischief they possibly could to distress the poor creatures they could not murder, and who were standing on the shoal before mentioned, obliged to be woeful spectators of their great, or perhaps irreparable loss.

After the Indians had completed this piece of wantonness we sat down, and made a good meal of fresh salmon, which were as numerous at the place where we now rested, as they were on the West side of the river. ... For the sake of form, however, after having had some consultation with the Indians, I erected a mark, and took possession of the coast, on behalf of the Hudson's Bay Company ...

One of the Indians' wives, who for some time had been in a consumption, had for a few days past become so weak as to be incapable of travelling, which, among those people, is the most deplorable state to which a human being can possibly be brought. Whether she had been given over by the doctors, or that it was for want of friends among them, I cannot tell, but certain it is, that no expedients were taken for her recovery; so that, without much ceremony, she was left unassisted, to perish above-ground.

Though this was the first instance of the kind I had seen, it is the common, and indeed the constant practice of those Indians; for when a grown person is so ill, especially in the Summer, as not to be able to walk, and too heavy to be carried, they say it is better to leave one who is past recovery, than for the whole family to sit down by them and starve to death; well knowing that they cannot be of any service to the afflicted. On those occasions, therefore, the friends or relations of the sick generally leave them some victuals and water; and, if the situation of the place will afford it, a little firing. When those articles are provided, the person to be left is acquainted with the road which the others intend to go; and then, after covering them well up with deer skins, &c. they take their leave, and walk away crying.

Sometimes persons thus left, recover; and come up with their friends, or wander about till they meet with other Indians, whom they accompany till they again join their relations. Instances of this kind are seldom known. The poor woman above mentioned, however, came up with us three several times, after having been left in the manner described. At length, poor creature! she dropt behind, and no one attempted to go back in search of her.

A custom apparently so unnatural is perhaps not to be found among any other of the human race: if properly considered, however, it may with justice be ascribed to necessity and self-preservation, rather than to the want of humanity and social feeling, which ought to be the characteristic of men, as the noblest part of the creation. Necessity, added to nation custom, contributes principally to make scenes of this kind less shocking to those people, than they must appear to the more civilized part of mankind ...

Among the various superstitious customs of those people, it is worth remarking, and ought to have been mentioned in its proper place, that immediately after my companions had killed the Esquimaux at the Copper River, they considered themselves in a state of uncleanness, which induced them to practise some very curious and unusual ceremonies. In the first place, all who were absolutely concerned in the murder were prohibited from cooking any kind of victuals, either for themselves or others. As luckily there were two in company who had not shed blood, they were employed always as cooks till we joined the women. This circumstance was exceedingly favourable on my side; for had there been no persons of the above description in company, that task, I was told, would have fallen on me; which would have been no less fatiguing and troublesome, than humiliating and vexatious.

When the victuals were cooked, all the murderers took a kind of red earth, or oker, and painted all the space between the nose and chin, as well as the greater part of their cheeks, almost to the ears, before they would taste a bit, and would not drink out of any other dish, or smoke out of any other pipe, but their own; and none of the others seemed willing to drink or smoke out of theirs.

We had no sooner joined the women, at our return from the expedition, than there seemed to be an universal spirit of emulation among them, vying who should first make a suit of ornaments for their husbands, which consisted of bracelets for the wrists, and a band for the forehead, composed of porcupine quills and moose-hair, curiously wrought on leather.

The custom of painting the mouth and part of the cheeks before each meal, and drinking and smoking out of their own utensils, was strictly and invariably observed, till the Winter began to set in; and during the whole of that time they would never kiss any of their wives or children. They refrained also from eating many parts of the deer and other animals, particularly the head, entrails, and blood; and during their uncleanness, their victuals were never sodden in water, but dried in the sun, eaten quite raw, or broiled, when a fire fit for the purpose could be procured.

When the time arrived that was to put an end to these ceremonies, the men, without a female being present, made a fire at some distance from the tents, into which they threw all their ornaments, pipe-stems, and dishes, which were soon consumed to ashes; after which a feast was prepared, consisting of such articles as they had long been prohibited from eating; and when all was over, each man was at liberty to eat, drink, and smoke as he pleased; and also to kiss his wives and children at discretion, which they seemed to do with more raptures than I had ever known them do it either before or since ...

On the eleventh of January, as some of my companions were hunting, they saw the track of a strange snow-shoe, which they followed; and at a considerable distance came to a little hut, where they discovered a young woman sitting alone. As they found that she understood their language, they brought her with them to the tents. On examination, she proved to be one of the Western Dog-ribbed Indians, who had been taken prisoner by the Athapuscow Indians in the Summer of one thousand seven hundred and seventy; and in the following Summer, when the Indians that took her prisoner were near this part, she had eloped from them, with an intent to return to her own country; but the distance being so great, and having, after she was taken prisoner, been carried in a canoe the whole way, the turnings and windings of the rivers and lakes were so numerous, that she forgot the track; so she built the hut in which we found her, to protect her from the weather during the Winter, and here she had resided from the first setting in of the fall.

From her account of the moons past since her elopement, it appeared that she had been near seven months without seeing a human face; during all which time she had supported herself very well by snaring partridges, rabbits, and squirrels; she had also killed two or three beaver, and some porcupines. That she did not seem to have been in want is evident, as she had a small stock of provisions by her when she was discovered; and was in good health and condition, and I think one of the finest women, of a real Indian, that I have seen in any part of North America ...

The singularity of the circumstance, the comeliness of her person, and her approved accomplishments, occasioned a strong contest between several of the Indians of my party, who should have her for a wife; and the poor girl was actually won and lost at wrestling by near half a score different men the same evening. My guide, Matonabbee, who at that time had no less than seven wives, all women grown, besides a young girl of eleven or twelve years old, would have put in for the prize also, had not one of his wives made him ashamed of it, by telling him that he had already more wives than he could properly attend. This piece of satire, however true, proved fatal to the poor girl who dared to make so open a declaration; for the great man, Matonabbee, who would willingly have been thought equal to eight or ten men in every respect, took it as such an affront, that he fell on her with both hands and feet, and bruised her to such a degree, that after lingering some time she died.

When the Athapuscow Indians took the above Dog-ribbed Indian woman prisoner, they, according to the universal custom of those savages, surprised her and her party in the night, and killed every soul in the tent, except herself and three other young women. Among those whom they killed, were her father, mother, and husband. Her young child, four or five months old, she concealed in a bundle of clothing and took with her undiscovered in the night; but when she arrived at the place when the Athapuscow Indians had left their wives (which was not far distant), they began to examine her bundle, and finding the child, one of the women took it from her, and killed it on the spot.

This last piece of barbarity gave her such a disgust to those Indians, that notwithstanding the man who took care of her treated her in every respect as his wife, and was, she said, remarkably kind to, and even fond of her; so far was she from being able to reconcile herself to any of the tribe, that she rather chose to expose herself to misery and want, than live in ease and affluence among persons who had so cruelly murdered her infant. The poor woman's relation of this shocking story, which she delivered in a very affecting manner, only excited laughter among the savages of my party.

In a conversation with this woman soon afterward, she told us, that her country lies so far to the Westward, that she had never seen iron, or any other kind of metal till she was taken prisoner. All of her tribe, she observed, made their hatchets and ice chisels of deer's horns, and their knives of stones and bones; that their arrows were shod with a kind of slate, bones, and deer's horns; and the instruments which they employed to make their woodwork were nothing but beavers' teeth. Though they had frequently heard of useful materials which the nations or tribes to the East of them were supplied with from the English, so far were they from drawing nearer, to be in the way of trading for iron-work, &c. that they were obliged to retreat farther back, to avoid the Athapuscow Indians, who made surprising slaughter among them, both in Winter and Summer ...

On the twenty-fourth [of February], a strange Northern Indian leader, called Thlew-sa-nell-ie, and several of his followers, joined us from the Eastward. This leader presented Matonabbee and myself with a foot of tobacco each, and a two-quart keg of brandy, which he intended as a present for the Southern Indians; but being informed by my companions, that there was not the least probability of meeting any, he did not think it worth any farther carriage. The tobacco was indeed very acceptable, as our stock of that article had been expended some time. Having been so long without tasting spirituous liquors, I would not partake of the brandy, but left it entirely to the Indians, to whom, as they were numerous, it was scarcely a taste for each. Few of the Northern Indians are fond of spirits, especially those who keep at a distance from the Fort: some who are near, and who usually shoot geese for us in the Spring, will drink it at free cost as fast as the Southern Indians, but few of them are ever so imprudent as to buy it.

The little river lately mentioned, as well as the adjacent lakes and ponds, being well-stocked with beaver, and the land abounding with moose and buffalo, we were induced to make but slow progress in our journey. Many days were spent in hunting, feasting, and drying a large quantity of flesh to take with us, particularly that of the buffalo; for my companions knew by experience, that a few days walk to the Eastward of our present situation would bring us to a part where we should not see any of those animals ...

Having a good stock of dried meat, fat, &c. prepared in the best manner for carriage, on the twenty-eighth we shaped our course in the South East quarter, and proceeded at a much greater rate than we had lately done, as little or no time was now lost in hunting. The next day we saw the tracks of some strangers; and though I did not perceive any of them myself, some of my companions were at the trouble of searching for them, and finding them to be poor inoffensive people, plundered them not only of the few furs which they had, but took also one of their young women from them.

Every additional act of violence committed by my companions on the poor and distressed, served to increase my indignation and dislike; this last act, however, displeased me more than all their former actions, because it was committed on a set of harmless creatures, whose general manner of life renders them the most secluded from society of any of the human race.

... [I]t is an universal practice with the Indian Leaders, both Northern and Southern, when going to the Company's Factory, to use their influence and interest in canvassing for companions; as they find by experience that a large gang gains them much respect. Indeed, the generality of Europeans who reside in those parts, being utterly unacquainted with the manners and customs of the Indians, have conceived so high an opinion of those Leaders, and their authority, as to imagine that all who accompany them on those occasions are entirely devoted to their service and command all the year; but this is so far from being the case, that the authority of those great men, when absent from the Company's Factory, never extends beyond their own family, and the trifling respect which is shown them by their countrymen during their residence at the Factory, proceeds only from motives of interest.

The Leaders have a very disagreeable task to perform on those occasions; for they are not only obliged to be the mouth-piece, but the beggars for all their friends and relations for whom they have a regard, as well as for those whom at other times they have reason to fear. Those unwelcome commissions, which are imposed on them by their followers, joined to their own desire of being thought men of great consequence and interest with the English, make them very troublesome. And if a Governor deny them any thing which they ask, though it be only to give away to the most worthless of their gang, they immediately turn sulky and impertinent to the highest degree; and however rational they may be at other times, are immediately divested of every degree of reason, and raise their demands to so exorbitant a pitch, that after they have received to the amount of five times the value of all the furs they themselves have brought, they never cease begging during their stay at the Factory; and, after all, few of them go away thoroughly satisfied ...

12

"The Worst and Most Dangerous Men"

A Profile of the Hudson's Bay Company

DOCUMENTS
A) Character Book, 1832
   George Simpson

The Hudson's Bay Company is, at over three hundred years of age, Canada's oldest commercial enterprise. A connection with the British royal family certainly helped its early chances of success, but the road forward remained rocky, twisted, and fraught with hazards. Commercial survival, let alone expansion, required shrewd and ruthless leadership. George Simpson's (1786/87–1860) *Character Book* provides a glimpse into the organization of the western fur trade.

Born in London an illegitimate son, Simpson was shepherded off to work for his uncles. Business mergers drew them toward the Hudson's Bay Company, and in 1820 they packed their nephew off to Montreal as a company employee. He did well, by chance arriving just as the epic struggle between the two great fur houses, the Northwest Company and the Hudson's Bay Company, drew to a climax in 1821. Simpson emerged as governor of the Northern Department, and this authority gradually increased until he became, in 1839, governor and chief of all Hudson's Bay Company operations. Nepotism alone did not facilitate his rapid rise through the ranks: Simpson had plenty of business acumen and used this to merge the two companies. By 1832, 18 out of 25 chief factors, and 14 out of 24 chief traders were still old Northwest Company employees.

A harsh judge of people, Simpson began a secret list of employees as early as 1821. Rumours leaked out, however, and he exchanged names for numbers in order to retain confidentiality. The following list dates from a particularly difficult period in his life which may have contributed to the grumpy tone. He caused a scandal by rejecting his "country wife" in favour of a more conventionally acceptable English woman who was apparently not very suited to the rough-and-tumble life at a fur trader fort. She made few friends, suffered frequent bouts of ill health, and went through a fragile pregnancy that caused Simpson endless sleepless nights. This, of course, ingratiated neither her nor her husband to the tight-knit community of Red River, and she eventually retreated to the bright lights of Montreal. By January 1832 he ranted in exasperation: "I could fill volumes with the details of the most Vindictive & Malicious intrigue that ever entered the mind of man which I have witnessed since I came here. In short I am sick and tired of Red River and would be off tomorrow if I currently could — indeed I am becoming quite disgusted with the country..." But Simpson could not leave. His financial situation, the result of poor investments, forced him to stay regardless of his feelings for the fur trade.

His *Character Book* remained a guarded secret until he died. It presumably contained information too sensitive for corporate eyes and public scrutiny. Regardless of his methods and characterizations, he certainly put the Hudson's Bay Company on firm footing and emerged as a captain of Canadian industry. He received a knighthood for his troubles in 1841.

A) Character Book, 1832
George Simpson

FIRST CLASS [CHIEF FACTORS]

No. 1 [Colin Robertson]

A frothy trifling conceited man, who would starve in any other Country and is perfectly useless here: fancies, or rather attempts to pass himself off as a clever fellow, a man of taste, of talents and of refinement; to none of which I need scarcely say he has the smallest pretension. He was bred to his Fathers Trade an operative Weaver in the Town of Perth, but was too lazy to live by his Loom, read Novels, became Sentimental and fancied himself the hero of every tale of Romance that passed through his hands. Ran away from his master, found employment for a few months as a Grocers Shopman at New York, but had not sufficient steadiness to retain his Situation, pushed his way into Canada and was at the Age of 25 engaged as Apprentice Clerk by the N W Co for whom he came to the interior, but found so useless that he was dismissed the Service. His age about 55 and his person of which he is exceedingly vain, large, soft, loosely thrown together inactive and helpless to infirmity. He is full of silly boasting & Egotism, rarely deals in plain matter of fact and his integrity is very questionable. To the Fur Trade he is quite a Burden, and a heavy burden too, being a compound of folly and extravagance, and disarranging and throwing into confusion whatsoever he puts his hand to in the shape of business. The concern would gain materially by allowing him to enjoy his situation a thousand Miles distant from the scene of operations instead of being taxed with his nominal Services in the Country.

No. 2 [Alexander Stewart]

An easy, mild tempered, well disposed little man about 52 Years of Age; speaks Cree well, and acquires influence over Indians by his kind treatment and patient attention to them; but his diminutive size and retiring diffident manner, unfit him very much for the 'rough & tumble' of the business. He is a man of strict integrity & veracity but 'tis strongly suspected is given to tippling in private.

No. 3 [John George McTavish]

Was the most finished man of business we had in the Country, well Educated, respectably connected and more of the Man of the World in his conversation and address than any of his colleagues. A good hearted Man and generous to extravagance, but unnecessarily dignified and high minded which leads to frequent difficulties with his associates by whom he is considered a 'Shylock' and upon many of whom he looks down; rather strong in his prejudices against, and partialities for individuals, which frequently influences his judgement, so that his opinions on men and things must be listened to with caution: is about 54 Years of Age, has of late Years become very heavy unwieldy and inactive; over fond of good living and I must fear is getting into habits of conviviality and intemperance.

No. 4 [John Clarke]

A boasting, ignorant low fellow who rarely speaks the truth and is strongly suspected of dishonesty; his commanding appearance & pompous manner, however, give him a good deal of influence over Indians and Servants; and his total want of every principle or feeling, allied to fair dealing, honour & integrity, together with his cruel & Tyrannical disposition render him eminently qualified for playing the lawless, cold blooded Bravo in opposition. He is in short a disgrace to the 'Fur Trade'; about 52 Years of Age.

No. 5 [George Keith]

About 48 Years of Age. A man of highly correct conduct and Character and much attention to his business; well Educated and respectably connected: Not wanting in personal courage when pushed altho' rather timid, nervous and indecisive on ordinary occasions. Speaks Cree and understands Chipewyan.

No. 6 [John Dugald Cameron]

About 58 Years of Age; Strictly correct in all his conduct and dealings, and possesses much influence over the Natives: Speaks Saulteaux well, and is one of our best Indian Traders; but in other respects not a man of business; not well Educated, yet possesses a good deal of general information having read almost every Book that ever came within his reach.

No. 7 [John Charles]

A plain blunt Englishman about 50 Years of Age, not well Educated, yet regular œconomical and attentive to his business: speaks Cree and Chipewyan and has a good deal of influence with Indians, but so irritable and violent at times, that 'tis feared he will some Day get into trouble with them. He is a man of veracity and integrity, but not bright, and would be easily led by any designing person who chose to take the trouble of Watching his peculiarities.

No. 8 [John Stuart]

About 57 Years of Age, calls himself 47 — 70 winters at least, however, are marked on his countenance, but still very tough & hardy; has undergone a good deal of privation and from his persevering character was at one time the fittest man in the country for exploring Service and severe duty. Had not the advantage of a good Education but being studious improved himself very much and having a very retentive memory is superficially conversant with many subjects. Is exceedingly vain, a great Egotist, Swallowing the grossest flattery, is easily cajoled, rarely speaks the truth, indeed I would not believe him upon Oath; lavish of his own means, extravagant and irregular in business and his honesty is very questionable: a good hearted man where he takes a liking but on the contrary Malicious & Vindictive: fancies himself one of the leading & most valuable men in the Country, but his Day is gone by, and he is now worse than useless being a cloy upon the concern: has many eccentricities, & peculiarities, yet few of them do credit either to the head or heart although they afford him a privilege of speech and of action which no other man in the Country possesses; in short he is a contemptible body altogether. (May be considered in his dotage and has of late become disgustingly indecent in regard to women.)

No. 9 [Edward Smith]

About 50 Years of Age. A very well meaning well behaved man, who through his kind conciliatory manners and upright conduct has acquired influence with Servants & Indians. Speaks Cree and Chipewyan, is an excellent Indian Trader and is most attentive to his business which is managed with regularity and œconomy.

No. 10 [John McLoughlin]

About 48 Years of Age. A very bustling active man who can go through a great deal of business but is wanting in system and regularity, and has not the talent of managing the few associates & clerks under his authority: has a good deal of influence with Indians and speaks Saulteaux tolerably well. Very Zealous in the discharge of his public duties and a man of strict honour and integrity but a great stickler for rights and privileges and sets himself up for a righter of Wrongs. Very anxious to obtain a lead among his colleagues with whom he has not much influence owing to his ungovernable Violent temper and turbulent disposition, and would be a troublesome man to the Compy if he had sufficient influence to form and tact to manage a party, in short, would be a Radical in any Country — under any Government and under any circumstances; and if he had not pacific people to deal with, would be eternally embroiled in 'affairs of honor' on the merest trifles arising I conceive from the irritability of his temper more than a quarrelsome disposition. Altogether a disagreeable man to do business with as it is impossible to go with him in all things and a difference of opinion almost amounts to a declaration of hostilities, yet a good hearted man and a pleasant companion.

No. 11 [James Keith]

About 47 Years of Age. A scrupulously correct honourable man of a serious turn of mind, who would not to save life or fortune, do what he considered an improper thing. Well Educated, very attentive to business in which he is regular & systematic, indeed both in business and private Life formal to a fault, his whole words and actions being governed by what he considers the strictest rules of propriety but withal I consider him the most faultless member of the Fur Trade.

No. 12 [Joseph Beioley]

About 50 Years of Age. A steady well conducted little man whose word can be depended upon; tolerably well Educated, and particular and œconomical in business to excess if possible, as his peculiarities in those respects adapt him better for operations on a contracted than an extended scale. He is not generally liked being considered vain touchy and vindictive, but I have always been most pleased with his whole demeanour conduct and management, and his strict integrity & veracity I think cover all his faults; in short, I consider him one of the most valuable members of the Fur Trade.

No. 13 [Angus Bethune]

A very poor creature, vain, self sufficient and trifling, who makes his own comfort his principal study; possessing little Nerve and no decision in anything: of a snarling vindictive disposition, and neither liked nor respected by his associates, Servants or Indians. His Services would be overpaid by the victuals himself & Family consume. About 48 Years of Age.

No. 14 [Donald McKenzie]

About 52 Years of Age. A large, heavy, inactive indolent Man, who makes a very bad use of the Talents he possesses, which in some respects are above mediocrity. In business he is perfectly useless and never gives it the smallest attention. His style of writing is Flowery and not inelegant, and in conversation he is smooth & plausible to such a degree that a Stranger or one unacquainted with his artifices is likely to be deceived in him: indeed his whole Life is one uniform system of art, deceit, falsehood, intrigue, suspicion, selfishness and revenge. When I brought him to this place it was in the most dismal state of dissension that can be conceived owing to the misconduct of Mr Bulger & Mr Clarke and to the wretched condition of the people; a good deal of address was therefore necessary to prevent them from cutting each others throats, so that his insinuating manner, together with his disingenuous subtlety and talent in lying, rendered him eminently qualified for smoothing them over, and doing such dirty work as a Straight forward honourable conscientious man would not descend to; he was therefore a convenient instrument in the hands of an other, but when left to himself, he had full scope of which he availed himself, for the indulgence of the bad qualities already enumerated to which may be added a degree of vanity, jealousy and malice which it is scarcely possible to conceive. For a length of time I was myself egregiously deceived by his specious reasoning, and he contrived to mystify and pervert facts and to shield himself by his hints, insinuations and falsehoods so effectively that when I came to examine into some of the charges brought against him I thought him more Sinned against than Sinning; but I now know him thoroughly, and have no hesitation in saying, that he is one of the worst and most dangerous men I ever was acquainted with. My presence alone keeps him sober, but when left to himself he will assuredly become a confirmed Drunkard.

No. 15 [Alexander Christie]

Never were two characters so different from each other as that of the Gentleman I am now describing and of the person I have just noticed. This is one of our best characters, an honourable, correct, upright good hearted man as can be found in any Country; beloved & respected by all who know him, attentive to business qualified to be useful in any branch thereof and a valuable member of the concern. About 49 Years of Age.

No. 16 [John McBain]

About 54 Years of Age. An ignorant, illiterate common kind of fellow, whose only talent consists of a little low cunning and falsehood. Has been a tolerable bruiser, was at one time a tolerable Snow Shoe walker and his imagination being fertile in little trick and artifice was some years ago useful in opposition, but he is now becoming indolent and unserviceable.

No. 17 [William McIntosh]

About 53 Years of Age. A revengeful cold blooded black hearted Man whom I consider capable of anything that is bad: possessing no abilities beyond such as qualify him to cheat an unfortunate Indian and to be guilty of a mean dirty trick: Suspicious, Cruel & Tyrannical without honour or integrity, in short, I have never been able to discover one good trait in his character.

No. 18 [William Connolly]

About 45 Years of Age. An active useful man whose Zeal and exertions have generally been crowned with success, whose Word may be depended on in most things, and whom I consider incapable of doing anything that is mean or dishonorable. His temper, however, is violent to madness when roused, he is at times Hypochondriacal, always tenacious of his rights privileges and dignity, disposed to magnify his own exploits and to over rate his Services which nonetheless are valuable, rather domineering and Tyrannical, but on the whole a respectable and useful Member of our Community.

No. 19 [John Rowand]

About 46 Years of Age. One of the most pushing bustling Men in the Service whose zeal and ambition in the discharge of his duty is unequalled, rendering him totally regardless of every personal Comfort and indulgence. Warm hearted and Friendly in an extraordinary degree where he takes a liking, but on the contrary his prejudices exceedingly strong. Of a fiery disposition and as bold as a Lion. An excellent Trader who has the peculiar talent

of attracting the fiercest Indians to him while he rules them with a Rod of
Iron and so daring that he beards their Chiefs in the open camp while surrounded by their Warriors: has likewise a Wonderful influence over his people. Has by his superior management realized more money for the concern
than any three of his Colleagues since the Coalition; and altho' his Education has been defective is a very clear headed clever fellow. Will not tell a lie
(which is very uncommon in this Country) but has sufficient address to evade
the truth when it suits his purpose: full of drollery and humour and generally liked and respected by Indians Servants and his own equals.

No. 20 [James McMillan]

About 49 Years of Age. A very steady plain blunt man, shrewd & sensible of correct conduct and good character, but who has gone through a vast
deal of severe duty and is fit for any Service requiring physical strength firmness of mind and good Management provided he has no occasion to meddle with Pen & Ink in the use of which he is deficient his Education having
been neglected. An excellent Trader, speaks several Indian Languages and is
very regular and œconomical in all his arrangements: a good practical man,
better adapted for the executive than the Legislative departments of the business. His plain blunt manner however cannot conceal a vast deal of little
highland Pride, and his prejudices are exceedingly strong, but upon the whole
he is among the most respectable of his class and a generally useful Man.

No. 21 [Peter Warren Dease]

About 45 Years of Age. Very steady in business, an excellent Indian Trader,
speaks several of the Languages well and is a man of very correct conduct and
Character. Strong, vigorous and capable of going through a good deal of Severe Service but rather indolent, wanting in ambition to distinguish himself
by any measure out of the usual course, inactive until roused to exertion and
over easy and indulgent to his people which frequently occasions a laxity of
discipline, but when his temper gets ruffled he becomes furiously violent. His
judgement is sound, his manners are more pleasing and easy than those of
many of his Colleagues, and altho' not calculated to make a shining figure
may be considered a very respectable Member of the Concern ...

2ND CLASS [CHIEF TRADERS]

No. 1 [Jacob Corrigal]

About 60 Years of Age. A quiet steady common kind of Man, who is
merely qualified to follow instructions in the management of a Trading Post;

timid, slow and better adapted to obey than to command. Sober & well conducted, more so, however, perhaps through fear of being brought to serious account should he break out than from principle. Has every reason to be well satisfied with the situation he fills and I imagine has no hope of advancement.

No. 2 [Thomas McMurray]

A loquacious, frivolous, good tempered sycophant, without steadiness or abilities to bring himself into notice. About 62 Years of Age and nearly worn out. Speaks Cree & Saulteaux tolerably well, but not respected by Indians nor has he any influence with the people under his command and made a butt of by his colleagues and Superiors. Has no prospects of advancement.

No. 3 [Donald McIntosh]

About 64 Years of Age. A very poor creature in every sense of the Word, illiterate, weak-minded and laughed at by his Colleagues. Very much offended, that he has not been promoted; and complains loudly of the neglect he has experienced in that respect altho' his only claim to advancement is his antiquity. Speaks Saulteaux, is qualified to cheat an Indian, and can make & set a Net which are his principal qualifications; indeed he would have made a better Canoe Man or Fisherman than a 'Partner'. 'Tis high time he should make room for a better Man. He is perfectly Sober and honest.

No. 4 [John Peter Pruden]

About 57 Years of Age. A man of good conduct and character and of respectable appearance and manner but weak minded vain & silly without decision in or knowledge of business beyond the simple process of dealing with an Indian across the Counter. Has no command over his people and but little judgement in other respects. Over fond of good living which he makes his principal study, and a fine Beef Steak is sufficient to solace him under the most Severe afflictions. Speaks Cree, and is a tolerable 'Plain Indian' Trader, but by no means bright; attached to old customs, an enemy to all innovations, easily led away or Cajoled, and when reminded of his own merits which is frequently the case by his colleagues ironically, very much offended that he has not been promoted; but in my opinion ought to consider himself fortunate in having obtained his present situation.

No. 5 [Hugh Faries]

About 56 Years of Age. A well conducted steady man, who is liked by Indians is respected by his people and has gone through a great deal of drudg-

ery in the country. Is considered Sensible and clear headed and is of an Independent spirit, but his temper is exceedingly irritable and he is everlast-
ingly grumbling snarling & repining: is a man of strict integrity and is
altogether a more respectable fellow than many belonging to the 1st class of
the old School, but his day for promotion I think is past, and his prospects
are not flattering unless he should accidentally be in nomination with more
objectionable candidates.

No. 6 [Angus Cameron]

About 48 Years of Age. A very active useful Man and steady, regular
and œconomical in business. Possesses a description of firmness allied to
obstinacy but sound of judgement in most things and on the whole, a shrewd
sensible correct man who will not do an improper thing nor descend to an
untruth: displays excellent management in any business entrusted to his
charge, speaks Algonquin, has much influence with Indians and is generally
respected: his prejudices are strong, but he is not blinded by them, and would
make a respectable Member of our board of Direction to a Seat in which he
aspires with fine prospects of success.

No. 7 [Simon McGillivray]

About 45 Years of Age. Possesses a good deal of superficial cleverness
and is very active but conceited, self sufficient and ridiculously high minded.
Very Tyrannical among his people which he calls 'discipline' and more feared
than respected by Men & Indians who are constantly in terror either from
his Club or his Dirk: Would be a very dignified overbearing man if he was
in power; fond of little convivial parties and would soon fall into intemper-
ate habits if he had an opportunity of indulging in that way. Has a good
deal of the Indian in disposition as well as in blood and appearance, and if
promoted would be likely to ride on the top of his commission and assume
more than it is either fit or proper he should have an opportunity of doing;
in short I think he would make a bad use of the influence he would acquire
by promotion, and be a very troublesome man.

No. 8 [John McLeod]

About 46 Years of Age. A correct well behaved well Meaning Man, who
is always most anxious to discharge the duties with which he is entrusted in
a satisfactory manner and would on no consideration do an improper thing.
Very firm when he finds it necessary to make a stand; but not bright, on the
contrary so confused that it is next to impossible to understand what he
means to be at either verbally or on paper. Deficient in point of Education

and quite a clown in address and should consider himself fortunate in his present situation which is more valuable than a man of his abilities could reasonably aspire to in any other part of the World.

No. 9 [Alexander Roderick McLeod]

About 50 Years of Age. Has been a stout strong active Man; a good pedestrian, an excellent shot, a skilful Canoe man and a tolerably good Indian Trader, but illiterate self sufficient and arrogant; does not confine himself to plain matter of fact, annoys every one near him with the details of his own exploits; 'I did this' 'I did that' and 'I did the other thing' continually in his mouth, but it unfortunately happens that he rarely does any thing well. Even his physical powers have been greatly over-rated and I have never been able to discover that he possesses beyond the most ordinary mental abilities: yet his own vanity and the partiality of Friends have made him an aspirant to a place in the 1st Class to which in my opinion he has very moderate pretensions as regards merit and if he did succeed in gaining that stand he would be a most overbearing Tyrannical fellow. Is capable of little mean tricks and I suspect is fond of a Glass of Grog in private. Would have made an excellent Guide altho' he adds little respectability to the 'Fur Trade' as a 'Partner'.

No. 10 [Alexander Fisher]

About 45 Years of Age. A trifling thoughtless superficial lying creature, who has no Steadiness or consistency, full of plans which are more Changeable than the Wind: has sufficient address to pass himself off as a sharp fellow with a Stranger, but is entirely an Eye Servant and cannot be entrusted with any business requiring the least management unless closely watched. Can make himself agreeable to Indians until they discover his falsehood which must very soon be the case, as he is totally regardless of truth, in fact, a habitual Liar without conduct or principle, and was becoming so much addicted to Liquor that I found it necessary to remove him a few years ago to one of our most Sober Stations.

No. 11 [Samuel Black]

About 52 Years of Age. The strangest man I ever knew. So wary & suspicious that it is scarcely possible to get a direct answer from him on any point, and when he does speak or write on any subject so prolix that it is quite fatiguing to attempt following him. A perfectly honest man and his generosity might be considered indicative of a warmth of heart if he was not known to be a cold blooded fellow who could be guilty of any Cruelty and would be a perfect Tyrant if he had power. Can never forget what he may consider a slight or insult, and fancies that every man has a design upon him. Very cool, resolute to desperation, and equal to the cutting of a throat with perfect deliberation: yet his word when he can be brought to the point may be depended on. A Don Quixote in appearance Ghastly, raw boned and lanthorn jawed, yet strong vigorous and active. Has not the talent of conciliating Indians by whom he is disliked, but who are ever in dread of him, and well they may be so, as he is ever on his guard against them and so suspicious that offensive and defensive preparation seem to be the study of his Life having Dirks, Knives and Loaded Pistols concealed about his Person and in all directions about his Establishment even under his Table cloth at meals and in his Bed. He would be admirably adapted for the Service of the North West coast where the Natives are so treacherous were it not that he cannot agree with his colleagues which renders it necessary to give him a distinct charge. I should be sorry to see a man of such character at our Council board. Tolerably well Educated and most patient and laborious in whatever he sets about, but so tedious that it is impossible to get through business with him.

No. 12 [Peter Skene Ogden]

About 45 Years of Age. A keen, sharp off hand fellow of superior abilities to most of his colleagues, very hardy and active and not sparing of his personal labour. Has had the benefit of a good plain Education, both writes and speaks tolerably well, and has the address of a Man who has mixed a good deal in the World. Has been very Wild & thoughtless and is still fond of coarse practical jokes, but with all the appearances of thoughtlessness he is a very cool calculating fellow who is capable of doing any thing to gain his own ends. His ambition knows no bounds and his conduct and actions are not influenced or governed by any good or honourable principle. In fact, I consider him one of the most unprincipled Men in the Indian Country, who would soon get into habits of dissipation if he were not restrained by the fear of these operating against his interests, and if he does indulge in that way madness to which he has a predisposition will follow as a matter of course. A man likely to be exceedingly troublesome if advanced to the 1st Class as the Trade is now constituted, but his Services have been so conspicuous for several years past, that I think he has strong claims to advancement.

No. 13 [Cuthbert Cumming]

About 48 Years of Age. A plain, blunt straightforward honourable man who would not do an improper thing nor descend to an untruth on any consideration. Sensible, Steady, œconomical as a Trader and altho' not a general man of business, nor a Pen and Ink man, would make a respectable member of our principal board, being a man of Sound principles and of correct conduct and character. Is the best Saulteaux Speaker in the Country, and is respected by Servants and Indians and esteemed by his Colleagues and Superiors. A very fit man to come forward.

No. 14 [Francis Heron]

About 46 Years of Age. A plausible man who can write a good Letter and is not deficient of abilities but makes an exceedingly bad use of them. Suspicious, designing and intriguing; seldom or never adheres to truth; lays himself out to sow the seeds of dissension among his acquaintances; Capable of any thing however mean dishonourable or improper to indulge his revenge or to gain a selfish end. Was getting into habits of Drunkenness but found they were likely to injure his prospects of advancement and therefore Changed from a Grog to a rigid Water Drinker but must sooner or later break through all his Sober resolutions: fancied that an appearance of Sanctity would bring him into notice but if I am at liberty to judge of his Sincerity by his conduct he is a perfect Hypocrite. I believe him capable of anything that is bad and consider him a very unfit man for promotion. In business he is indolent and inactive yet speculative & full of wild theory and in private life he is Gross Sensual and Licentious.

No. 15 [John Siveright]

About 50 Years of Age. A poor well behaved little man who is sickly Deaf & Worn out; was promoted to the rank of a Clerk from being a Gentleman's body Servant and to his present situation on account of his Age and infirmity, at least I suppose so, as I am not aware of any other particular claims he could have had: he is regular œconomical and attentive in the management of the little business entrusted to his care. He shot a man in cold blood a good many years ago and although little is now said about it, he is still looked upon as a Murderer by many of his colleagues, but in that affair I believe he was more influenced by personal fear and want of Nerve than by any worse feeling. The poor man is fitter for an Hospital than the charge of a Trading Establisht requiring any material exertion. 'Tis time he should retire.

No. 16 [Robert Miles]

About 40 Years of Age. The best Clerk in the Country as regards Penmanship and Knowledge of Accounts, but his Education does not qualify him for any thing beyond the Mechanical operations of a Counting House; he has had little or no experience in any other branches of the business and his judgement is of no great depth. Very fond of good living and if not kept at his Work would become indolent and devoted to his pot and his pipe. A man of good conduct generally speaking who will not tell a deliberate false-hood nor act improperly; but not so close and confidential as a person in his Situation ought to be, fond of finding fault; full of childish jealousy and ridiculously stiff and stately behind his Desk as also behind his pipe, in short, a wiseacre who would in England be a Pot House Politician.

No. 17 [Colin Campbell]

About 45 Years of Age. An Excellent Trader who speaks Several of the Native Languages well, and has the talent of conciliating the Friendship of Indians. Mild and unassuming in his manners, commands respect from his people and is esteemed by his colleagues and superiors; his conduct highly correct and proper, has had the advantage of a plain Education, writes a good hand, is a tolerable accountant and generally speaking a useful man who would make a more respectable figure at the Council Board than many who now occupy seats there.

No. 18 [Alexander McTavish]

About 48 Years of Age. A self sufficient would be Wise Man, who claims a vast deal of merit to which he has not the smallest pretension. A sly, smerking, plausible fellow who lies habitually, full of low cunning, suspi-cion and intrigue; continually laying himself out to rouse suspicions and to create dissentions; indolent, inactive, unhealthy arising from his own indis-cretions and very useless. Was a recruiting Sergeant, but more likely to show off on the Parade than in the Field, at least so 'tis thought in this country. Lays claim to a wonderful degree of foresight and exhibits a vast deal of after wisdom, finds fault with every thing and every body with a view to persuade others that he would improve upon the existing state of affairs if he had a voice in the management; but that, he is not likely to have unless an extraordinary change takes place in his habits conduct and character.

No. 19 [Archibald McDonald]

About 50 Years of Age. A shrewd, clear headed Man, who Studies his own interests in all things, obsequious in courting favour, but would be over-bearing if in power. Rather inactive and 'tis thought does not possess much nerve, but a generally useful Man who will not do any thing really bad nor tell a direct falsehood: fond of conviviality, enjoys a Glass of Grog and suspect would soon become addicted to Liquor if exposed to temptation and not under restraint. Expresses himself tolerably well on paper and is better informed, and would make a better figure on our Council board than many of his colleagues or even than the majority of those now Seated there ...

CLERKS

No. 1 Annance F. N.

About 40 Years of Age. 13 Years in the Service. A half breed of the Abiniki Tribe near Quebec; well Educated & has been a Schoolmaster. Is firm with Indians, speaks several of their languages, walks well, is a good Shot and qualified to lead the life of an Indian whose disposition he possesses in a great degree. Is not worthy of belief even upon Oath and altogether a bad character altho' a useful Man. Can have no prospects of advancement. Attached to the Columbia Deptmt. ...

No. 10 Birnie James.

A Scotchman about 35 Years of Age. 14 years in the Service. Useful in the Columbia as he can make himself understood among several of the Tribes and knows the Country well; but not particularly active, nor has he much firmness: deficient in point of Education; a loose talking fellow who seldom considers it necessary to confine himself to the truth. Has no pretension to look forward to advancement indeed is very well paid for his Services at £100 p Annum.

No. 11 Bryson L. M.

An Irishman. About 42 years of age 13 Years in the Service. Steady and tolerably well conducted, but not a good Clerk or Trader; does not speak Indian and is not particularly active. Was attached to the Commissariat in the Peninsular War, but I should think in one of the lowest capacities. Says he has been a 'Mercht' but was unfortunate: is evidently a fellow who has been accustomed to live from hand to mouth by his Wits. Deals in the Marvellous but his fiction is harmless: has no hopes of advancement. Attached to the Temiscamingue Deptmt. ...

No. 13 Corcoran Thomas.

About 38 years of age, has been 14 years in the Service. An Irishman of limited Education yet writes a fair hand and would be useful about a Depôt, but not so well adapted for the Indian Trade as he does not speak any of the Languages, is not very active and makes but an indifferent Voyager; is nevertheless in charge of a Small Post which he manages very well. Correct in conduct but furiously violent when roused and has little polish about him. Stationed at Albany.

No. 14 Cowie William.

A Scotchman about 23 Years of Age, has been 9 years in the Service. A steady well conducted Young Man and a tolerable Indian Trader. Speaks Chippewyan and manages a small Post very well. Rather deficient in regard to Education and not qualified for Counting House business. Was shamefully inveigled 3 years ago into an injudicious Marriage with a half breed Girl by Chief Factor McBain whose relation she was, which is likely to operate against his prospects. Stationed at Lake Huron …

No. 17 Douglas James.

A Scotch West Indian: About 33 Years of Age, has been 13 Years in the Service. A stout powerful active Man of good conduct and respectable abilities: tolerably well Educated, expresses himself clearly on paper, understands our Counting House business and is an excellent Trader. Well qualified for any Service requiring bodily exertion, firmness of mind and the exercise of Sound judgement, but furiously violent when roused. Has every reason to look forward to early promotion and is a likely man to fill a place at our Council board in course of time. Stationed in the Columbia Deptmt. …

No. 19 Davies William.

A half breed from the Southern Department. About 24 Years of Age, has been 7 years in the Service; neither a good Clerk nor Trader, trifling, superficial and does not confine himself to the truth. Not a man of any promise and can have no expectation of material advancement. Stationed at Mingan.

No. 20 Delormier George.

A Canadian. About 24 Years of Age, has been 2 Years in the Service: illiterate, superficial & trifling: Walks well on Snow Shoes and speaks a little Algonquin having been brought up in the Indian village of Cocknawagan opposite La Chine where his Father is the Government Interpreter. Considered merely a temporary Servant, having been engaged during the opposition for River St Maurice to fill an unexpected Vacancy. Will probably be allowed to retire this year.

No. 21 Erlandson Erland.

A Dane. About 42 Years of Age, has been 17 years in the service. Was bred a ship Carpenter in the Dock Yard of Copenhagen and entered the Service as a labourer from one of the Prison Ships at Chatham where he was a Prisoner of War. A steady painstaking well behaved man who has improved himself very much since he came to this country, writes a good hand, expresses himself well in English either Verbally or by Letter for a Foreigner and is a shrewd Sensible Man. Strong, active & useful, liked by his Superiors, esteemed by his Colleagues and respected by Servants and Indians; indeed a superior man in many respects to some of our Councillers, and whom I should like to see promoted in due time as a reward for his meritorious conduct and in order to shew that it is to Character & conduct we principally look in our Elections: but being a Foreigner and raised from the ranks I suspect it will be a difficult matter to get him the number of Votes necessary to put him in Nomination. Stationed at Ungava.

No. 22 Ermatinger Francis.

An Englishman about 32 Years of Age, has been 14 Years in the Service. A stout active boisterous fellow who is a tolerable clerk and trader and qualified to be useful where bustle and activity without any great exercise of judgement are necessary. Talks a little at random but will not descend to a deliberate falsehood. Got into disgrace lately in consequence of having employed one of the Company's Servants in cutting off the Ears of an Indian who had had an intrigue with his Woman, but which would not have been thought so much of, had it been done by himself in the heat of passion or as a punishment for Horse Stealing which is an offence of frequent occurrence at the establishment of which he had charge, the business of which he conducted very well until removed on account of the circumstances alluded to. Attached to the Columbia Department ...

No. 27 Gladman George.

A half-breed. About 36 Years of Age, has been 17 years in the Service. Is the principal accountant at Moose Factory, writes a good hand and understands our accounts. Has had no experience as a Trader and knows little about the general business of the Depot. Entertains a very high opinion of himself and would be presuming & forward if permitted. Exceedingly jealous of any little attentions shown his colleagues and disposed to assume authority over juniors: fancies that his time is thrown away in this country, and that he could do much better elsewhere — but I think he has brought his Services to an excellent Market and that he is fully paid for them.

No. 28 Gladman Joseph.

A half-breed brother of the before mentioned. About 38 Years of Age, has been 17 years in the Service. A more Steady and I think qualified to be a more generally useful man than the former. Speaks both Cree and Chipaway, understands the management of Indians and conducts the business of the Small Post of New Brunswick very well. Irritable, short tempered and like his Brother, has an excellent opinion of himself, and is very conceited which is a leading characteristic in the half breed race. His Services I should consider well paid for at £100 p Annum in any Country.

No. 29 Good Richd.

An Englishman about 55 Years of Age, has been 37 Years in the Country. A poor Drunken useless creature, in whom, no trust or confidence can be placed. Quite a Sot from whom it is impossible to keep Liquor as if he cannot purchase or pilfer it from the Stores, he will obtain it clandestinely through the Servants or Indians. Retained in the Service from a feeling of charity alone, as were he discharged he would either Starve or become a Pauper. Stationed at Moose ...

No. 31 Grant Cuthbert.

A half breed whose Name must long recall to mind some horrible scenes which in former Days took place at Red River Settlement in which he was the principal actor. About 38 Years of Age, during 20 of which he has been more or less connected with the Service. A generous Warm hearted Man who would not have been guilty of the Crimes laid to his charge had he not been drawn into them by designing Men. A very stout powerful fellow of great nerve & resolution but now getting unwieldy and inactive. Drinks ardent spirits in large quantities, thinks nothing of a Bottle of Rum at a Sitting but is so well Seasoned that he is seldom intoxicated altho it undermines his constitution rapidly. A sensible clear headed man of good conduct except in reference to the unfortunate habits of intemperance he has fallen into. Entirely under the influence of the Catholic Mission and quite a Bigot. The American Traders have made several liberal offers to him, but he has rejected them all being now a staunch Hudson's Bay man and we allow him a saly of £200 p Annum as 'Warden of the Plains' which is a Sinecure offered him entirely from political motives and not from any feeling of liberality or partiality. This appointment prevents him from interfering with the Trade on his own account which he would otherwise do in all probability; it moreover affords us the benefit of his great influence over the half breeds and Indians of the neighbourhood which is convenient inasmuch as it exempts us from many difficulties with them. He resides at the White Horse Plain about 16 miles up the Assiniboine River where he has a Farm and only visits the Establishment on business or by Invitation; but is always ready to obey our commands and is very effective when employed as a constable among the half breeds or Indians. Is perfectly satisfied with what has been done for him which is quite sufficient and has no prospect of advancement.

No. 32 Grant Richard.

A Scotch Canadian about 42 Years of Age, has been 17 years in the Service. Writes a tolerable hand but deficient in Education. Can manage the affairs of a small Trading Post very well, but does not speak Indian. Is active and bustling, but not Steady, would Drink if not under constraint, speaks at random and is scampishly inclined. Looks forward with confidence to a Chief Tradership and is well supported by many Factors who feel an interest in him. I have been strongly pressed by several of those Gentlemen for whom I have a great esteem to give him my support, but with every desire to oblige them, I do not feel myself at liberty to recommend his case as yet to the favourable consideration of the Govr & Committee. Stationed in the Saskatchewan Deptmt. ...

No. 42 Hamel Antoine.

A Canadian about 30 Years of Age — 4 Years in the Service. A stout strong illiterate common kind of fellow who was employed during the op- position in River St Maurice chiefly because he could walk well on Snow Shoes and had the name of being a tolerable bruiser. Can drink, tell lies and Swear. Will be discharged when his Engagement expires as we have no occa- sion for men of his stamp in peaceable times.

No. 43 Killock James.

A Scotchman. About 40 Years of Age, has been about 20 years in the Service. An active useful man in charge of a small post. Speaks Cree and keeps his accounts tolerably well, but possesses no particular recommendatory qualifications, on the contrary, likes a glass of grog yet does not get Drunk because he carries it well; would nevertheless I understand be addicted to it if not under restraint. It would be highly inexpedient to allow such Men possess an interest in the business.

No. 44 Kennedy John.

A half breed Native of Cumberland, about 26 Years of Age, has been 3 years in the Service in the capacity of surgeon at the Columbia. I know so little of this Young Man as yet that I cannot speak either in regard to his character or abilities: if he turns out well however, I shall be agreeably sur- prised as it is a lamentable fact that very few of his breed have hitherto con- ducted themselves with propriety ...

No. 49 McIntosh John.

A half breed of the Chippaway Nation. About 34 Years of Age has been 14 years in the Service. A stout strong low blackguard lying fellow, who is retained in the Service to prevent his being troublesome to us in Opposition on the shores of Lake Superior where he was born and brought up, and related to many of the Indians in that quarter. Stationed in Lake Superior Deptmt.

No. 50 McKay Donald.

A Temiscamingue half breed about 40 Years of Age, has been 21 years in the Service. An active useful Man at Kenigumissie, to the Indians of which place he is related and with whom he has much influence. Would be very troublesome if in the hands of opposition and therefore retained in the Service altho not steady fond of Liquor and given to falsehood. Stationed at Kennigumissie.

No. 51 McKay Edward.

A half breed from the Southern Shores of the Bay. About 35 Years of Age has been 17 years in the Service. Unsteady and of indifferent character. Was a deserter from the Hudson's Bay to the North West Coy during opposition and now retained in the Service to keep him out of the hands of Petty Traders: but like many of his breed would be discharged if we were not apprehensive that he would in that case give us trouble. Stationed at Lake Huron.

No. 52 McKay Wm.

A half breed. Brother of the above noticed. About 42 Years of Age 21 years in the Service. Nothing respectable about him either in conduct of character, and neither active nor useful — but retained in the Service to prevent his being troublesome to us. Stationed at Ruperts River. Nine out of Ten of those half breeds are little better than Interpreters, deficient in Education — bearing indifferent Characters and having no claim to a prospect of advancement ...

No. 57 McDougald George.

A Scotch Canadian. About 45 Years of Age, has been 17 years in the Service. A sly knowing low Vagabond who Drinks, lies, and I dare say Steals. Was an auctioneer in Montreal but swindled his creditors; entered the Hudsons Bay Service during the heat of opposition and deserted to the North West Service. An excellent Trader and a keen Shrewd fellow who is qualified to be very useful either at a Trading Post or Depôt, but a man of no principle who is retained in the Service merely because he could be very troublesome to us if attached to Opposition on the West side the Mountains from his knowledge of the Country and business. Stationed in the Saskatchewan Deptmt. ...

No. 60 McKenzie Donald.

A Scotchman about 45 Years of Age, has been 14 Years in the Service. Tolerably well Educated and has an imposing Manner and address, but a trifling useless superficial fellow who can Drink & pilfer and rarely speaks the truth. Was a Lieut in the Army but 'Sent to Coventry' and obliged to Sell out having Shewn the 'White Feather'. A blustering Cowardly poltroon who is retained in the Service through mere charity. Stationed in New Caledonia ...

No. 62 McKay Thomas.

A half breed of the Saulteaux Tribe, about 40 years of Age has been 20 years in the service. Lame in consequence of a Dislocation of the Knee notwithstanding which he is very active, one of the best Shots in the Country and very cool and resolute among Indians. Has always been employed on the most desperate service in the Columbia and the more desperate it is the better he likes it. He is known to every Indian in that Department and his name alone is a host of Strength carrying terror with it as he has sent many of them to their 'long home'; quite a 'blood hound' who must be kept under restraint. Possesses little judgement and a confirmed Liar, but a necessary evil at such a place as Vancouver; has not a particle of feeling or humanity in his composition. Is at the height of his ambition ...

No. 72 Ross Chs.

A Scotchman about 38 Years of Age, 14 Years in the Service. A good classical scholar and a man of very correct conduct but so nervous at times that it is quite painful to see him. Very Slovenly both in business and in his appearance. Has a smattering of the Saulteaux & Carrier Languages. I have often thought that he was not quite of Sound Mind and am much mistaken if he has not shewn decided symptoms of Madness altho it has been carefully concealed by those about him. Expresses himself very well on paper and has a certain cleverness about him — but not generally useful nor likely to become a rising man. Stationed at New Caledonia ...

No. 88 Barnston George.

A Scotchman, 12 Years in the Service, about 32 Years of Age. A well Educated man, very active, & high Spirited to a romantic degree, who will on no account do what *he* considers an improper thing, but so touchy & sensitive that it is difficult to keep on good terms or to do business with him, which frequently leads to difficulties: Seems to consider it necessary to make an 'affair of honour' of every trifling misunderstanding; has been a principal in one and a Second in another bloodless Duel and would fight anything or any body either with or without a cause. Has a high opinion of his own abilities which are above par, but over rates them. Is sometimes of a gloomy desponding turn of mind and we have frequently been apprehensive that he would commit suicide in one of those fits. It is evident that he is of unsound mind at times; but with all his failings & peculiarities we feel an interest in him. Retired from the Service last year fancying himself neglected or ill used but without any good grounds for so thinking, and readmitted this Season lest he might connect himself with the Americans and give us trouble or do worse in a fit of desperation (if reduced to distress) out of which a story might be made by designing people to the great annoyance of the Company ...

13

"A Great Humbug"

The Gold Rush in British Columbia

DOCUMENTS

A) News from British Columbia, *The Daily Globe*,
   January 2, 1860
   Charles Major

B) To the Editor of *The Islander*, November 17, 1858
   C.C. Gardiner

C) Journal, 1862
   S. G. Hathaway

D) Vancouver Island and British Columbia, 1865
   Matthew MacFie

G old fever can hit the most upstanding and conservative individuals, and can drive them, once smitten, to ridiculous and dangerous
ends chasing that seductive yellow glow. The gold fields of California attracted every sort: naïve city boys, hardened criminals, prostitutes, people
down on their luck, shrewd businessmen and women, new immigrants without better prospects, genuine miners, and the myriad of others. The boom,
of course, became a bust, leaving many dreamers high and dry, often in debt,
casting about for a new Eldorado, the next "mother lode."

Vague reports of gold along the Fraser River filtered south by boat as
early as 1855, from the little Hudson's Bay fort of Victoria. Rumours turned
to reality by the fall of 1857. Up came the fortune hunters, packed onto ships
or overland via Whatcom Trail through the Washington territory. Tiny Victoria
groaned under the strain of a transient and enthusiastic throng of some
30,000 miners who descended upon the unprepared company village. Most
miners remained just long enough to buy provisions at grossly inflated prices,
then set off for the sand bars along the Fraser, or later, to instant towns like
Barkerville in the Cariboo. What they lacked in experience, they possessed in
tenacity and enthusiasm — and they needed both.

Mining the bars along the Fraser was either relatively easy or impossible. Winter time and spring runoff covered the golden sandbars with a torrent of turbulent water that made panning infeasible, or at least desperately dangerous. Frustrated miners could only camp along the banks and watch the level slowly recede, worrying whether money and supplies would last until they could continue panning. Many, if not most, lost that race.

The British government worried about so many Americans in the undefended interior of present-day British Columbia. Colonial officials feared that the land might be annexed by sheer numbers if no action were taken. James Douglas, Governor of the Colony of Vancouver Island, did not wait for official consent before asserting British authority over the mainland colony in 1858. This was easier said than done, particularly after the first diggings petered out and miners moved from the Fraser and Thompson rivers north into the Cariboo.

New Cariboo strikes occurred at Keithly, Antler, Williams, and Lightning creeks, and instant towns like Barkerville sprang up like so many mushrooms. Unlike panning sandbars, however, this next chapter in British Columbia's mining history required plenty of capital to cover the costs of boring deep into the ground, refining the ore, and then transporting it to the coast. Unless a miner had money, he inevitably had to create partnerships or give up, drifting to the next gold discovery, ever hopeful of getting there early in the game. And what were the chances of success? A few, usually those staking early claims, made famous fortunes. The majority, however, eked out bare subsistences or drifted back to Victoria, broke and broken. Many never survived to tell their tales.

Thus the communities that sprang up often disappeared as quickly as they emerged. Barkerville, virtually overnight, became the biggest city west of Chicago and north of San Francisco. The instant towns were frontier places buzzing with activity as transient men shopped, did their business, played hard, or simply marked time. Neither education nor religion, two hallmarks of stable communities, usually existed. The lack of families made the social structure even less stable and predictable. Life in the little towns also tended to be very seasonal, frenzied summer activity tapering off to silent and frigid winter boredom.

S.G. Hathaway, like the majority, came from California. His story was not particularly unusual. He was a trained printer without mining experience, completely unused to the rigours of outdoor life and gold extraction, but utterly blinded by gold fever. C.C. Gardiner and Charles Major arrived from eastern Canada but unfortunately nothing else is know about them. Matthew MacFie seems to have had enough sense to stay out of the gold fields. He offers a broader, less jaundiced, perspective of British Columbia frontier society. Each man perceived events differently and their documents deal with the two different gold rushes.

A) News from British Columbia, *The Daily Globe*, January 2, 1860
   Charles Major

Fort Hope, Frazer River
Sept. 20th, 1859
Dear Sir: I am afraid you will think I had forgot my promise, — but I wanted to know something about the country before writing to you. In the first place, do not think that I have taken a dislike to the country because I am not making money; the dislike is general all over the country. To give you anything like a correct idea of it would take more paper than I have small change to purchase, and more time than I could spare, and then it would only be commenced.

The country is not what it was represented to be. There is no farming land in British Columbia, as far as I can learn, except a very small portion joining Washington Territory, and on Vancouver's Island, where there is one valley of 20,000 acres; but that cannot be sold until Col. Moody's friends come out from the old country, and get what they want.

It never can be a place, because there is nothing to support it, except the mines, and just as soon as they are done the place goes down completely, for there is absolutely nothing to keep it up; and I tell you the truth the mines are falling off very fast. There is nothing in this country but mines — and very small pay for that; they are you may say, used up. We have been making two, three and four dollars per day, but it would not last more than two or three days; and so you would spend that before you would find more. There has been great excitement about Fort Alexander, three hundred miles above this, and also about Queen Charlotte's Island. They have both turned out another humbug like this place. A party arrived here yesterday from Alexander, and they are a pitiful looking lot. They are what the Yankees call dead broke. They have been six hundred miles up the river. When they got down here they had no shoes to their feet. Some had pieces of shirt and trowsers, but even these were pinned together with small sharp sticks; and some had the rim of an old hat, and some the crown. They had nothing to eat for one week, and not one cent in money. This is gold mining for you!

I expect the Frazer River fever has cooled down by this time, at least I hope so; for I do pity the poor wretches that come out here to beg. They can do that at home; as for making money, that is out of the question. Since we came here (to use the miners' term) we have been making grub; and those who can do that, think they are doing well. If there are any making arrangements to come to this place, let them take a fool's advice *and stay at home*. I would just about as soon hear that anyone belonging to me was dead, as to hear they had started to come here. They say it wants a man with capital to make money here; but a man with money in Canada will double it quicker than he will here. And if I, or any other, was to work as hard and live as meanly, I could make more money in Canada than I can here. Since we have been on the River we have worked from half-past two and three o'clock in the morning till nine and ten o'clock at night (you can see the sun twenty hours out of the twenty-four in the summer season) and lived on beans! If that is not working, I don't know what it is. Besides this you go home to your shanty at night, tired and wet, and have to cook your beans before you can eat them. And what is this all for? For *gold* of course; but when you wash up at night, you may realize 50 cents, perhaps $1.

There have been some rich spots struck on this river, but they were very scarce, and they are all worked out; and the miners are leaving the river every day, satisfied there is nothing to be made. But now that I am in the country I will remain for a year or so, and if nothing better turns up by that time, I think I will be perfectly satisfied. I have met with some that I was acquainted with, and it is amusing to see those who felt themselves a little better than their neighbors at home, come here and get out of money, and have to take the pick and shovel, perhaps to drag firewood out of the woods and sell it, or make pack-mules of themselves to get a living. I do not mean to say that it is so all over the Colony, but it is from one end of Frazer River to the other. I dare anyone to contradict what I say; and I have good reason to believe it is as bad all over the country. I saw a patch of oats here the other day. They were out in head, only four inches in height, yellow as ochre, and not thick enough on the ground to be neighbours. Vegetables and other things are as poor in the proportion; and as for the climate, it is just as changeable as in Canada, if not more so. I can't say much about the climate on Vancouver's Island, but I think it is rather better.

I met T.G., the carpenter, from Sarnia, who left there about a year ago. He went round the Horn, and he was ten months and fifteen days in coming here. He is cutting saw logs making a little over grub. He says he is going to write to the Sarnia *Observer*, and give this place a cutting up! There are a great many Canadians here, and they would be glad to work for their board. A man could not hire out to work a day if he was starving. I have seen some parties from California; they say times are very hard there. There are just three in our party now, H.H., J.R., and myself. There were two of the H's; one was taken sick and had to leave the river; he is in Victoria, and is quite recovered again; has been there two months, and has not got a day's work yet. I was very sick myself when I just came here, but am quite healthy now, and so fat I can hardly see to write. The rest are quite well.

The Indians are not very troublesome at the mines; they are kept down pretty well. They are very numerous here and on the Island, the lowest degraded set of creatures I ever saw.

It is estimated that the number of miners who make over wages, is one in five hundred; and the number that do well in the mines is one in a thousand. So you see it is a very small proportion. If you know anyone that wants to spend money, why, this is just the place. Anyone bringing a family here would require a small fortune to support them in this horrible place, hemmed in by mountains on all sides, and these covered with snow all the year.

I have lived in a tent since I came up the river, and I have to lie on the ground before the fire and write; it gives a very poor light, so excuse the writing. It has been raining here steady one week, and the mountains are all covered with snow; for when it rains here it is snowing upon the mountains. It is a wild looking place. You will please tell our folks you hear from me, and that we are all well. I will write to some of them in about two weeks or so. I have wrote five letters already, but I have not heard from any of them; so many letters go astray in coming here and going from this place, that perhaps they do not get them at all. Give my respects to old friends, and tell them to be contented and stay at home.

I remain, yours truly,
Charles Major

B) To the Editor of *The Islander*, November 17, 1858
C.C. Gardiner

... No doubt you are aware that about the 1st of May last a great excitement arose, and spread quickly over the lands of California, Oregon and Washington Territories, proving equally infectious to men of all vocations — the merchant, the farmer, the mechanic and miner — that gold in abundance was found on the Fraser and Thompson Rivers. I being, perhaps, like many others, of somewhat an excitable disposition, left, on the 20th May [1858], a mining town in the interior of California, and proceeded to San Francisco, where I found the excitement even more intense than in the mountains — the greatest credence being given to the stability of the reports, they going unanimously to prove the country could not be surpassed in richness with gold.

... Some thousands men were waiting there at that time in the greatest dilemma not knowing which way to proceed to the new mines. Fraser River being so high could not be ascended for two months, a sufficient distance to reach the main diggings, on account of the current running so swiftly through the Big Canyon, forming rapids, which would be impossible to navigate at that stage of water. Nevertheless, many would form in companies, buy a canoe, lay in from three to six months' provisions, and start, working their way as far as possible, until the river fell. Others would assert they would wait for the trail, which was then in operation of being cut through the country, across the Cascade Mountains to Thompson River, at the expense of some Land and Town Lot speculators, who were determined to have the great depot and centre of trade, effected by the new mines, on American soil. The balance of the men were divided in opinion, the weaker, or perhaps I may now justly allow, the wiser, being disgusted with the chances of getting to the New Eldorado, resolved to return to California.

... The upsetting of our canoe was nothing more than an accident, which most every company experienced, many not only losing their grub, but their lives. We very nearly lost two of our men, but were providentially saved by catching hold of the branches of a leaning tree, as the current was taking them swiftly down.

... Every day of the 23 [days to get up the river] we were in the cold water most of the time, with our heads out, but very frequently with them under, an unpleasantness which could not be avoided, in passing the line outside the trees and brush which grew on the banks of the river, when the water was low, but were now submerged half way to their tops. Those nights we passed in sleeping in our wet clothes, or part of them only, as each in his turn had to keep watch, with revolver in hand, that the Indians did not steal our provisions, as well as Mamaloose [kill] us while asleep. Notwithstanding our guard, every few mornings one or the other of the companies would have something missing that the Red Skin had stolen at night. Indeed it is considered as impossible to keep them from or detect them stealing ...

We found quite a number of men camped on the river banks, the most of whom had come by trail from the Colville Mines in Washington Territory, and who were forced to kill their horses and mules, the flesh of which they had been subsisting on for the last 4 weeks. Flour we soon ascertained (if there was any for sale) was worth $125 per 100 lb., meat of all kinds $1.75, beans $1.00, and everything else in proportion.

Fraser River was still very high, and the miners informed us they could only make from two to five dollars per day, that not being sufficient to grub them the way provisions sold, and there was not a probability of it getting much cheaper for some time.

Five of us in Company pitched our tent, fixed up our mining tools, and went to work. We prospected up and down the river a distance of 40 miles each way, and could find gold in small quantities most anywhere on the surface of the bars, which were then getting bare, as the river fell. The gold is much finer than any found in California, and found in a different deposit. On Fraser River what has been dug has been found within three to eighteen inches of the surface, in a kind of sand being underneath a very pretty gravel, but no gold in it. In this country it is just the reverse, in sand like on Fraser, we can find nothing in California, but in the gravel, and the nearer we approach the bed rock, the coarser the gold, and the richer it pays. We found a bar which prospected better than any other in that section, and set in to try our luck. We worked early and late, averaging from $3 to $5 per day. We washed out dirt in rockers, using quick silver, not then being able to save all the gold, it being so fine, much would float off, and some rusty that would not amalgamate. After working there about six weeks our stock of provisions was getting nearly exhausted, and we concluded to pack up and start down stream. I for one was getting tired of living on bread and water alone, for long since the Indians had stolen the coffee. Not any of the miners within fifty miles of us at this time were making grub, at the price of provisions; indeed it was hard to get it at any price, as few had it to spare. The river had fallen quite low, and where we expected, as in California, to find it rich, we could make nothing. Men began to think it a great humbug, and the glowing accounts of Fraser River became gradually pronounced a fiction. The natives there were all so very troublesome, stealing and pointing guns at men was a prominent feature of their character ...

I am afraid, Mr. Editor, I have taken up too much space in your columns, and shall conclude by saying I should not advise anyone from P. E. Island to come to Fraser River, with the intention of making his fortune; and I'm quite sure, speaking from experience, nothing will be gained by going for anything else, as the trip is a very expensive and laborious one.

Michigan Bluffs, Placer County, California.

C) Journal, 1862
S. G. Hathaway

British Columbia, June 20, 1862.

On the 3rd June I left San Francisco in Steamship Brother Jonathan for Victoria. On the way up we went into the Columbia River up to Portland, Oregon. Remained there from Saturday noon till Monday morning, then out to sea again & on to Victoria arriving there Tuesday afternoon, June 10 — just one week on the trip. We pitched our tent in the edge of the woods, half a mile out of town & began camp life at once. We found that, owing to the snow still lying up in the mountains we were still early & so concluded to wait a while & learn more of the country before starting. On the 17 I and two other young men — one from Maine, the other from New Hampshire — concluded to try our luck as partners; so we bought a mule together & a load of provisions — enough to last six weeks at least — & on the 18th took another step for Cariboo, taking a steamboat for New Westminster on the Fraser River — Got in at evening & had to lie over till this morning, waiting for another boat to take ... and here we are now steaming along in a bright, warm day against a rushing, boiling current, winding this way & that through a rugged chain of snowy mountains, many of them rising up for thousands of feet so steep that no living thing can climb ... There are numbers of Indians all through this region, & we see an encampment now & then, & see them paddling their eggshell canoes. They are peaceable & depend much upon trade with the whites for their living —

Monday — June 23 — Little Lillooet Lake — after sailing up the Fraser river about 45 miles we turned into Harrison river, & 5 miles brought us to where it widened into a beautiful lake from one to 6 or 8 miles wide & 45 miles long. I wish you could see it. Snowy mountains & rocky cliffs rising straight up from the water, shutting out all the world but the blue sky overhead; islands & sharp points running out into the lake — making a picture of wild grandeur different from anything I ever saw before. We got to the upper end at 10 o'clock at night, where there is a shanty village called Port Douglas. Got our things ashore & blundered around in the dark to find a spot to camp, which we did without much trouble. From Douglas there is 29 miles of land travel to the next lake, where we are now. The next morning after landing we loaded the mule & made up packs for ourselves, each one carrying from 30 to 40 pounds, & away we went. It was very warm, my pack bore down heavy & my boots — iron heeled, soles nearly an inch thick & driven full of round headed nails — gave my poor feet a sorry rasping. I had too much clothing, & was soon drenched in sweat. We staggered along some 4 miles & stopped for dinner & a few hours rest; then we bucked to it again & stopped for the night after making altogether about 10 miles. The next day we did better — making 14 miles — though it was a rainy day and we were all sore — my feet the worst in the lot. We stopped at a wayside shanty for the night, paying two dollars apiece for our supper & breakfast. This morning we made the 5 miles to this lake in less than two hours, & here we must wait most of the day for a chance to sail up the lake to the next portage, as the strips of land separating the chain of lakes are called. We meet many men returning already. Most of them have not been through to Cariboo, but far enough to find out that they have not money enough to stand it. Most of those who have been there give the same reason for coming back — too early in the season & not money enough to be able to wait till the ground is in a fit state to work. For myself I expect nothing, & try to think as little as possible about it. I am in for it now & must see it out now if it takes my last dollar & leaves me "dead broke" in a foreign land —

June 26 — Anderson Lake — We came up Lillooet Lake on Monday evening in a big clumsy boat, sending the mule around by a trail. It was a short trip — only 7 miles, & we got through & crossed the land portage — less than 2 miles — to Pemberton Lake before dark. Made camp for the night. Next morning bundled aboard a ricketty little steam boat & came to Pemberton City about 2 o'clock. Got dinner & started on the 30 mile portage to Lake Anderson, getting here early this morning — Thursday. & we are wasting a few hours for the boat to be loaded — June 27 — Seaton Lake — Made the trip down to Anderson — about 16 miles — packed up & hurried across the narrow portage — less than 2 miles — to catch the Seaton lake boat, but found they had only waited for those who had horses to ride, & she was a quarter of a mile off when we got to the landing. We sent some hearty curses after them for the scurvy trick & camped to lie over till today. There are many Indians all along the route. They work pretty well, packing over the portages, loading wagons & boats, &c & the squaws bring us branches of grass to sell — They have some customs different from Indians I have seen before. They bury their dead up in the air! — that is, they build a crib & stick it up on poles 15 to 30 feet high, sometimes leaning it against a large tree, and they put the bodies in these. Over & around them they hang flags, blankets, kettles — sometimes a gun — whatever belonged to them when alive, I suppose — I have seen quite a number of these burial places during the last few days, almost always in some place overlooking the water. The water through the whole country here is cold as ice water from the melting of the snows from every hill. I went in for a wash today. One plunge was enough.

July 4 — well up on the Brigade route for Cariboo. No holiday for us, we must keep moving, though we would lie by & rest if the mosquitoes would not torment us. Night & day, at all times & all places they swarm upon us, — millions upon millions of all kinds. We are all but eaten by them, & yet we are told they are worse ahead — God pity us! — Came down Seaton Lake June 27 — Next morning on to Lillooet City. Here we had to cross the Fraser river — more than 1/4 of a mile wide & boiling & surging along at the rate of 20 miles an hour. Nothing larger than a whale boat to cross in. Took our load in, hitched poor mule to the stern, & away we went, my heart in my throat through fear of losing Billy. But we made the other shore all safe, half a mile or so further down, paid 25 cts apiece, & a dollar for the mule, & we were off at last, free from steamboats & dependent only on ourselves & Billy Mule. Every day we push ahead, over mountains, through green valleys, along lakes, & we have come at last into a region where we see no snowy mountains, nothing but low hills, grassy plains, & a great many ponds & small lakes. The days are very long — twilight till after 9 o'clock, & we travel early & late, resting 3 or 4 hours in the middle of the day. I have suffered much with my feet, but they are doing better now, & my health otherwise would be excellent, were it not for the colds I have caught, which have settled down to a troublesome cough.

My long spell in the printing office made me tender; but I think I shall soon harden to it.

Going to Cariboo is no play. We expect to be two weeks longer yet, & the worst of the road comes last. We still meet many poor fellows going back, a sorrowful looking set. They all went up too soon, & with too little money, so that high prices drove them back before the weather would allow them to prospect.

July 15 — Almost in the diggings — Dragging along day by day — wet, tired, hungry & sleepy, I felt hardly able to write a full description of our journey as I had meant to do at first.

Today we draggled along in the rain over a miry trail till we got well soaked, when we made camp for the afternoon and dried out by a rousing fire — From all the accounts we hear from those going back the prospect is a gloomy one — but on we go to try our luck. Provisions are very dear — at Williams Lake, nearly a hundred miles back we bought 50 lbs flour, 18 lbs Bacon, 32 lbs Beans — 100 lbs in all, for which we paid $90 — The next we buy will be a dollar a pound we expect.

Aug. 6. — Nelson Creek — Cariboo — Got in to the new town of Van Winkle on Lightning Creek, on Saturday, July 18th. Provisions dear & scarce. Flour $1.25 a pound — tea $3.00, salt $5 for a 3 pound bag, nails $3 a pound & hardly any to be had. My partners growled all the way up because I thought best to bring some nails along, — they wish now we had brought all nails! Sold Billy Mule at once for $140, & I found on dividing our goods that I had provision enough to last me 5 or 6 weeks. Next day, Sunday, we rested, & on Monday I took blanket & grub for two weeks, stored the rest in a cabin at $1 a week, & came over to Nelson Creek to prospect for diggings. First bought a license to mine, good for a year — $5 for that. My partners got discouraged in a day or two & went off, & I expect they are out of Cariboo by this time. I then went in with two sailor boys from Martha's Vineyard who travelled part of the way up with us & came over to Nelson at the same time. Found some men who have been prospecting on the creek for 2 months, sinking shafts (wells, you would call them) trying to hit upon the deepest part of the channel where the gold always settles. They have the best looking chance on the creek, & as they had just got out of money & provision, they offered us an equal share with them if we would join them

& feed two of them two weeks. We concluded to do so; so here we are, hard at work, the two weeks nearly up, & nothing certain known as yet. Yesterday I went back to Van Winkle & packed over all my things — 70 pounds. If anybody thinks that it is fun let them try it — 8 miles & back, over a mountain, deep sloppy mud nearly every foot of the way, & big logs to straddle & climb at every ten steps, it seems, & sometimes two or three of them together at that. Walk over that road in the morning & stagger back with a load of 70 pounds in the afternoon, & almost any lazy man would be satisfied with his day's work.

I am afraid Cariboo will swamp me as it has thousands of others. There are some few men who are getting out gold very fast. Some few claims are yielding as high as 150 pounds a week — report says more; but the great majority are getting nothing, most of the crowd, in fact, have been driven back by the high prices eating their money up before they had a chance to try for diggings. I have almost a mind to go back to California if I find nothing where we now are, but I hate to give up while there is yet a chance, however slight, — I have still about $440, left out of $613 that I had on leaving Suisun, & I can manage to stand it here for the balance of the season & have enough left to pay my way back to California & there begin anew. Not a pleasant prospect at that, but I suppose I shall have to stand it. However, if I stay here I shall not fail through lack of trying.

Aug 10. Sunday. Broke down yesterday as far as this creek is concerned. Water came into the bottom of our shaft so fast that we cannot dig deeper without making a wheel & pump, & the prospects are not good enough to satisfy us in going to the expense. Today the two men we have been feeding start out for Cala. together with one of the sailor boys, who leaves so that his partner may have money enough to stay longer. As for me I don't know what to do. Inclination & judgment, too, as far as that goes say "Go back to Cal." God knows this is a hateful country — rain nearly all the time & all the country covered with a thick, heavy growth of gloomy firs, with the swampy, miry ground buried under fallen trees so that it is almost impossible to get along. Everybody I see looks gloomy & discouraged, & it really seems hopeless to try to do more in Cariboo. In all my trials I never saw a darker time.

Sept. 8. — Still on Nelson — concluded to try to pick up a few dollars here, by scratching around where men worked last year rather than run around. Have made about $100 clear of expenses in the last month — rather slow for

Cariboo. Today we have had snow & I suppose we must soon leave. I have little hope of now getting back the cost of the trip to say nothing of pay for my time, but I am thankful that I have not lost all like so many others. I am working very hard, every day, Sundays & all, & I shall be glad when forced to give it up. I do not know that I can earn anything here more than a few days longer, & I think I shall go to Williams' Creek, where there are very rich diggings & new discoveries being made. Some of the claims there pay twenty-five pounds of gold a day to each man working! More money in one day than I want to make me happy for life. Well I must grind along till my lucky day comes, & gather in my slow dollars one by one, only too happy if old age don't nip me before I get a little resting place in this wide world.

Sept. 28 — On Nelson yet. Been scratching around steadily. Am now even on the cost of the trip & enough besides to take me back to Cala. Bad weather now — snowing & freezing nearly all the time. Most of the men have left the creek — only four left here now, & each one working & living by himself about a quarter of a mile from each other. Today my cabin mate went away. We started in to work together but he soon bought a bit of ground that was paying well — about $50 a day — giving $500. It fizzled out completely before he got half his money back, & now he strikes out for Williams' Creek. Would go myself & try for big diggings, but I cannot feel justified to leave $10 a day, & I am making that now with a fair show of doing so as long as I dare stay here — That cannot be many weeks more — Looks dubious now — If a deep snow comes on it will be a serious matter for me to get out. But my chief fear is of being robbed on my way down, — many have been robbed and some murdered on the down trails. This country is all a wilderness & it is very easy for robbers to escape. No doubt there are many lying in wait for the big purses that have been growing fat up here & will soon be on the way out for the winter.

Oct. 5. Nelson Creek—Bad weather lately. The sun is fast working south & we see but little of it even when fair. It is freezing cold & scarce an hour without a snow squall.

Have been troubled with a nervous fear lest I should get snowed in, but at last concluded to take the chance & brave it out. I got the man working alone above to join me & prospect a place on the hill high above the creek. I think it will pay & if it will we shall have a good claim for next year. So I went over to Lightning today after more grub & got enough to stand me two weeks. Let in to snow in the morning & has been at it hard & steady ever since. It rather frightens me, but I am in for it now & must take the chances whether I will or not. We have got to dig a ditch & bring water on the ground we wish to prospect, & it will take us three or four days to test it, if it looks dangerous then to stay longer we will make a break out, if not we shall stay till our grub is nearly gone.

Found the town today nearly deserted, most of the men having gone below for the winter. I expect hard times getting out, but that don't scare me, — it is the chance of getting blocked in & frozen or starved that makes me fearful. Wish now that instead of going for grub today I had packed up & got safely over the mountain that we have to cross at the head of Nelson. If it keeps on snowing this way there will be three feet of snow there tomorrow, & when we go we have to carry a load of blankets & grub. Hard to get in & harder to get out, this Cariboo.

Oct. 13. It was a bad night to us that of last date. Snow fell heavily & steadily all night. Could not sleep for nervousness, & about midnight the overloaded trees began to fall crashing down all around us. Went out & roused new partner Martin in cabin close by. Stood outside watching, & before he could find his boots a large tree which threatened us gave way by the roots. Yelled the alarm and out came Martin bare footed for dear life. He ran directly under the course of the tree, stumbled & fell & the tree crashed in the snow directly at his heels. A narrow escape & it seemed to frighten me more than it did him. After that we sat up till day in my cabin, rushing out at every crack & warning sound. I think we heard the fall of fifty trees & eight or nine fell that might have crushed us, but luckily they leaned the other way. The storm held up during the day & we went on with our work.

We got about discouraged on Tuesday the 7th & were about to make ready to leave, when we were surprised by the unexpected coming back of my old cabin mate from Williams Creek. He encouraged us to stand out a while longer, so we pitched in till yesterday, Sunday, & then went out after more grub, intending to stay ten days longer if possible. Most of last week we had snow & cold weather, — & on Friday it began to rain, & on Saturday there was a heavy freshet. Sunday was a fine day but we had a hard time breaking a trail out to Lightning. The rain seemed to have packed it hard & made it worse. Today Monday, it has set in to rain again so that after getting well drenched we quit work about the middle of the afternoon. This weather is a surprise all around. Almost everybody has left the country believing that everything would be frozen by this time. So far I am loser by staying. Have spent about $50 for grub since Sunday before last & have made nothing for it yet. We are trying a place now where we did expect to make $20 a day, but it does not look good now since we started in. Thought last evening when we got back to camp faint & worn out that I could never get out of this if another heavy snow should come, but after supper felt stronger & am taking the chances, now quite unconcernedly. By the way, the night of the great storm closed on the morning of my birthday I shall hardly forget it —

Oct. 17. Friday. Mild weather has held on till the snow is nearly gone. Diggings still turn out poorly — have not got our grub money back yet ... I am in a bad fix just now — got a raging boil coming — just at this particular time, & on my foot, too! — It seems as if the devil must have had a hand in it. Could not get out to work today — tried it — took me nearly an hour to get on my boot & hobble off 50 yards, then I just crawled back again. Right among the cords at the bend of the foot just above the instep — Who ever heard of such a thing — It is very late in the season for Cariboo, & if a big snow comes within a few days, how shall I, a cripple, get out? A serious question with me now.

Oct. 26. Sunday. Have had a sorry time since last date. My boil does not work well. Poulticed for 8 days till nothing more would run but blood & now I am dressing with salve. The skin has come off from a spot the size of a half dollar, leaving the raw flesh still swelled, hard, and sore. Pulled on my rubber boot yesterday for a trial, but was glad to squirm out of it again pretty quickly. Have suffered as much in my mind as in my body through fear of snow setting in. It holds off beyond all expectation. We have had some light falls, & Thursday & Friday last very cold, making anchors ice in the swift water. Yesterday was rainy clearing off in the night with a light snow, — today as usual, cold gray clouds threatening snow. The sun runs so low here now that we can see it only about two hours at & near midday even when fair. Don't remember seeing the sun three times in the last three weeks. O, that I were out of this gloomy wretched country! Were I not a cripple I should feel at ease, for if snow set in steadily I could pack up & leave, sure of being able to fight my way out, but now my fears get the better of me.

[Note in pencil by another hand: "From all accounts lost trying to make Williams Creek. R. C. S. Randall."]

D) Vancouver Island and British Columbia, 1865
Matthew MacFie

... Between March and June, in 1858, ocean steamers from California, crowded with gold-seekers, arrived every two or three days at Victoria. This place, previously a quiet hamlet, containing two or three hundred inhabitants, whose shipping had been chiefly confined to Indian canoes and the annual visit of the company's trading ship from England, was suddenly converted into a scene of bustle and excitement. In the brief space of four months 20,000 souls poured into the harbour. The easy-going primitive settlers were naturally confounded by this inundation of adventurers.

Individuals of every trade and profession in San Francisco and several parts of Oregon, urged by the insatiable *auri sacra fames*, threw up their employments, in many cases sold their property at an immense sacrifice, and repaired to the new Dorado. This motley throng included, too, gamblers, 'loafers,' thieves, and ruffians, with not a few of a higher moral grade. The rich came to speculate, and the poor in the hope of quickly becoming rich. Every sort of property in California fell to a degree that threatened the ruin of the State. The limited stock of provisions in Victoria was speedily exhausted. Flour, which on the American side sold at 2L. 8s. per barrel, fetched in Vancouver Island 6L. per barrel. Twice the bakers were short of bread, which had to be replaced with ship biscuit and soda crackers. Innumerable tents covered the ground in and around Victoria far as the eye could reach. The sound of hammer and axe was heard in every direction. Shops, stores, and 'shanties,' to the number of 225, arose in six weeks.

Speculation in town lots attained a pitch of unparalleled extravagance. The land-office was besieged, often before four o'clock in the morning, by the multitude eager to buy town property. The purchaser, on depositing the price, had his name put on a list, and his application was attended to in the order of priority, no one being allowed to purchase more than six lots. The demand so increased, however, that sales were obliged to be suspended in order to allow the surveyor time to measure the appointed divisions of land beforehand ...

The bulk of the heterogeneous immigration consisting of American citizens, it was not wonderful that they should attempt to found commercial depots for the mining locality in their own territory. Consequently, they congregated in large numbers at Port Townsend, near the entrance to Puget Sound and at Whatcom in succession. Streets were laid out, houses built, and lots sold in those places. But inconveniences of various kinds hindered their success. Semiahmo, near the mouth of Fraser River, was next tried as the site of a port; but this rival city never had existence except on paper. These foreign inventors of cities obstinately refused to acknowledge the superior natural advantages of Victoria compared with the experimental ports they had projected. It is not speculators in new towns, however, but merchants and shippers that determine the points at which trade shall centre; and it is only that harbour which combines the greatest facilities for commerce, with the fewest risks to vessels, which is patronised by them. Victoria, judged by these tests, was found most eligible of all the competing places of anchorage in the neighbourhood ...

While the majority — comprising Jews, French cooks, brokers, and hangers-on at auctions — stayed in Victoria for the purpose of ingloriously improving their fortunes, by watching the rise and fall of the real-estate market, several thousands, undismayed by dangers and hardships incident to crossing the gulf and ascending the river, proceeded to the source of the gold. When steamers or sailing-vessels could not be had, canoes were equipped by miners to convey them to British Columbia; but this frail means of transit, unequal to the risks of the passage, sometimes occasioned loss of life.

A monthly licence had to be taken out by all bound for the mines, and this gave them the right to take whatever provisions were required for individual use. At the outset steamers on the river allowed miners 200 lbs. and subsequently 100 lbs. free of charge; but they preferred in general to join in the purchase of canoes for sailing up the river as well as across the gulf.

The country drained by the Fraser resembles mountainous European countries in the same latitude, where streams begin to swell in June and do not reach their lowest ebb till winter. Those, therefore, who happened to enter the mining region in March or April, when the water was very low, succeeded in extracting large quantities of gold from the 'bars' or 'benches' not covered with water. The mass of immigrants not having arrived till a month or two later, found the auriferous parts under water. Ignorant of the periodic increase and fall of the stream to which I have adverted, their patience was soon exhausted waiting for the uncovering of the banks. Not a few, crestfallen and disappointed, returned to Victoria.

A gloomy impression began to prevail among the less venturesome spirits that tarried in this scene of morbid speculation. Gold not coming down fast enough to satisfy their wishes, thousands of them lost heart and went back to San Francisco, heaping execrations upon the country and everything else that was English; and lacing the reported existence of gold in the same category with the South Sea bubble. The rumour took wing that the river never did fall; and as placer-mining could only be carried on rivers, the state of the river became the barometer of public hopes, and the pivot on which everybody's expectations turned. This preposterous idea spread, was readily caught up by the press of California, and proved the first check to immigration. Another impediment was the commercial restrictions imposed by the Hudson's Bay Company in virtue of the term of their charter for exclusive trade in the interior not having yet expired.

A few hundred indomitable men, calmly reviewing the unfavourable season in which they had commenced mining operations, and the difficulties unavoidable to locomotion in a country previously untrodden for the most part by white men, resolved to push their way forward, animated by the assurance that they must sooner or later meet the object of their search and labour. Some settled on the bars between Hope and Yale, at the head of navigation; others advanced still higher, running hair-breadth escape, balancing themselves in passing the brink of some dangerous ledge or gaping precipice encumbered with provisions packed on their backs.

A new route was proposed via Douglas, at the head of Harrison Lake and Lilloet, that should avoid the dangers and obstructions of the river trial. But this did not at first mend matters; for the intended road lay through a rugged and densely-wooded country, and much time and money required to be consumed before it could be rendered practicable. Before the line for the Lilloet route was generally known, parties of intrepid miners, anxious to be the first to reap its benefits, tried to force their way through all the difficulties opposed to them. The misery and fatigue endured by them was indescribable. They crept through underwood and thicket for many miles, sometimes on hands and knees, with a bag of flour on the back of each; alternately under and over fallen trees, scrambling up precipices, or sliding down over masses of sharp projecting rock, or wading up to the waist through bogs and swamps. Every day added to their exhaustion; and, worn out with privation and sufferings, one knot of adventurers after another became smaller and smaller, some lagging behind to rest, or turning back in despair. The only thought seemed to be to reach the river ere their provisions should give out. One large party was reduced to three, and when they came to an Indian camp where salmon was to be had, one of these hardy fellows made up his mind to return ...

Nor was this case an uncommon one. Gold there was in abundance, but want of access prevented the country from being 'prospected'; and reckless men, without stopping to take this into account, condemned the mines and everything connected with them without distinction.

If the commerce of the interior had been thrown open, and private enterprise allowed to compete with the natural difficulties of the country, these would have soon been overcome. Forests would have been opened, provisory bridges thrown over precipices, hollows levelled, and the rush of population following behind, the country would have been rapidly settled, and the trader have brought his provisions to the miner's door.

Affairs in Victoria, meanwhile, grew yet more dismal. The 'rowdy' element that had assembled in the city, finding no legitimate occupation to employ their idle hands, were under strong temptation to create such disturbances as they had been accustomed to get up in California. Losing, for the moment, that wholesome dread of British rule which that class usually feel, a party of them rescued a prisoner from the hands of the police, and actually proposed to hoist the American flag over the old Hudson's Bay Company's fort. But the news that a gunboat was on her way from Esquimalt to quell the riot, soon calmed alarm and restored peace.

Large sums of money, sent up from San Francisco for investment, were shipped back again; and whole cargoes of goods, ordered during the heat of the excitement, were thrown upon the hands of merchants. Jobbers had nothing to do but smoke their cigars or play at whist. Some accused the company; others complained of the Government; others sneered at 'English fogyism;' and others deplored the want of 'American enterprise.' 'Croaking' was the order of the day.

The Governor, seeing the tide of immigration receding, managed to control his prejudice against the 'foreigners' from a neighbouring state, so far as to moderate the severe restrictions he had put upon goods imported to British Columbia, and adopted more active measures in opening trails to the mines. But his tardy decision came too late to be attended with immediate benefit.

At length, however, the river did fall, and the arrival of gold-dust foreshadowed a brighter future. But sailing vessels left daily, crowded with repentant and dejected adventurers, whose opposition to the country had become so inveterate, that they could not now be made to believe in the existence of gold from Fraser River, though proved by the clearest ocular demonstration. The old inhabitants imagined that Victoria was about to return to its former state of insignificance.

Yet it is asserted, on reliable authority, that in proportion to the number of hands engaged upon the mines — notwithstanding the unequalled drawbacks in the way of reaching them — the yield during the first six months was much larger than it had been in the same period and at the same stage of development in California or Australia ...

For a few intelligent and persevering men these facts and figures had weight. But amateur miners, romantic speculators, and 'whiskey bummers,' could not, by the most attractive representations, be detained in the country ... For such scouts of civilisation — had the 'castles in the air' which they built not been demolished — would have reenacted in our colonies such scenes of riot and bloodshed as disgraced California nine years previously. It was well that we should get rid of all who wanted impossibilities and indulged exaggerated hopes. The few hardy and enterprising settlers who remained ceased to pursue Will-o'-the-wisps, and composed themselves to the sober realities of life.

In September '59, when I first set foot in Victoria, the process of depopulation was still going on, though it soon after reached its lowest point. A healthy relation between supply and demand in every department was being effected. The tens of thousands that had pressed into the city in '58 were diminished to not more than 1,500, embracing 'the waifs and strays' of every nationality, not excepting a good many whose antecedents were not above suspicion.

Apart from the Government buildings, two hotels, and one shop, all the dwellings and houses of business were at that time built of wood. Many stores were closed and shanties empty. There was little business doing, and no great prospect ahead. This stagnant condition continued with but little abatement till the close of 1860, when intimations came of eminently productive mines being discovered at the forks of Quesnelle, which at that time seemed as difficult of access as the Arctic regions. A few scores of miners, arguing from the fineness of the gold dust found near Hope, Yale and the forks of the Thompson, that it was washed down from some quartz formation in the north, penetrated to the spot just referred to. Language fails to describe the trials these men endured from the utter absence of paths of any kind, the severity of winter climate, and often the scant supply of provisions. The theory by which the daring pioneers were guided was remarkably verified, and the toils of many of them were abundantly rewarded.

Their return to Victoria with bags of dust and nuggets rallied the fainting hopes of the community, and they were regarded as walking advertisements that the country was safe. Business immediately improved, the value of town property advanced; some who had been hesitating about erecting permanent buildings caught inspiration and at once plunged into brick-and-mortar investments.

The few scores that had worked on Antler Creek in '60 increased, in the spring of '61, to 1,500. Some addition to our population in the latter year came from California, and every man who could possibly make it convenient to leave Victoria for the season went to the new diggings. Of those who went, one-third made independent fortunes, one-third netted several hundreds of pounds, and one-third, from a variety of causes were unsuccessful ...

The chief misfortune connected with the influx of population at this period was that it comprised an excessive proportion of clerks, retired army officers, prodigal sons, and a host of other romantic nondescripts, who indulged visions of sudden wealth obtainable with scarcely more exertion than is usually put forth in a pleasure excursion to the continent of Europe. These trim young fellows exhibited a profusion of leather coats and leggings, assuming a sort of defiant air, the interpretation of which was, 'We are the men to show you "Colonials" how to brave danger and fatigue!' But their pretensions generally evaporated with the breath by which they were expressed, and many that set out with this dare-all aspect were soon thankful to be permitted to break stones, chop wood, serve as stable-boys, or root out tree-stumps. The vague imaginations with which they left home were soon dissipated, when, on the termination of the voyage, they discovered that 500 miles lay between them and Cariboo — a distance which must be passed over muddy roads and frowning precipices, with whatever necessaries might be required for the trip strapped to their shoulders. Hundreds went half way to the mines, and returned in despondency; hundreds more remained in Victoria, and were only saved from starvation by the liberality of more prosperous citizens. A much larger number came than the country, with a deficient supply of roads, was prepared to receive. Still a considerable number made large amounts of money, and the majority of those who have possessed sufficient fortitude to bear inconveniences and battle against discouragements are in a fair way for speedily acquiring a competency ...

It was remarked by an intelligent shipmaster, whom I met in Victoria, that he had not found in any of the numerous ports he had visited during a long sea-faring career, so mixed a population as existed in that city. Though containing at present an average of only 5,000 or 6,000 inhabitants, one cannot pass along the principal thoroughfares without meeting representatives of almost every tribe and nationality under heaven. Within a limited space may be seen — of Europeans, Russians, Austrians, Poles, Hungarians, Italians, Danes, Swedes, French, Germans, Spaniards, Swiss, Scotch, English and Irish; of Africans, Negroes from the United States and the West Indies; of Asiatics, Lascars and Chinamen; of Americans, Indians, Mexicans, Chilanos, and citizens of the North American Republic; and of Polynesians, Malays from the Sandwich Islands ...

In description of resources Vancouver Island may resemble the parent country, and thus merit the proud title of 'the England of the Pacific.' But the peculiar elements composing the nucleus of the population render it physically impossible for that exact form of national character we have been accustomed to ascribe to Great Britain to be perpetuated in the island of the Far West. Does the presence, so largely, of inferior races forbode the fatal tainting of the young nation's blood and signal its premature decay, or will the vitality of the governing race triumph over the contamination with which more primitive types threaten to impregnate it? This is the important enquiry that engrosses the attention of ethnological speculators in the nascent communities of the North Pacific ...

It is maintained also, that while by intermarrying with descendants of Europeans we are but reproducing our own Caucasian type, by commingling with eastern Asiatics we are creating debased hybrids; that the primary law of nature teaches self-preservation; and that such protective enactments as have been referred to are essential to the perpetuation and advancement of the nation.

Happily both these coloured races are admitted to the enjoyment of civil privileges in these colonies upon terms of perfect equality with white foreigners, and are alike eligible for naturalisation. Yet even on the British side of the boundary there is a disposition to look coldly upon the immigration of Celestials. It is alleged that so large an amount of Chinese labour must have the effect of reducing the price of white labour. But such an opinion is without foundation; for those Chinamen, who arrive without capital, are only capable of engaging in menial employments, such as cooking, hawking tea, and keeping laundries. It is but few skilled labourers, I presume, that would desire to compete with them in these callings. Nor can their presence at the mines at all interfere with the enterprises of the superior race; for it is well known that they are unable to resort to those mechanical appliances requisite in the working of rich diggings; that they always keep at a respectful distance from the whites, and are content with such small returns as may be yielded by abandoned 'claims,' from which the whites have already taken the cream.

As to the fear that, if access to the country were not made strait for them, they might ultimately overrun and devastate it like a plague of locusts, nothing could be more groundless. No people have a more intelligent acquaintance with 'the law of supply and demand.' They are generally under the direction of shrewd merchants among their own countrymen, who never encourage the poorer classes to leave China without being certain that a fair prospect of occupation exists for them in the parts to which they are imported; and in this respect the judgment of those leading Chinamen is rarely at fault. It must be acknowledged to their credit that in California, British Columbia, and Vancouver Island, an unemployed Chinaman is seldom to be met with, and a more industrious and law-abiding class does not reside in these dependencies. In their social and domestic habits, however, I frankly admit there is room for much improvement as far as cleanliness is concerned.

It is natural that a race so exclusive and so much avoided by their white fellow-citizens on the coast, should give preference to the manufactures of their own country. Much of the clothing they wear and many of their articles of food come from China. They contrive, it is true, to spend as little of their earnings as possible on their adopted soil — most of the money made by the humbler classes among them being remitted home for the laudable object of contributing to the support of needy relatives. But it is a mistake to regard the trade done and the capital acquired by them as so much wealth diverted from the channels of white industry, since but for their presence in the country the greater part of that trade would not have been created; nor would that capital have been accumulated. They cannot prevent commercial advantage accruing to the colonies from their influence, if they would. It is often British bottoms that convey them from China, and they are obliged to buy hardware, waterproof boots, and pork from us. Poultry, too, being esteemed a great luxury, is in great demand among them. When they have lived among the civilised for a time, it not unfrequently happens that they adopt the European and American costume entire ...

The Chinese of Vancouver Island and British Columbia, only numbering at present about 2,000, have not yet attempted the erection of any places of devotion. But when attracted in greater force, the pious among them, according to the Buddhist standard, may be expected to erect fanes in which to celebrate traditional rites ...

Whether, therefore, we consider the antiquity of these Mongols, their natural ingenuity, or the encouragement afforded by their national institutions to talent, integrity, and industry, the most cogent reasons exist for our extending to them a cordial welcome. Let the colonists show the fruits of a superior civilisation and religion, not in ridiculing and despising these Pagan strangers, but in treating them with the gentle forbearance due to a less favoured portion of the family of mankind, and they will continue to be useful and inoffensive members of society. The prejudice which characterises race or colour as a disqualification for the exercise of civil rights reflects dishonour upon the civilised community that indulges it.

The descendants of the African race resident in the colonies are entitled to some notice. About 300 of them inhabit Victoria, and upwards of 100 are scattered throughout the farming settlements of the island and British Columbia. The chief part came to the country some time previous to the immigration of '58, driven from California by social taboo and civil disabilities. They invested the sums they brought with them in land, and by the sudden advance in the value of real estate which followed the influx of gold seekers, most of them immediately found themselves possessed of a competency. It was not surprising, under these circumstances, that some, formerly habituated to servitude or reproached as representatives of a barbarous race, should, on being delivered from the yoke of social oppression, fail to show much consideration for the indurated prejudices of the whites, most of whom at that period were either Americans or British subjects, who sympathised with the ideas prevailing in the United States respecting the social status of the coloured people.

Whereas they had been restricted in California to worship Almighty God in their own churches or in a part of those frequented by whites, designed for the exclusive accommodation of persons of colour, they were permitted on coming to Vancouver Island free range of unoccupied pews, in the only church then erected in the colony. The church-going immigrants in the mass wafted to our shores in '58 were at once brought into a proximity with coloured worshippers which was repugnant to past associations. It is difficult to analyse this social prejudice between the races, and impossible to defend it. But I have been astonished to observe its manifestations in Christian gentlemen whose intelligence and general consistency were exemplary. The negro supporters of the church, regarding themselves as the 'old families' of the country and the monied aristocracy, and wincing under the recollection of social wrongs endured by them under the American flag, were not disposed to give way in the slightest to the whims and scruples of the whites. Many of the latter remonstrated with the clergyman against allowing the congregation to assume a speckled appearance — a spectacle deemed by them novel and inconvenient. They insisted that they were prepared to treat the "blacks" with the utmost humanity and respect, in their own place; but that the Creator had made a distinction which it was sinful to ignore, that the promiscuous arrangement might lead to the sexes in both races falling in love with each other, entering into marriage, and thus occasioning the deterioration of the whites without the elevation of the negroes being effected. The worthy parson, being direct from the parent country, and till then wholly inexperienced in the social relations of the conflicting races, felt at liberty to take only philanthropic and religious ground in dealing with the question. He maintained that the stains of men's sin, in common, were so dark, that mere difference in colour was an affair of supreme insignificance before the Almighty, in comparison, and that the separation desired by the whites was of carnal suggestion, which Christianity demanded should be repressed. He is said even to have gone so deeply into the subject in a particular sermon as to assert that the disposition of nerves, tendons, and arteries, and the essential faculties of the soul were alike in white and black — the sole distinction between them consisting of colouring matter under the skin, the projection of the lower jaw, and the wool by which the scalp was covered ...

The same prejudice of race continues, unfortunately, to interfere with harmony in social gatherings for the purposes of amusement. More than once has the presence of coloured persons in the pit of the theatre occasioned scenes of violence and bloodshed, followed by litigation. When, a few years since, a literary institute was attempted to be formed, and the signatures of one or two respectable negroes appeared in the list of subscribers, the movement came to an untimely close. A white member of a temperance society, which was eminently useful in the community, proposed the name of a coloured man for admission, intentionally avoiding to disclose at the time any information as to his race, and when it was discovered that the society had been beguiled, ignorantly, into accepting a negro as a brother teetotaller, it broke up.

There is nothing in the constitution of the colony to exclude a British born negro from the municipal council or the legislature, and yet, however well qualified he might be by talent and education for the honour, his election could not be carried in the present state of public feeling. The negroes are perfectly justified in claiming those civil rights which British law confers upon them, and they are resolved not to desist struggling till these are fully achieved.

Having by commendable zeal succeeded in organising a rifle corps and a brass band, they expressed a wish to appear in uniform, on occasion of a public procession formed to escort the present Governor to his residence on landing in the colony. But the prejudice of the whites ruled it otherwise. When they sought an opportunity of showing esteem for the retiring Governor at a banquet given to that gentleman, admission was refused them. When the 'common-school' system is introduced, in which the families of both races are equally entitled to participate, I foresee that storms will arise.

Many of this people in the country are necessarily endowed with very limited intelligence, while some are well-informed, and eloquent in speech. But, as a race, they compare favourably with whites of corresponding social position, in industry and uprightness ...

The Government officials constitute the centre of the social system (still in a formative state), and around it multitudes of broken-down gentlemen and certain needy tradespeople rotate. The most wealthy members of the community have, in general, more money than culture — a condition of things always incident to the early stage of colonial development. Many of them owe their improved circumstances simply to being the lucky possessors of real estate at a time when it could be bought for a nominal amount. Some who eight years ago were journeymen smiths, carpenters, butchers, bakers, public-house keepers, or proprietors of small curiosity shops in San Francisco or Victoria, are now in the receipt of thousands of pounds a year. Among this class there are those who bear their prosperity with moderation, while others indicate the limited extent of their acquaintance with the world by an air of amusing assumption.

There is a resident in the country who, in consideration of his past official relation to it, as first Governor of British Columbia, deserves passing notice in this place. I refer to Sir James Douglas. This gentleman is completely unknown in England, except at the Colonial Office and to a few directors of the Hudson's Bay Company. But being a local celebrity, the reader may not object to be introduced to so interesting a character. In stature he exceeds six feet. His countenance, by its weather-beaten appearance, still tells of many years spent in fur-trapping adventure, in the wilds of the interior. Introduced at the age of fifteen or sixteen from the West Indies, the reputed place of his birth, into the service of the company, and deprived, during the greater part of his life, of the advantages of society, except that of Indians, half-breeds, and persons like himself occupying humble situations in the employ of the company, every praise is due to him for not being indifferent to mental culture in those mountain solitudes in which the flower of his manhood was passed. The stateliness of his person — of which he always seems proudly conscious — and his natural force of character suggest the reflection to an observer, how vastly more agreeable would have been his address and powerful the influence of his character and abilities had he enjoyed in early life a liberal education and intercourse with persons of refinement and culture ...

His efforts to appear grand, and even august, were ludicrously out of proportion to the insignificant population he governed — numbering less than the inhabitants of many a country town in England. When he spoke to anyone within the precincts of the Government House, his Quixotic notions of his office, which he evidently thought splendid, prompted him to make choice of the sesquipedalian diction he employed in his despatches. The angle of his head, the official tone, the extension of his hand, the bland smile which never reached beyond the corners of his mouth — all these stiff and artificial arrangements were carefully got up and daily repeated by him under the delusion that the public imagined him to be natural and a perfect Brummell in politeness. His manners always gave one the impression that to make up for early disadvantages he had religiously adjusted his whole bearing to the standard of Lord Chesterfield, and it is needless to say how amusing was the combination of his lordship and this dignified old furtrapper.

His attitude toward the officials serving under his government was austere and distant. This he had acquired under the sort of military regime observed between the officers and servants of the Hudson's Bay Company. I have heard magistrates addressed by him in a pompous manner that no English gentleman would assume toward his porter. But Sir James solemnly felt that 'the machine of state' could only be kept in motion by his delivering commands, with head erect, and with that rotund and peremptory utterance which at once betrayed and excused vulgarity.

He was rarely visible at his desk or in the street without being arrayed in semi-military uniform; but the climax of his extravagance was probably capped by his being followed perpetually, whether taking an airing in the country or going to visit, by an imposing orderly, duly armed and in uniform. In so small and practical a town as Victoria, the temptation of the local wits to satirise so preposterous a spectacle was irresistible.

Petty diplomacy was a passion with Sir James — doubtless developed, from his youth, in the wheedling mode of transacting business with the Indians, adopted by the company in the interior. He never sent away any suppliant for governmental favours without holding out some hope, which, at the same moment, he, in many cases, determined to frustrate. A favourite plan of his with any whom he thus sought to keep in good humour was to exhaust their patience by expedient and indefinite postponement of the object desired ...

If the character of people is respectable, humble origin is felt to be much less a barrier to advancement in the colonies than in England. But in no part of the empire are shams so readily detected.

Let it not be supposed, however, that our female society is entirely composed of this or of any other class that is doubtful. It must be confessed, that there are too many females in both colonies as everywhere else, that reflect as little credit upon the land of their adoption as they did on the land of their birth. Still, we have among us ladies of birth and education, and, what is yet more important, of moral qualities that would render them an ornament to their sex in any part of the world.

Refugees from bankruptcy, disgrace, or family strife, suffered in some other part of the world, are to be met with in Victoria every few yards. But among the unfortunate are some of the most estimable men I have ever seen.

The tone of society has become decidedly more British since 1859; but still, as then, the American element prevails. Citizens of the United States may easily be known by their spare, erect, and manly figure. The business men among them are, for the most part, attired in superfine cloth, most frequently of a dark colour, and highheeled, broad-toed boots, of admirable fit. The coloured shooting-jacket, so frequently worn by Englishmen in the colony during the week, has no attraction for Americans.

For ethereal beauty, handsomeness, liveliness, and general intelligence, American ladies must be allowed to be eminently distinguished. That high refinement, which can only result from breeding and education, and is to be found in the foremost rank of British society, is without parallel among Americans. But it is my impression that the average of educated American ladies cannot be equalled, in interesting expression of countenance and brightness of intellect, by English ladies of the middle-class generally. The charming sweetness of the American beauty, however, fades prematurely, and at the age of 30, when a well-developed English lady is but in her prime, the smooth visage and transparent complexion of our fair cousin have been for years invaded by wrinkles.

Americans appear to me defective in conversational power. However rapid and distinct their speech may be, the diction employed by them is so stilted, and their forms of expression are so elaborate, as to contrast unfavourably with the terse idiomatic phraseology used by those Englishmen who are competent to wield their own language ...

The intense pitch to which the feelings of people are strung in a gold-producing country is a frequent cause of insanity. Whether that malady exist in a greater degree in this community than in one of a more settled description, I am not sufficiently versed in the statistics of the subject to aver. But certainly a much larger proportion of cases have been personally known to me here than in the same period I ever saw in the much denser populations of England. I can reckon up eight persons — all of whom I have been on speaking terms with, and most of whom I knew intimately, who, in four years and a half, have become lunatics, and as such are either living or dead ...

The immigrant accustomed to the distinctions of class obtaining in settled populations of the old world, will be struck to observe how completely the social pyramid is inverted in the colonies. Many persons of birth and education, but of reduced means, are compelled, for a time after their arrival, to struggle with hardship, while the vulgar, who have but recently acquired wealth, are arrayed in soft clothing and fare sumptuously. Sons of admirals and daughters of clergymen are sometimes found in abject circumstances, while men only versed in the art of wielding the butcher's knife, the drayman's whip, and the blacksmith's hammer, or women of low degree, have made fortunes ...

Society in the interior is very depraved. In Yale, Douglas, Lytton, Lilloet, Forks of Quesnelle, and the mining towns, little trace of Sunday is at present visible, except in the resort of miners on that day to market for provisions, washing of dirty clothes, repairing machinery, gambling, and dissipation. Out of the 5,000 souls in Victoria, a few may be found who respect the ordinances of religion. But at the mines, adherents of religious bodies have hitherto been numbered by scores and units.

Up to the present there have been but two places of worship in Cariboo — one connected with the Church of England, and the other with the Wesleyan Methodists. Till the fall of 1863, when these were built, the services of public worship were conducted in a bar-room and billiard-saloon. At one end of the apartment was the clergyman, with his small congregation, and at the other were desperadoes, collected unblushingly around the faro or pokah table, staking the earnings of the preceding week.

Profane language is almost universal, and is employed with diabolical ingenuity. The names of 'Jesus Christ' and the 'Almighty' are introduced in most blasphemous connections. Going to church is known among many as 'the religious dodge,' which is said to be 'played out,' or, in other words, a superstition which has ceased to have any interest for enlightened members of society ...

The slang in vogue in the mining regions is imported mainly from California, and is often as expressive as it is original. 'Guessing' and 'calculating' are exercises of perpetual occurrence. If one have the best of a bargain, he is said to have got 'the dead wood' on the other party in the transaction. A mean and greedy man is 'on the make;' and where a 'claim' is to be disposed of, the proprietor is 'on the sell.' A conceited man thinks himself 'some pumpkins;' and when any statement is made, the exact truth of which is doubted, it is said to be 'rayther a tall story.' When a claim disappoints the hopes of those interested in it, it has 'fizzled out.' Credit is 'jaw-bone;' and in one store on the road to Cariboo, the full-sized jaw-bone of a horse is polished, and suspended on the wall, with the words written under: 'None of this allowed here.' The ground of the allusion is evident, the product resulting from the motion of the jaw being the only security a needy purchaser has to offer. Another expression for wanting credit is 'shooting off the face.' Deceit in business is 'shananigan.' A good road, steamboat, plough, dinner, or anything else you please, is 'elegant.' When one has run off to avoid paying his debts, he has 'skedaddled,' or 'vamoosed the ranch;' or if hard-up, he wants to 'make a raise.' Owing to the remoteness of British Columbia from other centres of British population, it is called the 'jumping-off place' — another phrase for the end of the world. Any issue likely to arise from a given chain of events, is seen 'sticking out.' When two parties are playing into each other's hands, with a sinister object in view, it is a case of 'logrolling.' When the conduct of any one renders him liable to a whipping or something worse, he is 'spotted.'

Among the roughest of professional miners, exhibitions of kindness occur fitted to shame many of more moral pretensions. As a class, they are not avaricious. It is not so much the possessing of money, as the excitement attending the acquisition of it, that affords them satisfaction. It were more conducive to their welfare could they be induced to cultivate more thrifty habits. If the patronage they recklessly bestow upon public-houses were withdrawn, and the vast sums thus squandered diverted into productive channels, the spirit of legitimate enterprise would be fostered, and the resources of the country be more rapidly developed.

The sentiment of 'pure and undefiled religion' does not flourish at present in the colonies. In the Protestant world on the Pacific coast, the religious sect to which a man is attached may commonly be determined by the extent of his business. Small retailers and mechanics swarm among the Methodists; jobbers, who break packages, and the larger class of store-keepers, frequent the Presbyterian and Congregational chapels; and the bankers, lawyers, and wholesale dealers prefer the Church of England. Just as with their augmented resources they erect comfortable houses, so they seek to provide themselves with a church suited to their advanced social position. The utilitarian tendencies of the people are such, that eloquent or spiritual preaching by itself will not attract worshippers. Their comfort must be consulted, as it respects the place of worship erected, and their emotions must be appealed to through the medium of an organ and an efficient choir.

Religious scepticism prevails to a remarkable extent, as it does in all new countries. I have known cases in which Christian pastors have been turned away from the bedside of the dying colonist, and forbidden by him either to offer prayer to Almighty God for his restoration to health, or administer the consolations of the Gospel. But I trust such cases of extreme obduracy are not common ...

In a country where so many are governed by impulse, and rendered desperate by losses sustained in speculation, it is not surprising that instances of highway robbery and murder should occasionally happen. The commission of these crimes, however, as in California and Australia, has been hitherto confined to solitary intervals, between the towns of British Columbia, on the way to the mines. The proportion of crime, at present, is decidedly small, considering the character and number of the population ...

14

"Deaf to Their Cries"

Irish Immigration

DOCUMENTS

A) Journal, 1847
   Gerald Keegan
B) Three Years in Canada, 1829
   John Mactaggart
C) Report of the Roman Catholic Chaplain of the
   Provincial Penitentiary, January 24, 1853
D) "Protestant Organization", August 27, 1847
   The Loyalist, Saint John, New Brunswick

A part from the indigenous population, Canada was a nation of immigrants who began migrating across the Atlantic from Europe to our shores as far back as Champlain early in the seventeenth century. Although Europeans came from nations and cultures as diverse as England, France, and Ireland, they did share some common experiences. Many were what are now called economic refugees: people fleeing hard times in their "old countries" in favour of hope and promise in the new world. All shared the same pain of losing familiar surroundings among friends and family, and the shock of integrating into a new and often strange society at the other end. Many also faced hostility and suspicion as they stepped onto Canadian quaysides after miserable weeks at sea. The majority of newcomers came from the poorest classes in Europe, those most susceptible to the vagaries of recession, mechanization, urbanization, intolerance, and starvation.

Famine forced thousands of poor Irish men, women and children to British North America during the 1840s. The Irish population of tenant farmers, by mid-century, existed almost entirely on the potato. When a deadly blight all but destroyed the crop, peasants faced one of two choices: stay and die, or take a chance, struggle to the coast, find passage on a ship, and leave that hell. The catastrophe was so great that Ireland's population fell from 8 to 4 million, either from death or emigration. Most of those fleeing were Catholics from what is today the Republic of Ireland. There were, however, Protestant emigrants too, largely from the northern counties of Ulster. The two groups generally did not mix, feared each other, and periodically clashed violently. Bigotry was not unique to Ireland, and Irish Catholics also found themselves second-class citizens in Canada.

Many of those who survived the trek to the emigration ports and the voyage to North America never made it farther than the quarantine island of Grosse Isle in the St. Lawrence River. There thousands expired, packed cheek by jowl in unspeakable squalor, because Canada could not and would not offer them the help they needed. Nor was Canadian popular reaction particularly surprising. Disease, after all, soon wafted from immigrant ships to land, striking without warning, often with deadly results in an age without effective medicinal remedies. Locals came to fear and hate the disease-ridden Irish, shunning them, and forcing them out of range. This was not a new attitude. The English stereotype of an Irishman was a drunken, brawling, dirty, lazy, stupid, papist peasant. Thus new Irish Catholic immigrants, usually destitute and weak, survived as best they could, picking up tough labouring jobs on the canals, getting marginal work doing what others refused, or breaking the law. For these people, the land of opportunity was, at best, a sick joke.

That Gerald Keegan's journal survived is miraculous. A local school master in Ireland, he was a member of the literate minority, and a natural leader to his community. It is hardly surprising that he and much of his extended family left his native land and urged others to do so when the potato famine struck. What makes Keegan different from the vast majority, however, is that he chronicled his ordeal, in minute detail, even through the grimmest hours. His uncle, already resident in Canada, tragically arrived at Grosse Isle just hours before Keegan's death. At least he rescued the journal which now stands as one of the few inside glimpses of the "Irish Holocaust."

John MacTaggart (1791–1830) was an engineer trained at the University of Edinburgh, Scotland. A successful writer, he published an encyclopedia in 1824, and numerous articles on Canadian geology after immigrating in the mid-1820s. Then he became a surveyor for the Rideau Canal, a job he eventually lost for drunkenness. Back in England, he published his thoughts and observations on Canada, which included the notion that Britain should rid itself of colonists who were "as able a state of grumblers as you can meet in the world." In particular, he hated the gentry, legal profession, and the "low Irish" who constituted the bulk of the Rideau Canal's unskilled labour force.

The Chaplain whose report on the provincial penitentiary is included in this volume is unknown.

The Loyalist, a newspaper published in Saint John, New Brunswick, promoted Protestantism and, typical of radical anti-Catholicism, urged the establishment of more Orange lodges as a way to ensure Protestant supremacy in Canadian society.

A) Journal, 1847
Gerald Keegan

... For men and women to want is bad enough, but to have the children starving, crying for the food their parents have not to give them, and lying awake at night from the gnawing at their little stomachs; oh, it is dreadful. God forgive those who have it, and will not share their abundance even with His little ones. I came home from school this afternoon dejected and despairing. As I looked round me before opening the door of my lodging, everything was radiantly beautiful. The sunshine rested on the glory of Ireland, its luxuriant vegetation — its emerald greenness. Hill and valley were alike brilliant in the first flush of spring and the silver river meandered through a plain that suggested the beautiful fields of paradise. Appearances are deceitful, I thought; in every one of those thatched cabins sit the twin brothers, Famine and Death. As I opened the door, Mrs. Moriarty called to me that my uncle Jeremiah had been twice asking for me. Poor man, I said to myself, he will have come to borrow to buy meal for his children and I will not have a shilling in my pocket until the board pays me my quarter's salary. I respect Jeremiah, for both he and his brother in Canada were kind to my poor mother. How I wish all the family had gone to Canada; cold in winter and hot in summer, they say, but there is plenty to eat. I took up a book and had not long to wait for my uncle. He did not need to say a word, his face told me he knew what starvation meant. I called to my landlady to roast another herring; my uncle would share my dinner. He came neither to beg nor borrow, but to ask my advice. After high mass on Sunday the proctor got up on a stone and told them their landlord had taken their case into consideration, and went on to read a letter he had got from him. In it Lord Palmerston said he had become convinced there was no hope for them so long as they remained in Ireland, and their only means of doing better was to leave the country. All in arrears who would agree to emigrate he would forgive what they were due and pay their passage to Canada. Are you sure, I asked, this letter was really from Lord Palmerston?

… At my uncle's house I found a number of his neighbors waiting and we were soon discussing the subject that filled their heads. The agent had given out he had got another letter in which the landlord mended his offer, by promising that his agent at Quebec would pay ten shillings a head on their landing at that city, and saying the Canadian government would give each family a hundred acres free. There was to be no breaking or separating of families; all would go in the same ship. Against the lure of the free passage, the ten shillings, and the hundred acres, they put leaving Ireland for such a wild cold place as Canada, and to people in rags the thought of its frost and snow was terrible. My uncle fetched his only letter from his brother and I read it aloud. I had to do so several times, as they argued over particular statements and expressions in it. The account it gave of his comfort weighed with them. After a great deal of talk my uncle says, "Well, boys, my brother never told me a lie an I believe every word of his letter. If ye says, I'm for takin the offer an lavin at onct." His decision carried them by storm, and the listless downcast men became bright and energetic with the new hope born within them. As I walked home, I though it over. There was the possibility of their being deceived by the agent. They were ignorant of business and could easily be imposed upon. Should I not go with them and protect their interests? What was here to keep me in Ireland? Everything I had tried had gone against me. When I was in a fair way at Maynooth, the thought had possessed me the priesthood was not my vocation and I left its loved walls. Failure and disappointment had marked every effort made in other callings since. To give up my situation as teacher would matter little; its salary was a mockery. I would see Aileen.

Feby. 28, 1847. — Aileen consents. Like myself an orphan, she has no ties to bind her to dear old Ireland beyond those common to all her children. We will be married the week before the ship sails. Gave up my school today. As I mean to keep a journal of the voyage, I sat down tonight and wrote the foregoing, to remind me in future years of the causes that led to my decision.

March 8. — Uncle came to see me this morning. What he tells me raises doubts of the good faith of the landlord. The agent was round yesterday with an attorney who got them to put their mark to a paper. A ship is promised beginning of April.

10. — Walked to town to see the agent. He was not for showing the paper at first. It was a release of all claims on the landlord and a promise to give him peaceable possession on the 1st April. The remission of what is due for rent and the free passage are specified as the quid pro quo of the landlord, but not a word about the ten shillings a head to be paid at Quebec or the 100 acres per family from the Canadian government. Nothing can now be done; the poor people are at Lord Palmerston's mercy.

April 9. — We were married Monday morning, and spent three happy days with Aileen's cousin in Limerick. Arrived here in Dublin today. The ship is advertised to sail tomorrow. Took out our tickets for second cabin and drive tomorrow morning to where the ship is lying.

10. — When the car drove alongside the ship, instead of finding her ready for sea she was a scene of confusion, carpenters at work on her hull and riggers perched in her cordage. There is a mountain of freight to go on board, which she is not ready to receive. It was a shame to advertise her to sail today when she cannot leave for several days. Our second cabin proves to be a cubby-hole in the house on deck. We might as well have gone in the steerage and saved £5. It was late in the day when uncle and his neighbors arrived; they formed a large party, and were footsore with their long tramp. The captain refused to allow them to go on board and they will have to spend the night on the quay. The weather fortunately is dry.

11. — I spoke to the captain on behalf of the emigrants. I showed him they had come on the day advertised and had a right to maintenance. He curtly told me to go and see the ship's broker, who has his office far up in the city. I waited over an hour in an outer room to get an interview with the government emigration inspector. I implored him to put in force the law on behalf of the poor people shivering on the quay. He haughtily ordered me out of his office; saying he knew his duty and would not be dictated to by a hedge schoolmaster. Came away indignant and sore at heart. Looking over the emigrants I can see why Lord Palmerston confined his offer to those in arrears for rent and who had small holdings. Such persons must needs be widows or old men without proper help. His lordship has shrewdly got rid of those likely to be an incumbrance on his estates. The company is made up largely of women and children, with a few old or weakly men. The number of widows is surprising.

12. — The weather is cold and showery and the poor people are most miserable — wet, hungry, and shivering. I went to Dublin to see the ship's broker. He received me very smoothly and referred me to the charterer, with-

out whose instructions he could do nothing. The charterer I found to be out of town; the owner of the ship lives in Cork. I returned disconsolate. An infant died today from exposure. On going to see about the innocent's burial, the priest told me it was common for ships to advertise they would sail on a day on which they had no intention of leaving. It was done to make sure of getting all the passengers they could pack into the vessel. They get £3 a head from the landlords, children counting as half, and the more they can force on board the greater their profit. His experience had been that charterers of vessels for carrying emigrants were remorseless in their greed, and, by bribing the officials, set the government regulations at defiance. Scenes he had seen on the quays drew tears from all save those whose hearts were hardened by the lust of gain.

14. — The poor people are homesick and heartsick. Today a number of them tried to get on board and take possession of the berths between decks, which were finished yesterday. They were driven back by the mate and the sailors. One man was brutally picked on by the mate. It seems if the passengers go on board they would have a right to rations, hence their being denied shelter. Some of the men have got work along the quays, and every sixpence is a help to buy bread. Again ventured to remonstrate with the captain. He said he had nothing to say to an informer, referring to my visit to the government agent. I told him I would report his conduct to Lord Palmerston, and have just written a letter to his lordship.

15. — Matters have been going on from bad to worse. Two more children have died from cold and want. Not a soul in the crowd has had a warm bit since they left home. Their food is an insufficiency of bread, which is poor sustenance to ill-clad people camped in open sheds. The ship is ready for sea yet they will not let us go on board ...

17. — At daybreak we were roused by the clanking of the capstan as the anchor was weighed. There was a light air from the north-east. Sails were spread and we slowly beat out of the bay and took a long slant into the channel, dropping our pilot as we passed Kingstown. Stores were broached and biscuit for three days served. They were very coarse and somewhat mouldy, yet the government officer was supposed to have examined and passed them as up to the requirements of the emigration act. Bad as they were, they were eagerly accepted, and so hungry were the people that by night most of them were eaten. How shamefully the ship was overcrowded was now to be seen and fully realized. There were not berths for two-thirds of

the passengers, and by common consent they were given up to the aged, to the women and the children. The others slept on chests and bundles, and many could find no other resting place than the floor, which was so occupied that there was no room to walk left. I ascertained, accidentally, that the mate served out rations for 530 today. He counts two children as one, so that there are over 600 souls on board a ship which should not legally have 400, for the emigrant act specifics 10 square feet of deck to a passenger. Why was this allowed? …

20. — When I awoke this morning I became sensible of the violent motion of the ship. Going out I saw we were fairly on the bosom of the Atlantic and the ship was plunging through the ocean swell. The east wind still held and we were speeding on our course under full sail. I found my fellow-passengers to be in a deplorable condition. The bulwarks were lined with a number who were deadly seasick. Going between decks the scene nigh overcame me. The first time I went below I was reminded of a cavern — long and narrow and low in ceiling. Today it was a place for the damned. Three blinking oil lanterns cast light enough to show the outlines of forms that lay groaning on the floor, and give glimpses of white stony faces lying in the berths, a double tier of which surrounded the sides of the ship. A poignant wail of misery came through an atmosphere of such deadly odour that, for the first time, I felt sick, and had to beat a retreat up the narrow ladder. The cool ocean breeze revived me and Aileen, who proved a good sailor, had our modest breakfast ready when I joined her. On revisiting the steerage later in the day I found there were passengers down with more than sea-sickness. There are several cases of dysentery. I asked the steward to tell the captain. He informs me the captain can do nothing, having only a small medicine-chest for the crew. However he told him, and the captain ordered the steward to give them each a glass of whisky. I had plain proof today of my suspicions that drink is being sold, and on charging the steward he told me it was the custom for the mates of emigrant ships to be allowed to do so, and he would get me what I wanted at any time for sixpence a noggin. I told him I had taken the pledge at the hands of Father Matthew and considered drink unnecessary. My remonstrances fell on stony ground, for the steward, a decent, civil fellow sees no wrong in drinking or in selling drink.

21. — The first death took place last night, when a boy of five years succumbed to dysentery. In the afternoon a wail suddenly arose from the hold — a fine young woman had died from the same cause. Both were

dropped into the sea at sunset. There are fewer seasick today, but the number ill from dysentery grows. Cornmeal was served out today instead of biscuit. It was an injury instead of a sustenance, for it being impossible to make stirabout of it owing to no provision having been made for a galley for the passengers, it had to be mixed with water and eaten raw. Some got hot water, but most had to use cold. Such food when dysentery threatens is poison. Today was cold with a headwind that sent the spray flying over the bows. Had a long talk this afternoon with a very decent man who is going to Peterborough, Canada West. He thinks it is not disease that ails the children, but cold and hunger. Food and clothes is what they need, not medicine. The number of sick grows. Sighted 2 ships today, both too far away to speak to them.

22. — Why do we exert ourselves so little to help one another, when it takes so little to please? Aileen coaxed the steward to let her have some discarded biscuit bags. These she is fashioning into a sort of gowns to cover the nakedness of several girls who could not come on deck. The first she finished this afternoon, and no aristocratic miss could have been prouder of her first silk dress than was the poor child of the transformed canvas bag, which was her only garment ...

30. — Cold and rainy with fog. A north-west wind is blowing that drives the ship at a good rate, though not straight on her course. The fever spreads and to the other horrors of the steerage is added the cries of those in delirium. While I was coming from the galley this afternoon, with a pan of stirabout for some sick children, a man suddenly sprang upwards from the hatchway, rushed to the bulwark, his white hair streaming in the wind, and without a moment's hesitation leaped into the seething waters. He disappeared beneath them at once. His daughter soon came hurrying up the ladder to look for him. She said he had escaped from his bunk during her momentary absence, that he was mad with fever. When I told her gently as I could that she would never see him again, she could not believe me, thinking he was hiding. Oh the piercing cry that came from her lips when she learned where he had gone; the rush to the vessel's side, and the eager look as she scanned the foaming billows. Aileen led her away; dumb from the sudden stroke yet without a tear ...

May 2. — There had been a flurry of snow during the night, so that yards and deck were white when I went out. The gale still holds and boatswain said if the weather cleared we would see Newfoundland. Two small booms cracked but that has not deterred the captain from keeping on all the sail the ship will bear. At times her lee rail almost touches the water, and the deck slants so it is difficult to cross it. The captain is anxious to end the voyage, and no wonder, for the fever spreads. One child and two adults have died within the last twenty-four hours. Their bodies were dropped overboard when the ship was going 12 knots an hour. A cold, miserable day.

3. — The gale blew itself out during the night and today it is calm, the ship pitching and rolling on a glassy swell, and the sails flapping as if they would split. There is a mist, and it is very cold, which the boatswain tells me, indicates ice near. Lead cast and soundings found, showing we are on the Banks. Some of our people, who are fishermen, bargained with the cook for a piece of salt pork and using it as bait cast their lines. Their patience was tried for a while, until we struck a school of fish, when for half an hour they caught cod and dogfish as fast as they could haul them in. The school then left and few were caught afterwards. They gave a few of the best fish to the cook and in consideration he cooked what they had, so for one day all between decks had enough to eat. The drinking-water has been growing daily worse, and now the smell of it is shocking. The barrels must have been filled from the Liffey near a sewer. Repugnant as it is to sight, smell, and taste it continues to be doled out in such meagre measure that the sick are continually crying for water with not a drop to give them. The number now sick is appalling — the young of dysentery, the old of fever, the cause of both diseases starvation. Uncle's second boy died this afternoon of dysentery. Poor uncle, his lot is a sore one, yet he never complains. Wind came from southwest towards evening bringing milder temperature with light rain. Sighted several fishing schooners and saw sea-birds for first time since left coast of Ireland ...

Grosse Isle, May 31. — Fourteen days since I penned a line in this sorrowful record. I wish I had not lived to pen another. God's will be done, but, oh, it is hard to say it. Yet I ask myself, what right have I to repine? Grievous as has been my loss, what is it compared with that of many of those around me, whose quiet submission rebukes my selfish sorrow. Enough of this, let me resume my record. When the ship came abreast of the quarantine buildings, all fresh from a new coat of whitewash, the anchor was dropped. It was nearly an hour before the quarantine officer came on board, and I heard him on stepping from his boat apologize to our captain for the delay, owing to his waiting for breakfast. The captain took him down to the cabin and it was a long while before he re-appeared, when he stepped down to the main deck, where all the passengers, able to be out of bed, were waiting him. He walked round us, asked a few to hold out their tongues, and then went down into the hold, where he stayed only a minute or so. Passing a few words with the captain, he re-entered his boat and was rowed back to the island. No sooner had he left, than the boatswain got orders to have all boats made ready to take the sick ashore. First the dead were brought up. The sailors shrank back, there was a muttered consultation, and the boatswain, taking me aside, told me they would not touch them or even row a boat that held them, and I had better drop them overboard. "Never," I cried, "shall it be said that the bodies of the faithful did not receive Christian burial when it was possible to give it." Calling out from among my people four men whom I knew were fishermen, I asked them if they would row the dead ashore, and on saying they would, the boatswain let me have a boat. Decently the bodies were passed over and we made our way to the landing. We had trouble in getting them out of the boat, for the steps of the quay were out of repair, but we managed it and carried them to what, from the cross on it, we saw was a church. The priest came out and I told him our purpose. Leaving the dead in the church, we went back to the ship for the others. By this time the sick were being landed, and roughly handled they were. As it would be a while before the graves would be ready, I lent a hand — the most miserable, heartrending work I had ever engaged in. With indecent haste they were hurried from the ship deck into the boats, and tossed on to the steps of the quay, careless of what injury they might receive. Most were unable to help themselves in the least, a few were delirious. Men, women and children were all treated the same, as so much rubbish to be got rid of as quickly as possible. It was no better on land. The quarantine had only two men to spare to help the few relatives who came ashore to carry them from the wharf to the buildings, and many lay an hour in a cold pelting rain. It signified little as to their getting wet, for they were all doused by the waves in landing them on the quay. Small wonder two died on the quay, and were borne to the chapel to add to the number awaiting burial there. The priest was very considerate, and, although I did not ask it, said mass, which I knew would be a great consolation to the relatives. Leaving the cemetery with the priest, I thanked him from my heart, and ran to the quay. My heart was in my mouth when I saw on it Aileen, standing beside our boxes, and the ship, having tripped her anchor, bearing up the river.

"What makes you look so at me, Gerald? I have come as you asked."

"I never sent for you."

"The steward told me you had sent word by the sailors for me to come ashore, that you were going to stay here. They carried the luggage into a boat and I followed."

I groaned in spirit. I saw it all. By a villainous trick, the captain had got rid of me. Instead of being in Quebec that day, here I was left at the quarantine-station. "My poor Aileen, I know not what to do: my trouble is for you." I went to see the head of the establishment, Dr. Douglas. He proved to be a fussy gentleman, worried over a number of details. Professing to be ready to oblige, he said there was no help for me until the steamer came. "When will that be?" Next Saturday. A week on an island full of people sick with fever! Aileen, brave heart, made the best of it. She was soaking wet, yet the only shelter, apart from the fever sheds, which were not to be thought of, was an outhouse with a leaky roof, with no possibility of a fire or change of clothing. How I cursed myself for my rashness in making captain and mate my enemies, for the penalty had fallen not on me, but on my Aileen. There was not an armful of straw to be had; not even boards to lie on. I went to the cooking booth, and found a Frenchman in charge. Bribing him with a shilling he gave me a loaf and a tin of hot tea. Aileen could not eat a bite, though she tried to do so to please me, but drank the tea. The rain continued and the east wind penetrated between the boards of the wretched sheiling. What a night it was! I put my coat over Aileen, I pressed her to my bosom to impart some heat to her chilled frame, I endeavored to cheer her with prospects of the morrow. Alas, when morning came she was unable to move, and fever and chill alternated. I sought the doctor, he was not to be had. Other emigrant ships had arrived, and he was visiting them. Beyond giving her water to assuage her thirst when in the fever it was not in my power to do anything. It was evening when the doctor, yielding to my importunities, came to see her. He did not stay a minute and writing a few lines told me to go to the hospital steward, who would give me some medicine. Why recall the dreadful nights and days that followed? What profit to tell of the pain in the breast, the raging fever, the delirium, the agonizing gasping for breath — the end? The fourth day, with bursting heart and throbbing head, I knelt by the corpse of my Aileen. There was not a soul to help; everybody was too full of their own troubles to be able to heed me. The island was now filled with sick emigrants, and death was on every side. I dug her grave, the priest came, I laid her there, I filled it in, I staggered to the shed that had sheltered us, I fell from sheer exhaustion, and remember no more. When I woke, I heard the patter of rain, and felt so inexpressibly weary I could think of nothing, much less make any exertion. My eye fell on Aileen's shawl, and the past rushed on me. Oh, the agony of that hour; my remorse, my sorrow, my beseechings of the Unseen. Such a paroxysm could not last long, and when exhausted nature compelled me to lie down, I turned my face to the wall with the earnest prayer I might never awaken on this earth. How long I slept I know not. Some motion of one leaning over me brought back consciousness ... It was Father Moylan ...

"... [D]o what duty calls from your hand."

"There is no need of my help now."

"No need! I tell you every hour there are Irish men and women dying within a furlong of you for lack of the commonest help. Before I came here, I found sick who had not had their fever assuaged by a drop of water for 18 hours; children who had not tasted a bite since yesterday; the dead lying beside the living, and all because there is none to help."

"I do not understand why that should be on land. There is plenty of food and help in Quebec."

"Yes, and so there was on your ship, but a heartless captain and a greedy mate stood between the food and water and the passengers. There is abundance of everything within sight of here, yet our countrymen are perishing by the score, because the government of Canada is deaf to their cries."

"What interest can the Canadian government have in acting so?"

"No interest. It is more heedlessness than intent. The politicians are too absorbed in their paltry strifes to give heed to a few thousands Irish emigrants dying at their door."

"It sounds incredible."

"That is because you do not know politics and politicians here. I tell you, Gerald, I have been in Canada now three years, and (always barring the tools of the Irish landlords) if there be a more despicable creature than the office-hunting Canadian politician, I have yet to see him."

"If I must act, I should go first to Quebec to see after my people. They were promised ten shillings a head, to be paid by Lord Palmerston's agent at Quebec, and a deed from the Canadian government for a hundred acres a family."

"Faugh! Not a shilling, not an acre did they get. I saw them. Lord Palmerston has no agent in Quebec, the government will give no free grant of land. Mere lies told the poor crathurs to get them to leave Ireland."

"Well, then, I could at least make an example of the captain of our ship."

"Not a bit of it; you are deceiving yourself. The prosecution would have to be taken by the emigration agent, and he would not, if he could help it.

Then, where are your witnesses? You would be bled of your last dollar by the lawyers and do nothing. No, Gerald, there is no use of thinking of leaving here. Providence has guided you to Grosse Isle and here is your work. Come, man, get up and do it."

I sank back with a groan. I did not want to move, the father insisted, however, and, after many remonstrances, grasped my hand and raised me to my feet. He took me to where the resident priest lived, insisted on my washing myself and gave me, out of his bag, one of his clean shirts. Then we sat down to dinner, Fathers McGoran and Taschereau joining us. The conversation was of the deluge of emigrants, every day bringing new arrivals, and every ship with its quota of sick and dying. Every available place having become crowded, the ships had to remain and become floating hospitals. The calamity with which they were face to face was so unexpected and appalling that how to devise means to grapple with it staggered them. They spoke of the need of urging the government to erect sheds and send plenty of nurses and doctors. I listened in silence until Father Taschereau asked me for my opinion, as one who was an emigrant. I said many had died on the voyage and many more had been landed who would certainly die, but of this I was confident, there would not have been a death from fever or dysentery on the voyage or one sick of these diseases landed at Grosse Isle, had there been enough to eat. The solution of the difficulty therefore seemed to me simple. Give all who arrive plenty of wholesome food. Starvation is the cause of dysentery and fever. Remove the cause and these diseases will disappear. It is not medicine and nursing that are wanted, but food. The people fled from starvation in Ireland to be worse starved on board ship where their lot was made worse by the lack of pure air and water, of which they had no lack in Ireland ...

I asked Father Moylan about his visit to the ship the day before. He told me the man who shouted for him had a brother dying, who wanted the church's last rites. "It was my first visit to a fever-stricken ship," he went on to say, "and it was a revelation. I could not stand upright in her hold, for it was not much over 5 feet high, and there was little more elbow than head room. Every side was lined with berths and I saw dead lying in them with the living. The stench made one gasp, and the sight of the vermin crawling over dead and living made my flesh creep. An Irish priest is used to the sights of disease and want, but the emigrant-ship, fever-stricken, embodies every form of wretchedness and multiplies them ten-fold."

The quarantine-buildings are huddled together at the upper end of the island and each we examined during the day. Except the one in which uncle lay, they are flimsy affairs, a shelter from the heat of the sun and no more, for the boards are shrunken and the roofs leaky. In one the berths are in double tier, like those of a ship, the result being the patient in the lower berth is made uncomfortable by the one above, and he in turn, from weakness, can neither get out nor into it without help, which he seldom gets. Every place is crowded with sick, even the two churches being occupied. The government had prepared for 200 sick; already there are nigh a thousand, and many more on the ships who cannot be landed for want of room. Without regard to age or sex they are huddled together in the sheds, and left to die or recover. The attendance was hardly worth speaking of. At long intervals a man or woman would come round with drink and food, but there was no pretence at coming for their comfort. We were told by many nobody had been near them for hours. We saw the dead lying next the living, for the bodies are removed only night and morning, and in many cases there were two and three in a berth. Over all this sad scene, from which hope had fled, shone the virtues of patience and submission to the divine will. No querulous word was heard, no grumbling; the stricken flock bowed beneath the rod of affliction with pious assignation. Workmen were busy building a new shed and there were tents lying round, but all the preparations were woefully insufficient. Father Moylan agreed with me that the lack of nurses was even worse than the lack of shelter, and though a supply might be had from the healthy emigrants, I thought not; emigrants in health were too eager to escape after being bound to scenes of horror on shipboard for a month and more. We labored to do our best, and many a pail of water did the father carry from the river to serve out in cupfuls in the sheds.

The weather has been sorely against the sick, rain with high east winds, adding to their discomfort. Nearly every day there is a fresh arrival of a ship, and not one without sick on board. The wind had been from the east the day before and on the morning of the 25th a whole fleet was seen bearing up the river, of which a dozen had emigrants. At Father Moylan's request, I spent a day with him going from ship to ship, a boat having been lent him by a friendly captain. The passengers cried with joy when they saw him and clustered round the holy man, whose services in administering the last consolations of the church were needed at every step. I spoke with the passengers while he was below, and it was an unvarying tale of starvation on the voyage and cruel usage. I found the passengers on ships that had been lying at anchor over a week to be still starving, for the captains had not increased the rations and Dr. Douglas said he could not supply provisions from the shore unless authorized by the Canadian government. One of the new arrivals had 13 dead on board. The 40 ships now at anchor, have nigh 15,000 emigrants: of these I am sure one-third would not be passed as healthy. Sailors are at work on shore erecting a sort of shelter with spars and sails, where the ships will leave their healthy to perform quarantine, while they go on to Quebec.

June 3. — Father Moylan has left with the design of making representations to the government about the condition of things here. He intended, if his bishop consented, to go direct to Montreal, and speak to the ministers themselves. The forwarding of emigrants passed as healthy has begun. They are crowded on to the steamers until there is barely room to move. The reason for this is, the passage money is a dollar a-head and the more packed on board, the more profit. Truth to tell, this class of emigrants are eager enough to leave, and get away from this place. The meanness of the Canadian government in dealing with them is shameful. Instead of allowing healthy passengers to go on with the ship as at first, they are now landed. Being compelled to land and stay here by the government's orders, it would be reasonable to expect the government would provide for them. It does not; all it has done is to send an agent who offers to sell them provisions at cost. Uncle's recovery is hopeless; his strength has gone.

5. — Poor uncle is dead. He was buried yesterday. Ellen keeps hovering between life and death; she has youth on her side. Poor Bridget is worn to a shadow, waiting on the sick. Being told a ship that came in this forenoon was from Sligo, I watched a chance to get on board, expecting to find some I knew among her passengers. I found her deck crowded with emigrants, watching the sailors fish up from the hold with boathooks the bodies of those who had died since entering the river. I soon learned there was bad blood between the crew and passengers, all of whom who could do so had left the steerage two days before and lived on deck. The hold had grown so loathsome with the warm weather that it became unbearable. The crew resented their living on deck. The captain stood at the poop rail; and proved to be a civil man. He told me he had done his best for the passengers on the voyage, but the charterers had poorly provisioned the vessel and he could not therefore give them the rations he wished. For the bad feeling between the sailors and passengers he could not blame either. Staying on deck the

emigrants were in the sailors' way, yet he could not order them back to the hold. Three sailors had caught the fever during the week, which incensed their comrades against the emigrants. He was to pay the sailors a sovereign for each body brought up. I told him of Captain Christian of the ship Sisters, who, the week before, when emigrants and sailors refused for any money to go into the hold to bring up the dead, went down himself and carried them to the deck on his shoulders. I hope he may live to know that Irishmen are grateful, for he is now down with the fever. I recognized none of the passengers, for they were from the northeast end of Lord Palmerston's estates. Their poverty was extreme. They had no luggage and many had not rags enough to cover their nakedness. So haggard and white were they, so vacant their expression, that they looked more like an array of spectres, than of human beings. Coming back, I had painful evidence of the brutal indifference of the authorities in dealing with the sick. They continue to be brought from the ships to the quay in rowboats, and the line of ships being now two miles long, the journey is a long one, and often fatal in bad weather. A small steamboat for transferring them would be a godsend, but the government does not get one, does not even spend ten shillings to replace the broken planks of the steps on the quay, although the want of them causes many a feeble one to slip into the river.

6. — Dr. Douglas exemplifies how a man may be estimable as an individual yet unequal for his duties as an official. He is so obliging and gracious personally that it is unpleasant to find fault with him, yet it is apparent he does not grasp the magnitude of the affliction he has to deal with and is unable to devise means to meet it. All the steps taken are ridiculous in their petty nature. I have been told that it is not him but the Canadian government that is to blame, that it will not allow him a free hand in meeting the emergency, does not respond to his calls, and warns him to be careful in incurring expenditure. Probably that is true, but the government is not accountable for the foolish rules by which the island is governed. There is now a large colony of supposed healthy emigrants confined to the northwest corner of the island. When one falls sick, instead of being taken to the fever-sheds, he is conveyed to the ship in which he was a passenger, and from here is taken to the sheds. The delay and the fatigue of the journey by land and water, if it does not kill the patient makes his recovery more doubtful. Although the population of the island has doubled in a few weeks, the boat with supplies from Quebec continues to come once a week only. We may

be starving, many are starving this day, yet until the steamer comes there is no help. The dead are being buried in trenches, three tier deep. Men and women whose strong arms would add to Canada's wealth are being held here by its authorities to die of want when within sight of plenty. I look at the row of farm-houses on the opposite bank of the river, on the little town whose roofs I see, and knowing there is comfort and plenty over there, marvel at the stupidity, the criminal disregard, that leaves us without bread to eat or even straw to die upon. Steamers pass daily but they are not allowed to stop at the island; my poor people are kept prisoners to perish amid the rocks of this island. The Almighty will surely have a day of reckoning with the rulers of Canada, for it is Canada's territory we are on and it is Canada's quarantine in which we lie bound. The sick are everywhere and are neglected. I found the body of a man in a thicket where he had crawled like a scared beast to die in peace. Bodies are taken from the tents daily where the healthy are supposed to lodge. The sheds have become repugnant to every sense, and the sick are worse off than on ship, for few have relatives to attend them, and they lie for hours without being helped even to a drink of water. The inmates of a tent told me nobody had been near them for two days, and not one among them able to stand for a minute. Everything is against us, for the weather is windy and wet. I go to spend the night in the old shed. My brain is overburdened with the sorrows of my people, and I would I were at rest with Aileen.

10. — A steamer came in this morning to take away emigrants, and I am sure over a thousand were packed on board. Her purser brought a package of letters; one of them was for myself.

> Montreal, June 8, 1847.
>
> My Dear Gerald, — I had it in mind to have written you several days ago, but postponed taking pen in hand day after day in expectation of being able to convey to you the intelligence that would cheer your heart — that the government had decided on adopting a policy of adequate relief. That it grieves me to say, they have not done, although I have exerted myself to arouse them to a sense of their duty, but it is little a poor priest can do with our public men. When I reached here I went first to see the premier. After waiting my turn for an hour with a crowd of visitors, I was admitted. He was civil, but is a dull man, and did not seem

to realize what I was telling him. He told me to go to the provincial secretary, to whose department emigration belongs, and see him. I left in no good humor, to do as Mr. Sherwood bade me. Mr. Daly was not at his lodgings; he had gone to the back of the mountain to dine. I have learned since, he is better at dining and wining than attending to his duties. I had an interview with him next day. You may not know that Mr. Daly is of ourselves. He is a Galway man himself and his lady is from Kilkenny. Appealing to an Irishman and a Catholic I expected him to fall in with me — that all I had to do, was to seize him of the actual facts of the situation at Grosse Isle and he would act with energy. That was what I expected of him but all I got from him, Gerald, was soft words and promises, and neither the one nor the other will feed the starving or cure the sick. He told me to call next day, as he wanted time to go over the reports. When I went, his servant man said he was out, and I never found him in again for me. When the house opened, I managed to get in, to hear what the governor would say about the emigrants. The words put in his mouth about them made me angry. The government pretended they had made ample preparation for the expected influx and that everything was going on well. Beside him stood two men smiling among a bevy of ladies who knew better, for I had told them all. In the debate since then, when a member on the opposition side referred to the rumors of the state of matters at quarantine, Mr. Daly begged the house not to give heed to alarmist reports and to rest assured the government was doing everything that was required, had appointed a commission of three doctors to visit Grosse Isle and would act on their report. I had little respect before for Canadian politicians, I have less now. I was advised to wait on the new minister, John A. Macdonald, the youngest member of the government. I told my friend that if Mr. Daly would not do the decent thing by his countrymen, I was not going to ask the member for the Orange city of Kingston, who, like all the others of them, is engrossed in intrigues to keep his party in office. The talk of the city is whether the ministry will stand, for its majority is only one or two, and there is a good deal of excitement about it ... This will not be for long. The evil has come to the door of this city. The forwarding by wholesale of all emigrants able to move, has brought the fever. The emigration sheds are at Windmill point, an inconvenient place, for there is not water enough to permit the steamers to come up to the wharf, and the emigrants have to be landed by scows, which is sore on the sick. I am not going to say that the journey from Grosse Isle to here is as bad as the voyage across the Atlantic, but it has a few features worse than it. The steamers come in with emigrants packed on their lower deck like herrings in a fish-box. The steamers are chartered by the government from their supporters, and a few of them are old, worn-out tubs, that take two days to a trip that ought to be made inside 20 hours. Without food or cover, blistered by the sun in the day and chilled by the river breezes at night, the poor creatures are landed here more dead than alive. Many who went aboard feeling well, are carried off in a dying state. My curse and the curse of every Irishman be on the government that allows the helplessness of our countrymen to be traded upon to make money for their followers. If their transportation was left open to all ship-owners, the emigrants would be brought here in large and speedy steamers, and a limit could be put to the number they carry. Once landed, the emigrants are decently treated. I am thankful to be able to say that. It is the city and not the government that manages. For sick and well there is plenty of wholesome food, and no lack of doctors or nurses. The food, to be sure, is coarse and the cooking not good, but you know the saying, The poor drink wather and the rich sip tay. After Grosse Isle it is fine. What I have seen here has shown me the necessity of moving the quarantine to the flats below Quebec. If the sick were moved from Grosse Isle to near the city they would get all the supplies and service needed. I expect to return to Quebec in a day or so, and before leaving here hope to get the bishop to wait on the premier, to ask that the new fever sheds be placed on the outskirts of Quebec. I hear from the emigrants as they arrive of you, and as they speak they bless you. I hope to see you soon.

YOUR OLD PRECEPTOR.

12. — A ship that came in from Sligo has many of my old neighbors. They say after we left, the agents gave out that all who refused to emigrate would have the relief taken from them, which was all they had to keep life in them until next crop. The more that went, the more eager were those left behind to go. At the rate they are coming, Lord Palmerston will have his land clear of people by Michaelmas, and be able to lease it to Scotch cow-feeders. Most of the emigrants come expecting free land from the Canadian government and a pound a-head from the agents of their landlords at Quebec. Oh, the deceivers, to cheat these poor people with lies!

16. — Bridget is down with the fever, just when Ellen was recovering and likely to be able soon to leave with her sister for uncle's farm in Huntingdon. It seems as if exposure, if long enough continued, is sure to induce the disease. Doctor Douglas says few can withstand breathing the air of the sheds for a fortnight without being laid down. I expect my turn will come yet. A company of soldiers has arrived to act as a guard over the camp of what is called the healthy emigrants to keep them from going near the fever sheds. It is of a piece with everything else. The fever is in the camp as well as in the sheds. Had they sent a few hundred boards from Quebec to floor the tents, it would have been more sensible than to supply a guard. The weather is still wet, and the ground under the tents is soaking, yet the people have nowhere else to lie. I was telling the head of the Church of England clergymen, Doctor Mountain, of what my friend had said about quarantine being moved near the city. He agreed it ought to be done, although the people of Quebec would resist. The cellar of the marine hospital having become full to overflowing with emigrants, workmen came three days ago to erect sheds on the hospital grounds. The people of St. Rochs assembled, scattered the lumber, and drove away the workmen. Lamenting the lack of nurses, he told me it was partly due to the government's not offering sufficient wages. Placards on the Quebec streets asking for nurses at 60 cents a day met with no response. Doctors were offered only $3.50 a day. A dollar a day for nurses and $5 for doctors would get a supply, but the authorities would not consent. I can believe any-

thing of them. They will not send us a supply of straw, even, and many of the sick are lying without anything below them ...

26. — The weather has been steaming hot for a week, with heavy showers, and fog at night, making our situation worse and spreading infection. There is a stench both in and out of doors. Ships continue to come in and the number of sick to grow; a doctor told me there are over 2000. The nurses, both men and women, that come from Quebec, are a bad lot. They neglect their duties, smuggle in drink to those of the sick who can pay for it, and rob the dying. On this lone island, where everything else is so scarce, whisky can be got by whoever wants it. The greed of gain overcomes the fear of infection, and it is smuggled in by small boats from Quebec. Last night there was an uproar in the camp of the healthy, caused by drunkenness. The military guard is a hurt to the emigrants. Like soldiers everywhere, they have neither morals nor decency. Bridget grows worse and poor Ellen is making a bad recovery, for she exhausts her strength by trying to nurse her sister. Monaghan and Stanhope talk by the hour, and their converse has put new heart in them. Hope is better than medicine. Indeed, I have seen scores die from despondency or indifference to life, who, to all appearance, ought to have recovered ...

29. — Father Moylan has got back for a few days. There is need for more like him, but Irish priests are few in this part of Canada, and our people want them alone. The ships now arriving report larger mortality than those that came in May. This is due to the heat. The condition of the holds of the ships that come in is unspeakably revolting. Several buried over a hundred in the ocean, equal to a fifth of the number of their passengers.

July 2. — Father Moylan wanted me to go to Montreal as a witness before a committee of enquiry appointed by the legislature. I have no heart to leave here, and I told him if they would not believe him they would not believe me. There is no improvement in caring for the sick; the callousness of the Canadian government to the sufferings of God's poor on this island I cannot understand. The weather is not settled, and beyond the sun being scorchingly hot at midday is as fine as could be wished.

9th. — This evening I took a walk to the far side of the island and enjoyed the solitude and the peace of nature. Sitting on the beach, I watched the sun sink behind the hills. I have a feeling that my own sun will soon disappear, for I am sad and disheartened beyond all my experience. Dr. Fenwick told me the other day I should leave; that I needed a change. I cannot, indeed I will not, for I cherish the secret wish to die where my Aileen left me. A ship has arrived with 31 dead on board; she lost over a fourth of those who embarked on her at Liverpool. Another out of 470 emigrants, dropped 150 into the Atlantic. Sure, tragedies like these ought to direct the eyes of the civilized world to what is happening. My heart is broken at the sight of thousands of my own dear people, men, women, and little children, dying for lack of a crust on Canada's shore.

14. — I think the end has come. Tonight my head throbs and my bones are sore. Bridget, after hovering a long while between life and death, sank to rest this morning, and is buried. Ellen leaves by tomorrow's steamer, and will be in Huntingdon in a few days. I gave her a message to uncle. My life has been a failure. May God have pity on me and on my poor people. Oh, that Aileen were here; that I felt her hand on my racked forehead.

B) Three Years in Canada, 1829
John Mactaggart

Travellers in general have set their faces against poor people emigrating to Canada. There is nothing in which I am more willing to coincide in opinion with them than this. Food is not to be had there merely for the eating; it requires considerable exertion to make a living, as it does in almost every other place. Neither is employment readily obtained; a common labourer can find nothing to do for almost six months in the year, until he has learned how to wield the hatchet. He may then find employment in the woods; but it takes an Irishman a long time to learn the art of the hatchet, if he has been used chiefly to spade and shovel work, which is quite a different kind of occupation. When he first commences hewing down trees, he often hews them down upon himself, and gets maimed, or killed; and if he attempts squaring, he cuts and abuses his feet in a shameful manner. The common people of Ireland seem to me to be awkward and unhandy. What they have been used to they can do very well; but when put out of their old track, it is almost impossible to teach them any thing. A Glasgow weaver, although not bred to spade and pick-axe, as they are, makes a much better settler, can build a neat little house for his family, and learn to chop with great celerity, so that in a short time nobody could suppose that he had been bred amongst bobbins and shuttles.

It is a singular fact, too, with the Irish, that if they can get a mud-cabin, they will never think of building one of wood. At By-town, on the Ottawa, they burrow into the sand-hills; smoke is seen to issue out of holes which are opened to answer the purpose of chimneys. Here families contrive to pig together worse even than in Ireland; and when any rows or such like things are going on, the women are seen to pop their carroty polls out of the humble doors, so dirty, sooty, smoke-dried, and ugly, that really one cannot but be disgusted; and do what we will for their benefit, we can obtain no alteration. If you build for them large and comfortable houses, as was done at the place above-mentioned, so that they might become useful labourers on the public works, still they keep as decidedly filthy as before. You cannot get the low Irish to wash their faces, even were you to lay before them ewers of crystal water and scented soap: you cannot get them to dress decently, although you supply them with ready-made clothes; they will smoke, drink, eat murphies, brawl, box, and set the house on fire about their ears, even though you had a sentinel standing over with fixed gun and bayonet to prevent them.

Living then in such a manner, what must the consequence be in a climate such as Canada? It is bad in Ireland, but there it is worse. They absolutely die by the dozens, not of hunger, but of disease. They will not provide in summer against the inclemencies of winter. Blankets and stockings they will not purchase; so the frost bites them in all quarters, dirt gets into the putrid sores, and surgical aid is not called in by them, until matters get into the last stage. In summer, again, the intolerable heat, and the disregard they pay to their health, by living as they do, and drinking swamp waters, if there be none nearer their habitations, instead of spring or river water, bring on malignant fevers of all kinds ...

Emigration of the poor may probably answer a good end, as lessening the dense population of Ireland; but it certainly will never do well for Canada, unless some other methods be devised than those now observed. It may perhaps be argued, that they are necessary as labourers at public works; I would say, no such thing. If I had any work to perform in Canada of my own, I would not employ any Irish, were it not for mere charity. The native French Canadians are much better labourers, as they understand the nature of the country, can bear the extremes of the climate much better, keep strong and healthy, and always do their work in a masterly and peaceable manner; whereas the Irish are always growling and quarrelling, and never contented with their wages ...

Are they any better than if they had remained in Ireland? It is true that servants are required, and many would be very willing to employ a great number, but they are unable to pay them adequately for their labour; as agricultural produce will either not admit of being raised beyond what will support the family, or the chance of a crop, and expense of transport to market, deter them from making the attempt. Poor ignorant people too, when they arrive in such colonies, are apt to feel themselves considerably elevated, and will not condescend to toil for mere bread until reduced to the last stage of poverty. Besides, as they have land offered to them for a trifle, the idea of being proprietors has a most intoxicating effect. Under this influence, I have seen them hurrying into the woods with a very indifferent hatchet, a small pack on their back, followed by a way-worn female and her children, there to live for a time on air, (and if that rise out of the swamps, none of the best either) — we have met them again crawling out, — and where is the heart that would not melt at the sight — some of the children, most likely, dead, and the rest bit and blindfolded by musquitoes!

C)   Report of the Roman Catholic Chaplain of the Provincial Penitentiary, January 24, 1853

Persons may be startled at seeing that the great majority of the Catholic convicts are either Irish or of Irish extraction, whereas the Irish Catholics do not form much over one-fourth of the whole Catholic population of Canada; but this ought only to surprise a very superficial observer, and should lead no one to conclude that there is any more natural vicious disposition in the Irish character, than in that of any other people; for virtue, honesty, and absence from crime, the Irish farmers in this Country can bear a very fair comparison with either the Scotch or English, and Irish women are admitted on all hands, to be more virtuous than those of any other nation. A great allowance ought to be made for the early education and prejudices of the Irish; for centuries back they have been a persecuted and trodden down people in the land of their nativity; their forefathers have been plundered of their property, and until very late it was a capital crime for an Irish Catholic to teach even an Elementary School — under such rule, ignorance and poverty were the only inheritance to the Irish to hand down to their posterity, with this was mixed a pretty fair dose of hatred towards their persecutors. Place any nation in the world in the same position in which the Irish had to live for the last three hundred years, and I am convinced that after such an ordeal, it would not be half so virtuous as the Irish are; persons must not also judge of the Irish character from that of many of those we see in this Country, nor from the lying accounts with which the English Press generally teem. The great majority of the Irish who have selected Canada for the land of their adoption, arrive pennyless in it; they must for many a year depend upon employment in the Public Works, to obtain the means of keeping body and soul together; men of every description and disposition congregated together in large numbers have never been the best school of morality, and they must be more than men, if this has not a most deteriorating effect upon their conduct. Few of those employed in the mines of California are Irish, and yet, if we believe the daily accounts we receive from that country, there are more crimes committed in it in one week than there is in this country for years. I will be told that in this free Country, the Irish enjoy the same advantages as those of every other country, but generally speaking this is not the case. Few of the German settlers arrive in this country without being the possessors of some hundred dollars or pounds; large numbers of them, the moment they make up their minds to emigrate to Canada or the United States, send out Agents to procure large tracts of land, where numbers from the same locality can settle together. On their arrival they know where to direct their course, and they have means not only to pay for the land, but also to stock it, and support their families for two or three years. The first European settlers after the Conquest, received large tracts of land gratis, which enabled them to provide for the future settlement of their children and grand children; among these there were few or no Irish. The first Irish emigrants who came to Canada, were those brought out by the late Mr. Peter Robinson, and every one knows that, instead of being a proper selection, they were the very worst characters, of whom the people of the south of Ireland wanted to rid themselves. With all the advantages imaginable, persons of this description could not succeed; but the misfortune was, that from their idle and dissipated habits, they were the cause of creating very unfavorable prejudices against the whole Irish Nation; this prejudice was really carried so far, that I have known a certain Judge for whom the knowledge of one being an Irishman, and particularly an Irish Roman Catholic, was a sufficient evidence to obtain conviction ...

D) "Protestant Organization", August 27, 1847
The Loyalist, Saint John, New Brunswick

Let us now consider the present state of this Province, with the prospects ahead ... Emigrants who annually land upon our shores are (as we before observed) generally of the very lowest class. Perhaps after all it is well that they are so; for if they were an intelligent, quiet, orderly people, and still cherishing those hostile feelings which we have noticed, there is little doubt but the Protestant population would take them by the hand, and treat them with the greatest cordiality, and not awake to their danger until they found their liberties attacked, or a rebel boat in arms against British sovereignty. But unfortunately for our present peace — *fortunately* we hope for our future prosperity — these emigrants are the most inveterate scoundrels in creation, and no sooner obtain a footing among us than they fall to their old trade of breaking heads. In the South of Ireland, where there are scarcely any Protestants, they enjoy this national pastime by trying the strength of each other's skull; but here they find plenty of Sassenachs to practice upon, and the whole country is disturbed ...

This riotous and murderous conduct excited considerable attention some five years since, and sensible men began to inquire what was to be done to put a stop to it. "Get up a Protestant Conservative Association," says one. It was tried, and failed. "We have a remedy," said the man of Ulster, "one which has been tried in the North of Ireland, and proved;" and they immediately established some Orange Lodges. Many natives of this Province who, if not really alarmed at the progress of events, did not think it consistent with the character of Britons, who love their freedom, thus to be insulted, and trampled upon by a horde of ignorant and ragged savages, and that too in the land of their birth, joined heart and hand with the Irish Protestants, and the Orange Society has ever since been spreading and gaining strength in every part of the Province.

It becomes us now to look at this Society calmly, without prejudice for or against, and consider first the necessity for its organization, and the objections usually urged against it. The necessity, in our opinion, for Protestant organization in this Province, arose not more from the many murderous attacks committed upon quiet and unoffending Protestants, by Catholic ruffians, than from the dreary prospect which the future presented. The facts were these — several thousands of emigrants were annually landing upon our shores; they were clearly all Catholics, nearly all ignorant and bigoted, nearly all paupers, many of them depraved, and many became chargeable to the parochial authorities. The advent of so many emigrants of this order was a serious tax upon the inhabitants of the sea-ports; many of them got what they could from the poor overseers, and then betook themselves to the United States; others found their way into the interior, where for want of better men (we do not mean physically, for many of them are sturdy rogues) they were employed, a few in agricultural pursuits, and more in lumbering; those who were employed by agriculturists generally behaved pretty well, as they were thinly scattered over Protestant settlements and it is only when they herd together that they are so very turbulent and arrogant. Those who were engaged lumbering, took occasion every time they left the woods to get drunk, quarrel, fight, riot, cheat, smash windows, and break heads. But besides these, there were numerous herds of them located in York Point and Portland; these were "your humble servants" during the day while the backsaws were in their hands, but if they saw you by night they broke your head; and lately they had grown bold enough to assemble in force by daylight upon particular occasions, riot and murder, and dispute the possession of the public streets with the authorities! This, surely, was a state of society calling for immediate preventive measures, and if the authorities were either too weak, too indolent, or too much frightened, to suppress and punish the disorderlies of the peace, all lovers of order were at least justified in organizing.

Five years, however, have elapsed, and although the rioters have in several instances been checked — when they attacked the Hibernian Hotel; when they attacked a Protestant house in Portland, and recently at Woodstock, for instance — still they rally again and again, and more effectual measures for their suppression seemed absolutely necessary.

But the *future* (unless a remedy be soon applied) appears the most alarming. We have no statistics by which we can form anything like a correct estimate of the number of Irish Catholics in this Province, but will suppose these to be one fourth of the population. But if they continue pouring their thousands upon us from Ireland every year, they must gain rapidly in proportion, and not many years will elapse before they will form a majority! Should that be the case what have we to expect but murder, rapine, and anarchy, without any chance of redress? Our Legislature would then be overawed by letters from the notorious Captain Reck; mob law would usurp the functions of our Courts; and our elections would be conducted under the surveillance of a thicket of Irish Shillèlahs! Mercy on the Protestant minority who might then dare to plead their rights, or cross the path of the bigots! ... Let us ask, then — with this prospect in view — should not Protestants be united? Should they not organize?

Perhaps it may be urged that Government should protect us, keep the peace, and punish all offenders. But will Government do it? It is possible for Government (or municipal authorities) to organize a strong police force, and station them in the disturbed districts, but it is expensive. It might (and we think should) be adopted for the preservation of peace in St. John and Portland, but it could scarcely be carried out elsewhere. But even then it would prove much less efficacious than a general Protestant organization. Let the miscreants who disturb the peace of this Province, (where we believe there is not a single Protestant but ardently desires peace and good order) but know that the entire Protestant population have become so thoroughly disgusted with their misdeeds, (as, happily, is now the case in the County of Carleton) and they will shrink from a repetition of them, lest they draw down upon their heads the vengeance of an insulted and outraged community. Again, we have seen Magistrates and Crown Officers shrink from a proper discharge of their duties, apprehensive, no doubt, of the vengeance of the lawless hordes ...

Again, what remedy have we for the grim looking future? Government it is true, may encourage emigration, or discourage it; but we can scarcely ask or expect our local Government to adopt the latter course, while there are so many millions of acres of the public lands unsettled, and while it is so obviously the interest of Government, in a financial and commercial point of view, that the population should increase. Nor would Government, were it so disposed, pass any discriminating regulations, or restrictions, on emigration; it could not impose a tax, or "head-money" upon Catholics, and allow Protestants to enter free, — it could not wink at free grants of lands to the latter, and prohibit the sale of them to the former. Something, perhaps, Government could and should do, is establish agencies in the rural districts of England, Scotland and the North of Ireland, and thus induce a healthy ... population ...

But with our present prospects in view, as we have described them, it is by the Protestants, as an organized body, acting under one and the same impulse, and by them alone, that the dire calamity which threatens us can be averted. If they wish to save the country it is high time for them to adopt precautionary measures. Let them discourage by every means in their power a pauper Catholic emigration. Let the Legislature be compelled to pass a law forbidding the Captains of vessels from landing an emigrant upon our shores, unless he has a certain amount of capital, or can give bonds that he will not become chargeable to our authorities for a certain period; let this law be made known in Ireland; and by agents, and through the public press of that country, let it be made known that the Protestants of New Brunswick will neither harbour nor employ a Roman Catholic. At the same time let a fund be raised, by voluntary contribution, to assist able-bodied Protestants to emigrate, and let every encouragement be held out to them on their arrival. These are the only measures which can prevent New Brunswick from becoming a Catholic Province, and they must be adopted soon, or it will be too late; and these measures can only be carried into effect by Protestant Organization ...

[W]e will briefly notice the objections usually urgent against Orangeism. These are as follows: — first, that it is a *secret* society; secondly, that it stirs up strife entirely by exciting the Roman Catholics; and thirdly, that it is confined to the middle and lower orders of Protestants, and therefore is not *respectable*. Before we sweep away those silly objections, let us first premise that we joined the Orange Society several years since, because we perceived there was a necessity for Protestant organization, and because a Protestant Society of which we were previously a member, was broken up. We are not particularly wedded to the Orange Institution; any other Protestant association, — provided its objects were as laudable, its rules as good, and it possessed the same inherent elements of vitality — would be equally welcome to us. But the secrecy complained of is the very thing which ensures its life. Look at the history of Societies in general ... Men combine in the excitement of the moment, the excitement over they become careless, and the combination loses its vitality. But in the Orange society men enter; and while the act is voluntary, they are aware that they are taking a step which can never be resigned; they receive symbols which they can never divulge to the world; they are received into a brotherhood to which they are bound by the most solemn obligations; they are wedded to Protestantism (in the purest sense of the word) for life. It is this which accounts for its extraordinary vitality and adhesiveness; it is this which has defied every attempt of the enemies of Protestantism to crush it; it is this which is causing it to spread far and wide throughout the British dominions. It is this which will one day be found the main pillar of the empire, as it will be the means of perpetuating British rule in these colonies, and what is there secret about it? Nothing but the signs and passwords by which the members know each other, and which were instructed chiefly for a benevolent purpose, and such of the business proceedings as the Society may deem it prudent to keep among themselves, — generally of no importance whatever to the public.

That Orangeism may possibly excite a feeling of indignity in Roman Catholics we will not deny; but it is because it is a Society which keeps watch upon their actions, and because they are conscious their actions will not bear a scrutiny. Orangeism is not bigoted; neither is it intolerant; neither is it disorderly; and if Roman Catholics were neither of the three, they and Orangemen might go hand in hand together. But this excuse is of no weight. If there is any necessity for Protestant organization, the Society to which we attach ourselves may as well be this as any other, for there never was a Protestant Society in existence that did not draw down the ire of Roman Catholics ...

Already do we perceive a stir in the ranks of our aristocracy. Slow to move, they are at length convinced that organization is necessary. In the Counties of York and Carleton many new lodges have recently been installed, and the Protestant population — with very few exceptions — are united together as one man ...

15

"Equal in Every Respect"

Education for Natives, Blacks, and Women

DOCUMENTS

A) Report on the Affairs of Indians in Canada
Journal of the Legislative Assembly of the Province of Canada (1847), App. T.

B) "The Coloured People and the Common Schools"
The Leader, December 12, 1862

C) "A Reply from the Black Community"
Globe, January 3, 1863

D) Address to Parents on the Education of Girls, Toronto, 1865
Mrs. Holiwell, Elm House School for the Education of Young Ladies

E) Report of the Grammar School Inspector for 1865
George Paxton Young

The modern teaching profession is a product of the nineteenth and twentieth centuries. Before then, except for limited efforts by the Catholic church in New France, education, such as it was, occurred in the home. Standards varied wildly as parents taught their children what they knew or what they thought important. Formally educated parents — the minority — consequently offered their children far more training than the majority of illiterate or semi-literate families. This, of course, helped perpetuate Canada's clearly defined class structure. Private schools and tutors did exist for the wealthy, but the idea of a free, universal, publicly funded, and compulsory education system caught on slowly in an age of *laissez-faire* individualism. Public education finally gained some credibility after a dubious citizenry came to believe that it might cure society's growing ills of crime, poverty, vagrancy, disrespect for authority, secularization, and the potential for class warfare. Thus the idea of "public institutions" and "universal education" gained popularity.

But who should learn what and how? Could Black children master the same materials as whites? Should they? Could Native youths? Surely classrooms should not integrate different races. Where did religion fit? And what about girls? Should they study academic subjects, be restricted to traditional domestic arts, or both? Girls and boys must assuredly learn in segregated environments, must they not? "Universality" meant different things to different people, and a hornet's nest of debate burst once British North America cleared the hurdle of at least offering public education. In the end, separate schools with different curricula ruled the day.

Native education went back to the early days of New France and Marie de l'Incarnation — with universally dismal results. French authorities believed that education and literacy were the cornerstones of conversion, but their efforts were too ethnocentric to succeed. The military controlled Native affairs under British rule, and no formal policy on education existed until civil authorities took over in 1830. Administrators believed that semi-nomadic aboriginal people stood in the way of sedentary European agricultural settlement, but that could change if Natives became farmers. Thus the drift of much nineteenth-century Indian education was toward assimilation and preparing indigenous people for manual labour and farming. The best way to achieve this, so the church believed, was through residential schools that removed Indian children from their parents' cultural influence.

Many Natives, particularly the Ojibwa, supported this policy and hammered out an agreement in the mid-1840s between themselves, the churches, and government. They believed that the next generation must acquire European skills to survive the rapidly changing world. Some First Nations people sought education for their children as far back as the 1820s, and by 1827 complained that many American Natives received state schooling whereas British North American indigenous people did not. The sticking point usually remained the thorny question of religion and whether to allow it into the classroom. Ojibwa Christians like Reverend Peter Jones pushed the idea of European education as the will of God, and acted as a strong catalyst for social and religious change among his people. He supported residential schools, too, though he believed Natives must run them — but this did not occur.

Native leaders eventually acquiesced by July 1846, and accepted the American idea of manual schools for their children. The concept called for self-sufficient communities that graduated skilled Natives capable of taking their places in mainstream society. Here, students attended regular classes during the morning and spent the afternoon learning manual skills that simultaneously fed them and heated their institution. Many bands supported the schools and some even underwrote costs, but what were the results? An 1856 report concluded that the project lacked universal support, and that graduates fell far short of the ideal. Perhaps blame lay with the uncomprehending, largely unsympathetic, and insensitive European missionaries running the institutions.

Nova Scotian Black children attended segregated schools after the courts decided it was preferable to isolate them. That also occurred in Canada West where an 1849 statute authorized municipal governments to establish publicly funded separate Black schools. Any five Black families in a neighbourhood could petition and receive a grant, but they could not attend white schools. The legal system upheld this by excluding all Blacks from Chatham's public schools in 1861.

The segregation issue split the Black community. Many leaders wanted separate schools because their people did not understand the British curriculum and fugitive slaves often could not perform the work required by the Education Department. These pro-segregationists constituted a minority, however, and most Blacks resented their obvious second-class status. They challenged it in Hamilton, citing the inequity of paying municipal taxes when local authorities barred their children from public schools yet refused to provide alternatives. A legal victory at Simcoe in 1855 gained them the right to attend common schools, but only if no separate institution already existed. At least Black community leaders received promises of public funding, but the level of funding never adequately addressed the chronic shortage of competent teachers and the visibly inferior facilities. And what of those attending integrated schools? Prejudice gained momentum in the 1850s, and Black children had to sit on separate benches. Ontario's separate Black schools did not begin to disappear until 1910. The last one closed in 1965.

The Maritime situation both paralleled and differed from Canada West. New Brunswick and Prince Edward Island's small Black community generally did not face segregationist legislation nor separate schools. Blacks and whites apparently mixed quite readily, both in and outside school, but only in areas with few visible minorities. Local white pressure in Fredericton and Saint John (towns with sizable Black populations) denied spaces to Black children, thereby forcing their parents to choose between no school or opening their own. Legislated segregation in Nova Scotia ceased in 1963.

For girls of every class, education in the eighteenth and nineteenth centuries revolved around domestic training. Ordinary girls, so the stereotype went, were destined to become women charged with keeping home and hearth. Wealthy young ladies later managed household servants and the vital art of entertaining. Thus they learned everything from candle making to soap production, sewing, and culinary arts. All girls also usually learned the rudiments of reading, writing, and arithmetic, at least those whose parents could teach them.

Such limited training seemed inadequate in an increasingly sophisticated world that now perceived education as a panacea for all manner of social decay. This led to the establishment of a number of private girls schools where young ladies of characters, whose parents could afford to pay, at least gained some exposure to formal education. It was, however, not enough for many social critics who called for much wider access to a broad curriculum. But could girls attend classes with boys? Most communities in this period were too poor to provide separate schools for each gender, and girls, by default not choice, attended common public schools. Authorities kept the boys at bay by separating them to one side of the classroom or, in more extreme cases, teaching girls in the summer, boys in winter.

Many social critics and thinkers in the 1860s, and later, believed in separate spheres for men and women. Training for similar tasks, they argued, was unnatural when the sexes so obviously existed to perform different roles. Co-education did not sit well with this influential group. Concerns were also raised about the moral and physical dangers of close proximity between the sexes during adolescence, a time of effervescing hormones. Coeducation in the lower grades might be accepted, but not at high school (then called the grammar school).

The essence of the argument followed other dilemmas of the day. Grammar schools fed into the universities, for which females were supposedly not suited. Women should therefore not frequent either, or at least the public purse should not fund their presence. Opponents of this attitude demanded that women be allowed to prepare for the professions at public expense if they so desired. In the meantime and beyond much of the hubbub, wealthy young ladies attended their fashionable and exclusive private girls' grammar schools where they learned everything from etiquette to Euclid, thus neatly straddling the line dividing home from the outside world. Much like the issue over Blacks in mainstream schools, local school board trustees won the right to decide in the end. Some chose carefully controlled coeducation with separate entrances, playgrounds, recess and dismissal times and, of course, distinct seating arrangements in the classroom.

George Paxton Young (1818–1889) was a life-long bachelor who overcame his natural shyness to become an instrumental figure in the development of education policy in Canada West. Graduating with a master's degree in divinity from the University of Edinburgh, he immigrated to Canada West in the late 1840s to become minister of Knox Church, Hamilton. He eventually became Canada West's first school inspector, in which capacity he toured the colony, visited every school, examined teachers' and students' progress, and wrote numerous critical reports on the grammar school system. He later became professor of moral philosophy at Knox College, and chair of metaphysics and ethics at University College, Toronto. The private Paxton preferred the company of books to people, but in public he metamorphosed into a dynamic and charismatic teacher who became a legend among his students.

A) Report on the Affairs of Indians in Canada
Journal of the Legislative Assembly of the Province of Canada (1847), App. T.

It has been shown that, up to a recent period, the policy of the Government towards this race was directed rather to securing their services in time of war, than to reclaiming them from barbarism, and encouraging them in the adoption of the habits and arts of civilization. With this view, they were for many years placed under the superintendence of the military authorities in the Province.

Since 1830, a more enlightened policy has been pursued, under instructions of the Secretary of State, and much has been done in Upper Canada, both by the Government and various religious bodies, to promote their civilization, but the system, although improved, has had a tendency to keep the Indians in a state of isolation and tutelage, and materially to retard their progress.

The inquiries of your Commissioners, and their consideration of the numerous opinions submitted to them, have led them to the conclusion, that the true and only practicable policy of the Government, with reference to their interests, both of the Indians and the community at large, is to endeavour, gradually, to raise the Tribes within the British Territory to the level of their white neighbours; to prepare them to undertake the offices and duties of citizens; and, by degrees, to abolish the necessity for its farther interference in their affairs.

Experience has shown that Indians can no longer lead a wild and roving life, in the midst of a numerous and rapidly increasing white population. Their hunting grounds are broken up by settlements; the game is
exhausted; their resources as hunters and trappers are cut off; want and disease spread rapidly among them, and gradually reduce their numbers. To
escape these consequences, no choice is left, but to remove beyond the pale
of civilization, or to settle and cultivate the land for a livelihood. From this
cause, and under the influence of the Missionaries, few Indians remain unsettled in the inhabited parts of Canada.

But the settled and partially civilized Indians, when left to themselves,
become exposed to a new class of evils. They hold large blocks of lands,
generally of the most valuable description, which they can neither occupy
nor protect against the encroachments of white squatters, with whom, in
the vain attempt to guard their lands, they are brought into a state of constant hostility and collision. As they are exempt from any obligation to make
or maintain roads through their lands, these reserves are serious obstacles to
the settlement and improvement of the surrounding country, and their possessors become objects of jealousy and dislike to their neighbours; of these
the more unprincipled are always on the alert, to take advantage of the weakness and ignorance of the Indians, and of their partiality for spirits, in order
to plunder them of their improvements and other property; habits of intoxication are thus introduced and encouraged, destitution ensues, and general demoralization is the speedy consequence.

Against these latter evils, Christianity and religious instruction have been
found both a prevention and a remedy. The several experiments which have
been made with zeal, and followed up with perseverance, have proved eminently successful. The Indians have generally evinced much readiness to
embrace the Christian religion, and to receive instruction.

But, in order to enable them to compete with the whites, and to take
their position among them as fellow-citizens, some time and more comprehensive and active measurements are necessary. Sir Francis Head despaired
of every being able to effect this object, and, therefore, he proposed to remove them to a distance, and to fortify them, as much as possible, against
all communications with the whites. The evidence, also, which your Commissioners have received on this point, varies much, although they conceive
that the isolation of the Indian Tribes has generally been recommended, on
account of its convenience to the whites, and its supposed temporary advantage to the Indians, rather than from any enlarged or philanthropic views

for the ultimate benefit of the latter. But all Sir F. Head's attempts to induce the Indians to abandon their old settlements, failed, and every similar attempt is likely to fail. The Indians have usually a strong veneration and affection for their old haunts, and consider it a disgrace to abandon the bones of their ancestors, while the faith of the Crown, and every principle of justice, are opposed to their compulsory removal.

Experience has also taught that, while they remain among whites, it is impossible to prevent the closest communication between them. Laws have been passed to prevent whites from settling in their villages, to protect them from squatters, to restrain the sale of liquors among them, but all these enactments have been disregarded or evaded, and if it were possible for the Government to devise a system of separation, the Indians would be the first to break through it.

There is, therefore, but the one course left, which has been pointed out — to endeavour to raise them to the level of the whites. To this there appears to be no insurmountable impediment. It is the universal testimony, that there is nothing in the character of the Indian race which is opposed to such a result. They possess all the higher attributes of the mind; their perceptions of religion and their sense of moral obligations are just; their imagination is fertile; their aptitude for instruction, and their powers for imitation are great; neither are they wanting in a desire to improve their condition; they are sensible of the superiority of the whites, and of the disadvantages under which they themselves labour, from their want of knowledge, and the converted Indians are generally very anxious for the education of their children. Many are acting as Missionaries and Interpreters among their brethren in Canada and the Territories of the Hudson's Bay Company, with credit to themselves, and infinite advantages to those under their charge. Most, if not all those who have received a good education, are equal, in every respect, to their white associates; some lads of the Upper Canada College have distinguished themselves highly. Among the Chiefs are many intelligent, well conducted, religious men, quite competent to manage their own affairs, and very shrewd in the protection of their own interests.

The chief obstacles to the advancement of the race are, their want of self-dependence, and their habits of indolence, which have been fostered, if not created, by the past policy of the Government; their ignorance or imperfect knowledge of the language, customs, and mode of traffic of the whites; and that feebleness of the reasoning powers, which is the necessary consequences of the entire absence of mental cultivation. None of these difficulties appear

insuperable, and your Commissioners are of opinion, that all the measures of
the Government should be directed to their removal, and to the development
of those natural capacities which the Indian character exhibits. This may be a
difficult task, as regards the majority of the adults, whose habits have been
formed, with whom the time for instruction is passed, and who have become
familiarized with their condition, but with the youth it will be otherwise.

They are represented to be very apt in acquiring knowledge, and the
schools which have been established among them upon an efficient footing,
have proved very successful. It is by their education mainly that your Commissioners look to the future elevation of the Indian race; but much may
yet be done with a large portion of the adults, by instruction and encouragement. Their various recommendations will consequently have reference
to these main objects.

GENERAL RECOMMENDATIONS

1. That as long as the Indian Tribes continue to require the special protection and guidance of the Government, they should remain under
   the immediate control of the Representative of the Crown within the
   Province and not under that of the Provincial Authorities ...
2. That measures should be adopted to introduce and confirm Christianity among all the Indians within the Province, and to establish them
   in Settlements.
3. That the efforts of the Government should be directed to educating
   the young, and to weaning those advanced in life from their feelings
   and habits of dependence.
4. That, for this purpose, Schools should be established, and Missionaries and Teachers be supported at each Settlement, and that their
   efficiency should be carefully watched over.
5. That in addition to Common Schools, as many Manual Labour or
   Industrial Schools, should be established, as the funds applicable to
   such a purpose will admit.

Your Commissioners are satisfied, that if in England more elementary
instruction in reading and writing be found ineffectual to form the minds
and establish the character of the youth of the nation, the same difficulty
presents itself, with much greater force, in dealing with the Indian youth.
Their education must consist not merely of the training of the mind, but of
a weaning from the habits and feelings of their ancestors, and the acquirements

of the language, arts and customs of civilized life. Besides the ordinary routine of a primary School, the young men should be instructed in husbandry, gardening, the management of stock, and simple mechanical trades; the girls in domestic economy, the charge of a household and dairy, the use of the needle, &c; and both sexes should be familiarized with the mode of transacting business among the whites. It is by means of Industrial or Manual Labour Schools, in which the above branches of instruction are taught, that a material and extensive change among the Indians of the rising generations may be hoped for ...

The Chief Superintendent of Indian Affairs: "I am of opinion that a general Education should be provided for the Indian youths, both male and female, on a uniform system, something similar to the New England Company's Establishment. The children should reside at the Establishment, and be placed under the constant supervision of a competent and attached Tutor, who should pay to their habits the same attention as to their minds. The course of Education should consist of reading, writing, and arithmetic, and religious instruction under the superintendence of the Minister of the church to which they belong; they should also be instructed in such mechanical arts as they display an aptitude to acquire, and in the theory and practice of husbandry; the more talented should be encouraged, by a more liberal education, to enter into Holy Orders, and become the resident Ministers among their Tribe.

"The girls, besides a similar elementary Education, should be instructed in such useful acquirements as are possessed by white people of the inferior class. The proceeds of their labours, as well as of the boys, in the mechanical arts, might be profitably disposed of in the neighbouring towns and surrounding country. This constant employment of their intellectual and bodily faculties, will alone reserve the Indians from extinction, and elevate their condition" ...

The Reverend Peter Jones: "From the knowledge I have of the Indian character, and from personal observation I have come to the conclusion, that the system of education adopted in our Common Schools has been too inefficient. The children attend these Schools from the houses of their parents, a number of whom are good, pious Christians, but who, nevertheless, retain many of their old habits; consequently, the good instruction the children receive at the School is, in a great measure, neutralized at home.

"It is a notorious fact, that the parents in general exercise little or no control over their children, allowing them to do as they please. Being thus left to follow their own wills, they too frequently wander about the woods with their bows and arrows, or accompany their parents in their hunting excursions.

"Another evil arises from their not being trained to habits of industry whilst attending the Schools, so that by the time they leave they are greatly averse to work, and naturally adopt the same mode of life as their parents.

"Under these circumstances, I am very anxious to see Manual Labour Schools established amongst our people, that the children may be properly trained and educated to habits of industry and usefulness.

"I see nothing to hinder the entire success of such a plan, and, as the School in the Missouri country is answering the most sanguine expectations of its promoters, we may safely conclude, that the same success would attend the like operations amongst our Indians.

"I am happy to inform you, that all the Indians with whom I have conversed, highly approve of the project, and are very anxious to see such a School in immediate operation. They are ready and willing to give up their children to the entire control and management of the Teachers.

"I beg also to state, that, in my humble opinion, unless something be done in this way, the Indians will for ever remain in the half-civilized state, and continue to be a burden to the British Government and the Missionary Societies."

B) "The Coloured People and the Common Schools"
The Leader, December 12, 1862

The Board of School Trustees of the neighbouring city of London is the first to take up a subject which has attracted more or less attention in different parts of the Province — the mingling together of coloured and white children in the Common Schools. The Board has not acted hastily in the matter. The subject has been under consideration for several months; and it is only within the last few days that the board came to a final determination. Their report is one which does them credit. It goes over the whole question, suggests difficulties and meets objections in a way which shows that they have not acted in a hasty manner or an ungenerous spirit; but on the contrary, that they have brought a careful study and calm deliberation to bear upon the various points which came before them. As the subject is one of provincial importance, we shall state as briefly as possible the views taken by the Board, and the recommendations they make in their report.

Let it be premised that the number of colored children of school age in London is 96. Of those 50 attended school on an average during the past year, and as many as 80 attended at various times. It is upon such data as this that the Board had to work. They set out by stating that a feeling exists in the community that from climatic reasons or organic causes, there is a repugnance in the minds of the white population to a close or intimate relation between their children and those of colored parents. The children themselves sympathize in this feeling or prejudice, whichever one may wish to call it; and the result is not infrequently "a bandying of offensive epithets, embittered acrimonious feelings and juvenile quarrels. In these petty disputes the parents frequently take part, complaints are made, and will continue to be made by both parties, that their children have been insulted; and, by the colored parents, that theirs have been harshly and perhaps unjustly treated." The Board then touch upon another point, which they think a false delicacy should not prevent them from noticing; and this is, that during the summer months an "effluvium" arises from these children "which is highly offensive to many of the children, and still more so to many of the teachers." Then, there is naturally a want of sympathy between the colored children and the teachers. It is possible that the teachers endeavour to avoid the appearance of acting toward one scholar in a different manner from another; but there is nevertheless a want of sympathy, to use no harsher term, between the white teacher and the colored child, which the latter, with the natural shrewdness of its race, is not slow to perceive. This feeling of estrangement between teacher and scholar, the Board think cannot be the best means of elevating the Negro, as the jealousy called into play in childhood must result in mutual dislike in later years. "When educated apart they will not be educated for evil; they will not have some of the worst passions of the human heart called daily into play and thus strengthened by exercise; they will have no taunts and insults to remember; and when they enter life as men, they will be enabled to meet their white fellow-citizens without a single acrimonious feeling, arising from the recollections of wrongs suffered or injuries retaliated."

This is the whole case as offered by the Board: these the arguments which they give for recommending that a separate school for the colored children should be established in London. Difficulties connected with the legal construction of the statute appeared to them at first in the way of carrying out their recommendation, but on looking into the different cases on which judgments have been given in the courts, they came to the conclusion that there is nothing in the Statute to prevent their establishing a separate school for the colored population. This is not the most serious point, however. The questions of a social or organic nature which the Board have ventured to touch upon, and handled in such a practical manner are those which are most likely to provoke discussion. Will the ultra advocates of the public schools denounce the recommendation of the London Board as an innovation upon our common school system? Will the ultra philanthropists, the firm believers in the doctrine that all men are born free and equal, independent of color or of race, direct their bitter shafts against the guardians of education in London the less? And last, though, to use an old expression, not least, how will the colored people themselves view the discussion of these London school trustees? We shall see.

In the meantime we have a little hesitancy in expressing our own opinion. We see no single reason for questioning the course which has been taken by the London Board. Physiological questions and questions of race may be thrown aside for the nonce and this subject viewed in the practical light of everyday experience. In those parts of the Province where there is a large colored population the difficulties arising out of the admixture of children of black and white parents give rise very often to unpleasant bickerings and creates a strong feeling of hostility between the two sections of the population. In some westerly parts of the Province the black children are entirely excluded from the common schools; and it was only the other day that an intelligent colored woman from that section of the country was in this city soliciting aid for the education of her race. Perhaps some person will say this ought not to be so. Such an argument is fully met by the fact as it exists. There is no use in trying to turn a stream against its head; and there is as little use in endeavoring to educate white and black children in the same school room. Natural causes, if no other, are opposed to it; but there is besides, an inbred feeling of repugnance in the breast of almost every white person at hybridism, which must to some extent be the result of a commingling of the races. We say this with no hard feeling toward the black population in our midst. They have received shelter here, and are safe under the protection of that flag which treats all men alike, no matter what their color, all other things being equal. But when a forcible and practical objection presents itself to an indiscriminate mingling together of black and white children in the same school rooms, we are sure to see a repetition of what has occurred in parts of the country of Essex, in London and other places west. There is but one way of meeting this difficulty. The children of black men are entitled to the benefits of education as well as those of the whites; but it does not necessarily follow that they both should be taught together. The conclusion of the London Board appears to be the only just way in which to meet the difficulty. It is hard to believe that the colored people will object to this. They prefer distinctive churches for themselves rather than to assemble together in the same edifices with their white brethren. This is not unnatural if they consider their own self-respect, which, whether rightly or wrongly is sure to be more or less hurt when they thrust themselves into positions which are not agreeable to them. And why should they not desire to receive education under similar circumstances? They ought to value rather than spurn a concession to a feeling which is impossible to overcome or remove; and in this view it is to be hoped that the recommendation of the London Board of School Trustees will be carried out not only in that city, but in all other places where a similar difficulty arises.

C) "A Reply from the Black Community"
Globe, January 3, 1863

Sir, I noticed lately in the *Leader* an editorial headed, "The Colored People and the Common Schools," and must say of all the articles that have appeared in that sheet against the colored people, it is the most despicable and malicious. The article commences by stating what the School Trustees of London are doing to degrade the colored people of that city, but it is only a pretext still further to pander to the prejudices of the "mudsills." As to the action of the London Trustees, their course is certainly most singular, for while the Americans, who were the first to establish separate schools and other institutions for colored people, are emerging from the dark ages of their prejudices, the enlightened school trustees and teachers of London are making a retrograde movement, and are relapsing into the slough of "Negrophobia." As it is in all cases where men espouse a bad cause, these trustees and teachers are obliged to descend to sophistry to make out their case. The *Leader* says: "They set out by stating that a feeling exists in the community that, from climatic reasons or other organic causes, there is a repugnance in the minds of the white population to a close or intimate relation between their children and those of colored parents." Now, that there are persons in London who are so tainted with "Negrophobia" as to object to colored children, however decent, going to the same school that they send theirs to, I have no doubt; and that these same persons instill these same feelings into their children and that there are teachers base enough to permit their prejudices to prevent them from discharging their duties to their scholars on account of their color; but I cannot believe that the people of Canada will at the caprice of such sycophants deprive us of our educational privileges. They say also that the result of the children being educated together, is not unfrequently a bandying of offensive epithets, embittered acrimonious feelings, and juvenile quarrels. In these petty disputes the parents frequently take part, complaints are made, and will continue to be made by both parents, that their children have been insulted; and by the colored people, that theirs have been harshly treated. Well, such may be the state of things in London, but it is a little singular that in Toronto, where we have a much larger population, and one, too, I have no doubt, quite as intelligent and refined as in London, the colored and white children go to the same schools together, and we hear of no such complaints and bickerings here. The very reverse is the case. The best feelings are cultivated among the scholars themselves and between scholars and teachers ...

Numerous cases might be cited to prove, that here, in many instances, the strongest ties of friendship exist betwixt the scholars and between the teachers and colored scholars; and we would particularly invite the London trustees and teachers, to pay our schools a visit during the examination, and at times when prizes and certifications are given, and they will see colored children receive both amidst the plaudits of the white scholars, and the parents and friends who attend on those occasions. Then, again, say the trustees, "an effluvium arises, during the warm weather, that is disagreeable to both teachers and scholars." Well, as to the children, they must have been trained by their parents, like the bloodhounds down South "in Dixie," to enable them to smell their colored schoolmates from the white ones. And as to the teachers, they must have extraordinary organs of scent to enable them to distinguish which of their scholars it is from whom the "disagreeable effluvium arise," without a personal scenting of each one separately. If they can, I, for one, would advise our city fathers to employ them to scent out the "pig nuisance" that is so much complained of in our city, for it is certainly an occupation more suited to them than common school teaching. And I would further recommend to the Teacher's Association, to expel all such members as being unfit to associate with them. And still further, they say, "When the colored people are educated apart, they will not be educated for evil; they will not have some of the worst passions of the human hearts called daily into play, and thus strengthened by exercise; they will have no taunts and insults to remember; and when they enter life as men, they will be enabled to meet their white fellow-citizens without a single acrimonious feeling, arising from the recollection of wrongs suffered or injuries retaliated." A gentleman, now a candidate for Mayor of this city, stated some years since, at the nomination when he was a candidate for Parliament, that while travelling Europe he saw a man with a cage filled with all types of animals, both ferocious and harmless, fondling with each other in the best of friendship. He asked the man how did he manage to train them to treat each other so friendly; he replied by saying that he put them together when young, and they grew up as friends and remained so. Now, sir, I think the London trustees and teachers might learn a useful lesson from the man and his cage of animals.

Then, as to the law on the subject, it is evident that the trustees have no more right to establish separate schools for colored people than they have to establish them for Catholics, unless they ask for them; and according to the sixty-third chapter, section 1st, of the Consolidated Statutes for Upper Canada, the request must come from the twelve heads of families. It is said also, that the trustees feared that the law did not permit them to carry out their nefarious schemes, but that certain decisions will. Now, the only one that can with any color justify them, is the case of Dennis Hill against the trustees of Dresden. It seems the separate schools for colored people were very badly conducted, and Hill preferred to send his children to the schools other than the one for colored people. The trustees ejected them. He brought an action against them in the Court of Queen's Bench, Chief Justice Robinson presiding; and the judge decided that, as the colored people in that particular locality had asked for a separate school, they must send their children to it; and, consequently, the trustees had a right to exclude them from the other schools; and that the colored people must seek redress from the Legislature. This may be law, but it is certainly not justice; for if it is, then, upon the same principle, no Roman Catholic can send his children to any of the common schools of this city, because they have asked for and obtained separate schools. But suppose for argument's sake that they have the power to establish these separate schools for colored people, in consequence of the small number of colored children, they could not erect one in every ward, and, consequently, they would have to establish one in the centre of the city, and therefore the colored children would be obliged to travel a long distance past many common schools, however inclement the weather may be, to get to the separate school. See, then, how unjust such a course would be if it was generally adopted. The *Leader* asks how will the colored people view the discussion of these London school trustees. Well, sir, I will tell him how we view it. We will seek redress at the hands of the Legislature, by petition and otherwise, and we will never rest satisfied until it is out of the power of any set of school trustees to impose upon us separate schools against our will; and not only so, but we will agitate the subject for the purpose of getting those already established, abolished. And, sir, if the intelligent colored lady, or as the *Leader* has it, *woman*, was to exert herself to half the extent she does to beg money for a school "for the especial benefits of refugees and other colored people in Chatham," to get the school law so altered as to secure equal school privileges, she would not need to go round the country every year begging, but would do much to elevate her race, and less to put arguments in the mouths of their enemies to traduce them and build up barriers to their advancement ... The *Leader* says, "natural causes, if no other, are opposed to the admixture in the schools of the two races; but there is, besides, an in-bred feeling of repugnance in the breast of almost every white person at the hybridism which must to some extent be the result of their commingling." Now, sir, I must say, that if we look to the South, to the West Indies, and even to Canada, it does not appear that white people are so much opposed to hybridism after all, unless they practice one thing and believe another. It is further argued, that we should not object to the action of the London trustees, because colored people have separate churches. Well, the two cases are not at all analogous; for it would be absurd to say, because some few colored people in the exercise of their freedom choose to establish a Methodist or a Baptist Church, that all other colored people, whether they belong to any other denomination or not, must go to the colored churches, and be excluded from those of the white. I say, Mr. Editor, if this principle is to be carried out, a colored young man who headed his classes in the Upper Canada College while there, and now leads them in the Toronto University, and who never allows a convocation to pass without his name being mentioned in connection with some prize or mark of distinction, must be thrust from its halls, and driven into obscurity and degradation. Likewise other colored young men that are in the University, the Medical Schools, the Theological Seminaries and Colleges, those attending the law courts and lectures, and colored young ladies attending the public and private seminaries, all must be turned out to have their hopes blasted, and perhaps come to destruction. For while it might be possible to establish Separate Schools, it would not be to establish Separate Colleges. Mr. Editor, I must now conclude this already too lengthy communication, by appealing to an educated and Christian community, and ask is it right, is it according to the principles of freedom, is it in unison with the character of Britons, that, while the colored people are trying to elevate themselves in the scale of humanity, after having been brutalized by the white man for so many ages, and are both in the colleges and public schools, gaining so much distinction, a few obscure men in the community should try to pick flaws in the laws, and hunt up decisions to deprive us of our school privileges; and that newspapers, which should be the palladium of freedom and good order, should stoop so low as to stir up the prejudices of the white population against the colored? And, sir, to the colored people I will say that, while I am quite certain the school trustees of Toronto, as well as the local superintendent, are perfectly sound on the schools as they exist relative to the colored people, it becomes them to look well to their interest, and especially to the election of School Trustees, for their enemies are going about seeking how they may destroy their liberties. Nor need those colored people who do not identify themselves as such, think they will escape these disabilities on that account; for they may depend upon it, that whether they hail from either West or East Indies, it is as well know here who are colored as it is in the South where they came from, and the same rule that will exclude a child from the common schools because he is black, will exclude him because he is a mulatto or anything else but white.

I remain Sir,

Your obedient servant,

DIOGENES.

Toronto, Dec. 12, 1862

D) Address to Parents on the Education of Girls, Toronto, 1865
Mrs. Holiwell, Elm House School for the Education of Young Ladies

... We are now somewhat prepared to answer the enquiry — What is expected from a young girl to render her a Lady, in the most comprehensive and proper sense of the term?

First, then, a fair acquaintance with the various departments and branches of knowledge, as combined in a thorough course of study.

Second, — Respectable attainments in the several accomplishments, or at least excellence in some.

Third, — An intimate knowledge of the requirements and usages of good society, and such refinement of manners as can be acquired only by mixing freely in it.

Fourth, — Such a knowledge of the practical duties of life as will enable her, when arrived at a proper age, to undertake with confidence and discharge with success the responsibilities of the household and the family.

The two first qualifications are particularly the work of teachers and schools; the foundation of the third must be laid at the same time, but differs from the others, inasmuch as home co-operation is indispensable. Gentleness and refinement must prevail in the domestic circle, or school discipline and example are quickly forgotten. This department must be perfected, and the fourth entered upon, when the time comes for the usual routine of study to be dispensed with.

By the first qualification, I mean so much familiarity with History and Geography, Ancient and Modern, that she will readily understand most historical allusions, and the connexion of the present age in its politics and philosophy with the past, and I would have her acquire such a method of studying these subjects as would make it easy at any time to take up a particular history of a particular period or country, and master it with the least waste of time. Also such knowledge of her own language that her correspondence may be correct and elegant; her diary, memorandum book, and album mirrors that reveal an educated mind. I would have her Arithmetic comprehensive, that in business transactions she would control results, and not feel herself at the mercy of the shopkeeper and the workman, as is often the case. I would add to these attainments, an acquaintance with the Sciences and Literature, that she may not look with an ignorant eye on the wonders of that world of which she forms a part, and when thrown among the learned and scientific she may follow the conversation with pleasure, even when forbidden to assist.

By the second: — A good knowledge of the Theory and Practice of Music, and such cultivation of the voice as the individual talent will permit. My own taste would lead me to desire no other accomplishment, if the musical talent were really superior, and very highly cultivated; should it, however, be only moderate, if would be as well to add Drawing or Painting, or both; and if musical taste were altogether wanting, I would prefer that a pupil devote herself altogether to Drawing, as the time spent over the Piano will be only wasted. The Modern Languages should never be neglected in a thorough course of education. French has a particular claim on us as Canadians, with half our fellow-subjects speaking that tongue, and Italian and German might be added advantageously, especially if the young pupil showed no preference for art.

Dancing, and various kinds of Needle Work, are easily attainable by all, and should rather be looked upon as amusements, than matters requiring serious application.

The foundation of the third department of education should begin from the cradle, and depends more strictly on moral training than anything else. A perfect control of temper, a consideration for the feelings of others, respect for age and virtue, a modest estimate of self — these are the attributes of the true lady, and must be taught from infancy. The usages of the polite world — an easy and graceful demeanor — are readily gained by intercourse with good society, when the basis is constructed on Christian principles and Christian love. Without this, polish is a spurious coinage, detected from the genuine ore at a glance by those whose admiration and praise are an honor.

The fourth branch is altogether the mother's department, and should be entered upon as soon as the school routine is completed. Among the wealthy aristocracy of the European world, this branch of education might be dispensed with, without ill effect; but in this favored country, where few are so rich as not to be the happier and the better for excellence in domestic management, it should form an important part of a girl's training. Should the blind goddess lavish her favors on her, then will her efficiency in housekeeping add a charm to her menage, that wealth merely could not give; and money that would be ignorantly spent, without benefit to any one, would, under her administration, supply food for the hungry and clothes to the naked. If, on the contrary, comparative proverty should be her lot, what a jewel in her matron's crown would be economy! We need no magnifying glass to see the evils around us of bad management and extravagant housekeeping; families that might be respected are brought to beggary through it, and men that ought to enjoy competency and freedom from care are bowed down with the burden of supporting ill-ordered and spendthrift households. Mothers sometimes retain too tenaciously the reins of domestic government; if they would devolve some of their duties on their grown-up daughters, it would prove beneficial to both. A few errors must be overlooked at first; a few failures in marketing, a foolish investment now and then in shopping, must be expected, and cheerfully endured; but a little practice soon enables the tyro to choose and purchase with almost the success of her elders, while her mother has the happy consciousness that when the time comes for them to part, it is not as an inexperienced child she sends her away to learn her lesson in bitterness and alone, but hopeful and confident of the future.

It now remains for us to enquire what are the best means within our reach of providing this education for our daughters. Many persons, who estimate education highly, entertain a deep-root distrust, if not an aversion to schools. Much could be said on both sides of the question; and arguments in favour of home training, or school discipline, can be furnished in abundance by the advocates for either system: theoretically, I think, perhaps the admirers of home education have the best of it; but I believe the discipline of schools to have been crowned with the most practical success.

It is a beautiful picture that of a young girl reared in the pure atmosphere of the domestic circle, accustomed to live in the sunshine of parental love; to hear nothing but the refined conversation of her mother's select society, no reproof severer than *her* gentle admonitions, no word or sentiment but approved by her anxious censorship. With an amiable disposition, fair talents, and intellectual and refined parents, one can imagine a young girl bred up to womanhood in artless ignorance of all that is wicked and deceitful in the world, a charming study for those who are versed in its wiles, a creature to love and cherish, to watch and guide ... [But] the maiden that has never had an opportunity of comparing her mental and moral qualifications with those of others, is sure to enter life with false views, is likely to mistake specious vice for genuine virtue, and could never detect the gloss of superficial elegance from real worth. It might be asked, "How is this experience to be gained at school?" I would answer, that wisdom consists very much in forming a proper estimate of self, considered both absolutely and relatively, and in the power of applying that knowledge with discrimination to the various positions in which we may be placed; and that a school, from its very constitution, its numbers, and mixed character, affords a better opportunity for attaining the necessary information than the retirement of home. She can there compare her mental powers and standing with others of her age; she discovers her moral shortcomings; she cannot help finding out that she is peevish or passionate, and that the respect and love of her schoolfellows depend on overcoming her failings. In spite of the foolishness of youth, she will see that the popular and best liked are the truthful and independent; and if a high moral tone pervades the establishment, there will be the pressure of public opinion on a small scale which will work very beneficially on the character of the children. There is an atmosphere of impartiality about a school that is almost unattainable at home, which is admirably adapted to dissipate any false impression of superiority; ... There is no doubt that submission and discipline might be taught at home, as well as at school, but are they, generally? It is good for a child to be so many hours of a day under control; she learns to govern her temper, and be forbearing; she has not the same inducements to idleness and disobedience, for all are busy and all obey; and youth cannot help moulding itself on the model offered for imitation. Now, this training is not be arrived at in private tuition ... A child reared altogether under the paternal roof is somewhat similarly situated to a young Prince, in danger of never hearing the truth; it is the interest of those surrounding her to keep her self-satisfied; she is quite aware that her relations have a high opinion of her capacity and progress, she feels that she is an object of anxiety to her family: her efforts are magnified, her talents praised, and every step appreciated. The result of such a course must be disappointment ...

E) Report of the Grammar School Inspector for 1865
George Paxton Young

... As far as I can see, no evil arises from having little Girls and little Boys taught in School together. But in many of our Canadian Grammar Schools, Girls of 15, 16, or 17 years are associated with Boys of the same ages. This feature in the Grammar School System has been often strongly objected to, — apart altogether from the questions, whether the studies most proper for grown up Girls are the same as those which are most proper for grown up Boys, — on the ground of its moral tendency. I think it right to state the impressions in regard to this subject, which have been left on my mind by what I have had an opportunity of observing.

In Schools conducted by Teachers possessing weight of character, I have no reason to believe that the general moral tone of the Pupils is injuriously affected by Boys and Girls being taught together. Perhaps, on the contrary, the result is beneficial. Schools of the kind described, partake somewhat of the character of families, or of well regulated social circles, within which the free intercourse of young persons of different sexes with one another is universally admitted to be salutary.

But out of a hundred Grammar School Teachers, there will necessarily be a few who do not possess weight of character; and, under their rule, there is a danger of grown up Girls suffering as respects the formation of their moral character, from attending School along with grown up Boys. In the rough sports of Boys, where not the slightest impropriety is intended, Girls are liable to be subjected to a familiarity of treatment, which is apt insensibly to blunt their instinctive feelings of delicate reserve. I remember one instance, in which, on entering the School unexpectedly, during the interval of recess, when the Teacher was not present, I saw some big Boys chasing, and even dragging, big Girls, about the Room, in simple innocent amusement, no doubt, but still in a manner which, probably the Parents of the Girls would not have been delighted to behold. And a far more serious thing is, that, under Teachers who are without due weight of character, Girls who may have enjoyed no domestic advantages and who do not understand the beauty of a "meek and quiet spirit," are in danger of being drawn, by the feeling that they are playing their part in the presence of Boys, into an unfeminine rudeness of behaviour towards their Teacher. To the credit of our Schools, I will say, that I found that this evil, manifesting itself in an extreme degree was observed in only a single instance, but shades of it appeared elsewhere. In the instance to which I refer, a class of Girls, about 14, or 15 years of age, when questioned by their Teacher, answered him with an undisguised carelessness, amounting to contempt. They were ignorant of their Lessons, but seemed to assume that they were young Ladies, he had no right to presume to be displeased with them; they were pert and bold. It may perhaps be said that this offensive vulgarity had not any connection with the presence of Boys in the School, but was a result simply of the incompetency of the Master, and of the absence of proper domestic training at home; but I am of a different opinion. A Girl, who is destitute of refinement of nature, more readily becomes insolent, or sullen, at having her self-love wounded in the presence of Boys, than she would if surrounded merely by Companions of her own sex. And, at any rate, the important practical point remains, that when a Girl does so far forget herself as to be disrespectful to a Teacher, this is a vastly greater evil in its permanent effects on her character, when the fault is committed before Boys, than it would be under other circumstances.

16

"The Evils of Combination"

Working on the Beauharnois Canal

DOCUMENTS

A) Report into Disturbances upon the Beauharnois
Canal, 1843

It is ironic that a people with a long agriculturalist history formed Canada's first real proletariat. That, however, happened to Irish-Canadians during the early to mid-nineteenth century. This period marked the shift toward industrialization in Canada, an era in which small craft enterprises and independent workers disappeared in favour of enormous factories and companies employing first hundreds, then thousands, of labourers. Alienated workers lost control of their lives and work, and became increasingly bound to the unrelenting dynamism of faceless big capital and the steam age. Canal navvies, those thousands who dug the new waterways cutting through the colony of Canada, were among the first to feel the shift, and thereby formed the vanguard of what eventually became organized labour. Company owners, invariably *laissez-faire* capitalists, did not dispute the right of individual workers to bargain for their best contract, but they hated combinations: proletarians banding together into unions that then fought for collective agreements between worker and boss. Collectivism, the antithesis to nineteenth-century liberalism, threatened and, according to capitalist mythology, counteracted Charles Darwin's idea of natural law: the survival of the fittest. Entrepreneurs generally enjoyed government support, and workers faced a long and bitter struggle for recognition, better wages, and working conditions.

Construction of the Lachine Canal near Montreal began in 1821. Here hundreds, then thousands, of workers laboured from six in the morning until six at night with two hours for meals. Then they trudged "home" to shanties lining the canal banks that they often rented from the company at extortionate rates. By the 1840s, 10,000 navvies worked on the Welland Canal between Lake Erie and Lake Ontario, 3,000 dug the Beauharnois upstream of Montreal, and countless others toiled at the other great construction sites across the land.

They worked in appalling conditions. Men received their meagre pay once a month, sometimes in the form of scrip, a chit that they could only redeem for products sold at exorbitant prices in the company store. Diseases such as unspecified fevers, cholera, and typhoid periodically scythed through their ranks, and missing days for illness led, as often as not, to firing. There were no sick benefits, job site safety requirements, pensions, or provisions for unemployment insurance during the long cold winter months when work ground to a halt. Local residents often hated and feared the navvies and occasionally attacked them. Supply and demand kept wages desperately low, and contractors periodically melted away in the dead of night with the month's pay packet. Why work in conditions like that? Did newly arrived Irish immigrants have a choice? They had no skills, no money, no connections, and they faced a hostile reception from citizens.

The canalers regularly rebelled at their harsh treatment by rioting and striking, and even by threatening company managers. They also objected to labour-saving machinery that would cost jobs, and to outsiders threatening to depress wages. This was an early form of working class political expression, in this case evolving from a long history of action against British repression in their native Ireland. Nor were their acts random or undisciplined. Navvies carefully orchestrated their activities, and although they violated the letter of the law against combinations, generally pushed only far enough to gain improvements while keeping public opinion as sympathetic as possible. Threats of force became, in their eyes, legitimate bargaining tactics.

How could such appalling and dangerous conditions exist? Partly it was the prevailing socio-economic structure. Unique circumstances, however, further facilitated the process. Canal construction originally came under the auspices of Public Works, but that shifted to private enterprise after 1843. This saved the government money, but canal construction was a precarious business. Companies often lacked sufficient capital to do the job properly, materials were frequently difficult and expensive to obtain, and governments sometimes reneged on payment or paid late. Contractors had to charge high rents for lousy accommodations, they argued, because that might be their only profit. Canals also cut through the isolated hinterlands, far from the prying eyes of the public, and permanent housing could not exist in situations where job sites slowly moved. Navvies bear some responsibility for their own misfortune. They often continued old regional squabbles imported from Ireland, which kept them distracted, divided, and conquered.

The situation worsened in the mid 1840s after a decision was made to work year round in an effort to complete the canals quickly enough to compete with American waterways. Unfortunately, this coincided with a depression in the United States that sent thousands of Irish-American navvies scrambling across the Canadian border in search of winter work. Wages inevitably dropped in the off-season, but the new situation compounded the problem and led to heightened tensions along Canada's canals. The government called in the army, which, in itself, caused problems. Civilian and military authorities bickered over the use of troops as civil "police," senior officers arguing that soldiers should defend colonies against external enemies, not internal dissent. Indignant officers also believed that governments shirked their public responsibilities by refusing to hire police as long as they enjoyed free access to the army. Troops might also have to fire on their own citizens, or worse, refuse to do so after recognizing kindred souls in the navvies. This all led to the 1845 Act for the Preservation of Peace Near Public Works, the first of a long string of pieces of regulatory legislation aimed directly at controlling canal and railway workers.

The issue climaxed during the summer of 1843 when the Beauharnois Canal project experienced one clash after another between workers and establishment. The navvies ultimately returned to work at their original wage, but at least gained a good deal of public sympathy. The following documents reflect that turbulent summer and express the views of labour, contractors, and local government authorities. By this time, even government and the clergy recognized that canalers could not possibly exist on their meagre wages, regardless of thriftiness and ingenuity, and that conditions must change. Things improved, but very slowly, and inevitably required two steps back for every three forward.

A) Report into Disturbances upon the Beauharnois Canal, 1843
i) Deposition of Martin Donnelly

On the first day of July, 1843, came and appeared before Charles Wetherall, Esquire, one of the Justices of the Peace for the District of Montreal, and the Commissioners appointed by His Excellency the Governor General of this Province for enquiring into the causes, &c. of the disturbances which took place lately on the line of the Beauharnois Canal, Martin Donnelly, of Beauharnois, Labourer, who being duly sworn on the Holy Evangelists deposeth and saith: — I am a native of the County of Mayo, in Ireland; I arrived in this Province from my native Country on the 7th day of July last. On the 20th day of the same month I began to work on this Canal, from that time until the month of March last, I continued to work for the Board of Works so long as they had employment to give me, at the rate of 3s. per day, during the whole time the works were in active operation. From the month of March last, until the first of last month I remained in the employ of Messrs. Crawford, at the eastern extremity of the Canal. During that period there have been about 250 men at work on this section. The larger portion of these men are Irishmen who have worked in the United States. The remaining portion are with very few exceptions, Emigrants from Ireland, recently arrived in this Province. In the month of March last, I received 2s. a day, the price generally paid for that month. In April I received 2s. 3d. a day, and on the 1st of May, at the request of the other men employed on that section, I applied to Mr. Crawford, Senior, to ascertain what amount of wages he intended to give us during the ensuing month; he told me he would give 2s. 6d., for which price, we all agreed to work during that month. The hours of work on this section being from five in the morning, till seven in the evening, one hour being allowed for breakfast and one hour and a quarter for dinner. The payments were made at the end of each month in cash after deduction made of the value of articles supplied from the contractor's store. I was never compelled to take goods out of the store kept by Mr. Crawford, but I found the goods in that store cheaper than in two or three other stores in that neighbourhood and equally convenient where I could have got credit, had I required it. I believe few of the other men could obtain like credit, but I was well known and was generally better treated by the Store keepers and others, on account of the orphan children I have to support, and on account of my own character. For such articles as I had occasion to purchase from Crawford's store, the following prices were charged. 4 lbs. loaf, 5d., 1 lb. sugar, 5d., 1 lb. tea, 3s. 8d., there was also, tea sold at that store for 4s. 6d., 1 lb. tobacco, 10d., 1 lb. coffee, from 10d. to 1s. 3d. I cannot say how butter was sold at this store as I never purchased any there, and no beer or spirituous liquors of any kind. The men on that section are generally temperate. There are some men, especially among the unmarried, who drink occasionally. These men obtain liquor at two or three shanties, near the section where it is sold at 9d. a quart, and freely given on credit. I received payment regularly, at the close of each month, and no deduction was in any instance made from the amount of wages due me, except for such supplies as had been furnished me from the store, and such voluntary contributions as I occasionally made for the support of fellow labourers during sickness. We only receive payment for the days during which we have been engaged in labour. The works are frequently suspended by bad weather. I do not consider that half a dollar is a sufficient remuneration, for the following reasons:– Firstly, the work is not continuous, as the following statement will show. In the month of August last, I worked, and was paid for only 18 days.

In	September	14	days
	October	19	"
	November	4	"
	December	3	"
	January	4	"
	February	2	"
	March	6	"
	April	18	"
	May	24	"
		112	"

Secondly — House rent and provisions are higher here than in the cities. I should prefer 2s. a day in Montreal to 3s. here. And thirdly, we are here compelled to make small contributions for the support of suffering fellow labourers a burthen which we would be exempt from in the cities. The expenses of a labouring man on the canal per day are as follows, to wit:–

	S.	D.
Shanty rent	0	8
Expenses for his food, &c	1	3
Average of charitable contributions		½
	1	11½
Leaving a balance of		6½
	2	6

for fuel, clothing and other contingencies including lost time. During the time when the operations on the canal are suspended by unfavorable weather or other causes, there are no means of obtaining other employment without abandoning the works entirely. This is a calculation of the average expenses of a single man which I have made from my own experience. A large portion of the labourers are married men, many of whom have families: their expenses must of course increase in proportion with their families. The unmarried men usually pay from eight to nine shillings per week for boarding, lodging, washing and mending. My wife is dead; but I have three children to take care of, whom I am obliged to keep, and a servant woman, to whom I pay 10s. a month; but I only pay 2s. 6d. a month for my shanty as I built it myself with money I brought from Ireland, and only have to pay for the ground rent. The general impression amongst the labourers is, that the daily work of each man on the Canal is worth from six to seven shillings to the contractors. This is also my opinion; but I cannot be certain, as I have not seen the contracts. Four good labourers can quarry from two to three square yards, and can excavate in clay or mixed soil from six to seven yards a day. About the first of May last, a body of men, above 100 in number, came down from the head of the line: amongst them I recognised some of McDonald's men. They said their object in coming down was to induce us to join them in a strike for higher wages, urging upon us that 2s. 6d. was an insufficient price: but, having been promised 2s. 6d. for that month by our employers, we refused to turn out; at the same time we promised to join a general strike at the close of that month (May), unless the contractors raised the wages to 3s., for the ensuing month, along the whole line. The men from above appeared satisfied, and returned to work at their own sections. On the 15th of the same month, about 100 of Black's men, at work on the section adjoining Crawford's, at the east end of the Canal, came down and ordered us to get out of the pit where we were working, and join them, as they had struck for higher wages and shorter hours. Their hours were, and had been from some time in April, from dark to dark, so that in May they were compelled to set at work at about four in the morning, and to continue at work until eight in the evening, with the usual hours of intermission for meals. We refused to turn out with them, on the ground that we had agreed with our contractors for the month at half a dollar a day. They called us cowardly two and three penny men; but after some discussion, and after receiving from us a promise to turn out at the end of that month, unless our wages were raised to 3s., they returned to their section and continued to work until the first of June, their hours having been made the same as ours, that is to say — from five in the morning until seven in the evening. On the last day of May, all the labourers down the whole line gave up their tools to their respective foremen, and gave notice that they would not return to work until the wages were raised to 3s. From that evening until the 10th of June they all remained quiet in their shanties. Directly the men struck, the stores on Crawford's section were closed, and the ordinary means of getting supplies and the necessaries of life were thus taken away from us; and I have a personal knowledge that great distress prevailed in many of the shanties during that interval. On Saturday the 10th a large body of men from the upper sections of the line came down to this end: their object was to induce Crawford's and Black's men to go to their respective contractors, and demand higher wages. The larger portion of our men accompanied these men from above; but I remained in my shanty. On their return, I heard them agree to meet on the following Monday, at the Mills, in St. Timothée, for the purpose of ascertaining whether the contractors along the whole line would or would not raise the wages to 3s. On that day, Monday the 12th of last month, Crawford's men, with very few exceptions, went up towards the Mills; but, as I remained below with my little family, I cannot say what occurred there. The general feeling amongst the labourers on the Canal is against the system of keeping stores by the contractors. I, however, am of opinion, that provision would be more expensive along the line of the Canal, if the contractors were prohibited from keeping stores; and I feel confident that all the evils arising out of that system would be remedied by paying the men weekly for their labour in cash, and leaving them free to purchase either at the contractor's stores or at any other. No compulsion has been directly used by the contractors to make the labourers purchase at their stores, as far as I have been able to observe; but, from the facts of the payments being made monthly, those who cannot get credit elsewhere (and, as I have stated above, there are few who can), are obliged to supply themselves and their families with the necessaries of life out of the contract's stores; moreover, the men are thus obliged, in many instances, to live upon more expensive food, such as tea, coffee, &c., while, if they had money in hand, they might supply themselves with potatoes, milk, oatmeal, butter, and other such food, which would go much further in a large family. When I arrived here in July last, I had about seven sovereigns and a half remaining from the funds I left Ireland with. I have never lost the chance of a day's labour from sickness since I came to this country. The only time I lost was about twelve days, during my wife's illness and at the time of her death. I belong to the Temperance Society, having been a member of it for these three years past, so that I have never spent six-pence unnecessarily since I came to this country; and yet I have barely sufficient remaining out of the money I have brought here, and that I have earned here, to meet the little debts I have contracted on the Canal for the necessaries of life. I am aware that there have been no disturbances on this Canal, between the Cork and Connaught men: and further I say not. This present deposition being read to me, I declare the same to contain the truth, persist therein, and have made my mark,

MARTIN DONNELLY, his mark.

ii) Deposition of Thomas Reynolds

… Thomas Reynolds, of Beauharnois, labourer, who being duly sworn, doth depose and say. — I have been three years in this country, and am a native of King's County in Ireland. I was engaged in July last by the Board of Works, to work on this Canal at 3s. a day. I was paid at this rate until I was discharged on the 1st of November last. I remained out of employ, from that time until January, when Mr. Crawford began to open the Canal at the east end. Besides the time lost in the winter, the labourers on the Canal are frequently thrown out of employment during the spring, summer and autumn months by unfavorable weather. The works are always suspended on the Canal during rainy weather. I think on an average, healthy labourers who lose no chances of day's work, can get employment two days out of three in Canal work during the year. During the suspension of labour on the Canal, the men employed there, cannot go elsewhere in search of work, without exposing themselves to lose their places on the Canal. I have never heard any altercations or disputes between the Cork and Connaught men employed on the Canal since the month of March last. In January and February last, I received 2s. a day, in March and April, 2s. 3d. and in May 2s. 6d. In January, February and March, we wrought from dark to dark in Crawford's section. In April and May, from 5 in the morning until 7 in the evening. Black's men always began the work before us and continued after we had ceased. Black's is the next section to Crawford's, at the east end of the Canal. On the first of May last, some of the men of one of the neighbouring sections, I am not sure whose men they were, came down to induce us to strike for higher wages and shorter hours, but as we had made an agreement with our employers for that month, we refused to join the strike. On the 15th of the same month, Black's men came down to us, with the same object in view. Our employer was absent, and as we had heard, sick in Montreal. Moreover we had agreed for the month, and we declined joining, whereupon they returned their work, after having had their hours assimilated to ours. The last strike which was general along the whole line of the Canal, took place on the last day of May, on the evening of which day we quietly deposited our tools in the boxes made for them, delivered them to the foremen, and repaired to our shanties. Since that time no work was done on the Canal, until some day of last week, when employment was given to labourers on two sections, towards the west end of the Canal by Larocque, and by Brown and Finley, at 3s. a day. From the 1st day of June until the 10th, the labourers remained quiet, along the line, but on that day, it was a Saturday, a body of men from the upper line of the works came down and invited us to meet them on the following Monday, at the St. Timothée Mills, for the purpose of going along the whole line, and ascertaining whether or not the contractors were willing to give 3s. and regular hours. Immediately on ascertaining that the men had struck, contractors Crawford and McDonald closed their stores. Black allowed his to remain open, and behaved well towards his men, whom he allowed to have supplies therefrom as usual. Numbers of the labourers on Crawford's section were thus deprived of the necessaries of life, and lived on the charity of others. The general opinion of the labourers is, that the contractors should not be allowed to keep stores, and they would wish to be paid weekly so as to be free to purchase food and other necessaries wherever they might consider it most advantageous for themselves. The contractors' stores do not contain the articles of food which are most suited to the means and habits of the laborers, such as oatmeal, eggs, potatoes, milk, fresh meat, &c. I have known various instances where families and single men have been obliged to live on what the stores supplied, namely: bread, butter, tea, coffee, &c., while had they possessed ready money, they would have advantageously substituted potatoes, oatmeal, eggs, milk, &c. I have known many labourers who were obliged to eat bread three times a day, because they had no means of purchasing potatoes. I have worked in the City of Montreal as a labourer, and should prefer 2s. a day, with constant employment to 3s. here. I am unable to state the precise amount required for the daily support of a labourer on this Canal, at the present time, and I have been boarding for several months past with my father, on advantageous terms; but when, previous to that time, I tried to board myself upon 2s. a day, I could not succeed, but got into debt. And further I say not. This present deposition being read to me, I declare the same to contain the truth, persist therein, and have made my mark.

THOMAS REYNOLDS, his mark.

iii) Deposition of D.A. McDonald, 12 July 1843

I am one of the contractors of the Beauharnois Canal for sections 7 and 8, and employed about 200 labourers, before the 1st of June last. I allowed them 2s. 3d. in the month of April and 2s. 6d. in the month of May. The hours of work were from five to seven and work twelve hours, the payments being monthly. I had a store for the supply of such men as chose voluntarily to resort to it, there was no understanding that provisions or other store goods should be taken in payment or part payment of the labour. The following are the prices charged for the articles sold at my store during the month of May: 4 lb. loaf, fine flour, 6d.; mess pork, 4d.; tea, 3s. 6d.; coffee, New York, 10d.; oatmeal per stone, 1s. 3d.; sugar from 5d. to 5½d.; tobacco, 10d.; soap, 4d. I do not remember that the men ever complained of the articles sold at my store. I have no shanties, and know nothing about them, nor are my overseers permitted to board or lodge any of the men. The labourers have been paid according to the agreement. In the beginning of May, they struck for higher wages, namely: 3s. a day and shorter hours, from 6 to 7. I understood from them that their shanties being so far from the work, the time was too short for them to go and come for their meals. I declined making any alterations in the hours, but raised their wages to 2s.

6d. which had always been my intention, two thirds of them left, and nearly all of them returned and begged work from me, and that nothing but force would induce them to turn out for higher wages than 2s. 6d. They continued to work on these terms until the first of June, when they struck for 3s. I am convinced that the strike for 3s. was a general understanding throughout the line. No application was made to me during the month of May to give 3s. On Saturday, the 10th of June last, a party of about 300 men coming from the western sections, among whom I recognized 10 or 12 of my men advanced opposite Mr. Grant's hotel where I resided, one of the party advanced and asked me what I was going to give per day to my men, to which I replied, that as he was one of my men, he knew my terms, his name was William Glover, he then said, are you not going to pay more than 2s. 6d., to which I replied, that I would not. A voice in the crowd, said that I would be compelled to pay 3s. or give up my contract, I replied that I would not give up my contract, nor would I give 3s. a day. Then they said that unless I would raise the wages on the Monday following, I would be served as they intended to serve all the contractors, be killed or thrown in the rapids. I said that they might kill me, but that they could not force me to yield to their demand. They left and expressed that they intended visiting Mr. Crawford, whom they threatened with violence, promising to return and visit me on the next Monday. On the Monday morning a party from the eastern end, evidently not the same party who visited me on the Saturday, made its appearance about 10 o'clock before noon, and called for me to come out of Mr. Grant's hotel, I went out and found the mob in a very excited state. A man who advanced, asked me whether or not I would give the 3s. per day, I answered that I had nothing to do with them, as I could not recognize one of my own men among them. At this moment one of the mob made a rush at me, armed with a stick about four feet long: they were all armed in the same way. This man was held back by the man who first addressed me, saying that nothing should be done to me until I had given him further explanation, I think I could recognize the first spokesman by a cut on his left hand, I replied that unless all the contractors agreed to give 3s. I would not give more than 2s 6d. A general rush was then made at me, with cries of "kill him" — "murder him." I retreated into Mr. Grant's hotel, and secreted myself in the cellar. I know nothing more about it. I subsequently went down to the Mill, where Major Campbell advised me to leave the place for the moment. I am a Roman Catholic myself, and from the influence I know the Clergy possesses and occasionally exercises over their flocks, I am convinced that if Mr. Falvey had been present on the 12th of June last, my property would not have been destroyed, nor Mr. Grant's — and further I say not, and have signed.

(Signed) D. A. McDONALD

iv) Deposition of G.N. Brown, 13 July 1843

I am one of the contractors on the Beauharnois Canal, in partnership with one Finley, for Section 6. I employed a number of labourers, about 300, from the first of April last until the 1st of June last, at the rate of 2s. 6d. On the 1st of June last, I was forced by the workmen to give them 3s. a day, which sum I paid to them during that month. I keep a store for the convenience of the labourers. No one is compelled to purchase at my store. The prices of my store never exceeded that of other stores in the place. The men were always settled with monthly. Any balance coming to the men, after deduction of such articles as they had been provided with out of my store, was regularly paid to them in cash. I never had any complaints from my men as to wages, hours, or prices of goods in the store. I have hired a piece of land, which I sub-let to the workmen. Five shillings was the highest price I agreed to charge them for the ground rent, which rent was to be reduced according to the number of shanties built upon it; but I have never charged them with that rent. I have supplied them with boards to build their shanties, at £2 for a hundred. On Saturday, the 10th day of June last, a party of men, about 200 in number, came to my house from the western sections, and asked for me. I came out; and they demanded of me if I was disposed to give them 3s. a day. A number of them came, I believe, from Mr. Dunn's section. They halted by the sound of a horn. I replied "No" to their demand — that I would not give 3s. They went round the store, and broke two panes, when a man called out "Halt," and ordered them to stand back, to hear what I had to state. They then said, "We will give him till Monday, at 11 o'clock, to comply with our wishes." On the Monday following, early, I heard that my store was to be attacked; and on that morning a mob, amounting to about 2000, armed with bludgeons, surrounded the house. Some of them had stones in their hands to break open the store. A man, whose name I believe to be Daly, stepped forward, and called for me to come out. I stood forward on the step of the door, when he demanded 3s. a day for the men; or, if I hesitated in giving it, I would not have my life in three minutes, and my store would go in the same time. Whilst he made use of these words, a party of the mob held their sticks over my head. I firmly believe that, if I had not acceded to their demands, they would have put their threats into execution. I accordingly consented to give the 3s. They then took me on their shoulders and cheered me. On the Saturday and Sunday I acquainted Mr. Laviolette with what had taken place, and asked him for military protection. After the mob had left my house, to proceed to Mr. Larocque's, they came back again, and ordered a "halt" before my house. Three or four of the leaders came to the house, and ordered me to sign my hand to what I had agreed, which I did. They then stated they would have Crawford's and McDonald's (two of the contractors) lives, if they would not comply to their demands — that they had the whole line above, and that they did not thank us for our agreement, and that they would have the same on the other part, or have the lives of the contractors. It is usual to have different rates of wages, according to the length of the days and the seasons. And the deponent has signed.

(Signed) G. N. BROWN

v) Deposition of Andrew Elliott, 14 July 1843

I am contractor for section two of the Beauharnois Canal, and give employment to 217 men. The general rate of pay was 2s. 6d. per day, but I gave to some 2s. 9d. and to a few, 3s. — 11 and a half hours being the actual time of work required. I keep a store, from which the men could supply themselves at the same prices as at any other store even could they pay cash. They have always had what the store could supply altho' money was not due them and I have never refused to give cash to those to whom it was due whenever they required it. On the night of Sunday, the 11th of June last, I was sitting with two of my foremen when I heard a knock at the door; one of the foremen immediately opened it. I heard say: "Are you the contractor?" He replied no. I then went to the door. Immediately 4 men armed with guns presented them to my breast, they were not my men, and I should not know again. They said: "Walk out." I asked them what they had against me. They said: "Walk out and we will let you know." They were very violent and swore much; they were not drunk. I said: "Men, you are not brutes. I have had great many dealings with the Irish and they never injured one hair of my head." Then I went out. The muskets were continued to be held to my breast and the question put to me whether I would give the 3s. and hours from 6 to 6, and if I did not, I had but two minutes to consider of it or to live. I said: "I am sure you will not put these threats into execution." I heard a voice from the rear of my house, call out, "fire," whilst many of the mob were urging them to do so. The trigger of one of the muskets was pulled, but it flashed in the pan. I begged of them to give me till the morning when I should give them a decided answer. A man then ran and poked his musket through a pane of the glass, as I supposed, with the intention of shooting me if I ran into the house. Several men then rushed on me and gave me a blow on the head and another one on the side, which left me senseless. This is all I can recollect. I believe that this strike was a general combination along the whole line for a rise of wages. They returned to the store which is opposite my dwelling house on the Monday morning when my foremen Peter Onterson and George Rae came into my house where I was lying and said that the property would be destroyed unless I granted their demands. Under these circumstances I acceded. I paid them for eleven days and a half that they worked in the month of June, at the rate of 3s. a day, and those that are now working are doing so with the understanding that they will be paid at the same rate as the others along the line. I should have no objection to pay the men in cash once a fortnight. I believe at this moment there are about 2,200 men employed on this Canal, and that there are nearly 1,000 unemployed and further I say not and have signed.

(Signed) ANDREW ELLIOTT.

vi) Deposition of John Whitlaw, 17 July 1843

I have held various contracts under Government for public works, and been in the habit of employing from 500 to 800 men. In the year 1840, I was employed on the Chambly Canal. I paid to the labourers, in the early part of the season, 2s. 9d. per man: towards the fall of the year, when the labourers became scarce, the rate of payment was increased from 2s. 9d. to 3s. 6d. At that time, the provisions were much dearer than at present: the hours were from six in the morning until six in the evening, allowing one hour for breakfast, and one hour for dinner. In the year 1841, the rate of wages on the same work was from 2s. 6d. to 2s. 9d., with the same hours. In the year 1842, the rate of wages was 2s. 6d. — hours the same. During the whole of this time we had but two strikes for higher wages, viz., 3s. These strikes invariably arise among one or two, who incite the others to strike, and prevent the others from working. In May, last year, when the first strike took place, and intimidation and violence made use of to prevent others from working, application was made to the Police Magistrate of the District, who ascertained the names of the leaders, arrested them immediately, and committed them for trial; upon which the others immediately returned to their work, and no disturbance has since taken place on that section of the work. I am of the opinion, that the prompt interposition of authority, in ascertaining and securing the ringleaders, is the only effectual means to check the evils of combination, which would otherwise invariably lead to violence. I have given my attention to the subject of the quantity of labour that can be performed advantageously to both contractor and labourer; and I am of opinion that a labourer can perform as much labour in ten hours as he would in twelve. I know this from having actually tested the thing. A store was kept on the line for the convenience of the labourers. There were other stores in Chambly to which they might resort. At first we had no stores, and were requested by the labourers to keep one for their convenience. We sold at the market price, and had the same profit that other retailing stores had. We always paid our labourers every fortnight. In Montreal I paid every week. I consider the payment every fortnight to be in favor of the labourer, but against the interest of the contractor, as the men generally lose one or two days at each payment; therefore I consider the fewer the payments are made the better. We were not bound to provide shanties for the labourers, but we did so at our own expenses, and charged them 1s. per week for each, which would contain from twelve to fifteen men, and was about twelve feet square. No men were boarded by my foremen, and I consider the system to be open to great abuses. With reference to the prices of the times, I consider 2s. 6d. per day for ten hours' work, to be a fair price, and equal to 2s. 9d. and 3s. 6d. paid in the previous years. And further I say not; and have signed.

   (Signed) JOHN WHITLAW.

vii) Deposition of S. and S.R. Andres, 17 July 1843

We had $11\frac{1}{2}$ miles of the Chambly Canal to excavate, under two different contracts, and gave occupation to from 500 to 1000 men during four years. The rates of payment varied according to circumstances from 2s. 6d. to 3s. Our hours were first from five to seven, allowing one hour for breakfast and one hour for dinner. Afterwards, in consequence of discontent, we altered the hours from six to six. Ten hours actual work we consider to be as much labour as a man can advantageously perform. Our payments were made monthly in cash. We had stores conveniently situated along the line for the supply of provisions and necessaries to the workmen. We consider that the interests of both the contractors and the men are best consulted by the semi-monthly payments. With regard to stores, in many instances they are absolutely necessary. We can cite many instances where men who sought work were unable to procure on credit the means of subsistence, and without stores would starve. Notwithstanding the benefit thus derived from the establishment of stores, we know the general feeling of the labourers to be opposed to them. Our opinion is that they are beneficial to the labourers if conducted on proper principles. But if we undertook any public work on an extensive scale, with a knowledge of the feeling above described, we would not establish them until their convenience had been proved to the full conviction of the men. In short, whatever evils may exist in the store system, they are remedied by payments in cash, and that at the shortest practicable periods, which we have already stated to be the semi-monthly. We have always supplied the men with shanties. We have had several strikes arising from various complaints. They invariably can be traced to a few turbulent individuals; the great object in these cases is the immediate apprehension and punishment by committal or otherwise on the spot, one good example being sufficient to arrest the evil. The great difficulty under which the contractors labour, is the want of an efficient magistrate and paid constabulary, to arrest the evil at its outbreak, and before it gains head, when the mob becomes formidable, and violent measures must be resorted to. No local magistrate, unpaid, will ever act on such occasions. There is a moral effect produced on the minds of the men by the presence of an authorised Government Officer. The average working days of a labourer may be computed from eighteen to twenty days a month. We have no public works in hand now. We consider 2s. 6d. to be a fair price of daily labour, the hours being from six to six, two hours deducted for the meals. We prefer Canadians to Irish labourers. Our foremen had authority to discharge and engage men, and in some instances they boarded some of the men. And further we say not; and have signed.

(Signed) SAMUEL ANDRES, STEPHEN R. ANDRES.

viii) Deposition of Joseph Bergevin, 19 July 1843

I am a native of this Parish. I cultivate a land which belongs to me, and which is divided by the Canal. I know the price of provisions and the value of labour in this neighbourhood. The loaf of six pounds, is sold at present for ten pence. During the spring, and thence until about the beginning of this month, it was sold at, from eight pence to nine pence. Pork sells at from four pence to four pence half-penny; potatoes at from fifteen to eighteen pence the bushel; eggs, six pence a dozen; milk, about two pence the quart; butter, from six pence to seven pence half-penny; moist sugar, from five to six pence; hay, from five to five and a half dollars the hundred; oats for thirteen pence. My father has a fine land adjoining mine, on which he rears a great quantity of live stock; and having milk in abundance he wished to sell it on the Canal. I wished to do the same, and the contractors sent us away, telling us, if we wished to sell to go and sell at home, or else to go and sell it at their stores: in the same way we wished to sell eggs and other provisions on the Canal, but we were prevented from so doing in the same manner. I am of opinion, as well as all those of my neighbours, with whom I have conversed on this subject, that day-labourers cannot support themselves when they receive only half a crown a day. I know that the contractors in this vicinity have more than once suspended the work, even in fine weather: and the only reason we have been able to assign for it is, that they wished to compel their people to get farther in debt at the store, so as to have less money to pay them. It is impossible during these suspensions for the workmen to find work elsewhere, without abandoning altogether their work on the Canal. I know that the contractors have very often refused to employ the inhabitants of the place: I myself have been refused at the price they were then giving; we see no other reason for that than the certainty which the contractors have of making money on the provisions which they furnish to strangers; while the inhabitants of the place provision themselves; and also because they receive rents from those who come from a distance. The day-labourers ought to have three shillings a day, and they cannot support themselves on less. If less is given them they cannot live honestly. As they are paid at present, they cannot pay their lodging money, being barely able to exist, and reduced at times to eat boiled herbs. And further the deponent sayeth not, and declares himself unable to sign — this deposition having been read over.

ix) Deposition of J.B. Laviolette

… I was requested by Major Campbell, commanding the troops which were formed before the gallery [of Mr. Grant's hotel], to return down stairs on the first gallery, which I did. I went down, and standing on the left hand of Major Campbell I ordered the mob to disperse, and return to their homes or to their business, which they did not; and seeing that they were surrounding the house, I lost no time in proceeding to read the proclamation contained in the Riot Act, which proclamation I read in a loud and distinct voice, after which I again enjoined them two or three times to disperse — this they refused to do, saying that they were about their business, and would go when they chose, and some of them shouting and hissing, and continuing to advance towards the troops and round the house: their first line was about 17 or 20 yards distant from where the Infantry stood, drawn up in a line in front of the hotel, and flanked on both sides by the Cavalry, which had divided itself into two parties, equal in number. Seeing the determination of the mob not to disperse, but, on the contrary, seeing that they were advancing, and pursuaded that it was their intention to close in, and overpower us, as they had done at Mr. Larocque's, I ordered the troops to fire. The Infantry discharged their muskets. I have no knowledge that the Cavalry fired on the mob, but I heard Capt. Jones command his men to charge the mob, which they did. I did not order the charge of the Cavalry, nor did I hear Major Campbell, the senior Officer present, give any order to that effect. No more than 3 or 4 minutes elapsed, between the reading of the Riot Act Proclamation and the order I gave to the Officer in command, to fire upon the mob. The rapids run in front of the hotel. Between them, however, there is a fence and a thick brush wood, and they are distant between three or four acres. I saw the Cavalry charge the mob up and down the road, which is at a distance of about 25 yards from the front of Grant's hotel, diverging to the right and to the left of the house to reach the road. One man was killed on the spot, by the fire from the Infantry. There were six men buried after the Coroner's Inquest, which took place some 3 or 4 days after the Riot, from wounds received by the fire of the Infantry. Troops, with the Police, surrounded the Bush between the road and the river, and made twenty-seven prisoners, who were given in charge of the Military at the Mills, where they were kept for five or six days. I did not examine them, having no deposition against them, and having been assured on the contrary by the contractors, and by Mr. Shanly, one of the assistant-engineers, that there was nothing against them, and that they had been forced into the Riot, I thought my best course was to discharge them, which I did the more readily, as I was convinced that the one-half of the poor men who had shewn themselves in the mob, had been compelled to do so against their wishes. Since the riots, I have caused three men to be apprehended and committed to the Montreal Gaol, without any previous examination, as I did not consider myself competent to enquire into offences of the nature of those with which they stood charged by the depositions made against them. The names of the men so committed are Daniel Barron, Neil McCulloch, and Michael Cochran. I issued no warrants for the apprehension of these men, or any of them, but merely gave verbal orders to the Special Constables who arrested them ...

(Signed) J. B. Laviolette

x) Commissioners' Report

Report of the Commissioners appointed to inquire into the Disturbances upon the line of the Beauharnois Canal, during the summer of 1843; and Statements of the Expenses attending the suppression of the Riots on the Beauharnois and Lachine Canals; laid before the Legislative Assembly, by Message from His Excellency the Governor General, on the 16th October, 1843 ...

The hours of labour required from the workmen, each day, were never made to extend beyond twelve: some say the day's labour usually began at six a.m. and closed at six p.m., while two hours of intermission were allowed for meals. The labourers were invariably paid in cash, at the rate of three shillings per day, and they usually received their wages semi-monthly. Under this system, the men employed were quiet and apparently content. But when, subsequently, the same labourers, with many others, were employed by the various individuals, who have entered into contracts with the Board of Works for the completion of the work which remained to be performed on the Canal, their condition was greatly altered. Their hours of daily labour were extended; their wages became payable at the close of each month, and were reduced to the following rates per day — two shillings in March; two shillings and three pence in April; and two shillings and six pence in May.

The Contractors kept Stores, to which the men, when unprovided with money and credit to purchase elsewhere, were compelled to resort for such articles of food and clothing as they supplied.

In these Stores, few, if any, of the provisions which constitute the necessaries of life amongst the labouring classes, were to be found; so that the workmen were obliged to live almost exclusively upon food of an expensive description, such as bread, butter, tea, coffee, sugar, &c. Accounts of the supplies thus furnished to the men, were kept and at the close of each month, they usually received in cash, any balance that might be due to them ...

High rents were also paid to the contractors by the laborers for the small wooden huts called shanties which afford them shelter, although in each contract, the person undertaking it, binds himself towards the Board of Works "to provide the workmen on the Canal with suitable lodgings."

The general discontent which grew out of this new order of things soon became apparent. On the first day of May a body of men, amounting in number to about one hundred, proceeded from the western extremity of the Canal, along the whole line, for the purpose of effecting a combination amongst the laborers, but failing to induce all their fellow workmen to adopt at once the course proposed, they obtained a promise, that a general strike should be made on the thirty-first of May, throughout every portion of the works, and that no more labor should be performed after that time until they had obtained three shillings per day ...

The intention the laborers had formed, to strike for higher wages at the close of May, became generally known in the neighbourhood of the Canal, and had at an early period of that month, reached the ears of Mr. Laviolette, the Stipendiary Magistrate appointed by Your Excellency's lamented predecessor, for the purpose of maintaining order amongst the workmen on the Canal ...

On the evening of the thirty-first of May, all the labourers employed on the Canal, gave up their tools and notified their employers, that they would not resume their labors until wages had been increased to three shillings per day.

From this time until the tenth of the following month all remained quiet; although want and distress prevailed in various quarters, but more especially, on Mr. Crawford's sections, where the provision Stores were closed, so soon as the men withdrew from their labours.

Meantime a requisition for military assistance, was addressed to Colonel England, by Mr. Laviolette and Mr. Crawford, (the contractor above alluded to, who had been commissioned to act as Magistrate for the purpose of assisting Mr. Laviolette in the performance of his duties) and a party, consisting of fifty men and one subaltern, under the command of Major Campbell, was consequently detached from the 74th Regiment, and stationed at St. Timothée where they arrived on the morning of the tenth of June.

On the same day, a large body of men, amounting in number to three hundred, went down from the upper sections, to the eastern extremity of the Canal, and obtained a promise from a number of the labourers on each section, to the effect that they would assemble at the Mills in the Parish of St. Timothée on the following Monday, for the purpose of proceeding thence, in a body, to demand higher wages, from each of the contractors.

On their return towards the western end of the Canal, these men stopped at Grant's Hotel, where Mr. McDonald, one of the contractors then resided, and enquired of him if he would consent to pay his men more than two shillings and six pence per day: Mr. McDonald answered this question in the negative, whereupon a voice, from the crowd, was heard to say, that he (Mr. McDonald) would be compelled to do so, or give up his contract, and that if on the following Monday he did not consent to give three shillings per day, he should be killed or thrown into the rapids.

They then advanced towards Brown & Finlay's section when having met with a similar refusal, they broke a few panes of glass in the store, and intimated to Mr. Brown, that they would grant him delay, until the following Monday, at eleven o'clock to reflect upon the expediency of complying with their demands. It would appear that these men, a number of whom it is to be remarked, were recognized as having been in the employ of Mr. Dunn, soon after dispersed.

During the night of Sunday the eleventh, Mr. Andrew Elliott, contractor for section No. 2, was attacked in his dwelling house, by a number of men, four of whom were armed with muskets, which were placed at his breast, while the question was put to him, whether he would or would not raise the wages to the required price; and while he hesitated to reply, the trigger of one of the muskets was drawn, but the priming flashed in the pan. Mr. Elliott's assailants did not disperse until they had beaten him so severely, as to leave him senseless on the ground, and had committed some other acts of violence.

Mr. Laviolette in the deposition made by him on the nineteenth ultimo states in detail what occurred at Mr. Larocque's, at an early hour on the following morning (Monday the twelfth of June) when after the proclamation of the Riot Act had been read, a party of thirty soldiers, under the command of

Lieutenant Debutts, was surrounded and rendered powerless, by a mob collected from the western section of the Canal, who taking advantage of their success, compelled Mr. Symonds, Mr. Larocque's partner, to consent to the demanded increase of wages. During the absence of Mr. Laviolette in this quarter, a body of men from the eastern end of the Canal, crowded tumultuously around Mr. Grant's Hotel, situate at the place of Rendez-vous, chosen on the preceding Saturday. Mr. McDonald stepped forward on being called for, and having refused to accede to the demand which was made for higher wages, he was pursued and compelled to seek refuge in the cellar of the hotel, to protect himself from the fury of the mob, who when baffled in their pursuit, broke several windows in Grant's house, and turning towards Mr. McDonald's store, entered it by force, and destroyed or scattered all its contents.

After these men had disappeared, in the direction of the western extremity of the Canal, Mr. Laviolette returned to Grant's hotel at about noon, with the party of Infantry under the command of Lieutenant Debutts. They were accompanied by Mr. Crawford and Captain Jones at the head of a Troop, consisting of thirty horsemen, by whom they had been joined on the way from Mr. Larocque's section.

Mr. Laviolette on his arrival preferred a requisition to Major Campbell, for assistance, to protect Mr. Crawford's property at the eastern extremity of the Canal. The party which was detached for that purpose, consisting of forty men and a subaltern, under the command of Major Campbell, was drawn up on the high road, waiting for Mr. Laviolette, when the approach of a large body of men, formed as it is natural to infer, by a junction of the two mobs, who had appeared to Grant's, and at Mr. Larocque's in the morning, induced the Officer in command of the detachment to place his men in a position of safety.

They were accordingly drawn up in line before Grant's house, immediately in front of the gallery; the Infantry was stationed in the centre, facing the highway and was flanked by the cavalry on either side.

The mob halted by word of command, on the highway, in front of the hotel, their first line being at the distance of from twenty five to thirty paces from the troops; no fire arms were seen amongst them, they made no attempt to advance, but kept moving up and down the high road, and "there was a little shouting and hissing amongst them."

Mr. Laviolette after having requested them, in vain, to disperse peaceably, placed himself on a line with the troops, read the proclamation contained in the Riot Act, and again enjoined them to disperse; seeing however, that they evinced no disposition to withdraw and apprehending with Major Campbell, that, by means of a manoeuvre similar to that which was so successfully practised, but a few hours previous, on Mr. Debutt's detachment, at Mr. Larocque's house, the troops might be surrounded and overpowered. Mr. Laviolette, commanded the latter to fire. This order was repeated by Major Campbell, to the troops under his command; whereupon a volley was fired by the cavalry, as well as by the infantry and the former charged the mob with drawn swords ...

The mob fled in all directions at the first fire, and were pursued by the Cavalry and Infantry. It is said that the Infantry discharged no more than one round, yet several shots were fired subsequently, not only around Grant's Hotel, but also in the neighbourhood of the Mills. It has been ascertained that six men, at least, were killed by the fire of the musketry; a person whose body was found at Lachine, some days afterwards, as stated in the Coroner's certificate is supposed to have leaped into the river on that occasion to evade his pursuers and to have been drowned in the rapids.

The number of persons wounded remains unknown, as we have received no information on this point from any other quarter, than the English Hospital into which five of them were admitted.

During the pursuit, twenty seven prisoners were made, but after having remained under the charge of the Military at the Mills, during some five or six days, these men were all discharged by Mr. Laviolette, without examination, for the reasons assigned in the deposition given by him on the nineteenth ultimo.

We have clearly traced the origin of the disturbances, which terminated in the fatal manner above described, to the universal dissatisfaction entertained by all the labourers on the Canal, with the rate of wages allowed them by their employers.

This obvious fact naturally suggested the enquiry, whether these men had any just ground of complaint in that respect; and feeling the importance of this branch of our investigation, we amassed a volume of evidence relative thereto, which will fully bear us out in the opinion we have formed, namely: that the price paid by the contractors to their labourers, even when increased to two shillings and six pence per day, was not only an inadequate remuneration for the services of the latter, but was insufficient to afford them the means of subsisting.

It appears evident to us that a labourer employed on a Canal, remote from his ordinary place of abode, should always receive a remuneration higher by one fourth than the current wages of the season. The Canal labourer can seldom, if ever, obtain employment during more than twenty days in one month, even during the most favorable season and the works are not unfrequently suspended during weeks in succession, in consequence of rainy weather, and other accidents. During these intervals he cannot leave the neighbourhood to seek temporary employment without incurring the risk of being thrown out of employment for the season; as, a sudden resumption of the works may induce the contractor to employ another in his stead; moreover, provisions are invariably higher in the neighbourhood of public works, and, if he be a married man, his wife instead of contributing by her industry to the support of the little household, as she might do, were she in the neighbourhood of a City, becomes merely an additional burthen. Indeed we have no doubt that two shillings and six pence per day, even when paid in money at the most convenient intervals, is a remuneration of less value to the Canal man, than one shilling and eight pence would be to a labourer in a City, who is permanently employed, at least through the whole of the working season.

But, in addition to the disadvantages common to all labourers on Canals, the workmen on this line were compelled, by the system of monthly payments, to resort to the stores of the Contractors for all the necessaries of life. Here the small pittance of those who were burthened with families was usually exhausted before the day of reckoning, in the purchase of bread, pork, tea, coffee, sugar, and other such expensive articles of food, for which they would have advantageously substituted potatoes, meal, milk, eggs, &c., had the payments been made at such convenient intervals as to leave them a free choice. Heavy rents had also to be paid by these men, notwithstanding the 8th clause of the contracts, by which, according to our interpretation, the contractors were bound to furnish all the workmen on the Canal with suitable lodgings, free of expense.

The dissatisfaction which sprung out of the feeling that their labour was not sufficiently remunerated was increased by the unreasonable length to which their daily hours of labour were extended, especially on certain sections; and, when discontent had ripened into tumult and disorder, we find standing prominently forth, amongst the first instigators of aggressive measures, the men who were reduced to a state of destitution by Mr. Dunn's inability to pay them.

In the month of May, the Canal gave employment to between two and three thousand workmen, the great majority of whom were natives of Ireland, some of them had recently emigrated; others had been for several years engaged in public works in Canada and the United States.

The discontent occasioned by the various causes of complaint above adverted to, being fostered by neglect, soon roused the angry feelings of the more easily excited portion of these men, and they determined upon urging their fellow labourers to combine for the purpose of compelling the contractors to better their condition.

So early as the first of May a disposition had been publicly manifested, by the men employed on some of the western sections, to effect a combination. On the fifteenth of that month, the men employed on Pierce, Black and Co.'s section, rose with the same object in view; and about that time it became publicly known throughout the whole neighbourhood, that a strike for higher wages was to take place, on the first of June, along the whole line of the works. Meanwhile, the Stipendiary Magistrate, who was appointed for the sole purpose of maintaining peace and order amongst these ignorant and excitable men, remained inactive. In fact, the gentleman who acted in that capacity seems to have wholly misunderstood the object for which he was appointed ...

The impropriety of resorting to the employment of Military assistance, except in cases of absolute and imperious necessity is a topic which we would deem it unnecessary to dwell upon in addressing Your Excellency, even though our instructions had gone further than to require of us *such information* only as we could furnish, respecting the lamentable catastrophe which occurred on that day.

Whether a Magistrate can legally order troops to fire into an assembly of men who are not at the moment engaged in the perpetration of any Act of violence against persons or property and when no more than four minutes have elapsed after reading the proclamation contained in the Riot Act, is a question which with various others of minor importance arising out of the occurrences of that fatal day, as narrated above, is left for the consideration of the Executive.

In lamenting above all, the necessity, real or supposed, which demanded a sacrifice of several lives on that occasion, we deem it our duty to record also the regret which we have experienced on discovering that whenever the assistance of the civil power was invoked during these disturbances, it has been invariable rendered by ignorance or neglect, either an instrument of oppression or an object of derision.

The twenty seven prisoners who were taken upon the dispersion of the mob by the united attack of the Infantry and Cavalry, on the twelfth day of June, were detained during five or six days in close confinement under a Military guard, and then discharged without examination. If these men had rendered themselves guilty of an offence against the laws, why were they allowed to escape punishment? If on the other hand they were innocent why detain them a single hour? ...

17

"The Bold Scheme"

Confederation

DOCUMENTS

A) Confederation Debates, 1865
   - i) Tuesday, February 7
     Hon. George Etienne Cartier (Attorney General) [Montreal]
   - ii) Friday, February 3
     Hon. Sir Etienne-Pascal Taché (Premier, Receiver-General, Minister of Militia)
   - iii) Wednesday, February 8
     Hon. George Brown (President of the Council) [South Oxford]
   - iv) Thursday, February 16
     Hon. Antoine Aimé Dorion [Hochelaga]
   - v) Monday, February 27
     Christopher Dunkin [Brome]
B) Speeches and Letters, 1866
   Joseph Howe
C) Annexation or Union with the United States is the Manifest Destiny of British North America, 1868
   Alex Munro

Was this country a good idea? Was it even possible to fuse independent-minded British colonies into one giant territory with a tiny population spread unevenly along the southern perimeter? Canada still exists, but does that make it either good or viable? Quebec clearly remains unhappy in the national marriage, and library shelves bulge with books on western Canadian alienation. Perhaps Réné Lévesque was right: Confederation was a shotgun wedding doomed to fail, and we should admit it, get on with the divorce, and be friends. And yet what about the unity rally in downtown Montreal in 1995? How about those thousands who wept at the thought of Canada torn asunder? Our present debate on national unity rolls on, just as it did during the 1860s.

George Etienne Cartier (1814–1873) came from the comfort of a wealthy French Canadian family. He graduated from a Montreal college and began his legal career two years before the outbreak of the 1837 rebellions. This was a turbulent time and he, along with many other young French Canadian idealists, joined the militant underground *Fils de la Liberté* organization. Unlike many of his fellow rebels, however, Cartier fought the openly authoritarian local British administration, not the British crown. He became a wanted man after the rebellions failed, and fled to the United States where he remained until 1839. Ever defiant, he dared British administrators to prove their charges of treason against him. They could not, lacking solid proof, and he returned to his law practice.

Almost ten years later, now part of the French Canadian establishment, Cartier successfully ran for the Legislative Assembly. There he lobbied hard on behalf of the Grand Trunk Railway, for which he also worked as legal advisor. He easily survived charges of collusion and kept advancing, first becoming Attorney General, then joint Premier with John A. MacDonald in 1857. "Conflict of interest" was clearly not a major issue then. So why did Cartier, the old rebel, favour federation? He played a key role at the Charlottetown conference of September, 1864, and helped sway the delegates away from maritime union toward a wider federation of all British North America. Cartier's part in creating modern Canada should not be underestimated. He later served in the country's first federal cabinet as Minister of Militia, and much of Canada's vital expansion into the west occurred through his prodigious efforts.

Etienne Taché (1795–1865) traced his family roots far back into the history of New France. He, too, became a passionate promoter of federation, and like Cartier, arrived at that position via French Canadian nationalism. Thus it is hardly surprising that he supported the *Patriotes* during the rebellions. He feared the United States enough to take up arms during the War of 1812, but admired the U.S. sufficiently to do his medical training in Philadelphia. Medicine was perhaps too small a vocation for his ego, and he entered politics. There, as a prominent French Canadian, he shared the premiership with Allan McNab in 1855 and with John A. MacDonald the following year. His efforts helped create the highly successful Liberal-Conservative party that united conservatives from Canada West with their counterparts from Canada East. Taché came out of retirement to join the coalition of 1864 and presided over the Quebec Conference in October. Not exactly self-effacing, he eventually concluded that his efforts alone all but created Canada.

George Brown (1818–1880) also came from wealth, in his case a successful Edinburgh commercial family. His father, however, faced ruin when he muddled his own bank accounts with those of the municipality. The family fled to the United States, but influential Canadian Scots successfully lured him to settle in Canada in 1843. George Brown eventually started the Toronto *Globe,* which became the highest circulation newspaper in British North America. He quickly rose to prominence as a leading business figure and champion of political reform, particularly over the thorny issue of religion. Church and state should remain separate, Brown wrote in his editorials, and clergy reserves must be secularized. His controversial stance gained him an anti-Catholic, anti-French Canadian reputation that helped him politically. He won a seat in the Legislative Assembly in 1852, and soon set to acquiring all Hudson's Bay Company lands for Canada. Then, as leader of the revamped Clear Grits, he focussed on breaking the political deadlock plaguing Canada. This he attempted by spearheading the 1864 pro-federation coalition with his old rival, John A. MacDonald, and venturing to both the Charlottetown and Quebec conferences where he played a prominent role. He, unlike so many other Canadians, wanted closer relations with the United States, and this unpopular stance caused his departure from active politics. He remained behind the scenes of the Liberal Party throughout the 1870s, and accepted a Senate seat in 1874. A senator's life, which some have come to regard as the perfect venue for a long, comfortable, and lucrative semi-retirement, came to an abrupt end. Brown, who fought union activity throughout his life, was finally shot by a disgruntled employee. He died of the ensuing complications in 1880.

Joseph Howe (1804–1873) is perhaps best known for his "Botheration Letters," which he published as part of his political crusade against federation. Howe's primary allegiance was to the British empire and to Nova Scotia's independent place in it. Thus it is hardly surprising that he rebelled against the idea of a pan-British North American union. What, after all, could Nova Scotia gain? Would it not become a pawn pushed around by central Canada? He certainly supported a more integrated British Empire, but Howe believed that each colony should retain its autonomy within it. Howe refused to attend the Charlottetown and Quebec conferences of 1864, and instead led a local anti-Confederation delegation to London. They fought hard, but the British government wanted Canada united and paid little attention to them. They returned empty-handed but made their point when only one pro-Confederation candidate won his seat in the 1867 Nova Scotia election. Reinvigorated, he tried again, but London remained adamant. Many of his followers, in frustration, slowly drifted toward more radical solutions: rebellion or annexation to the United States. Howe, ever loyal to England, bowed before the inevitable and reluctantly accepted Confederation as a *fait accompli*. He finally accepted a cabinet post in the new federal government as Secretary of State. His last political appointment could be considered a fitting tribute: he became Lieutenant Governor of Nova Scotia.

Antoine Dorion (1818–1891) studied classics at a local seminary and then turned to law and politics. Though steeped in conservative Quebec culture, he strongly believed in universal suffrage and public education, and even admired American political institutions. This did not sit well with his fellow Quebec nationalists with whom he retained an uneasy alliance. Dorion eventually led the important French Canadian *Rouge* party, but always felt uncomfortable with its radical anti-clerical, nationalist wing. A bizarre agreement between him and Montreal's capitalist anglophone community led to an unlikely alliance, in 1849, calling for annexation to the United States. Remarkably, this was not political suicide, and he eventually led a short-lived government with George Brown in 1858, thereby outraging many of his nationalist supporters. Later his party rejected the 1864 coalition and actively campaigned against federation. His position on this issue did not prevent him from becoming a prominent member of both the provincial and federal Liberal parties. He became Minister of Justice in 1874, and later a federal judge.

Christopher Dunkin (1812–1881) grew up in a wealthy English household. He studied at the universities of London and Glasgow before drifting to the United States where he tutored Greek and Latin at Harvard. He then went on to Montreal, arriving in 1837, the year of the rebellions. There he worked as a journalist and later, as a high-ranking civil servant. Dunkin next took up law and became one of the highest paid and most respected lawyers in Canada East. His first dabble in politics ended in failure, but his second won him a seat for the Eastern Townships from 1857–61 and again from 1862–67. Cold, conceited, and insufferably self-righteous, he rammed through a prohibition bill in 1864. His Anglo supporters still accused him of cozying up to the French Canadian majority when he became treasurer of Quebec following Confederation. He eventually entered federal politics and became Minister of Agriculture in 1869. Dunkin ended his days on the bench of Quebec's superior court.

When Barnes and Company published his pamphlet, they described Alex Munro as an author of several works on the history, geography, and statistics of British North American. Literary and other searches have thus far failed to unearth any further publications or information about him.

A) Confederation Debates
i) Tuesday, February 7, 1865
Hon. George Etienne Cartier (Attorney General) [Montreal]

... The question for us to ask ourselves was this: Shall we be content to remain separate — shall we be content to maintain a mere provincial existence, when, by combining together, we could become a great nation? It had never yet been the good fortune of any group of communities to secure national greatness with such facility. In past ages, warriors had struggled for years for the addition to their country of a single province ... Here, in British North America, we had five different communities inhabiting five separate colonies. We had the same sympathies, and we all desired to live under the British Crown. We had our commercial interests besides. It was of no use whatever that New Brunswick, Nova Scotia and Newfoundland should have their several custom houses against our trade, or that we should have custom houses against the trade of those provinces. In ancient times, the manner in which a nation grew up was different from that of the present day. Then the first weak settlement increased into a village, which, by turns, became a town and a city, and the nucleus of a nation. It was not so in modern times. Nations were now formed by the agglomeration of communities having kindred interests and sympathies. Such was our case at the present moment. Objection had been taken to the scheme now under consideration, because of the words "new nationality." Now, when we were united together, if union were attained, we would form a political nationality with which neither the national origin, nor the religion of any individual, would interfere. It was lamented by some that we had this diversity of races, and hopes were expressed that this distinctive feature would cease. The idea of unity of races was utopian — it was impossible. Distinctions of this kind would always exist. Dissimilarity, in fact, appeared to be the order of the physical world and of the moral world, as well as of the political world. But with regard to the objection based on this fact, to the effect that a great nation could not be formed because Lower Canada was in great part French and Catholic, and Upper Canada was British and Protestant, and the Lower Provinces were mixed, it was futile and worthless in the extreme. Look, for instance, at the United Kingdom, inhabited as it was by three great races. (Hear, hear.) Had the diversity of race impeded the glory, the progress, the wealth of England? Had they not rather each contributed their share to the greatness of the Empire? Of the glories ... how much was contributed by the combined talents, energy and courage of the three races together? (Cheers.) In our own Federation we should have Catholic and Protestant, English, French, Irish and Scotch, and each by his efforts and his success would increase the prosperity and glory of the new Confederacy. (Hear, hear.) He viewed the diversity of races in British North America in this way: we were of different races, not for the purpose of warring against each other, but in order to compete and emulate for the general welfare. (Cheers.) We could not do away with the distinctions of race. We could not legislate for the disappearance of the French Canadians from American soil, but British and French Canadians alike could appreciate and understand their position relative to each other. They were placed like great families beside each other, and their contact produced a healthy spirit of emulation. It was a benefit rather than otherwise that we had a diversity of races ...

ii) **Friday, February 3, 1865**
     ***Hon. Sir Etienne-Pascal Taché (Premier, Receiver-General,
     Minister of Militia)***

... The honorable member then referred to the artificial communications of the country, viz., our Canals, which, he said, were on a scale unequalled in America, or, indeed, in the world. Our Railway system too, in proportion to our means and population, was as extensive as could be found anywhere else; yet with all these advantages, natural and acquired, he was bound to say we could not become a great nation. We labored under a drawback or disadvantage which would effectually prevent that, and he would defy any one to take a map of the world and point to any great nation which had not seaports of its own open at all times of the year. Canada did not possess those advantages, but was shut up in a prison, as it were, for five months of the year in fields of ice, which all the steam engineering apparatus of human ingenuity could not overcome, and so long as this state of things continued, we must consent to be a small people, who could, at any moment, be assailed and invaded by a people better situated in that respect than we were. Canada was, in fact, just like a farmer who might stand upon an elevated spot on his property, from which he could look around upon fertile fields, meandering streams, wood and all else that was necessary to his domestic wants, but who had no outlet to the highway. To be sure he might have an easy, good-natured neighbor, who had such an outlet, and this neighbor might say to him, "Don't be uneasy about that, for I will allow you to pass on to the highway, through my cross road, and we shall both profit by the arrangement." So long as this obliging neighbor was in good humor everything would go on pleasantly, but the very best natured people would sometimes get out of temper, or grow capricious, or circumstances might arise to cause irritation. And so it might come to pass that the excellent neighbor would get dissatisfied. For instance, he might be involved in a tedious and expensive law suit with someone else; it might be a serious affair — in fact, an affair of life or death, and he might come to the isolated farmer and say to him, "I understand that you and your family are all sympathising with my adversary; I don't like it at all, and I am determined you will find some other outlet to the highway than my cross road, for henceforth my gate will be shut against you." In such a case what is the farmer to do? There is the air left, but until the aerostatic science is more practically developed, he can hardly try ballooning without the risk of breaking his neck. (Laughter.) Well, that was precisely our position in reference to the United States … The people of the Northern States believed that Canadians sympathized with the South much more than they really did, and the consequences of this misapprehension were: first, that we had been threatened with the abolition of the transit system; then the Reciprocity Treaty was to be discontinued; then a passport system was inaugurated, which was almost equivalent to a prohibition of intercourse, and the only thing which really remained to be done was to shut down the gate altogether and prevent passage through their territory. Would anyone say that such a state of things was one desirable for Canada to be placed in? Will a great people in embryo, as he believed we were, coolly and tranquilly cross their arms and wait for what might come next? …

On the whole, he thought that the Confederation of all the Provinces had become an absolute necessity, and that it was for us a question of to be or not to be. If we desired to remain British and monarchial, and if we desired to pass to our children these advantages, this measure, he repeated, was a necessity. But there were other motives and other reasons which should induce us to agree to the scheme. Every honorable gentleman in the House knew the political position of the country, and were acquainted with the feelings of irritation which have prevailed for many years. They knew it happily not by their experience in this House, but by the tone of the public press, and by the discussions in another place where taunts and menaces were freely flung across the floor by contending parties. They knew what human passions were, and how, when bitter feelings continued for a long time, the distance between exasperation and actual conflict was not very great. They had now before their own eyes an example of the effects of such disagreements. It was persistently believed by many that the rival interests would never come to a rupture, but for three years they had been waging a conflict which had desolated and ruined the fairest portion of the country, and in the course of which acts of barbarity had been committed which were only equalled by the darkest ages. We in Canada were not more perfect, and the time had arrived when, as he believed, all the patriotic men in the country ought to unite in providing a remedy for the troubles we had to contend with. It might be said that the remedy proposed was not required, but he would like to know what other could be proposed. Legislation in Canada for the last two years had come almost to a stand still, and if any one would refer to the Statute Book since 1862, he would find that the only public measures there inscribed had been passed simply by the permission of the Opposition. This was the condition of things for two years, and if this were an evil there was another not less to be deplored; he referred to the administration of public affairs during the same period. From the 21st May, 1862, to the end of June, 1864, there had been no less than five different Governments in charge of the business of the country ...

Lower Canada had constantly refused the demand of Upper Canada for representation according to population, and for the good reason that, as the union between them was legislative, a preponderance to one of the sections would have placed the other at its mercy. It would not be so in a Federal Union, for all questions of a general nature would be reserved for the General Government, and those of a local character to the local governments, who would have the power to manage their domestic affairs as they deemed best. If a Federal Union were obtained it would be tantamount to a separation of the provinces, and Lower Canada would thereby preserve its autonomy together with all the institutions it held so dear, and over which they could exercise the watchfulness and surveillance necessary to preserve them unimpaired ...

iii) Wednesday, February 8, 1865
Hon. George Brown (President of the Council) [South Oxford]

... Well, sir, the bold scheme in your hands is nothing less than to gather all these countries [Newfoundland, Nova Scotia, New Brunswick, Lower Canada, Upper Canada, and British Columbia] into one — to organize them all under one government, with the protection of the British flag, and in heartiest sympathy and affection with our fellow-subjects in the land that gave us birth. (Cheers.) Our scheme is to establish a government that will seek to turn the tide of European emigration into this northern half of the American continent — that will strive to develop its great natural resources — and that will endeavor to maintain liberty, and justice, and Christianity throughout the land.

Mr. T. C. Wallbridge — When?

Hon. Mr. Cartier — Very soon!

Hon. Mr. Brown — ... We imagine not that such a structure can be built in a month or in a year. What we propose now is but to lay the foundations of the structure — to set in motion the governmental machinery that will one day, we trust, extend from the Atlantic to the Pacific. And we take especial credit to ourselves that the system we have devised, while admirably adapted to our present situation, is capable of gradual and efficient expansion in future years to meet all the great purposes contemplated by our scheme. But if the honorable gentleman will only recall to mind that when the United States seceded from the Mother Country, and for many years afterwards their population was not nearly equal to ours at this moment; that their internal improvements did not then approach to what we have already attained; and that their trade and commerce was not then a third of what ours has already reached; I think he will see that the fulfilment of our hopes may not be so very remote as at first sight might be imagined — (hear, hear). And he will be strengthened in that conviction if he remembers that what we propose to do is to be done with the cordial sympathy and assistance of that great Power of which it is our happiness to form a part. (Hear, hear.) Such, Mr. Speaker, are the objects of attainment to which the British American Conference pledged itself in October. And said I not rightly that such a scheme is well fitted to fire the ambition and rouse the energies of every member of this House? Does it not lift us above the petty politics of the past, and present to us high purposes and great interests that may well call forth all the intellectual ability and all the energy and enterprise to be found among us? (Cheers.) I readily admit all the gravity of the question — and that it ought to be considered cautiously and thoroughly before adoption. Far be it from me to deprecate the closest criticism, or to doubt for a moment the sincerity or patriotism of those who feel it their duty to oppose the measure. But in considering a question on which hangs the future destiny of half a continent, ought not the spirit of mere faultfinding to be hushed? — ought not the voice of partisanship to be banished from our debates? — ought we not to sit down and discuss the arguments presented in the earnest and candid spirit of men, bound by the same interests, seeking a common end, and loving the same country? (Hear, hear, and cheers.) Some honorable gentlemen seem to imagine that the members of Government have a deeper interest in this scheme than others — but what possible interest can any of us have except that which we share with every citizen of the land? What risk does any one run from this measure in which all of us do not fully participate? What possible inducement could we have to urge this scheme, except our earnest and heartfelt conviction that it will inure to the solid and lasting advantage of our country? (Hear, hear.) There is one consideration, Mr. Speaker, that cannot be banished from this discussion, and that ought, I think, to be remembered in every word we utter; it is that the constitutional system of Canada cannot remain as it is now. (Loud cries of hear, hear.) Something must be done. We cannot stand still. We cannot go back to chronic, sectional hostility and discord — to a state of perpetual Ministerial crises. The events of the last eight months cannot be obliterated; the solemn admissions of men of all parties can never be erased. The claims of Upper Canada for justice must be met, and met now. I say, then, that every one who raises his voice in hostility to this measure is bound to keep before him, when he speaks, all the perilous consequences of its rejection, — I say that no man who has a true regard for the well-being of Canada, can give a vote against this scheme, unless he is prepared to offer, in amendment, some better remedy for the evils and injustice that have so long threatened the peace of our country. (Hear, hear.) ...

But, Mr. Speaker, the second feature of this scheme as a remedial measure is, that it removes, to a large extent, the injustice of which Upper Canada has complained in financial matters. We in Upper Canada have complained that though we paid into the public treasury more than three-fourths of the whole revenue, we had less control over the system of taxation and the expenditure of the public moneys than the people of Lower Canada. Well, sir, the scheme in your hand remedies that. The absurd line of separation between the provinces is swept way for general matters; we are to have seventeen additional members in the house that holds the purse; and the taxpayers of the country, wherever they reside, will have their just share of influence over revenue and expenditure. (Hear, hear.) We have also complained that immense sums of public money have been systematically taken from the public chest for local purposes of Lower Canada, in which the people of Upper Canada had no interest whatever, though compelled to contribute three-fourths of the cash. Well sir, this scheme remedies that. All local matters are to be banished from the General Legislature; local governments are to have control over local affairs, and if our friends in Lower Canada choose to be extravagant, they will have to bear the burden of it themselves. (Hear, hear.) No longer shall we have to complain that one section pays the cash while the other spends it; hereafter, they who pay will spend, and they who spend more than they ought will have to bear the brunt. (Hear, hear.) It was a great thing to accomplish this, if we had accomplished nothing more, — for if we look back on our doings of the last fifteen years, I think it will be acknowledged that the greatest jobs perpetrated were of a local character — that our fiercest contests were about local matters that stirred up sectional jealousies and indignation to its deepest depth. (Hear, hear.) We have further complained that if a sum was properly demanded for some legitimate local purpose in one section, an equivalent sum had to be appropriated to the other as an offset, — thereby entailing prodigal expenditure, and unnecessarily increasing the public debt. Well, sir, this scheme puts an end to that. Each province is to determine for itself its own wants, and to find the money to meet them from its own resources. (Hear, hear.) ...

I am persuaded that this union will inspire new confidence in our stability, and exercise the most beneficial influence on all our affairs. I believe it will raise the value of our public securities, that it will draw capital to our shores, and secure the prosecution of all legitimate enterprises; and what I saw, while in England, a few weeks ago, would alone have convinced me of this. Wherever you went you encountered the most marked evidence of the gratification with which the Confederation scheme was received by all classes of the people, and the deep interest taken in its success ...

But secondly, Mr. Speaker, I go heartily for the union, because it will throw down the barriers of trade and give us the control of a market of four millions of people. (Hear, hear.) What one thing has contributed so much to the wondrous material progress of the United States as the free passage of their products from one State to another? What has tended so much to the rapid advance of all branches of their industry, as the vast extent of their home market, creating an unlimited demand for all the commodities of daily use, and stimulating the energy and ingenuity of producers? Sir, I confess to you that in my mind this one view of the union — the addition of nearly a million of people to our home consumers — sweeps aside all the petty objections that are averred against the scheme. What, in comparison with this great gain to our farmers and manufacturers, are even the fallacious money objections which the imaginations of honorable gentlemen opposite have summoned up? All over the world we find nations eagerly longing to extend their domains, spending large sums and waging protracted wars to possess themselves of more territory, untilled and uninhabited. (Hear, hear.) Other countries offer large inducements to foreigners to emigrate to their shores — free passages, free lands, and free food and implements to start them in the world. We, ourselves, support costly establishments to attract immigrants to our country, and are satisfied when our annual outlay brings us fifteen or twenty thousand souls. But here, sir, is a proposal which is to add, in one day, near a million of souls to our population — to add valuable territories to our domain, and secure to us all the advantages of a large and profitable commerce, now existing ... [H]ere is a people owning the same allegiance as ourselves, loving the same old sod, enjoying the same laws and institutions, actuated by the same impulses and social customs, — and yet when it is proposed that they shall unite with us for purposes of commerce, for the defence of our common country, and to develop the vast natural resources of our united domains, we hesitate to adopt it! If a Canadian goes now to Nova Scotia or New Brunswick, or if a citizen of these provinces comes here, it is like going to a foreign country. The customs officer meets you at the frontier, arrests your progress, and levies his imposts on your effects. But the proposal now before us is to throw down all barriers between the provinces — to make a citizen of one, citizen of the whole; the proposal is, that our farmers and manufacturers and mechanics shall carry their wares unquestioned into every village of the Maritime Provinces; and that they shall with equal freedom bring their fish, and their coal, and their West India produce to our three millions of inhabitants. The proposal is, that the law courts, and the schools, and the professional and industrial walks of life, throughout all the provinces, shall be thrown equally open to us all. (Hear, hear.)

But, thirdly, Mr. Speaker, I am in favor of a union of the provinces because — and I call the attention of honorable gentlemen opposite to it — because it will make us the third maritime state of the world. (Hear, hear.) When this union is accomplished, but two countries in the world will be superior in maritime influence to British America — and those are Great Britain and the United States. (Hear, hear.) ... Well may [the French-Canadian people] look forward with anxiety to the realization of this part of our scheme, in confident hope that the great north-western traffic shall be once more opened up to the hardy French-Canadian traders and voyageurs. (Hear, hear.) Last year furs to the value of £280,000 ($1,400,000) were carried from that territory by the Hudson's Bay Company — smuggled off through the ice-bound regions of James' Bay, that the pretence of the barrenness of the country and the difficulty of conveying merchandise by the natural route of the St. Lawrence may be kept up a little longer. Sir, the carrying of merchandise into that country, and bringing down the bales of pelts ought to be ours, and must ere long be ours, as in the days of yore — (hear, hear) — and when the fertile plains of that great Saskatchewan territory are opened up for settlement and cultivation, I am confident that it will not only add immensely to our annual agricultural products, but bring us sources of mineral and other wealth on which at present we do not reckon. (Hear, hear.) ...

But, sixthly, Mr. Speaker, I am in favor of the union of the provinces, because, in the event of war, it will enable all the colonies to defend themselves better, and give more efficient aid to the Empire, than they could do separately. I am not one of those who ever had the war-fever; I have not believed in getting up large armaments in this country; I have never doubted that a military spirit, to a certain extent, did necessarily form part of the character of a great people; but I felt that Canada had not yet reached that stage in her progress when she could safely assume the duty of defence; and that, so long as peace continued and the Mother Country threw her shield around us, it was well for us to cultivate our fields and grow in numbers and material strength, until we could look our enemies fearlessly in the face. But it must be admitted — and there is no use of closing our eyes to the fact — that this question of defence has been placed, within the last two years, in a totally different position from what it ever occupied before. The time has come — it matters not what political party may be in power in England — when Britain will insist on a reconsideration of the military relations which a great colony, such as Canada, ought to hold to the Empire. And I am free to admit that it is a fair and just demand. We may doubt whether some of the demands that have been made upon us, without regard to our peculiar position at the moment, and without any attempt to discuss the question with us in all its breadth, were either just or well-considered. But of this I think there can be no doubt, that when the time comes in the history of any colony that it has overcome the burdens and embarrassments of early settlement, and has entered on a career of permanent progress and prosperity, it is only fair and right that it should contribute its quota to the defence of the Empire. What that quota ought to be, I think, is a matter for grave deliberation and discussion, as well as the measure of assistance the colony may look for, in time of war, from the parent state — and, assuredly, it is in this spirit that the present Imperial Government is desirous of approaching the question. (Hear, hear.) I am persuaded that nothing more than that which is fairly due at our hands will be demanded from us, and anything less than this, I am sure, the people of Canada do not desire. (Hear, hear.) In the conversations I had, while in England, with public men of different politics — while I found many who considered that the connection between Canada and England involved the Mother Country in some danger of war with the powerful state upon our borders, and that the colonial system devolved heavy and unreasonable burdens upon the Mother Country — and while a still larger number thought we had not acted as cordially and energetically as we ought in organizing our militia for the defence of the province, still I did not meet one public man, of any stripe of politics, who did not readily and heartily declare that, in case of the invasion of Canada, the honor of Great Britain would be at stake, and the whole strength of the Empire would be unhesitatingly marshalled in our defence. (Hear, hear.) But, coupled with this, was the invariable and most reasonable declaration that a share of the burden of defence, in peace and in war, we must contribute. And this stipulation applies not only to Canada, but to every one of the colonies. Already the Indian Empire has been made to pay the whole expense of her military establishment. The Australian Colonies have agreed to pay £40 sterling per man for every soldier sent there. This system is being gradually extended — and union or no union, assuredly every one of these British American Colonies will be called upon to bear her fair share towards the defence of the Empire. And who will deny that it is a just demand, and that great colonies such as these, should be proud to meet it in a frank and earnest spirit. (Cheers.) Nothing, I am persuaded, could be more foreign to the ideas of the people of Canada, than that the people of England should be unfairly taxed for service rendered to this province. Now, the question presented to us is simply this: will these contributions which Canada and the other provinces must hereafter make to the defence of the Empire, be better rendered by a hardy, energetic population, acting as one people, than as five or six separate communities? (Hear, hear.) There is no doubt about it. But not only do our changed relations towards the Mother Country call on us to assume the new duty of military defence, our changed relations towards the neighboring republic compel us to do so. For myself, I have no belief that the Americans have the slightest thought of attacking us. I cannot believe that the first use of their new-found liberty will be the invasion, totally unprovoked, of a peaceful province. I fancy that they have had quite enough of war for a good many years to come — and that such a war as one with England would certainly be, is the last they are likely to provoke. But, Mr. Speaker, there is no better mode of warding off war when it is threatened, than to be prepared for it if it comes. The Americans are now a warlike people. They have large armies, a powerful navy, an unlimited supply of warlike munitions, and the carnage of war has to them been stript of its horrors. The American side of our lines already bristles with works of defence, and unless we are willing to live at the mercy of our neighbors, we, too, must put our country in a state of efficient preparation. War or no war — the necessity of placing these provinces in a thorough state of defence can no longer be postponed. Our country is coming to be regarded as undefended and indefensible …

iv) Thursday, February 16, 1865
Hon. Antoine Aimé Dorion [Hochelaga]

… If the scheme proposed to us were an equitable one, or one calculated to meet the wishes of the people of this country; but, as I said a minute ago, the scheme was not called for by any considerable proportion of the population. It is not laid before the House as one which was demanded by any number of the people; it is not brought down in response to any call from the people; it is a device of men who are in difficulties, for the purpose of getting out of them. (Hear, hear.) ... I come now to another point, viz., is the scheme presented to us the same one that was promised to us by the Administration when it was formed? This, sir, might be but of slight importance if the manner in which this proposed Constitution was framed had not a most unfortunate bearing on the scheme itself; but it is a grave matter, since the scheme is so objectionable, especially as we are gravely told that it cannot be amended in the least, but that it is brought down as a compact made between the Government of this country and delegates from the governments of Nova Scotia, New Brunswick, Newfoundland, and Prince Edward Island — as a treaty which cannot be altered or amended in any particular. (Hear.) The plain meaning of this is, sir, that the Lower Provinces have made out a Constitution for us and we are to adopt it ...

The whole scheme, sir, is absurd from beginning to end. It is but natural that gentlemen with the views of honorable gentlemen opposite want to keep as much power as possible in the hands of the Government — that is the doctrine of the Conservative party everywhere — that is the line which distinguishes the tories from the whigs — the tories always side with the Crown, and the Liberals always want to give more power and influence to the people. The instincts of honorable gentlemen opposite, whether you take the Hon. Attorney General East or the Hon. Attorney General West, lead them to this — they think the hands of the Crown should be strengthened and the influence of the people, if possible, diminished — and this Constitution is a specimen of their handiwork, with a Governor General appointed by the Crown, with local governors also appointed by the Crown; with legislative councils, in the General Legislature, and in all the provinces, nominated by the Crown; we shall have the most illiberal Constitution ever heard of in any country where constitutional government prevails. (Hear.) The Speaker of the Legislative Council is also to be appointed by the Crown, this is another step backwards, and a little piece of patronage for the Government. We have heard in a speech lately delivered in Prince Edward Island or New Brunswick, I forget which, of the allurements offered to the delegates while here in the shape of prospective appointments as judges of the Court of Appeal, Speaker of the Legislative Council, and local governors — (hear, hear) — as one of the reasons assigned for the great unanimity which prevailed in the Conference.

Hon. Mr. Holton — They will divide all these nice things amongst them. (Laughter.)

Hon. Mr. Dorion — ... Now, sir, when I look into the provisions of this scheme, I find another most objectionable one. It is that which gives the General Government control over all the acts of the local legislatures. What difficulties may not arise under this system? Now, knowing that the General Government will be party in its character, may it not for party purposes reject laws passed by the local legislatures and demanded by a majority of the people of that locality ... But how different will be the result in this case, when the General Government exercises the veto power over the acts of local legislatures. Do you not see that it is quite possible for a majority in a local government to be opposed to the General Government; and in such a case the minority would call upon the General Government to disallow the laws enacted by the majority? The men who shall compose the General Government will be dependent for their support upon their political friends in the local legislatures, and it may so happen that, in order to secure this support, or in order to serve their own purposes or that of their supporters, they will veto laws which the majority of a local legislature find necessary and good. (Hear, hear.) We know how high party feeling runs sometimes upon local matters even of trivial importance, and we may find parties so hotly opposed to each other in the local legislatures, that the whole power of the minority may be brought to bear upon their friends who have a majority in the General Legislature, for the purpose of preventing the passage of some law objectionable to them but desired by the majority of their own section. What will be the result of such a state of things but bitterness of feeling, strong political acrimony and dangerous agitation? (Hear, hear.)

... [T]his scheme proposes a union not only with Nova Scotia, New Brunswick, Prince Edward Island, and Newfoundland, but also with British Columbia and Vancouver's Island ... I must confess, Mr. Speaker, that it looks like a burlesque to speak as a means of defence of a scheme of Confederation to unite the whole country extending from Newfoundland to Vancouver's Island, thousands of miles intervening without any communication, except through the United States or around Cape Horn. (Oh!) ...

I now come to another point. It is said that this Confederation is necessary for the purpose of providing a better mode of defence for this country. There may be people who think that by adding two and two together you make five. I am not of that opinion. I cannot see how, by adding the 700,000 or 800,000 people, the inhabitants of the Lower Provinces, to the 2,500,000 inhabitants of Canada, you can multiply them so as to make a much larger force to defend the country than you have at present. Of course the connection with the British Empire is the link of communication by which the whole force of the Empire can be brought together for defence. (Hear, hear.) But the position of this country under the proposed scheme is very evident. You add to the frontier four or five hundred more miles than you now have, and an extent of country immeasurably greater in proportion than the additional population you have gained; and if there is an advantage at all for the defence of the country, it will be on the part of the Lower Province, and not for us ... Within a period of four years the Northern States have called into the field 2,300,000 men — as many armed men as we have men, women and children in the two Canadas — and ... we hear every day of more being raised and equipped. It is stated that, in view of these facts, it is incumbent upon us to place ourselves in a state of defence. Sir, I say it here, candidly and honestly, that we are bound to do everything we can to protect the country – (Hear, hear.) – but we are not bound to ruin ourselves in anticipation of a supposed invasion which we could not repel, even with the assistance of England. The battles of Canada cannot be fought on the frontier, but on the high seas and at the great cities of the Atlantic coast; and it will be nothing but folly for us to cripple ourselves by spending fifteen or twenty millions a year to raise 50,000 men for the purpose of resisting an invasion of the country. The best thing that Canada can do is to keep quiet and give no cause for war ...

v)   Monday, February 27
Christopher Dunkin [Brome]

It is impossible for me, occupying the position in which I now stand, not to feel that I am opposed to powerful odds, and that there is a sort of foregone conclusion, here, against the views which I desire to press upon the House ...

I desire to perpetuate the union between Upper and Lower Canada. I desire to see developed the largest union that can possibly be developed (I care not by what name you call it) between all the colonies, provinces and dependencies of the British Crown ... I am a unionist, who especially does not desire to see the provinces of Upper and Lower Canada disunited. To my mind, this scheme does not at all present itself as one of union; and if honourable gentlemen opposite will admit the truth, they will acknowledge that, practically, it amounts to a disunion between Upper and Lower Canada ... I desire to see them brought into closer union; and far from regarding this scheme as cementing more closely the connection of these provinces with the British Empire, I look upon it as tending rather toward a not distant disunion of these provinces from the British Empire ... I hold that proper means ought to be taken to prevent our disunion from the British Empire and absorption into the United States, and that this scheme by no means tends that way. I have no fancy for democratic or republican forms or institutions, or indeed for revolutionary or political novelties of any sort. The phrase of "political creation" is no phrase of mine. I hold that the power to create is as much a higher attribute than belongs to man, in the political world, as in any other department of the universe. All we can do is to attend to and develop the ordinary growth of our institutions; and this growth, if it is to be healthy at all, must be slow ...

Mr. Speaker, it is rather curious that hon. gentlemen, in recommending this scheme of theirs, seem never to be tired of speaking of its excellencies in general, and of modestly eulogizing the wisdom, and foresight, and statesmanship of those who got it up. I cannot wonder that their judgment in this behalf should be led a little astray by their surprise at the success which has so far attended their project. Their "officious" visit to Prince Edward Island took but a very few days, and it resulted in the scheme of a legislative union for the Lower Provinces being (as I think, unfortunately) laid aside; and then followed the Conference at Quebec, where these twelve honourable gentlemen, representing Canada, and twenty-one other gentlemen representing the Lower Provinces, sat together for the long period of nineteen days — seventeen working days and two Sundays — and as the result of these seventeen days of but partial work, by the way, we have from these thirty-three gentlemen a scheme of a Constitution which they vaunt of as being altogether better than that of the model republic of the United States, and even than that of the model kingdom of Great Britain. Neither the model republic nor yet the model kingdom of whose glorious traditions and associations we are all so proud, is for a moment to be compared to this work of theirs. (Hear, hear.) So perfect do they seem to regard their pet measure, that they tell us that we must not take time to discuss it. Even though Her Majesty's Secretary of State has told us that there are features of it that require further consideration and must be revised, yet they tell us that we must not change a letter or a line of it. (Hear, hear.) And yet, we are at the same time told that the details of this scheme, if examined at all, must be examined and viewed as those of a compromise. It is not, they freely admit, as satisfactory in its details as any of us would desire to have; but it is all we can get, and must be accepted or rejected as a whole ...

There has been exhibited, in this one respect, an all but impossible perfection. Every feeling, every interest, every class, is bid for in the cleverest way imaginable. The seat of the Federal Government is to be at Ottawa, of course. The Governor-General, or other head, of this magnificent future vice-royalty, or what not, will hold his court and parliament at Ottawa; but a handsome sop is thrown to Quebec and Toronto, also. They, too, are each to have a provincial court and legislature and governmental departments. Everything for everybody! As to the state that is to be created, its style and rank are left in most delightful ambiguity. We may be honoured with the dignity of a kingdom, or of a vice-royalty, or of we know not what. All we are assured of is, that it is to be a something better, higher and more grand than we now have. Perhaps the Sovereign herself will occasionally come over and exercise her authority in person; or, perhaps, a throne will be created for some member of the royal family ... It has been spoken of as an impropriety, almost treasonable, to hint at it as a bait thrown out to gentlemen who have been elected to the Legislative Council for a fixed period, that by voting for this scheme they may get themselves made legislative councillors for life ... In another place, on the other hand, we hear from another minister of the Crown that those gentlemen who hold patents of appointments for life may feel quite as safe, for certainly their claim to be retained in their present position is sure to have full weight. Further, in Lower Canada, each locality is told that it may rest satisfied it will not be overlooked, for each is to be represented in the Legislative Council by a gentleman residing or holding property in it; and both origins and both creeds alike are thus to have representation and full protection ...

Well, turning then to matters which affect this House, the same sort of thing is still observable. Representation by population is given to meet the grand demand of Upper Canada; but the people of Lower Canada are assured, in the same breath that it will not hurt them; that their institutions and privileges are made perfectly safe; that they will even have as many members in the Lower House as before, and that they will, in a variety of ways, be really better off than ever. A delightful ambiguity is found, too, upon the point as to who will make the future appointments of the constituencies.

The leader of the Government, in explaining the scheme the other night, admitted that the decennial revisions of our representation districts are really not to be left to the local legislatures, but are to be dealt with altogether by the Federal Legislature. Till then, most people, I believe, had held the contrary; but all had admitted the text of the resolutions to be equivocal, and each party had of course interpreted them as it wished. The postponement of the local constitutions is of the same character ... The appointment of lieutenant-governors is again a bait, and perhaps not a small one for a few of our public men. The power of disallowance of local bills, and also that of reserving them for the sanction of the General Government, are on the one hand represented as realities — powers that will really be exercised by the General Government to restrain improper local legislation — to make everything safe for those who want a legislative rather than a Federal union; but on the other hand, to those who do not want a legislative union, it is represented that they mean nothing at all, and will never be exercised. (Hear, hear.) ...

The financial portion of the scheme, equally with every other part, is presented to everybody in whatever light he would like to view it in. It will surely bring about economy, because the local governments will have so little to expend unless they resort to direct taxation; but yet, on the other hand, it is as surely to carry us through all sorts of wild expenditure — to give us new and exhaustless credit in England — to make possible vast defensive works throughout the country — to construct the Intercolonial Railway — to enlarge our canals westward — to create no one knows how vast a scheme of communication with the far North-West.

The sweeping rule is laid down, in the abstract, of basing representation on mere population; and that rule is sure to be followed out — not only as between the several provinces, but also as within each; and here again, not only as for Federal, but also as for provincial legislation. For all legislative purposes we must look to have all our territorial divisions open to frequent, one might say perpetual, reconstruction; and this subject perpetually to the disturbing influences of the party warfare of the hour ... At home, while the constituencies are wisely kept as lasting as they can be, the members they return are all held members of the one House of Commons, as little distinguished by the English, Scotch, Irish or Welsh location of their constituencies as they well can be. Here, again, this United States system which we are asked to copy, is the reverse, and the reverse of sound judgment. The House of Representatives in an aggregate of state delegations, and our mock House of Commons is to be an aggregate of provincial delegations. Each man is to come to it ticketed as an Upper or Lower Canadian, a New Brunswicker, a Nova Scotian, a Prince Edward Islander, or what not. These distinctions, which, if we are to be a united people, we had better try to sink, we are to keep up and exaggerate …

Well, then, Mr. Speaker, I turn next to our Legislative Council — too little like the House of Lords, to bear even a moment's comparison in that direction. It must be compared with the Senate of the United States; but the differences here are very wide. The framers of this Constitution have here contrived a system quite different from that; and when we are told (as it seems we are) that the Legislative Council is to represent especially the Federal element in our Constitution, I do not hesitate to affirm that it is the merest sham that can be imagined. (Hear, hear.) To show the contrast. The Senate of the United States consists of just two senators, freely chosen by the Legislature of each State of the Union … Well, sir, the Senate of the United States, thus constituted of two picked men from each state, and presided over by the Vice-President or by one of themselves, freely chosen by themselves, have devolved upon them the important function of impeachment. Even the President of the United States may be impeached before them for treason or malversation in office … Every treaty and every important appointment must go before them, and may be disallowed by them. They further exercise co-ordinate legislative functions, as to expenditure and taxation, with the House of Representatives. From all these circumstances combined, the Senate of the United States is, I believe, on the whole, the ablest deliberative body the world has ever known … As intended for the Federal check in the system of the United States, it is a machine simply perfect … Look now, on the other hand, Mr. Speaker, at the Legislative Council under the proposed Confederation; what is it? There is a sort of attempt to prevent its numbers from resting on a population basis; and this is about the only principle I can find in it … And these Legislative Councillors, thus limited in number, are to hold their seats for life. They are not to be even freely chosen, in the first instance, at least, from the first men in each section of the country. They are to be selected, as far as possible, from the small number of gentlemen holding seats in the present Legislative Council, either by the accident of their having been nominated to them some time ago, or by the chances of popular election since; and until that panel is exhausted, no other person in any province is to be taken; and hereafter, Mr. Speaker, as vacancies occur, they are to be filled as we are now told — and this is the strangest thing of all — not by the provincial legislatures, nor by any authority or any avowed influence of the local kind, but possibly by the General Government ...

But how do we stand here, Mr. Speaker, as to the attributes of our own provincial legislatures and governments on the one hand, and those of the Federal power on the other? Do we follow American example and give so much to the union and the rest to the provinces; or so much to them and the rest to it? Either rule would be plain; but this plan follows neither. It simply gives us a sort of special list for each; making much common to both, and as to much more, not shewing what belongs to either ... Take the subject of marriage and divorce for one — a subject on which there is a great deal of local prejudice and feeling, and into which even religious convictions largely enter. That matter is given to the General Legislature. But on the other hand, the larger matter, civil rights — of which this of marriage and divorce, from one point of view, forms a mere part — is given to the local legislatures ...

Why, there is even a special refinement of confusion as to criminal matters. Criminal procedure is to be federal; civil procedure, provincial; criminal legislation, proper is to be federal; but with a most uncertain quantity of what one may call legislation about penalties, provincial; civil rights, in the main, provincial; but with no one can tell how much of federal interference and overruling, and all with courts provincial in constitution, but whose judges hold by federal tenure and under federal pay ...

Talk, indeed, in such a state of things, of your founding here by this means "a new nationality" — of your creating such a thing — of your whole people here rallying round its new Government at Ottawa. Mr. Speaker, is such a thing possible? We have a large class whose national feelings turn towards London, whose very heart is there; another large class whose sympathies centre here at Quebec, or in a sentimental way may have some reference to Paris; another large class whose memories are of the Emerald Isle; and yet another whose comparisons are with Washington; but have we any class of people who are attached, or whose feelings are going to be directed with any earnestness to the city of Ottawa, the centre of the new nationality that is to be created? ...

There is a further salient contrast between the American system and the system proposed for our adoption. The people of the United States, when they

adopted their Constitution, were one of the nations of the earth. They formed
their whole system with a view to national existence. They had fought for their
independence and triumphed; and still in the flush of their triumph, they were
laying the foundations of a system absolutely national. Their Federal Government was to have its relations with other nations, and was sure to have plenty
to do upon entering the great family of nations. But we, what are we doing?
Creating a new nationality according to the advocates of this scheme. I hardly
know whether we are to take the phrase for ironical or not. Is it a reminder
that in fact we have no sort of nationality about us, but are unpleasantly cut
up into a lot of struggling nationalities, as between ourselves? Unlike the people
of the United States, we are to have no foreign relations to look after, or national affairs of any kind, and therefore our new nationality, if we could create it could be nothing but a name ... Half a dozen colonies federated are
but a federated colony after all ... The tie connecting us with the Empire,
and which ought to be a federal tie of the strongest kind, is too slight, is not,
properly speaking, so much as a federal tie at all. These provinces, with local
responsible government, are too nearly in the position of independent communities; there is not enough of connection between them and the parent state
to make the relations between the two work well, or give promise of lasting
long ... For disguise it how you may, the idea that underlies this plan is this,
and nothing else — that we are to create here a something — kingdom, vice-
royalty, or principality — something that will soon stand in the same position towards the British Crown that Scotland and Ireland stood in before they
were legislatively united with England; a something having no other tie to the
Empire than the one tie of fealty to the British Crown ... I say again, we had
far better hold firmly to the policy of thus maintaining and strengthening our
union with the parent state, than let ourselves, under whatever pretext, be
drawn into this other course, which must inevitably lead to our separation
from the Empire. (Hear, hear.) ...

B) Speeches and Letters, 1866
Joseph Howe

Let us see what these Canadians desire to do. They are not, as we have shown,
a very harmonious or homogeneous community. Two-fifths of the population are French and three-fifths English. They are therefore perplexed with
an internal antagonism which was fatal to the unity of Belgium and Hol-

land, and which, unless the fusion of races becomes rapid and complete, must ever be a source of weakness They are shut in by frost from the outer world for five months of the year. They are at the mercy of a powerful neighbour whose population already outnumbers them by more than eight to one, and who a quarter of a century hence will probably present sixty eight millions to six millions on the opposite side of a naturally defenceless frontier. Surely such conditions as these ought to repress inordinate ambition or lust of territory on the part of the public men of Canada ... While they discharge their duties as unobtrusive good neighbours to the surrounding populations, and of loyal subjects of the empire, Great Britain will protect them by her energy in other fields should the Province become untenable but it is evident that a more unpromising nucleus of a new nation can hardly be found on the face of the earth, and that any organized communities, having a reasonable chance to do anything better would be politically insane to give up their distinct formations and subject themselves to the domination of Canada.

Thus situated, and borne down by a public debt of $75,000,000, or about $25 in gold per head of their population, the public men of Canada propose to purchase the territories of the Hudson's Bay Company, larger than half of Europe. They propose to assume the government of British Oregon and Vancouver's Island, provinces divided from them by an interminable wilderness, and by the natural barrier of the Rocky Mountains; and they propose to govern Nova Scotia, New Brunswick, Prince Edward Island and Newfoundland — countries severally as large as Switzerland, Sardinia, Greece, and Great Britain, appointing their governors, senators and judges, and exercising over them unlimited powers of internal and external taxation ...

Anybody who looks at the map of British America, and intelligently searches its geographical features in connection with its past record and present political condition, will perceive that it naturally divides itself into four great centres of political power and radiating intelligence. The Maritime Provinces, surrounded by the sea: three of them insular, with unchangeable boundaries, with open harbours, rich fisheries, abundance of coal, a homogeneous population, and within a week's sail of the British Islands, form the first division; and the Ashburton Treaty, which nearly severed them from Canada, defines its outlines and proportions. These Provinces now govern themselves, and do it well, and Canada has no more right to control or interfere with them than she has to control the Windward Islands or Jamaica.

These Provinces have developed commercial enterprise and maritime capabilities with marvellous rapidity. Three of them can be held while Great Britain keeps the sea. Newfoundland and Prince Edward Island are surrounded by it, and the narrow isthmus of fourteen miles which connects Nova Scotia with the mainland can be easily fortified and can be enfiladed by gunboats on either side. But what is more these Provinces can help Great Britain to preserve her ascendency on the ocean. While far-seeing members of the House of Commons are inquiring into the causes which diminish the number of her sailors and increase the difficulty of manning her fleet, is it not strange that the great nursery for seamen which our Maritime Provinces present should be entirely overlooked, and that flippant writers should desire to teach 60,000 hardy seafaring people to turn their backs upon England and fix their thoughts upon Ottawa; and should deliberately propose to disgust them by breaking down their institutions and subjecting them to the arbitrary control of an inland population, frozen up nearly half the year, and who are incapable of protecting them by land or sea.

Referring to the statistics of trade and commerce, it will be found that Nova Scotia employs 19,637 mariners and fishermen; Newfoundland, 38,578; and Prince Edward Island, 2,113. Nova Scotia alone owns 400,000 tons of shipping.

Here are colonies within seven days' steaming of these shores, floating the flag of England over a noble mercantile marine, and training 60,000 seamen and fishermen to defend it, and yet the House of Commons is to be asked to allow some gentlemen in Ottawa to draw these people away from the ocean, which for their own and the general security of the empire they are required to protect, that their hearts may be broken and their lives wasted on interminable frontiers incapable of defence. Parliament, it is hoped, will think twice about this proposition, and of the scheme for launching a prince of the blood into a sea of troubles for the glorification of the Canadians.

Canada forms the second division of British America, in order of sequence as we ascend from the Atlantic. It is a fine country with great natural resources, and may develop into some such nation as Poland or Hungary. Hemmed in by icy barriers at the north, and by a powerful nation on the south, shut out from deep sea navigation for nearly half the year, with two nationalities to reconcile, and no coal, who will predict for her a very brilliant destiny at least for many years to come? The best she can do is to be quiet, unobtrusive, thrifty, provoking no enemies, and not making herself disagreeable to her neighbours, or increasing the hazards which her defence involves, by any premature aspirations to become a nation, for which status at present she is totally unprepared ...

But it may be asked, do not the Maritime Provinces desire this union? and, if the question includes the Quebec scheme of confederation, it is soon answered. Every one of them rejected it with a unanimity and decision not to be misunderstood. In Prince Edward Island, both branches of the Legislature being elective, but five members could be got to vote for it. In Newfoundland it was condemned by the people at the polls. In Nova Scotia the leader of the Government was compelled to come down to the House and declare it "impracticable"; and in New Brunswick the electors, animated by the instinct of self-preservation, rushed to the polls, swept the delegates aside, and trampled it under their feet. Here the matter would have rested had all the Provinces been treated with the justice and impartiality to which they were entitled ...

C) Annexation or Union with the United States is the Manifest Destiny of British North America, 1868
Alex Munro

In the following pages, we purpose showing that centralization and political union is the manifest destiny of British North America and the United States; that the physical character of the country, and the genius of forty millions of people, clearly point to the union of these two countries ...

A large party in the Provinces were in favour annexation to the American Republic, as the only safeguard from invasion, and the surest means of securing commercial progress and the development of the resources of the country. After nearly three years incessant labour, Canada, divided into two Provinces — Quebec and Ontario — with Nova Scotia and New Brunswick, has been federately united into one dominion, called the Dominion of Canada. The first session of the first Dominion Parliament closed in 1868. The acts of this memorable Parliament — memorable for wasting the resources of the country, and imposing onerous taxes on the people; indeed, nothing but general dissatisfaction has ran throughout the maritime colonies. Contrary to the pledges made by the union leaders in the Lower Provinces, and in accordance with the predictions of the anti-unionists newspaper postage, stamp and excise duties, and other heavy fiscal burthens are imposed, which the people, especially in Nova Scotia and New Brunswick, are very unwilling to bear.

British North America is not climatically and geographically adapted to form a Nation.

The productive parts of British North America are comprised in a few isolated spots, scattered along a ridge or belt of land, varying in width from one hundred to two hundred miles, and stretches across the American Continent, between the Atlantic and Pacific Oceans, three thousand miles in extent. On the southern boundary of this ridge, lies the United States; and its northern side is bounded by a great extent of uninhabitable country, sealed in frost and snow for the greater part of the year. From this terra incognita, the cold is driven over the Provinces and adjoining States, with chilling effects on agricultural and other operations. A careful examination of the country, clearly shows that British North America is not adapted to constitute a nation, and maintain its independence. Its boundaries are not rightly adjusted for national existence, and for the extension of the human race — the arts of industry, commerce, and for protection. Its chief rivers, lakes, mountains, and other attributes, are so interwoven with those of the conterminous States, that it is almost impossible to develop the resources of the Provinces, except by permission of the adjoining Republic; of which, by nature, British North America forms a part. The Columbia Rivers in the interior; the Red and Saskatchewan Rivers in the interior; and the great chain of lakes on the St. Lawrence, connect both countries.

The natural outlet for the products of the ten millions of inhabitants who now occupy the Western States — a population which, in a few years, may be doubled, is by the St. Lawrence. This is the way ships of a thousand tons might, by enlarging the canals, be brought from Chicago, the grain mart of the West, to the ocean, in place of by the long route by the Erie Canal. Unite the two countries under one government, and the St. Lawrence would at once become the highway of nations to the centre of North America. And by a divergence from the St. Lawrence route to Lake Champlain, the Eastern States could also be supplied with Western produce much cheaper than at present. And the river St. John, in New Brunswick, for a part of its distance, is in both countries; so that nearly all the great natural arteries of communication form a part of both countries ...

From the facts here adduced, it is obvious that a large part of British North America is not adapted for continuous settlement; its fertile districts are comparatively small, and separated from each other by extensive tracts of barren lands. Still, its natural resources are vast and varied, which, in union with the United States, would be developed, and the country become the seat of manufacturing industry; money would be more plenty; and emigrants would flock to the country by thousands, in place of leaving it, as at present, by hundreds ...

It is obvious that the agricultural capabilities of these Provinces will not be developed until the country becomes the seats of manufacturing industry, which it is highly capable of; and this cannot be done, as we shall attempt to show, without the Provinces are united to the States. Agriculturally considered, these Provinces are far inferior to the United States; while in a commercial point of view they have resources, equal if not superior to the Republic. But without the States for a market, the resources of the Provinces will not be developed, the history of the past clearly proves. It was during the existence of the Reciprocity Treaty that the Provinces made the greatest progress ...

Union with the United States would give life to manufacturing industry in the Colonies, and extend the commerce of both Countries

... But the want of compactness in the colonies, and consequent concentration of their population, with climatic obstructions, and the want of homogenity of the two great races, English and French, with numerous other causes, unfit the colonies to develop their resources. The country is so fragmentary in its geographical character, and the great distance the populations are apart — the centre of Nova Scotia is twelve hundred miles from the centre of the Ontario population; consequently, the trade between the Upper and Lower Provinces will only be limited ...

Previous to the Reciprocity Treaty between the Republic and the Provinces, the trade of the latter was unprofitable, indeed, in a depressed state, as it has been since the abrogation of that treaty. Though the treaty was considerably one-sided, it gave the Republic important advantages over the Provinces; still, during its existence, the trade of the Provinces was brisk; life was infused into most every department of provincial industry. The commerce of these Provinces with the States rose, in the ten years of the Reciprocity Treaty, from seventeen millions to eighty-two millions of dollars. The coal, limestone, gypsum, grindstones, building stones, lumber, fish and other products of the Provinces were sent to the States in large quantities and highly profitable returns were received ...

There are few countries in the world whose free trade with each other would be of more benefit than a reciprocal trade would be between British North America and the United States. The Provinces have the products in abundance the States really require; and the latter have hundreds of articles needed by these Provinces. So that a free trade between these conterminous countries could not fail to be of mutual benefit. Nature has constituted them one country and with one destiny.

The Provinces are defenceless

The territorial formation of British North America presents an insurmountable obstacle to its defence against the United States. With three thousand miles of a frontier bordering upon a populous nation, with whom a *causus beli* might arise at any time, it would be utterly impossible to defend this country. This view of the subject is corroborated by numerous reliable authorities. The Government of the two Canadas in 1862, in reply to a dispatch from the Imperial Government requesting Canada to erect defences and organize her militia, declared, that "No portion of the Empire is exposed to sufferings and sacrifices equal to those which would inevitably fall upon the Province in the event of a war with the United States. No probable combination of regular troops and militia would preserve our soil from invading armies; and no fortune which the most sanguine dare hope for would prevent our most flourishing districts from being the battle field of the war. Our trade would be brought to a stand still, our industry would be paralyzed, our richest farming lands devastated, our towns and villages destroyed; homes, happy in peace, would be rendered miserable by war; and all the result of events for the production of which Canada would be in no wise accountable."

The Parliament of Canada concurred in the foregoing statement of the Ministry. The conclusion here hinted at is — the country is defenceless, and therefore, it would be useless for Canada to expend her revenues in the training of her Militia and in the erection of fortifications, when it held that no probable combination of regular troops and Militia could save the country in the event of a war with the United States ...

Indeed, no country is more exposed to another, in a defensive point of view, than British North America is to the United States. From the Bay of Fundy to Lake Ontario, six hundred miles, there is only an imaginary line, without a natural or artificial barrier to obstruct the passage of the armies of the Republic into the midst of the most flourishing towns and settlements of these Provinces. The country adjoining the great lakes is also defenceless ... If British North America cannot be defended, it cannot exist as a dependent or separate state. The history of all countries clearly show the correctness of this principle.

What could four millions of people, scattered over a territory stretching from ocean to ocean, three thousand miles apart, do in defending such a frontier? Simply nothing. All the defences they could erect, and all the militia they could train would be powerless compared to the million and a half of armed men, that the thirty-five millions of conterminous people, with all the appliances and accustomed to all the hardships of war, could at a short notice rush into these Provinces. And England, three thousand miles from our borders, and the St. Lawrence sealed in ice for half the year, could not bring her fleet to aid the interior Provinces. The proposed Intercolonial Railroad, skirting the enemy's country for hundreds of miles, would be liable to be destroyed at numerous places; and rendered useless as a means of conveying men and munitions of war from Halifax to the interior ...

The surest system of defence the Provinces can adopt is a Union with the United States. Then, and not until then, will the Colonies be safe from invasion; and be able to arrest the stream of adolescent population which is continually flowing from their shores. As soon as our young men arrive at manhood they emigrate in large numbers to the Republic ...

The inhabitants of these Provinces are really American; their modes of thinking and speaking, their habits of living and acting, their moral attributes and general progress in civilization, has made them one with the people of the States. And politically, the inhabitants of these Colonies are fast losing sight of the symbols of European royalty; not, through any hostility to Great Britain. There are no rebellious feelings in the Colonies against the Parent State, neither should there be. If these Colonies desire union with the conterminous States, it cannot be through hostility to the Imperial State, but to secure their peace, improve their condition, and hasten the development of their vast latent resources ...

It is obvious that the climatic character and territorial formation of British North America, presents insurmountable obstacles in the way of governing it. And when we are officially informed that no probable combination of forces could save the country from destruction, in the event of a war with the United States; and when we know that the foundation of disaffection has been deeply laid, we conclude, that British North America, either as a dependancy or as a separate state never can have a prosperous history: it never can pass through this formative and critical period, and consolidate its remote parts. The geographical formation of the country does not admit of it, or adapt it for a nation. And the conflicting interests of its parts; their dependance on the United States; the aggressive character of the latter, taken in connection with the inability of the Provinces for defence, combine to show that the only means of securing peace, prosperity, and the development of the resources of the Provinces, is by uniting their destinies with those of the United States ...

The youth of these Provinces, like their birds in autumn, are leaving them in large numbers for the Republic. Such has been the run of population from Quebec, that the Legislature of that Province, at its last sitting, was asked "to devise some means for the arrest of the same." And a large part of the moneys of the Provinces is sent to the United States. Without manufactories are established in the Provinces, and the markets of the Republic freely opened to us, it is vain to expect these Provinces to progress. The Provinces however have drawn heavily upon the States. Many of their enterprises are in the hands of their American neighbours, who work our mines and telegraph lines, who found our factories, manufacture a large part of our lumber, and supply the farmers and mechanics with the chief part of their implements, and the masses of our people with the greater part of the necessaries of life.

Sources

Chapter 1. "Make More Haste Homeward"

G. Beste, "Account of the Second Voyage," from Richard Hakluyt, *The Principall Navigations, Voiages and Discoveries of the English Nation* (London: Bishop and Newberie, 1589). Jens Munck, "Navogatio Septentrionalis," reprinted in C.C.A. Gosch (ed.), *Danish Arctic Explorations, 1605 to 1620,* Vol. 2 (London: Hakluyt Society, 1897).

Chapter 2. "An Inconvenient Wind"

Christien Le Clerq, reprinted in William Ganong (ed. and trans.), *New Relation of Gaspesia* (Toronto: Champlain Society, 1910). Joyce Marshall (ed. and trans.), *Word From New France: The Selected Letters of Marie L'Incarnation* (Toronto: Oxford University Press, 1967). Reprinted with permission, © Oxford University Press 1996/CANCOPY.

Chapter 3. "Advantages and Inconveniences"

Champlain's accounts were reprinted in H.P. Biggar (ed.), *The Works of Samuel De Champlain*, Vol. 2 (Toronto: The Champlain Society, 1925); Pierre Boucher, *True and Genuine Description of New France Commonly Called Canada* (Paris: 1664) was translated by E.L. Montizambert under the title and reprinted as *Canada in the Seventeenth Century* (Montreal: 1883). Talon's memoir of 1673 can be found reprinted in *Rapport de l'Archiviste de la Province de Quebec 1930–31* (Québec: Imprimeur du Roi, 1931). In the 1992–23 annual report of the same journal can be found D'Auteuil's memoir of 1715. Duchesneau's letter of November 10, 1679 can be found reprinted in S.D. Clark, *The Social Development of Canada* (Toronto: 1955), and Denonville's correspondence was reproduced in E.G. O'Callaghan (ed.), *Documents Relative to the Colonial History of the State of New York*, Vol. 9 (Albany: Weed Parson and Company, 1855). P.F.X. de Charlevois, *Journal of a Voyage to North America*, Vol. 1 (London: 1761). Hocquart's instructions were reproduced in Y. Zoltvany (ed.), *The French Tradition in America* (New York: Harper and Row, 1969), and his memoir can be found in J. Reid, K. McNaught and H. Crowe (eds.), *A Source-Book of Canadian History* (Don Mills: Longmans, 1964).

Chapter 4. "An Afflicted People"

Paul Mascarene's "Description of Nova Scotia 1720," the Board of Trade correspondence of 1755, and J.B. Galerm's "Relation of the French Neutrals, 1758" were reprinted most recently in N.F.S. Griffiths, *The Acadian Deportation: Deliberate Perfidy or Cruel Necessity* (Toronto: Copp Clark, 1969). The circular letter from Gov. Lawrence to the Governors on the Continent, and Winslow's journal of the Acadian expulsion were reprinted in Public Archives of Canada, *Report*, Vol. 2 (Ottawa: King's Printer, 1905).

Chapter 5. "The Ruin of Canada"

Documents A, B, D, E, and G reprinted in E.B. O'Callaghan (ed.), *Documents Relative to the Colonial History of the State of New York*, Vol. X (Albany: Weed Parson and Company, 1858); de Capellis and de Beaucat's accounts were reproduced in K. MacKirdy, J. Moir, and Y. Zoltvany *Changing Perspectives in Canadian History* (Don Mills: J.M. Dent and Sons, 1971). "Narrative of the doings during the Siege of Quebec, and the conquest of Canada; by a nun of the General Hospital of Quebec transmitted to a religious community of the same order, in France" was first published in English in 1826 and most recently reprinted in Jean-Claude Hebert, *The Siege of Quebec in 1759: Three Eyewitness Accounts* (Quebec: Ministry of Cultural Affairs, 1974).

Chapter 6. "The Abundant Blessings of British Rule"

Murray's "Report of the State of the Government in Canada" was reprinted in Adam Shortt and Arthur G. Doughty (eds.), *Documents Relating to the Constitutional History of Canada, 1759–1791* (Ottawa: King's Printer, 1907). Briand's speech was reprinted as an appendix in G. Lanctot, *Canada and the American Revolution 1774–1783* (Toronto: Clarke Irwin, 1967); Plessis's address appears in H.D. Forbes (ed.), *Canadian Political Thought* (Toronto: Oxford University Press, 1977); John Lambert, *Travels through Lower Canada and the United States of North America , in the Years 1806, 1807 and 1808*, vol. 1 (London: Richard Phillips, 1810); Craig's letter was reprinted in A.G. Doughty and D.A. McArthur (eds.), *Documents Relating to the Constitutional History of Canada, 1791–1818* (Ottawa: King's Printer, 1914).

Chapter 7. "For the Sake of Humanity"

All documents reprinted in J.P. Howley (ed.), *The Beothuks or Red Indians: The Aboriginal Inhabitants of Newfoundland* (Cambridge: Cambridge University Press, 1915).

Chapter 8. "A Place Where Rum Is As Cheap As Beer"

John Macgregor, *Historical and Descriptive Sketches of the Maritime Colonies of British America* (London: Longman, Rees, Orme, Brown and Green, 1828).

Chapter 9. "Our Robinson Crusoe Sort of Life"

Susanna Moodie, *Roughing It in the Bush* (London: Richard Bentley, 1852); Anna Brownell Jameson, *Winter Studies and Summer Rambles in Canada* (London: Saunders and Otley, 1838); Catherine P. Trail, *The Backwoods of Canada* (London: Charles Knight, 1836).

Chapter 10. "The Long and Heavy Chain of Abuses"

"The Six Counties Address," *The Vindicator*, Oct. 31, 1837 reprinted in H.D. Forbes (ed.), *Canadian Political Thought* (Toronto: Oxford University Press, 1977); "The Toronto Union to the Reformers of Upper Canada," 31 July 1837 originally published in the *Constitution*, August 2, 1837, reprinted in C. Read and R. Stagg, *The Rebellion of 1837 in Upper Canada* (Ottawa: Carleton University Press, 1985); Joseph Howe's letters are to be found in J.A. Chisholm (ed.)., *The Speeches and Public Letters of Joseph Howe*, vol. 1 (Halifax: 1909).

Chapter 11. "To The Barren Grounds"

S. Hearne, *A Journey from Prince of Wales's Fort in Hudson Bay to the Northern Ocean* (London: A. Strahan and T. Cadell, 1795).

Chapter 12. "The Worst and Most Dangerous Men"

This document was first published in G. Williams (ed.), *Hudson's Bay Miscellany 1670-1870*, vol. 30 (Winnipeg: Hudson's Bay Record Society, 1975). Reproduced with permission of the Hudson's Bay Company Archives, Provincial Archives of Manitoba.

Chapter 13. "A Great Humbug"

Charles Major, "News from British Columbia," *The Daily Globe*, Toronto, January 2, 1860, reprinted in *British Columbia Historical Quarterly*, 4 (July 1941); C.C. Gardiner,"To the Editor of The Islander," reprinted in R. Reid, "To the Fraser River Mines in 1858," *British Columbia Historical Quarterly*, 1 (1937); S.G. Hathaway's journal was printed in I. Bescoby, "Notes and Documents," *Canadian Historical Review* (September 1932); Matthew

MacFie, *Vancouver Island and British Columbia* (London: Longman, Green, Longman, Roberts and Green, 1865).

Chapter 14. "Deaf to Their Cries"

The journal of Gerald Keegan originally published in R. Sellar, *The Summer of Sorrow* (Huntingdon: 1895); reprinted in R. O'Driscoll and Lorna Reynolds (eds.), *The Untold Story* (Toronto: Celtic Arts of Canada); John Mactaggart, *Three Years in Canada*, vol. 2 (London: Henry Colburn, 1829); Report of the Roman Catholic Chaplain of the Provincial Penitentiary, *Journals of the Legislative Assembly of Canada*, 1852–3, Appendix III; "Protestant Organization," *The Loyalist* (August 27, 1847).

Chapter 15. "Equal in Every Respect"

"Report on the Affairs of the Indians in Canada", *Journal of Legislative Assembly of the Province of Canada* (1847), App. T.; "The Coloured People and the Common Schools," *The Leader* (December 12, 1862); "A Reply from the Black Community," *The Globe* (January 3, 1863); Mrs. Holiwell, "Address to parents on the education of girls" (Toronto: 1865); Report of the Grammar School Inspector for 1865, George Paxton Young. All of these documents were reprinted in S. Houston and A. Prentice, *Family, School and Society in Nineteenth Century Canada* (Toronto: Oxford University Press, 1975).

Chapter 16. "The Evils of Combination"

"Report of the Commissioners appointed to inquire into the Disturbances upon the line of the Beauharnois Canal, during the summer of 1843; and Statements of the Expenses attending the suppression of the Riots on the Beauharnois and Lachine Canals… 16th October 1843," *Journals of the Legislative Assembly of Canada* Appendix T (1843).

Chapter 17. "The Bold Scheme"

All of the initial speeches originally published in Province of Canada, Legislature, *Parliamentary Debates on the Subject of the Confederation of the British North American Provinces, 1865*, were reprinted in Canada, *Confederation Debates* (Ottawa: King's Printer, 1950); Dunkin and Dorin's speeches can be found in J. Reid, K. McNaught, and H. Crowe (eds.), *A Source-Book of Canadian History* (Don Mills: Longmans, 1964). Howe's remarks were published in J.A. Chisholm (ed.), *The Speeches and Public Letters of Joseph Howe*, vol. 2 (Halifax: 1909). Alex Munro, *Annexation of Union with the United States is the Manifest Destiny of British North America* (St. John: Barnes and Company, 1868).

The Editor of this book and the Publisher have made every attempt to locate the authors of the copyrighted material or their heirs or assigns, and would be grateful for information that would allow them to correct any errors or omissions in a subsequent edition of the work.